Romano-British Industries in Purbeck

Excavations at Norden by Nigel Sunter
Excavations at Ower and Rope Lake Hole by
Peter J. Woodward

All three sites in the parish of Corfe Castle, Dorset

with an introduction by Peter J. Woodward

1987
Dorset Natural History and Archaeological Society
Monograph Series Number 6
Series Editor Jo Draper

© The Dorset Natural History and Archaeological Society 1986.
Printed by The Friary Press Ltd, Bridport Road, Dorchester, Dorset.

This volume is published with the aid of a grant from
English Heritage, Historic Buildings and Monuments Commission for England,
and from British Petroleum; the Gas Council (Exploration) Ltd;
Major D. C. D. Ryder and Rempstone Estates; and Major J. C. Mansel.

Cover: an archaeological reconstruction of the settlement at Ower in the 3rd century AD, *from the west. A pencil drawing by Peter J. Woodward for the Dorset County Museum archaeological gallery, 1983.*

CONTENTS

Excavations at Norden by Nigel Sunter

Introduction and acknowledgements	9
Excavation report	9
The pottery – coarse ware	22
fine ware	28
Samian ware by Kevin Greene, BA, PhD	29
The worked stone by Claire Thomas, BA, FSA(Scot)	30
Discussion	43

Microfiche

M1 Tabulated summary of features and finds by period
M2 The complete pottery catalogue (figs 10-17)
M3 Samian ware catalogue by Kevin Greene, PhD
M4 Catalogue of worked stone by Claire Thomas, BA, FSA(Scot)
M5 Glass by Jennifer Price, PhD
M6 The coins by P. J. Casey, FSA
M7 The small finds (figs. 26-28) by Katherine Johns
M8 The worked flints (fig. 29) by Richard Bradley, BA, FSA
M9 The animal bones by J. Startin

The Excavation of a Late Iron-Age Trading Settlement and Romano-British BB1 Pottery Production Site at Ower, Dorset by Peter J. Woodward

Introduction and site description	44
The excavations	50
The report and archive	50
The chronology and phasing	51
Site description and stratigraphy	52
Site industries and occupation characteristics: as defined by material remains, structures and phasing	66
Discussion	69
The finds	69
The Samian by Hedley Pengelly	69
First century imports and native fine wares, by Jane Timby with a contribution by D. F. Williams	73
The Amphorae by D. F. Williams	79
The mortaria	81
The New Forest Wares	82
The Oxfordshire Wares	82
The Black Burnished (category 1) Wares	83
The briquetage and kiln material by John Hawkes	92
Petrological analysis of the Pottery and Clays by Jane Timby and D. F. Williams	93
The coins by Richard Reece	95
The brooches by D. F. Mackreth	95
The bronze objects by Martin Henig	98
The Ironwork	98
Lead objects	100
The coloured glass by M. Guido, J. Bayley and Leo Biek, with a contribution from G. R. Gilmore	100
The Roman vessel glass by J. Price	102
The bone pins and worked bone	104
The spindle whorls and loom weights	104
The building materials and architectural fragments and miscellaneous stone objects by Peter Cox and Peter Woodward	104
The Kimmeridge shale	105
The flint	110
The slag and cinder	113
The human skeletal remains with a contribution on the Romano-British burial by Liz Cox and John Beavis	113
The animal bones by J. Coy	114
The marine molluscs by J. Coy and J. Winder	118
The charcoal identifications by Richard Thomas	119
The soils by John Beavis and Gena Porter	120
The geophysical survey and the archaeomagnetic susceptibility of soils by Andrew David	120
The archaeomagnetic sample from kiln 540	122

The carbon dates   122
Neutron activation analysis of some BB1 from Ower and Redcliffe by Jeremy Evans   122
M10 Fiche Appendix 1: The archive contents
M11 Fiche Appendix 2: The geophysics reports

The Excavation of an Iron Age and Romano-British Settlement at Rope Lake Hole, Corfe Castle, Dorset by Peter J. Woodward

Summary   125
Introduction and site description   125
The 1979 excavations   127
The chronology and phasing   128
Period 1 occupation (Early Iron Age)   131
Period 2 occupation (Middle Iron Age)   133
Period 3 occupation (Later Iron Age)   137
Period 4 occupation (Romano-British)   139
Period 5 field lynchets (Early Medieval)   143
The site industries and trading characteristics   145
The settlement, general considerations   148
The finds   150
The samian by Hedley Pengelly   150
The coarse pottery by Susan M. Davies   150
The petrological analysis of the 'haematite ware' by D. F. Williams and S. Tolfield 158
The briquetage by John Hawkes   158
The coins   159
The brooches by D. F. Mackreth   160
The copper-alloy objects, the identifications provided by Martin Henig   161
The lead objects   162
The ironwork   162
The glass   163
The worked antler, horn and bone   163
The architectural fragments, and portable stone objects   163
The Kimmeridge shale by P. J. Woodward and P. W. Cox   165
The flint by P. J. Woodward and P. W. Cox   171
The slag and cinder by Leo Biek   177
The human skeletal remains by Juliet Rogers   177
The animal bones and marine molluscs by Jennie Coy   178
The charcoal identifications by Richard Thomas   180
The 'foreign stone' and pebbles based on macroscopic identifications by
    Paul Ensom and a contribution on the iron pyrites by Leo Biek   180

Acknowledgments   180

FRONTISPIECE: Upper: Cleavel Point and the Ower peninsula from the east, probably taken in the summer of 1980. The water-pump station and pipe to the oil wells are complete. The site occupies much of the three fields of the peninsula; Newton Bay is to the left. Part of the Fitzworth Peninsula, site (56), can be seen in the middle distance with the Corfe River beyond. A marquee for sea scouts can be seen in the foreground to the left of the water-pump station (photograph courtesy of British Petroleum). Lower: The head of the Ower Peninsular and Cleavel Point with Newton Bay in the right foreground; beyond lie Green, Furzey and Brownsea Islands (photograph courtesy of British Petroleum).

INTRODUCTION

The archaeological excavations published here describe three Purbeck settlement sites of the Iron-Age and Romano-British periods; Rope Lake Hole, Norden and Ower. These three sites are viewed against a background of past and current research into an area which is topographically discrete, and provided a range of 'minerals' which were important to human populations throughout the prehistoric and historic periods. The Iron Age and Romano-British settlements known to be exploiting the mineral resources of the Isle of Purbeck and Poole Harbour (on an industrial scale) are depicted and described in Figure 1, which is a synthesis of data currently being collated, researched and gathered (Cox and Hawkes, in preparation). A full gazetteer of these sites is not published here, however most locations can be identified in relation to the data and sites published in the survey by the Royal Commission on Historical Monuments (1970).

Our present data base for the Iron Age and Romano-British periods in Purbeck owes much to Bernard Calkin (1892-1972), who in 1948 published the first distribution map of Iron Age settlement. This was the product of intensive fieldwork by himself and others from 1931 onwards, and the collation of nineteenth century discoveries (Calkin, 1948). Since this first map of prehistoric settlement was pubished, the data base has been greatly expanded by field survey and small scale excavation; the continued and pioneering work of Calkin himself, together with R. A. H. Farrar for the Royal Commission on Historical Monuments, John Beavis, Tony Brown, and Norman Field amongst others. Much of this work has been published in the Royal Commission's inventory for Dorset (R.C.H.M., 1970), and most of the sites discovered and explored have been noted in the *Proceedings of the Dorset Natural History and Archaeological Society*.

This data base provides a wealth of material for more detailed study of the settlement patterns, industrial characteristics, and the trading economy of Purbeck until the demise of Roman administration in the province. Research and synthesis of this data in conjunction with fieldwork has given us a great deal of information at many levels on specific aspects of Purbeck settlement and industry, and most importantly: the shale armlet industry (Calkin, 1953), the Purbeck Marble industry (Beavis, 1971), salt-winning (Farrar, 1975), the production of Black-Burnished pottery (BBI) (Farrar, 1977 and Williams, 1977). These studies recognise the unique position Purbeck, and its immediate hinterland around Poole Harbour, held in southern Britain. By the late Iron Age shale, salt and pottery can be identified as being traded out of Purbeck; inland, and along the coast. Poole Harbour provided shelter for shipping, and sites in the Harbour, such as Ower, Hamworthy, and Green Island, were certainly part of a trading network centred on Hengistbury further along the coast, which was concerned with trade inland, with northern France, and ultimately the Mediterranean (Cunliffe, 1980 *et seq*). After the Roman Conquest the mineral resources of Purbeck were increasingly exploited and exported, now including its fine stone for building materials and architectural ornament. The BB1 pottery trade grew rapidly at an early stage, probably as a result of early military contact. Supplies for military ordnance were possibly negotiated with local entrepreneurs, who would then have quickly expanded the production of BB1 pottery which may have provided added ballast or containers for the boats shipping supplies to the north. In addition the production of BB1 pottery was quickly expanded for the new civilian markets together with other items such as: marble mortars; shale tables, trays and ornament; limestone roof tiles; stone tesserae; and marble veneers. The mechanisms of the developing industries and trade are as yet not clearly understood, but have been discussed in a number of papers, more importantly: the Late

Iron Age trading patterns (Cunliffe, 1982), the military contact and induced trade (Greene, 1979), and the internal trading status of Purbeck sites (Woodward, 1980).

The three sites described here, Rope Lake Hole (9), Norden (46) and Ower (57) cover the range of Purbeck industries (apart from limestone exploitation), although many of the processes of each particular industry were not all in evidence on these particular excavations (Figure 1). These three sites can in some respects be seen as being representative of the topographic/resources zones in which they are located. However their internal structure, development, and status can also be seen to have been moulded by the developing patterns of trade within Purbeck, which in turn was influenced by the increasingly centralised economies of the Late Iron Age, the coastal trading contact with Hengistbury and the continent, and the new military and civilian markets induced by the Roman Conquest.

In this volume each site is presented separately, since they were originally prepared by individual authors for separate publication; the site at Norden by Nigel Sunter (1978), the site at Ower by Peter Woodward (1981), the site at Rope Lake Hole by Peter Woodward (1983). Each site has engendered its own individual discussion and conclusions, and these are published as they were prepared with each separate report. However it is perhaps worthwhile summarising here inter-relationships as seen against the patterns of settlement and induced trade that have so far been presented in this introduction.

In the Late Iron Age, Rope Lake Hole and similar sites can perhaps be viewed as rural settlement sites supplying materials and products to hillfort centres; locally to Flowers' Barrow, Woodbury Hill, and Bulbury; to hillforts further inland; and to coastal trading centres such as Ower, Hamworthy, and Green Island, for connecting trade to Hengistbury and further afield. After the conquest this site at Rope Lake Hole appears to have pushed into the specialist production of shale armlets, perhaps at the expense of its farming economy. The profits of this trade were either slight or more probably went elsewhere, perhaps to the villas which congregate along either side of the northern ridge; Bucknowle (35), East Creech (45), and Brenscombe (47). The sites (of which Rope Lake Hole is one) within zones A and B, which are located on some of the more tractable agricultural soils and also contain important mineral resources, can in general be considered as the suppliers of the raw materials and unsophisticated basic products, which are to be sent, perhaps via middlemen, to markets and factory centres for conversion to more sophisticated products and factory centres. Norden (46) was certainly one of these market centres in the post-conquest period and also apparently developed from a wealthy Late Iron Age settlement (Woodward 1980). The movement of material and products northwards to sites on Poole Harbour, which engaged in inland, coastal, and continental trade in the Late Iron Age is now known; and Ower (57) is certainly one of these sites (Cover and Frontispiece). However this site, which was primarily concerned with pottery and salt-production after the conquest and whose primary concern was probably to ship material to military and then civilian markets, does not appear to develop any permanent buildings of status. It is possible, although not proven, that the pottery, salt production, and shipment may have been seasonal with the profits being invested elsewhere (on the same estate?); perhaps on the nearby villa site to the north at Brenscombe (47).

This basic socio-economic interpretation relies on detailed inter-site comparisons. At present most of the detail available for the sites in Figure 1, has only been realised from surface collection, erosional sections, and small trial excavations. It is clear that more detailed excavations, such as those at Ower and Norden, increase the known range of industries present on sites, and in turn their relative

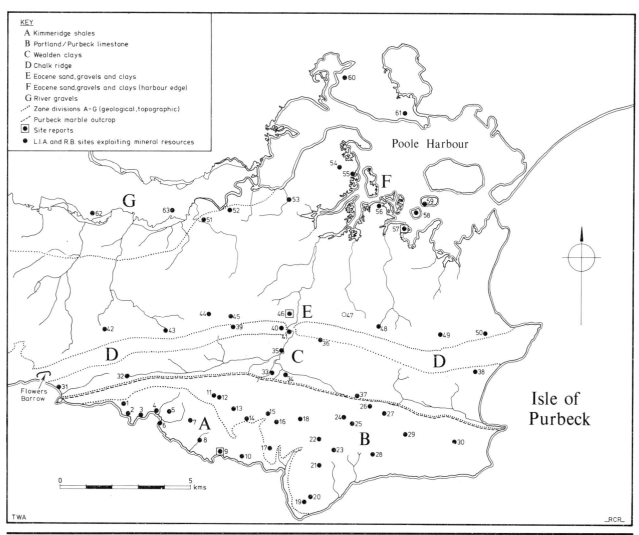

KEY
A Kimmeridge shales
B Portland/Purbeck limestone
C Wealden clays
D Chalk ridge
E Eocene sand, gravels and clays
F Eocene sand, gravels and clays (harbour edge)
G River gravels
....·· Zone divisions A–G (geological, topographic)
....· Purbeck marble outcrop
▣ Site reports
● L.I.A. and R.B. sites exploiting mineral resources

		SHALE	SALT	POTTERY BB1	MARBLE	LIMESTONE	OTHER STONE
ZONE A	SITES	1, 2, 3, 4, 5, 6, 7, 8, 9, 10.	1, 2, 3, 4, 6, 9.				9 Rope Lake Hole
	TOTAL	10	6	—	—	—	—
ZONE B	SITES	11, 12, 13, 14, 15, 16, 17, 18, 19, 20, 21, 22, 23, 24, 25, 27, 28, 29, 30.			18, 26, 27, 28.		
	TOTAL	19	—	—	4	—	—
ZONE C	SITES	31, 32, 33, 34, 35, 36, 37, 38.	31		31, 37.	31	
	TOTAL	8	1	—	2	1	—
ZONE D	SITES	39, 40, 41					
	TOTAL	3	—	—	—	—	—
ZONE E	SITES	42, 43, 44, 45, 46, 48, 50.	49	43, 46.	46, 50.		46. 46 Norden
	TOTAL	7	1	2	2	—	1
ZONE F	SITES	57, 58, 59, 61	53, 55, 56, 57, 59, 60, 61.	51, 52, 53, 54, 55, 56, 57, 61.			57 57 Ower
	TOTAL	4	7	8	—	—	1
ZONE G	SITES	62		63			
	TOTAL	1	—	1	—	—	—

Figure 1. Distribution and industrial character of Iron Age and Romano-British sites known to be working the 'mineral' resources in the Isle of Purbeck and around Poole Harbour (this distribution does not include all find spots or features indicative of settlement).

importance within the Purbeck economy (Figure 1). The synthesis table must therefore be regarded as basic and preliminary, in both the number of sites represented, and the number of industrial characteristics identified for each site. The need for more detailed inter-site comparisons at a series of levels to examine organisation and trade is obvious. The comparison of coinage-loss between sites has demonstrated the value of such an approach (Woodward, 1980). However at this early stage conclusions must to some extent be speculative. It is not yet possible with certainty to isolate 'type sites', or a 'site hierarchy' related to status and trade.

These three excavations are only a small part of the excavation and survey work undertaken since the last comprehensive survey of Purbeck was published in 1970 by the Royal Commission (R.C.H.M., 1970). Since then many sites have been discovered, mapped, and part excavated, and most have been at least noted in the *Proceedings*. The excavation of many of these sites has been undertaken, including those published here, as rescue excavations in advance of building development, agricultural improvements (ploughing), coastal erosion, and mineral extraction. Although these agencies of threat and destruction have resulted in the discovery of many of the sites, they are also rapidly destroying what remains. Since at least 1948, when Calkin first published his Iron Age settlement sites, Purbeck has been recognised as containing a range of well preserved archaeological landscapes which are of regional and national importance. This was implicitly recognised in a regional policy document published by the Wessex Archaeological Committee in 1981 (Ellison 1981, 18). The document as a whole provided a research framework for rescue archaeology in Wessex, and in particular drew attention to and summarised the current work in Purbeck. Since this publication an intensive archaeological survey in the Isle of Purbeck with reference to impending threats has been undertaken by the Wessex Archaeological Committee (now Trust for Wessex Archaeology) for the Department of the Environment (now H.B.M.C.(E)). This survey project is being undertaken for the Trust by Peter Cox and John Hawkes, and Fig 1 is a synthesis of period information derived from the full survey record. Against this background of Rescue and Survey several excavations are at present being carried out; at Bucknowle (35) by Norman Field, Jeff Collins, and Tony Light; those at Redcliffe (53) by Ray Farrar for the Dorset National History and Archaeological Society; and the evaluation excavation/survey at Norden (46), and Fitzworth (56) by Peter Cox for the Trust for Wessex Archaeology. It is also likely as a result of current threats that further excavation will be necessary at Fitzworth (56), Norden (46), in addition to the continual need for rescue excavation and evaluation of coastally eroded sites such as Rope Lake Hole (9), Warbarrow (31), and Hobarrow (2) in particular. More recently, in the summer of 1985, survey and excavations have taken place on Furzey Island (59) (Cox, 1986) in advance of the construction of a production well for the Dorset oilfield, and this may in turn precipitate further pipe-line developments across the site at Ower.

Settlement development, farming, mineral extraction and exploitation have induced many subtle and more obvious changes in the environment of Purbeck, and these continue today. All the archaeological sites described here have contributed indirectly to the form and texture of the present Purbeck landscape, and indeed are an intrinsic part of it. It is through their careful study that the character and organisation of past societies will be identified, and the processes of landscape change understood. This is well illustrated at Ower, where excavations in conjunction with geomorphological and historical studies combine to suggest that the range of Ower, Green and Furzey Islands (Frontispiece, lower) may well have been joined at one time by low-lying land and salt marsh as a single peninsula. It is now possible to suggest that the present islands may have been formed as a result of erosion and land inundation, caused in part by harbour silting and rises in sea level since the Iron Age. However, excavations, survey and historical study also suggest that this may well have been precipitated or at least accelerated by the construction of salt-pans across, and the cutting of water channels through, low-lying land for access to the Ower settlement and its products (cover illustration). The material and settlement remains from Ower give an historical context for these events which begin in the first centuries BC. By comparative archaeological study this data contributes to our broader understanding of the development of trade, settlement, and industry in the region. In conjunction with the studies at Norden and Rope Lake Hole, it has been possible to contribute much to our understanding of the Purbeck Landscape and beyond.

Peter J. Woodward
October 1983, with additions May 1986

Acknowledgments

I was invited to provide an introduction to this volume by the Editor because of my direct responsibility for two of the sites published here, and my involvement in the area as a whole when working as Dorset Field Officer for the Dorset Archaeological Committee from September 1977 to September 1980. Subsequently the two excavation reports were completed whilst employed by what is now the Trust for Wessex Archaeology. I would wish to acknowledge the great assistance and encouragement that I have been given by the committee and staff of the Trust, the Department of the Environment, and the many ideas contributed by individuals which enabled this Monograph (or perhaps Tetro Graph) to reach this final form, and in particular the individual contributors to the excavation reports published here; also Peter Cox, John Hawkes and Martin Papworth for providing and preparing data from the Purbeck Survey (T.W.A. 1982-1985), prior to publication. I can only hope that I have done justice to this area in an introduction of such quick flourish. I can but apologise for any lack of academic precision, and thank the Editor for allowing me the opportunity of writing the introduction to an area of such outstanding importance.

Excavations at Norden, Corfe Castle, Dorset, 1968-1969

NIGEL SUNTER, BArch, RIBA

INTRODUCTION

The Isle of Purbeck has a rich and varied geology; its coastal position was an important factor in the popularity of its mineral deposits (especially marble, limestone and Kimmeridge Shale) which have, over the centuries, been transported well beyond Dorset. A continuous ridge of chalk, the Purbeck Hills, divides the predominantly limestone scenery to the south from the low-lying heathland to the north. Only two gaps of any significance break through the Purbeck Hills, the most spectacular being at Corfe Castle which is conveniently centrally positioned along the ridge. The medieval castle, on a high cone of chalk, impressively commands the passage to and from the Isle of Purbeck. Witin the area generally known as Norden, 450m north-west of the castle, is the Roman site (SY 95648271) which is the subject of the present report.

The site lies to the north-west of an area which has long been suspected of having been a sizeable Roman industrial settlement (Farrar 1951a). The extraction of white clay from the Bagshot Beds during the last century unearthed a number of Roman finds. A map showing the distribution of recorded find sites is illustrated in fig. 2B, and detailed in the accompanying gazetteer in Table 1. Overlying the clay is a deposit of extremely light white sand. Modern ploughing tends therefore to be relatively deep, disturbing any upper stratified layers. This potential danger was recognised by Mr. P. A. Brown who had established that the site was Roman and of some complexity. The excavation took place during the summers of 1968 and 1969, with a week after Christmas 1968. Interpretation of this complex site was hampered by the problems inherent in excavating a sandy soil; particularly the lack of definition between stratified layers. The action of worms and burrowing animals further blurred any distinctions. It has therefore been necessary to be particularly mindful of this disturbance whilst dating layers with the help of apparently stratified finds.

ACKNOWLEDGEMENTS

Thanks must first and foremost be offered to Mr M. S. Ramm of Norden Farm, owner of the site, and Mr Tony Brown without whose help, co-operation and knowledge of local archaeology it would not have been possible to carry out the excavation and interpret its result. I am grateful to Mr Brown also for allowing me to pubish drawings of: pottery (fig. 1 nos. 570-572; fig. 12 nos. 565-569); worked stone (fig. 24 nos. 2-3; fig. 25 nos. 2, 5) and small finds (microfiche M7 fig. 26 nos. 1, 6; fig. 28 nos. 19-21, 24). I would like to thank Professor B. W. Cunliffe who not only drew attention to the existence of the site, but who subsequently offered much help and encouragement.

I must thank those friends who toiled so hard to make the excavation a success: Ruth Marris, William Frend, Jude Henstridge, Brendan O'Connor, Anne Read and Bill Startin. Many people in Corfe Castle extended their friendship to us, but in particular we were grateful to Mr and Mrs MacRae who offered warmth and comfort during our Christmas excavation.

The then Ministry of Public Building and Works assisted the excavation financially, and the Department of the Environment has kindly contributed to the cost of preparing this report. The Dorset County Museum provided tools, and I am am indebted to both Mr Roger Peers and Mr Rodney Alcock for their assistance during the excavation and since. Southampton University conserved the copper alloy and shale objects, and I am particularly grateful to Mrs Jo Chaplin for her contribution.

In addition to those contributors to this report who are acknowledged separately, I would like to thank Miss Jane Griffiths who drew the flints, Mr R. W. Sanderson of the Institute of Geological Sciences for several enlightening discussions about the Isle of Purbeck and its rock formations; and finally Mrs Susan Walker and Mr R. A. H. Farrar who kindly read through this report in typescript and made several constructive suggestions for its improvement.

EXCAVATION REPORT

(N.B. In the following report the trench numbers preface the layers thus: 1.44 refers to Trench 1, Layer 44.)

The two areas north and south of the field boundary (fig. ZC) are described separately (microfiche M1). Apart from Trench 9 and parts of Trench 1, all those north of the field boundary were completely stripped down to the natural subsoil. The detailed excavated evidence is presented in tabular form (microfiche M1) and summarized below as a chronological sequence which is divided into eight periods, starting with the earliest. It should be emphasized that the grouping of features under one period is not necessarily an indication that they were strictly contemporary. The aim of excavating south of the field boundary was primarily to establish, if possible, the southern limit of the presumed road discovered in Trench 1 and attributed to period 4. Those features south of the field boundary are only mentioned briefly here where excavation yielded results directly relevant to those north of the field boundary.

Summary of Discoveries

Periods 1 and 2

The first period of occupation (fig. 3), represented by burnt layers (1.51, 2.20; fig. 8 sections A, F) and voids (1.88, 1.45, 8.12, 8.19, fig. 8, section E, 1.44) which may indicate the initial clearing of the site and uprooting of trees, appears to have taken place by AD 70 (on the basis of the Dr37 samian sherd, fig. 17 no. 2, from the primary scorched earth). The overlying layer of abundant chalk chippings (1.57, fig. 8 section E), interpreted as a workfloor for the manufacture of chalk tesserae, is also dated to soon after AD 70.

A rounded V-shaped ditch (1.37, fig. 8 sections D, E, F, plate I) of Period 1 continued to act as a boundary in Period 2, separating the turf layers to the west (1.43, 2.16, 2.19, 7.10, 8.9; fig. 8 sections A, D, E, F, G) from the more mixed layers (1.59, 4.9, 4.25; fig. 8 sections C, D; fig. 8 section H), possibly indicative of a ploughsoil, to the east. Wall footings (2.25; fig. 8 section A) and a substantial chalk floor (4.23; fig. 8 section C) are the only evidence of an upstanding structure of unknown function in either Periods 1 or 2.

Both Periods were characterised by an admixture of pure Durotrigian native wares, such as those illustrated by Brailsford (1958, 35) and Wheeler (1943, 230-241), with Roman fine wares including a large proportion of samian and some sherds from the Claudian kiln at Corfe Mullen. There is insufficient structural or other evidence associated with this early activity to establish the extent to which these wares were being used either by a native community, in which case there would, no doubt, be an indication of local wealth resulting possibly from the manufacture and supply of consumer goods for the new Roman markets; or by a settlement of Roman craftsmen who for their everyday kitchen ware would have bought from the local potters.

Period 3 (fig. 3)

The small scale activity of Period 3 is marked by levelling (1.49; fig. 8 section E) over the now apparently redundant silted-up Period 1 ditch (1.37). Two pits (1.39, 7.13; fig. 8 section D), a gully (7.11) and a trench (1.59, 1.67, 4.10; fig. 8 sections A, C, D, E, F) of unknown function, were identified. Apart from some later pottery from the layers beneath the chalk make-up for the Period 4 road (1.69, 8.5; fig. 8 sections F, G), all the evidence is consistent with a first century date.

Period 4 (fig. 2)

Period 4 is marked by the construction of a road (1.25, 2.18, 8.4,

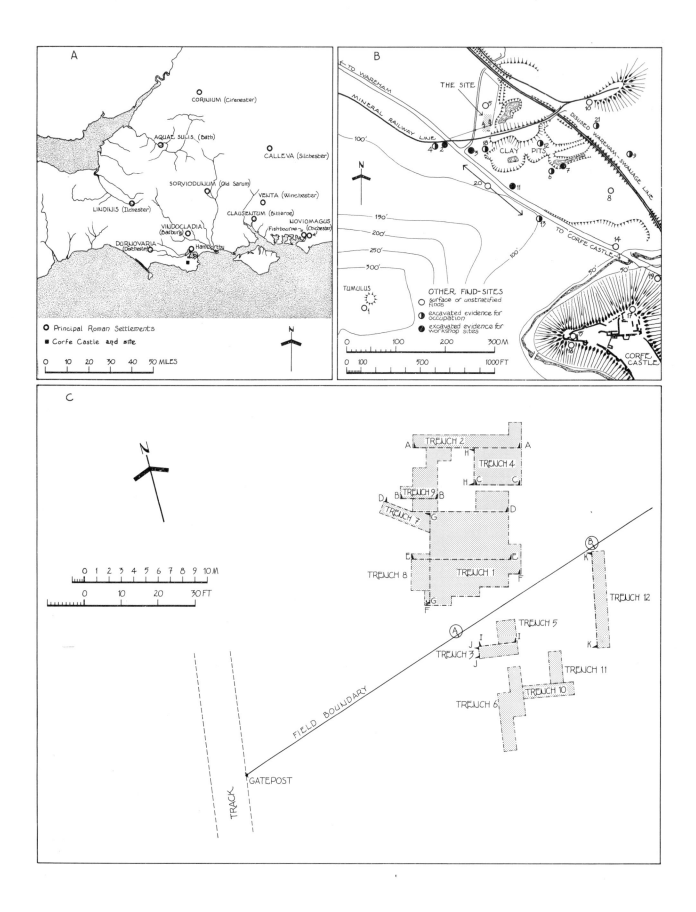

Figure 2. A – Location of Roman Corfe Castle. B – Norden and neighbouring find sites. C – Plan of the trenches.

Gazetteer of sites in the environs of Norden (fig. 2B)

1. SY 95408233 Romano-British sherds (Farrar, 1952, 93); rough-out for handmade shale armlet; 14 bronze coins (Farrar, 1959, 105).
2. SY 95568266 Part of shale table-leg, twenty small grey cubes (unused tesserae?) knapped from slightly calcareous siltstone, samian and Romano-British pottery (Farrar, 1964, 116).
3. SY 95628264 Floor (?) surfaces, shale offcut together with approximately two hundred flat shale discs varying in diameter 2.5 to 3cm and approximately 0.5cm thick, Romano-British pottery (Farrar, 1970, 156).
4. SY 95558266 Chalk road (?), incised shale panel or tray (Farrar, 1964, 116; 1965, 111).
5. SY 956827 Romano-British sherds (Farrar, 1951a, 86-91).
6. SY 95788261 Stone-paved floor, sherds of New Forest fluted beakers (Farrar, 1951a, 86-91); iron buckle and decorated samian (Farrar, 1970, 157).
7. SY 958826 Sacred well dating to the third and fourth centuries AD, evidence for shale-working (waste from shale armlet manufacture and other offcuts), numerous chalk tesserae (Hughes, 1972, 76; 1973, 91).
8. SY 95908257 Fragment of quernstone (Farrar, 1966, 119-20).
9. SY 95948264 Chalk and limestone floor, Romano-British pottery dating from first to fourth centuries AD, fragment of shale (Farrar, 1955, 126).
10. SY 95858276 Romano-British pottery from the banks of the clay-workings (although may have been derived from elsewhere; Farrar, 1970, 157).
11. SY 95698257 Romano-British pottery including Samian and New Forest Ware, a pestle of Purbeck stone, a Classic C shale core and many tesserae of chalk and 'ferruginous' shale (Farrar, 1972, 88; 1973b, 102).
12. Matcham's Pits 'A fine collection of Romano-British pottery' discovered in 1882, along with some 'coins, a bronze weapon and buckle, together with some stone coffins' and a 'road' 45.7cm below the surface. Moule (1906, 44) refers to a pottery factory at Norden presumably based on the 1882 evidence (Stuart, 1887, xxxix-xi, Farrar, 1955, 126).
13. SY 95738253 Flag-stones associated with Romano-British sherds and a coin of Nero in or near a water mains trench (inf. P. A. Brown).
14. A pair of bronze dividers and two shale plaques discovered in 1859 whilst lowering the road (Austen, 1859-60, 53; 225).
15. Corfe Castle Second century AD samian and coarse ware and a fragment of flue (?) tile (R.C.H.M., 1960, 38).
16. Surface finds of coarse Romano-British pottery (R.C.H.M., 1970, 599).
17. SY 95948233 Romano-British pottery (Farrar, 1963a, 104).
18. SY 95648265 Small Romano-British stone cist (Farrar, 1967b, 145).
19. SY 95998240 Romano-British sherd (Farrar, 1963a, 104).
20. SY 95568266 To SY 95788250 Surface finds of Romano-British pottery (R.C.H.M., 1970, 598).
21. SY 95858270 Building stone over an ashy layer containing a bronze fibula and a coin of Trajan (Inf. P. A. Brown).

Plate 1. Trench 1 looking north; Period 1, ditches 1.69 and 1.37.

9.6; fig. 8 sections A, B, D, F; fig. 9 section G; plate II) along the south and west of the excavated area, the surface of which had a pronounced camber. Along the south side the road was bounded by a V-profile limestone slab-lined ditch (1.27; fig. 9 section G; plate II) which turned the corner and terminated about a metre to the north. The pottery from the chalk hardcore (with the exception of that from 7.4, which may have been disturbed) is dated to sometime after *c*. AD 125. However if the chalk hardcore excavated in Trench 3, south of the field boundary (3.8, 3.3, 3.5, 3.4, 3.13; fig. 10 sections I, J), is part of the same road then the mortarium from 3.3

(fig. 13 no. 548) gives a date later in the century, from *c*. AD 140. The apparent lull in the occupation of the site at the end of the first and the beginning of the second centuries is not reflected by the overall sequence of samian (see p. 28 and microfiche M3) whose density is greatest between *c*. AD 43 and 120, and it follows that the density of occupation in the areas bordering the site presumably continued unbroken. However, apart from three unstratified coins: one of Domitian, one of Hadrian and one of Marcus Aurelius, all the coins (microfiche M6) belonged to pre-AD 73 or to the late third century and after. It could have been the result of either a drop in

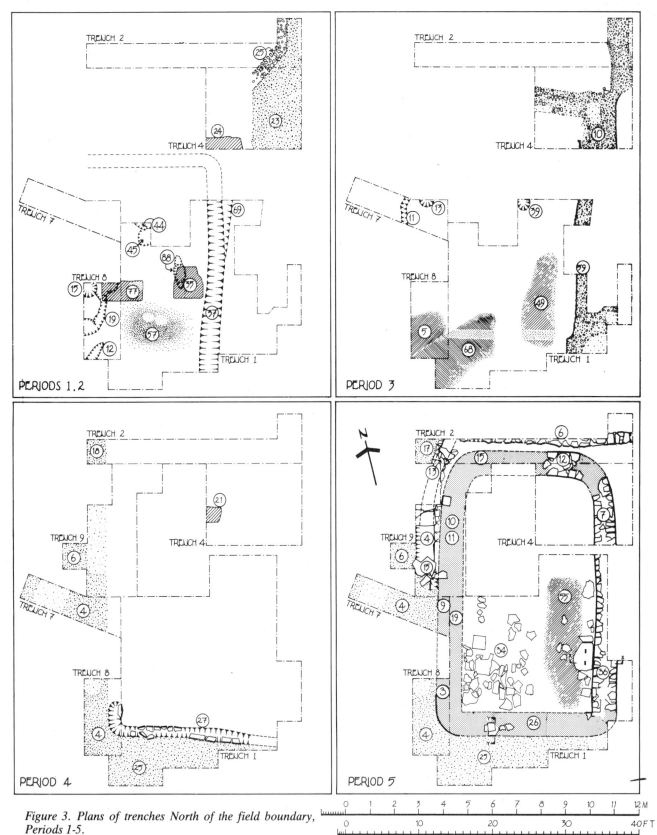

Figure 3. Plans of trenches North of the field boundary, Periods 1-5.

Plate 2. Trench 1 looking west; Period 4 Ditch 1.27 with road metalling 1.25 to the left and Period 5 paving on the right.

the density of occupation, in the economic well-being of the community or a period of intense activity as suggested below (see p. 43).

Period 5 (fig. 3)

In Period 5 the land bounded to the south and west by the Period 4 road was now developed, and the south wall of the new buildings was built over the road ditch. The lower courses of the east wall (1.36; fig. 8 section D) and much of the north east corner (2.12, 4.7; fig. 8 section A, C) remained intact to a height of approximately 20cm above the contemporary floor level. The other walls had been almost entirely robbed (1.19, 1.26, plate V; 2.15, fig. 8 section A; 8.3, 9.10). The wall was an average of 90cm thick, and built of rubble and limestone mortared together with soil. The northern corners were curved internally and externally, whilst what survived of the southern corners indicated that they were internally right-angled but externally curved. There is no obvious explanation for the differing north and south corners, although the resulting plan does impose certain limitations on the form of the recon-structed building. The one remaining stone of shelly Purbeck limestone at the base of the south facade was roughly moulded and presumably unfinished (fig. 4 section Y-Y). It seems unlikely that it was designed for use in this building and it is assumed to be either re-used from elsewhere or more likely a waste product from the stone workshops.

The overall size of the building would have been 11.3m long by 7m wide, leaving a clear internal space 9.3m long by 5.3m wide. It is not known where the entrance would have been, although it clearly was not in the east wall, and it is unlikely to have opened onto the uncovered gully (2.6; plate IV) to the north. There was no evidence for any partitions nor any roof supports inside the main walls, and in these respects the building found at Encombe Obelisk (Calkin 1953, 54; Farrar 1954, 80-1), which appears to have been used for industrial purposes, was similar.

Central to the problem of reconstructing the possible architectu-ral form of the building is the thickness of its walls relative to its size. Buildings constructed entirely of rubble masonry with earth as

a mortar are certainly not exceptional (Innocent, 1916, 121), but ideally walls built in this manner should be rather less than 60cm thick so that the inner and outer skins can be adequately interlocked (Brunskill, 1971, 35). At Norden there is no such bond through the thickness of the wall, and even assuming that regular bands of through-stones held the wall together, this is an extravagant use of building stone, all of which would have had to be transported some considerable distance from the limestone quarries south of Brenscombe Hill.

The Royal Commission notes that, in its surviving vernacular buildings (R.C.H.M., 1970, 42, 268), the difference between building materials used south of the chalk ridge, and the limited choice available to the north, where there is little building stone and where many buildings were as a result constructed of cob. Even in

Plate 3. Trench 2; Period 5 culvert.

Corfe Castle parish (*ibid*, 91-96), where the gap through the chalk hills would have made north-south transport more easy, there is still a notable number of cob buildings. Cob walls were generally built on a low stone plinth and this may indeed be what has survived at Norden; 90cm is not an uncommon thickness for walls built of cob (Clifton-Taylor, 1972, 298). Rounded corners are a distinct advantage since square corners are liable to crack and are vulnerable to physical damage (cf. Addy, 1898, 38-9). As an alternative to cob which is a 'wet' technique, 'pisé' a dry method in which suitable earth was compacted between boards of timber or wattle (cf. Pliny, XXXV, xiviii) may have been used. It is suggested that the 15 to 20cm of sandy soil which accumulated over the site (1.14, 1.28, 1.29, 4.8; fig. 8 sections C, D, E; fig. 9 section G) probably derived from such cob or pisé walls. Furthermore, it is possible that in addition to chalk and straw, broken pottery was added in order to achieve a workable mix. Hence perhaps the very large quantity of pottery distributed evenly throughout the layer.

Around the north and west sides of the building the Period 4 road had been cut away to accommodate a flat bottomed covered culvert (2.13, 9.4; fig. 8 sections A, B; plate III). Although no direct evidence was found of any suitable roofing material, it is likely that thatch which is relatively light, and can easily provide the generous eaves overhang essential to protect cob walls, was used. Thus the V-shaped gully (2.6, plate IV) to the north may have been designed to take water from the eaves, giving an overhang to the centre of the ditch of approximately 50cm.

Inside the building the ground had again subsided into the Period 1 ditch, and the surface was levelled with chalk and limestone hardcore (1.55; fig. 8 section D). Much of the interior was floored with limestone slabs and, judging by the rather haphazard layout and in places the lapping of one over the other, one is prompted to suggest that they were laid as and when necessary over a period of time (plate V). Against the east wall a large block of shelly Purbeck limestone 10cm thick had been set into the floor upon a foundation of limestone and chalk (fig. 4 section X-X; plate VI) and beside it a smaller slab of fine-grained limestone from the Purbeck-Portland beds. In the top surface of the larger block were two rectangular holes 50cm apart (centre to centre), each 7cm deep. Their sides were vertical and they were therefore not designed to be lewis-holes. It is suggested that this may have formed the base for a lathe or similar machine (see below).

The earliest probable date for the erection of the building is *c.* AD 150, and the vast majority of sherds could well have been in use before this date, indeed many could be of first century origin, which lends support to the suggestion of cob or pisé walls with an admixture of pottery. The pottery found in the fill of the Period 4 road ditch was of little help in dating the buiding whose south wall sealed it. From the chalk footings for the wall came only a small quantity of pottery; a flanged bowl is post *c.* AD 125 in date, and apart from one late Antonine sherd, the latest samian is Hadrianic to early Antonine. It is assumed that the former (from 9.11) was later in date than the building and trodden into the footings by the wall robbers. From within the wall came another flanged bowl and

one sherd of Antonine samian. It is suggested below that the building had been abandoned and its site used for dumping refuse well before *c.* AD 225. If the shortage of mid-Antonine samian sherds (observed by Dr Greene see p. 30) can indeed be attributable to the period of time when the whole of the excavated area was occupied either by a building or by roads, both of which would have been in use, then the approximate period *c.* AD 150-180 could very well represent the life span of the building.

The Period 5 building went out of use and household and industrial refuse were deposited on the site. If the walls of the building were built of cob they would doubtless have had to be in a very advanced state of decay before it would have been worth

Plate 4. Trench 2 looking west; Period 5 wall and gully 2.6 containing complete vessel, earlier layers partially removed.

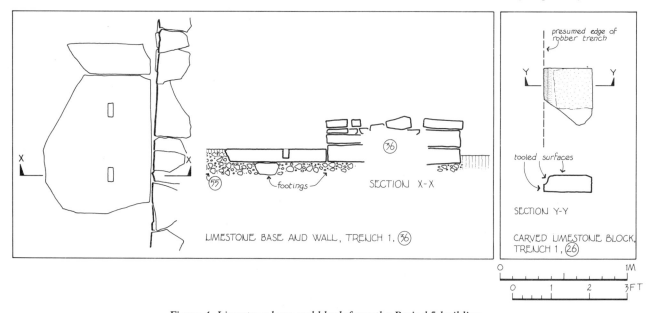

Figure 4. Limestone base and block from the Period 5 building.

Plate 5. Trench 1 looking south-west; Period 6 footings 1.16, together with remains of Period 5 wall 1.26 and Period 5 floor paving, both to the right of the figure.

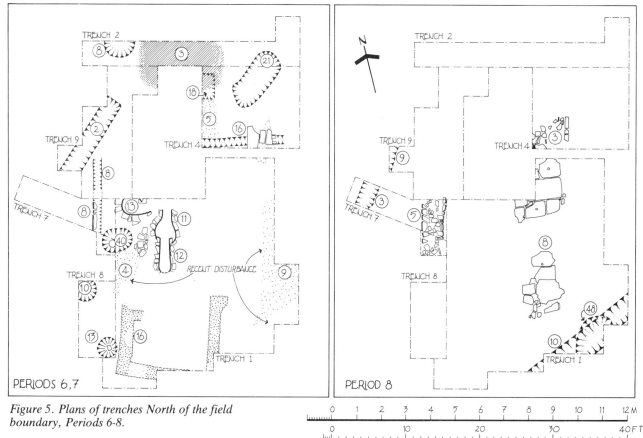

Figure 5. Plans of trenches North of the field boundary, Periods 6-8.

robbing the plinth of its stone for use elsewhere, and it may be for this reason that so much of the east wall has survived. Consequently it is from the level of soil accumulation that the walls were robbed. Most of the large quantity of pottery from this layer could well date to before c. AD 150, or c. AD 200 at the latest (apart from isolated sherds). The later sherds could easily have been intrusive, since only clearly defined features were recognisable in the uniform grey sandy soil which had been much disturbed by burrowing animals. Thus the robber trenches could have dated to the first quarter of the third century or earlier.

Period 6 (fig. 5)
In Period 6 a thin spread of soft chalk (1.4, 1.9, 4.5; fig. 8 section D; fig. 9 sections G, H) possibly indicates the re-use of the site for purposes other than dumping refuse. Cut through this was a partially slab-lined gully (4.16; fig 9 section H; plate VII) containing a large quantity of pottery including many fragments from individual vessels, totalling 10.8kg (fig 13a). It is suggested that many of these vessels must have been whole at or not long before the time they were deposited in the gully. There would appear to be no reason to date any of the forms represented to much later than c. AD 200. Indeed, over half of the fragments from the roughcast beaker (fig. 15 no. 17) were recovered from the gully, and this is unlikely to have been manufactured after c. AD 150. Even allowing for the 10 to 15 years suggested by Webster (1973, 1) as a normal period of use before breakage for coarse ware and even a longer period of time for more valuable vessels, the roughcast beaker, in particular, must have survived an exceptionally long time before being discarded. To suggest a date of c. AD 225 for the deposition of the pottery in the gully must surely be considered as the latest date reasonable as a *terminus post quem* for the chalk layer and in turn for the soil accumulation beneath it. In that case it is logical to suggest that the flanged and beaded bowl which was found with the chalk must also have been intrusive.

The probable footings of a small building (1.16; fig. 8 section H; plate V) have also been designated to this period. They enclosed three sides of a rectangle 3m wide, but nothing remained of its floor. A possible hearth (4.27; fig. 9 section H) which was never fired was also discovered.

Period 7 (fig. 5)
It is difficult to assign particular features of Period 7 to any clear chronological sequence, but they would appear to represent a varied use of the site over a number of years.

A group of three ovens or kilns (1.11, 1.12, 1.13; fig. 5; plates, VIII, IX, X; see also microfiche M1), was found in Trench 1, each differing in character from the others. Kilns 1.11 and 1.12 were excavated by Mr P. A. Brown, and 1.13 by the writer. The walls of all three were constructed of both shelly and fine-grained limestone set in a mortar of clay. The exposure to intense heat had caused many stones to become friable, cracked and grey-blue in colour, with the clay turning orange-red. Kiln 1.11 (plate VIII) had been partly demolished to form the stoke-pit for 1.12 which replaced it (plate IX). The mouth of the east facing fluc of 1.13 (plates VIII, X) was placed a little to the south of the mouth of 1.11. Therefore

they were presumably not in use at the same time. Kiln 1.11 (1.13m long by 70cm wide overall) was of pear-shaped plan with a clay floor. Kiln 1.12 (approx. 1.4m long by 50cm wide) was unusual in having no recognisable distinction between the flue and the body of oven; the floor was constructed of limestone slabs. 1.13 was assymetrical in plan (1.25m long by 70cm wide). It had a predominantly clay floor with a limestone slab set into it at the mouth of the flue.

These three ovens or kilns, though different in shape, presumably all belong to the common 'up-draught' type of key-hole shaped kiln. 1.13 is similar to the oven/kiln found at Broadmayne (Young 1973, 47) and apparently also to those found on the new library site at Colliton Park, Dorchester. However, worthy of note is the coarse ware found inside this oven which dates to the end of the third century and which has collectively a distinctive character which differentiates it from most pottery found elsewhere on the site (fig. 13b). These sherds were generally of the common Black-Burnished type, but with surface brush-marks applied before firing. Whilst surface brush-marks are not uncommon on later BB1 pottery (Farrar, 1973, 76) this characteristic is represented on only a very small proportion of the later ware at Norden. Whilst the majority of the types in this group would not be uncommon in any late third century context, a number do portray somewhat individual or less common features. For example, the vessel in fig. 13, no. 468 has an unusual form for its type, and decoration (i.e. an acute rather than obtuse lattice, with brush-marks beneath). The handled version of the jar/beaker (fig. 14 no. 342) is certainly uncommon (cf. Field, 1958, 109 fig. 4 no. 1 and Calkin, 1959, 123, for the decoration). The storage jar sherds with brushed exterior surfaces are too poorly represented on this site and elsewhere to suggest they are exceptional, although it should be noted that almost all the surfaces are oxidised externally; Farrar, (1977, 207) has suggested that the blackening process may have been a

Plate 6. Trench 1; limestone base set against east wall of Period 5 building.

Plate 7. Trench 4 looking west; Period 6 gully showing cover-slabs and Period 5 wall.

Plate 8. Trench 1 looking north-west; foundations of kilns 1.11 and 1.13.

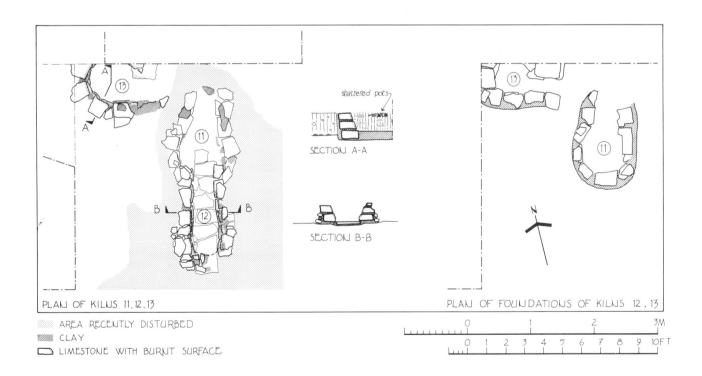

PLAN OF KILNS 11.12.13

PLAN OF FOUNDATIONS OF KILNS 12.13

SECTION A-A

SECTION B-B

shattered pots

AREA RECENTLY DISTURBED
CLAY
LIMESTONE WITH BURNT SURFACE

Figure 6. Kilns from Period 7.

separate stage in the initial firing. One flat base from an oval 'fish' dish (cf. fig. 14 no. 473) has an unusually large diameter. There are also insufficient numbers of late lids known to be able to say with any certainty that the example (fig. 14 no. 477) with a rough unburnished interior is an unsual feature. A date of post *c.* AD 275 is suggested for this distinctive group of pottery.

A small bar of pottery, also found in the oven/kiln and made in the same fabric as the vessels, with a trapezoidal section, it is unlikely to have been part of a vessel. Calkin (1948, 57) suggests that the clay bars found at Fitzworth may have been kiln bars, although Farrar (pers. comm.) has not been able to trace them. It is possible that the Norden example has a similar use, perhaps as a spacer or 'setter' in a kiln. Mr Brown, however, considered this fired clay object was too small and thin to have been effective as a fire bar and suggested it may have been a crude figurine.

It is clearly worth considering whether the structures with which the pottery was associated are indeed kilns. However, it should be stressed that no direct evidence which would normally be indicative of pottery manufacture (such as the presence of wasters) was found, and such evidence as the proportion of less common or unusual forms, and the 'setter'(?) can only add weight to the suggestion that pottery was manufactured on or near the site. All three 'kilns' are considerably smaller than the normal size for pottery kilns, but they are by no means unique in this respect. Although the floor of the firing chamber of 1.11 may have been supported upon a tongue or pedestal, even this, which is the widest of the three, is well within the maximum size given by Corder for kilns of Type IA(i) which had a permanent unsupported floor of perforated clay (Corder, 1959, 15); 1.12 and 1.13 would certainly belong to this category. At Crambeck a series of similar small kilns were found which apparently had no internal supports (Corder, 1928, 16, 17). A group of small kilns was also found at Little Chester, Derby, although all of these had central pedestals which supported the firing chamber floor (Brassington, 1971, 40). Whilst the firing chamber, which would have been totally above ground, could have been built to a larger diameter than the combustion chamber

below, it is unlikely that it was very much larger since the distribution of heat would not have been even throughout the oven. As a result none of the kilns would have been able to hold many vessels at one firing, and the excavator of the Derby kilns suggested that his kilns may have been experimental. The design differences between the 'kilns' at Norden could also have been the product of experimentation.

It is suggested then, that there was a pottery industry of some kind at Norden around the end of the third century. Apart from the Claudian kilns at Corfe Mullen (Calkin, 1935, 42ff), the horizontal-draught kiln found at Ower (Farrar, 1951b, 91-2) and a possible kiln site at Fitzworth (Farrar, 1949, 62-3; 1973a, 92), there is no confirmed evidence for any further kiln structures in the area, although there is much evidence for the production of pottery in South Dorset on a large scale. Farrar (1973a, 91) suggests that much of this may have been fired in bonfires. In or around 1882 a 'fine collection of Roman pottery' was found in Matcham's Clay Pits at Norden (Stuart, 1887, xxxix-xl). The finds were deposited at Encombe, but have since disappeared. The pottery was described as 'black in colour; it occurs principally in the form of urn-shaped vessels, decorated with a lozenge pattern around the neck', and it was suggested that these were all jars or cooking pots of the

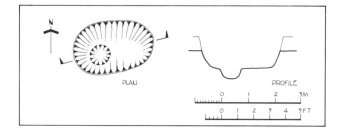

Figure 7. Pit 1.40, Period 7.

Plate 9. Trench 1 looking north-west; kiln 1.12.

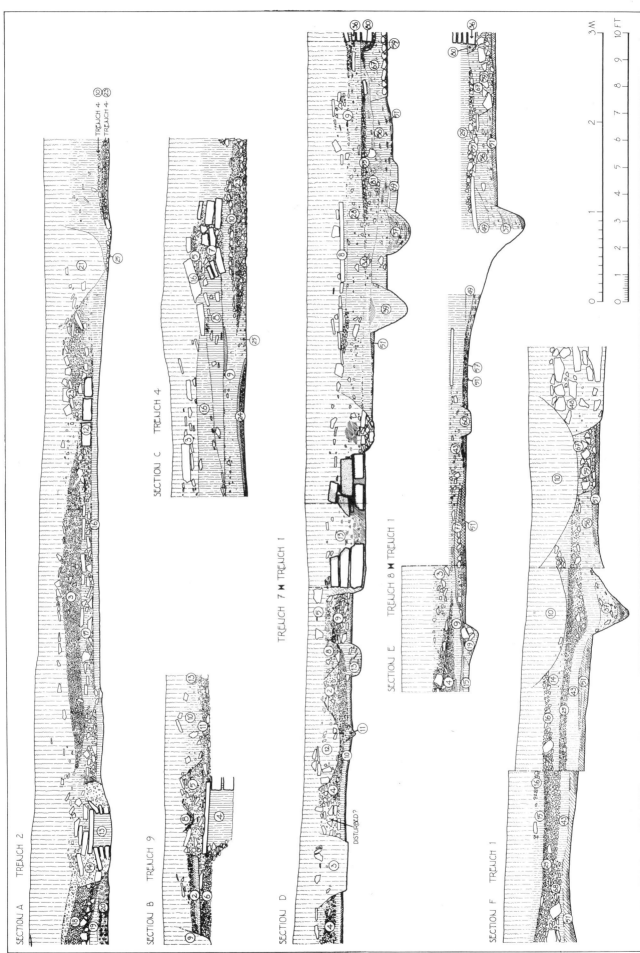

Figure 8. East-West sections of trenches North of the field boundary.

common Black-Burnished variety, although the description of the pattern around the neck is a little ambiguous. The 'lozenge pattern' probably refers to the lattice decoration so common on these vessels, but found generally around the body rather than around the neck. It seems most likely that the position of the decoration rather than the decoration itself was inaccurately described, in which case there is no clue as to its probable date. Nevertheless, if this pottery was indeed made at Norden, then it adds weight to the the suggestion that the structures discovered in the present excavations were in fact kilns. A dump of chalk and other material (2.3; fig. 8 section A; fig. 9 section H) had been deposited in the north of the excavated area and this had partly slumped into the robber-trench of the north wall of the Period 5 building. It consisted of layers of Purbeck Marble rubble, including

Plate 10. Trench 1 looking west; kiln 1.13, showing shattered vessel.

some which had been sawn and worked; some slag (probably blacksmithing waste, information P. Wilthew, Ancient Monuments Laboratory), burnt clay and sawn chalk, as well as much hard shale and mudstone, many fragments of which had worked surfaces and saw-marks. The large quantity of hard chalk, varied in size, and apart from many fine chalk chippings was all roughly cubically split (and similar in shape and size to the tesserae found in Period 1). Without doubt, this represents the waste from a nearby workshop (see microfiche M4). This layer contained a coin of Maximianus, and must therefore date to post AD 296-7.

The shallow trench (9.2; fig. 8 section B) may have been the footings for a building the rest of which would have stood to the north-west. It contained sherds from New Forest beakers and Oxford ware bowls as well as discarded waste products from the chalk and shale industries (fig. 22, nos. 48-50). The remaining features belonging to this period, apart from a gully (7.8, 9.8; fig. 8 section B, D) which may have been Period 6, are all pits. The most interesting is 1.40 (fig. 8, section E), 1.5m long by 1m wide with sides sloping to a base about 55cm below the contemporary ground level. A small depression 40cm diameter and 20cm deep was dug into the bottom of the south-western half of the pit. As a word of caution, there was evidence that the lower fill of this pit had been disturbed by burrowing animals.

Within the lower fill of the pit were the remains of about twelve sheep which were killed when they were between 10-24 months old (I am grateful to J. Startin for her assessment of the bones: see microfiche M9). None showed any signs of having been butchered, and many of the bones were still articulated when found, but the meat must have been missing from the bones when they were deposited in such a small pit, especially since most of them were found in the north-eastern half. In addition to the bones a fragment of a bone pin and a 12mm cube of a soft dark brown clay which is hitherto unique on this site were found. The black soil layer was sealed by limestone slabs and chalk, and the upper fill of the pit consisted of a mixed layer containing sandy soil, chalk and lumps of clay. The excavation did not throw any light on the possible function of the depression in the base of the pit, but if it was a post-hole related in some way to the pit, the post seems likely to have been removed at some stage rather than left *in situ* since the hole contained a number of non-articulated bones. These could have fallen into the void as the post was withdrawn. There is no obvious explanation for the use to which this pit might have been put and it must be concluded that the evidence points in the direction of some ritual activity; whether as part of some culinary process or post-mortem treatment of a diseased flock is of course mere speculation. Conclusions of a more concrete nature might have been drawn had more complete retrieval taken place. We can only conclude that the sheep, 79 per cent of which were at roughly the same stage at death, were buried finally in a partly articulated state for reasons unknown.

A total of 1,067 fragments of bone came from this pit, which has been roughly dated to the late third or fourth centuries AD, on the basis of a small amount of pottery found within it.

The only other notable pit (2.8) is datable to post AD 337-41 on account of the four coins found within it. The overall dating evidence provides a range between *c.* AD 275 and post *c.* AD 340 for Period 7.

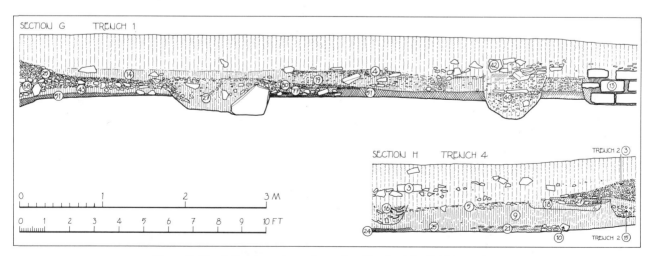

Figure 9. North-South sections of trenches North of the field boundary.

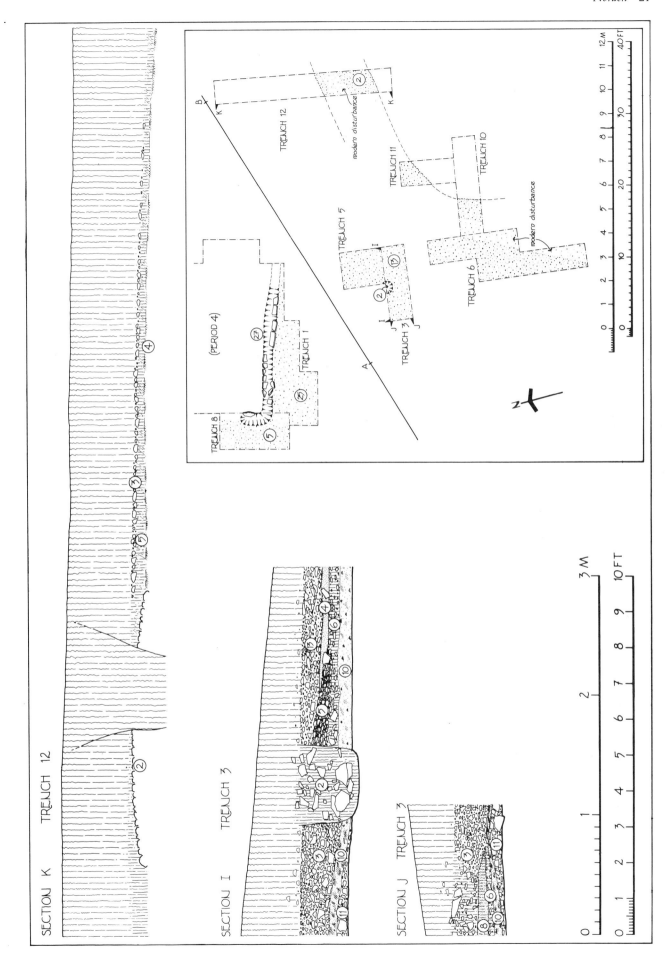

Figure 10. Trenches to the South of the field boundary.

Period 8
The miscellaneous features described under Period 8 are not themselves datable, although no finds stratified beneath them need be more recent than late Roman. The two areas of paving (1.8, 4.3; fig. 8 sections C, D and plate XI) were possibly part of a single floor, although there was no positive evidence for any standing structure relating to them. However, the three narrow stones aligned north-south in Trench 4 could quite convincingly denote the position of a wall which might have extended southwards along the east edge of the paved floor. Three of the slabs have circular holes in them, each approximately 6cm diameter; these seem to have been drilled from both faces. One additional hole, which was not quite so perfectly circular, was drilled through the edge of a slab in the northern group. These holes do not seem to have any logical relationship to one another.

The remains of the lowest course of a drystone wall (7.5; fig. 8 section D), 90cm wide may also relate in some way to the paving slabs.

THE POTTERY
The illustrated pottery is described in detail under the following headings: Coarse Ware (figs 11, 12, 13 and 14), Fine Ware (fig. 15) Samian Ware (fig. 17). The Coarse Ware includes such wares as mortaria whose identifications and descriptions have kindly been contributed by Mrs K. F. Hartley and the Fine Ware and Samian Ware identifications Dr K. T. Greene.

Coarse Ware
A considerable quantity of coarse ware was unearthed and consequently it has been possible to illustrate only a limited number of vessels. These are largely vessels which do not conform to common types, where they are either particularly complete or good examples of a type, or where they are of special importance as a group. Other vessels are described in detail by phase in the full catalogue (microfiche M2).

By far the majority of coarse ware sherds from Norden can be described broadly as being within the tradition of the 'Black-Burnished' pottery industry. These 'Black-Burnished' wares can, for the purpose of fabric description, conveniently be divided into two main groups, Fabrics 1 and 2:

Fabric 1: a gritty fabric, frequently containing quartz grits and occasionally lumps of quartz. The texture varies according to the coarseness of the grit, which may be a very coarse sand or sand and quartz, or a rather finer sand producing a more homogeneous 'spongy' fabric. The colour naturally varies considerably as a result of different firing conditions, but commonly the ware is dark grey or brown-grey. Burnishing generally produces a dullish finish, although well-burnished examples can be relatively shiny.

Fabric 2: a finer and more consistent fabric than Fabric 1. Generally a much darker colour, often black, but not uncommonly the ware can have a thin light grey 'skin' lying immediately under the black surface. Burnishing often produces a much shinier finish, and frequently, though not invariably, Fabric 2 vessels are better made than those of Fabric 1.

The distinction between Fabrics 1 and 2 becomes blurred at the finer end of the scale, and borderline cases are described as belonging to Fabric 1/2. Areas of burnishing are indicated by stipple on the illustrations, and are only described where the nature of its execution is considered significant.

Figure 11 (Coarse Ware)
9 Rim of jar, fabric 1, grey, unburnished. Period 1, primary scorched earth (1.51, 2.20).
45 Base of jar out-turned foot, fabric 1, grey, fired black on surface. Period 1, ditch (1.37).
47 Base of jar with splayed footring, fabric 1, grey, fired black on surface, burnished externally on base and body. Period 1, ditch (1.37).
61 Jar with angular rim, fabric 1, black, fired brown/black on surface. Period 2, turf layers (1.43, 2.16, 2.19, 7.10, 8.10).
79 Vertical-sided jar with slightly out-turned rim, fabric 1/2, grey. Period 2, turf layers (see no. 61).
80 Globular jar with simple rim, fabric 1, grey fired black on surface. Period 2, turf layers (see no. 61).
91 Straight-sided bowl or large beaker with bead rim, fabric 1, grey, fired black on surface, well burnished. Period 2, turf layers (see no. 61).

Plate 11. Trench 1 looking north-west; Period 8 paving slabs 1.8.

134 Jar with upright, outward-curving rim, fabric 2, black, well-burnished. Period 3, chalk rubble (1.68).

186 Beaker or small jar with upright rim and small shoulder, fabric 2, grey, fired buff on the surface. Period 4, ditch (1.27).

187 Globular jar with upright rim and verical appliqué strips around the body, fabric 1, grey. Period 4, ditch (1.27).

201 Jug, fabric 1, black. Period 5, foundations for walls (1.80, 7.9, 9.11).

206 Jar with angular rim with a slight hollowing around the inside of the top of rim; fabric 1/2, black, fired black/brown on surface. Period 5, walls (1.36, 2.12, 4.7).

226 Globular jar with upstanding bead rim with slight hollowing inside rim; fabric 1, grey, fired black on surface. Period 5, robber trenches for walls (1.19, 1.26, 2.15, 8.3, 9.10).

257 Jar with upright rim and no prominent shoulder, fabric 1/2, black, fired grey/brown on surface, with zone of decoration around body. Period 5, gully (2.6).

322 Small jar with simple rim, fabric 1, black, with burnished arcading around body. Period 6, soil accumulation (1.14, 1.28, 1.29, 4.8).

325 Jar with simple out-turned rim, fabric 1, grey, lightly burnished. Period 6, soil accumulation (1.14, 1.28, 1.29, 4.8).

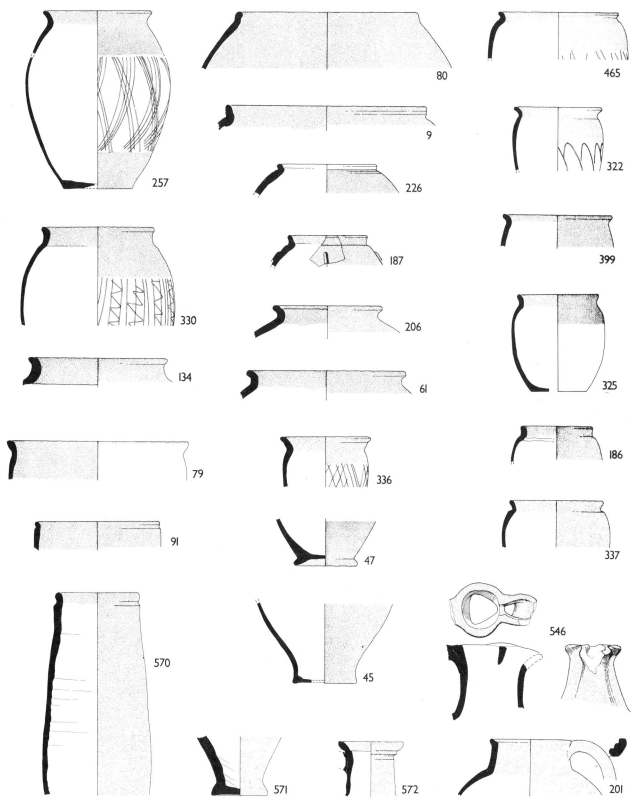

Figure 11. Coarse Ware: jars, beakers and flagons, scale 1:4.

330 Jar with upright rim similar to no. 257; fabric 2, grey, fired black on surface, well burnished with decoration around body. Period 6, soil accumulation (see no. 325).

336 Jar with straight out-turned rim, fabric 2, grey, laminated, fired black on surface, lattice decoration around body. Period 6, soil accumulation (see no. 325).

337 Jar with short upright rim, fabric 1/2, grey/orange, laminated, fired black on surface. Period 6, soil accumulation (see no. 325).

399 Jar with vertical sides and out-turned lip, fabric 1/2, grey, fired black on surface. Period 6, disturbed rubble (7.2, 9.5).

465 Jar with prominent shoulder and curled-over lip, fabric 2, black, well burnished with burnished lattice decoration around body.

546 Flagon with pinched spout and single handle, fabric 1, grey, fired black on surface. Period 8, (1.48).

570 Tall cylindrical vessel with bead rim, fabric 1, black/brown, fired grey on surface, burnished externally and only roughly internally. Unstratified.

571 Base of jar out-turned at the foot, coarse black ware containing prominent quartz and sand grits, fired black/brown on the surface, roughly burnished externally, only very crudely finished internally. Unstratifed.

572 Jug with single handle at neck, fabric 1, black, fired brown/black on surface. Unstratified.

Figure 12 (Coarse Ware)

24 Bowl with thick, square rim, fabric 1, laminated, black, fired brown on surface; large, but undetermined rim diameter. Period 1, primary scorched earth (1.51, 2.20).

25 Rim of bowl or pedestal foot, fabric 1, grey, fired black on surface, well burnished. Period 1, primary scorched earth (1.51, 2.20).

28 Base of bowl or jar with holes punched through base before firing, presumably a collander, fabric 2, black. Period 1, irregular shaped depressions (1.44, 1.45, 1.88, 8.12, 8.19). Fits with Coarse Ware no. 525 Period 7, pit 8.10.

29 Bowl with internally hollowed rim, horizontal rib or flange around the body, and pedestal foot-ring, fabric 2, black, well burnished. Period 1, irregular shaped depressions (see no. 28).

57 Bowl with thickened and internally hollowed rim, fabric 1, black, well burnished and decorated with burnished diagonal lines around body. Period 1, ditch (1.37).

60 Round-bodied bowl or jar with out-turned rim, and probably with handle just beneath the rim, fabric 1, black/brown, fired black on surface, well burnished exterior, slightly burnished inside. Period 1, hearth (1.77). Fits with Coarse Ware no. 523, period 7, pit 8.10.

103 Small dish or lid with slightly out-turned bead rim with hollowing internally, fabric 2, black, well burnished. Period 2, turf layers (1.43, 2.16, 2.19, 7.10, 8.9).

105 Carinated bowl or tazza, fabric 1, black, fired buff internally and buff/orange externally. Period 2, turf layers (see no. 103).

135 Base of bowl with pedestal foot, fabric 1, black. Period 3, chalk rubble (1.68).

199 Dish or jar with horizontal rim, fine hard micaceous fabric, burnt to a grey colour but originally pink, with red slip which is now mostly worn off. Period 5, wall foundations (1.80, 7.9, 9.11).

262 Flat-rimmed dish with vertical sides and a beading around the base, fabric 1, grey, laminated, fired black/brown on surface. Period 5, gully (2.6).

269 Flat-rimmed bowl, fabric 1, light grey, laminated, burnished inside, lightly burnished outside. Period 5, rubble (1.55, 1.81).

372 Straight-sided bowl with small flat rim, fabric 1, grey, burnished lattice decoration externally. Period 6, soil accumulation (1.14, 1.28, 1.29, 4.8).

375 Bowl with thick horizontal rim and slight bead on lip, fabric 1, black, coarse, with white inclusions, eroded burnished surface.

376 Small flat-rimmed bowl with hollowing on top of rim, fabric 2, grey, fired black on surface, zone of burnished lattice decoration around body. Period 6, soil accumulation (see no 372).

446 Base of bowl (?) with footring, fabric 1, grey, fired black/brown on surface. Period 6, shallow trench (4.18).

520 Bowl with small out-turned lip, fabric 1, black, well burnished. Period 7, pit (1.40).

521 Bowl with double bead rim, fabric 1, grey/brown, laminated, fired black/brown, on surface, only roughly burnished internally. Period 7, pit (1.40).

539 Small dish, fabric 1, grey, laminated. Period 7, pit (2.21).

541 Curved-sided bowl with thick rim, fabric 1, grey, laminated, fired black on surface, traces of brush-marks internally applied before firing. Period 8, layer sealed beneath floor (1.8, 4.3).

542 Flanged bowl with stubby flange and bead rim, fabric 1, black. Period 8, layer sealed beneath floor (1.8, 4.3).

547 Bead-rimmed bowl or beaker, fabric 1, black. Period 4 road (3.3, 3.4, 3.5, 3.8, 3.13).

565 Flat-rimmed bowl with applied decoration on rim, fabric 2, grey. Unstratified.

567 Straight-sided dish with spout, fabric 1/2, grey/pink, fired grey/brown on surface. Unstratified.

568 Base of (?) bowl with external beading, fabric 1, black. Unstratified.

569 Round-sided bowl with grooved rim and prominent handle(s), fabric 1, grey fired light grey on surface, burnished inside and lightly outside where lattice decoration is superimposed. Unstratified.

Figure 13 (Coarse Ware)

51 Bowl or lid with slight beading at rim, fabric 2, light grey, fired light grey/brown on surface. Period 1, ditch (1.37).

104 Lid or bowl with bead rim, hard grey fabric with fine quartz grits. Period 2, turf layers (1.43, 2.16, 2.19, 7.10, 8.9).

107 Base of amphora, pink/buff fabric. Period 2 turf layers (see no. 104).

123 Lid with internally beaded rim, fabric 1, black, with quartz grits. Period 2, ? ploughsoil (1.56, 4.9, 4.25).

125 Mortarium, very well-worn and burnt, in fine, cream fabric, tempered with sandy particles and some grey flint, black and quartz grit surviving. This mortarium form in this fabric was made by such potters as Q. Valerius Se--- and others whose work can be confidently dated *c.* AD 55-80. Their fabric and grit indicate manufacture in Gaul or south-east Britain. Period 2, ? ploughsoil (see no. 123).

130 Bead rim lid or bowl with curved wall and hollowing inside rim, fabric 1, brown, fired black/brown on surface. Similar to Corfe Mullen type 47 but with beading externally. Period 3, rubble filled trench (1.59, 1.67, 4.10).

249 Rim of amphora, buff fabric with white and grey grits. Period 5, covered culvert (2.13, 9.4).

265 Mortarium, well-worn in hard, pink-brown fabric with cream slip and quartz and red-brown. Period 5, gully (2.16).

383 Domed lid with internally hollowed rim, fabric 1, black, with burnished vertical lines on the exterior. Period 6, soil accumulation (1.14, 1.28, 1.29, 4.8).

384 Domed lid with small flange, fabric 1, grey, laminated, well burnished internally. Period 6, soil accumulation (see no. 383).

385 Mortarium, rather poorly made of form Gillam 238 (Gillam 1970), in fine yellowish cream fabric with concentric scoring inside and on top of the flange combined with flint, black and probably quartz grit. None of the kilns producing mortaria of this type have been found but their distribution and the kind of fabric used point to manufacture in Gaul or south-east Britain. There is abundant site-dating evidence form Agricolan sites in Scotland like Camelon and Cardean, from Richborough (Bushe-Fox, 1949, 92, Pit 125), and other sites, to provide a basic date for manufacture of *c.* AD 70-100, although many would of course have remained in use after this. Period 6, soil accumulation (see no. 383).

406 Many fragments of one amphora, light grey fabric, slightly gritty, fired pink/buff on surface. Period 6, disturbed rubble (7.2, 9.5).

407 Rim of amphora, buff fabric with white and grey angular grits. Period 6, disturbed rubble (7.2, 9.5). Fits with coarse ware no. 531, period 7, pit 2.8.

408 Mortarium, many pieces forming a large portion from a well-worn vessel in a granular cream fabric with brownish buff slip and white and grey flint with black and red-brown trituration grit. The counterstamp (FECIT) and a fragment from the name-stamp are preserved to each side of the spout. These stamps are from one of the dies of Matugenus who worked at Brockley Hill, Middlesex, and the die used to impress these stamps is either the one found there early in this century or one from the same matrix (Suggett, 1955, 60). There is abundant evidence from the kiln-site of his activity there (Suggett, 1954, 259ff). Well over a hundred mortaria of his are known from sites in England and Wales (Castle and Warbis 1973, 104). Matugenous is recorded on stamps as the son of Albinus, and the similarity of work confirms that it was

the mortarium potter of that name whose work is dated *c.* AD 65-95. The complete absence of Matugenus' stamps from Scotland and from Hadrian's Wall is significant with such a prolific potter and it supports a primarily Trajanic date, *c.* AD 90-125. Period 6, disturbed rubble (7.2, 9.5).

513 Domed lid with small flange, fabric 1, black, white grit inclusions, decorated externally. Period 7, shallow trench (9.2).

584 Mortarium flange fragment in granular cream fabric, probably made in the potteries south of Verulamium (including kilns at Verulamium, Brockley Hill and Radlett). *c.* AD 140-200. Period 4 road? (3.3, 3.4, 3.5, 3.8, 3.13).

Figure 14 (Coarse Ware)

342 Vertical-sided jar with a slight shoulder and a simple rim, coarse black laminated fabric containing large chips of mudstone quartz and other inclusions, diagonal 'combed' zones of decoration around body, and brush-marks around inside which were applied before firing; this vessel may be intrusive, and belong to the same vessel as no. 469. Period 7, kilns (1.11, 1.12, 1.13).

425 Jar with countersunk handle, fabric 1, grey. Period 6, gully (4.16).

434 Jar, fabric 1, black, with white inclusions, fired grey/pink on

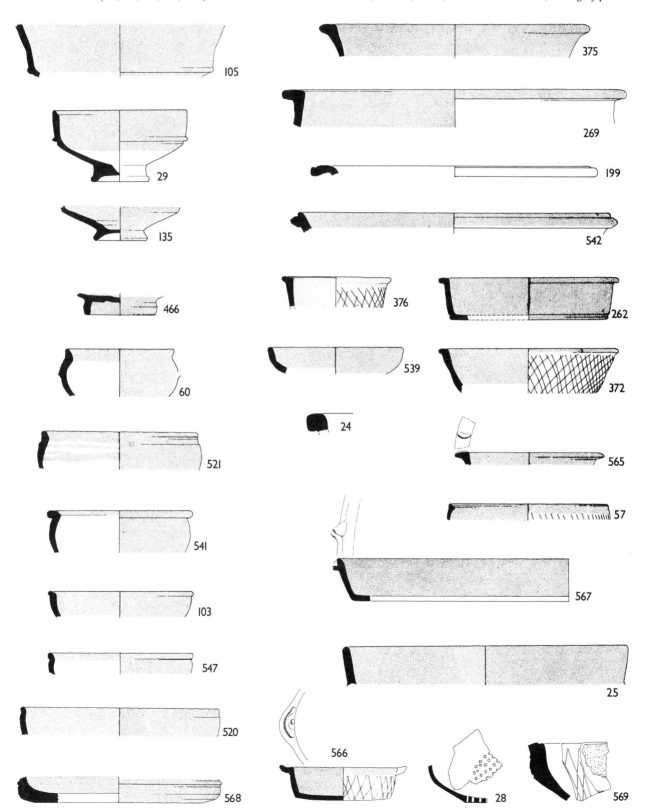

Figure 12. Coarse Ware: bowls, scale 1:4.

surface, zone of lattice decoration around body. Period 6, gully (4.16).

435 Jar with upright out-curved rim and no shoulder (cf. fig. 10, no. 257), fabric 1, grey with white grit inclusions, with zone of lattice decoration around body. Period 6, gully (4.16).

438 Jar with upright rim, no pronounced shoulder, and with straight sides, fabric 2, grey, fired black on surface, with lattice decoration around body. Period 6, gully (4.16).

439 Jar of similar form to no. 438, fabric 1, grey/brown, fired black/brown on surface, with zone of vertical burnished lines around body. Period 6, gully (4.16).

442 Jar with upright rim and angular lip, fabric 1, black, with quartz grits, fired black/brown on surface. Period, gully (4.16).

443 Jar similar to fig. 10 no. 322; red gritty fabric, fired brown on surface well burnished rim and exterior, zone of lattice decoration below horizontal line around body. Period 6, gully (4.16).

444 Globular jar with short upright rim and internal hollowing, fabric 1, grey, fired black on surface, well burnished rim and exterior, zone of lattice decoration below horizontal line around body. Period 6, gully (4.16).

447 Jar or beaker with short upright rim with handle(s), fabric 1,

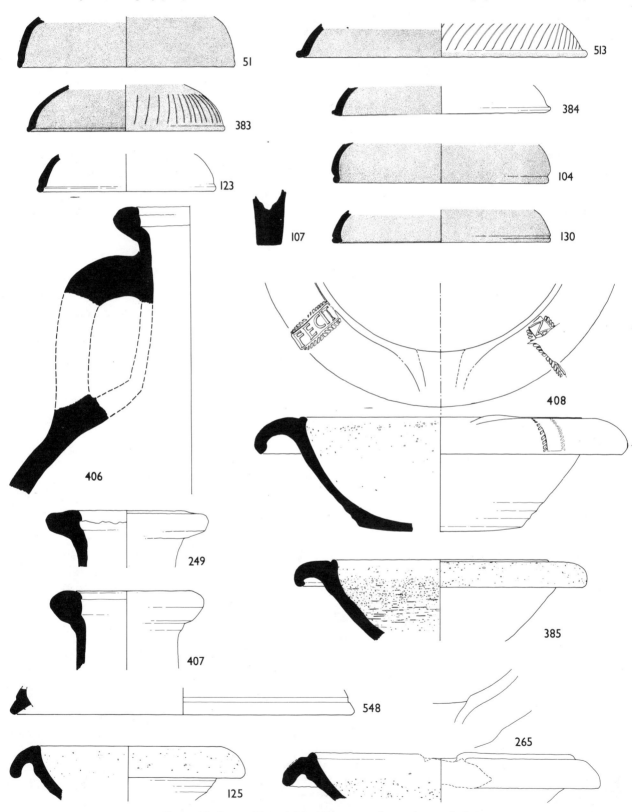

Figure 13. Coarse Ware: lids, amphorae and mortaria, scale 1:4.

grey/red, fired black on surface. Period 6, gully (4.16).

450 Jar with short upright rim, fabric 1, grey, fired red/brown on surface, zone of lattice decoration around body. Period 6, gully (4.16).

468 Jar with everted rim, similar to Gillam (1970) types 147/8, fabric 1, grey, narrow band of lattice decoration below horizontal line around body, possible traces of a cream slip around lower part of sherd, also possible brush-strokes visible below the decoration (applied before firing). Period 7, kilns (1.11, 1.12, 1.13).

471 Flanged bowl with high bead similar to Gillam (1970) type 228,

fabric 1/2, grey, fired black on surface well burnished internally and on flange, brush-marks externally. Period 7, kilns (1.11, 1.12, 1.13).

472 Flanged bowl with high bead similar to Gillam (1970) type 228, fabric 1, grey, fired black on surface, arcaded decoration externally. Period 7, kilns (1.11, 1.12, 1.13).

473 Straight-sided dish similar to Gillam (1970) types 329-30, but oval and with handles, fabric 1, black, brush-marks externally, traces of white slip; rim diameter varies from 20cm to 30cm around oval shape. Period 7, kilns (1.11, 1.12, 1.13).

474 Straight-sided dish with vertical sides, fabric 1, black, fired

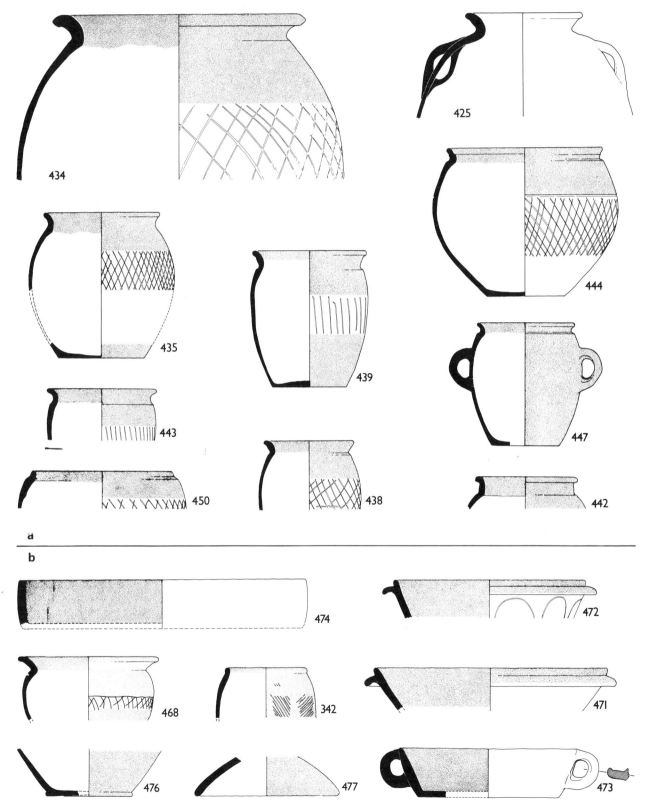

Figure 14. Coarse Ware: a – from Period 6 gully 4.16; b – from Period 7 kiln/oven 1.13, scale 1:4.

grey on the surface. Period 7, kilns (1.11, 1.12, 1.13).

476 Base of jar with bead around base; fabric 1, black, with mud-stone inclusions, fired black on the surface. Period 7, kilns (1.11, 1.12, 1.13).

477 Steep-sided lid, fabric 1, grey, fired black/grey on surface. Period 7, kilns (1.11, 1.12, 1.13).

Figure 15 (fine ware)

6 Beaker, smooth orange fabric; probably not an import, certainly first century and probably post-conquest. Period 1, chalk chippings (1.57).

10 Base of beaker, smooth fawn fabric. Period 3, rubble-filled trench (1.59, 1.67, 4.10).

11 Carinated bowl or tazza, possibly from the Corfe Mullen kilns, smooth white fabric; form common in Terra Nigra, continuing into Flavian period. Period 4, ditch (1.27).

14 New Forest bowl, ultimately based on Samian form 31R, 'soapy' pink laminated fabric with traces of red slip left on the surface. Period 6, soil accumulation (1.14, 1.28, 1.29, 4.8).

15 Oxford colour-coated imitation Dr. 38 bowl, smooth orange fabric, red slip; *c.* AD 250-400. Period 6, soil accumulation (see no. 14).

16 Corfe Mullen strap-handle from large two-handled flagon(?), smooth cream fabric, first century AD. Period 6, soil accumulation (see no. 14).

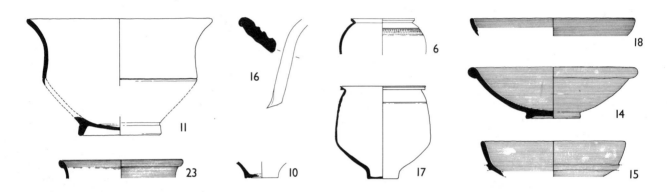

Figure 15. Fine Ware: scale 1:4.

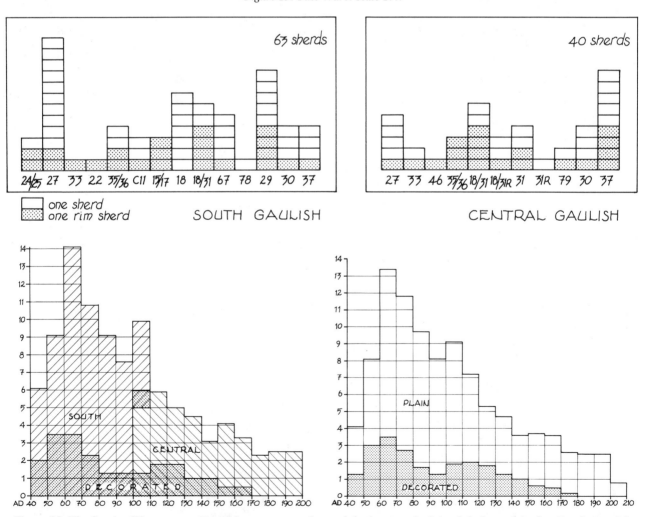

Figure 16. The Samian Ware – quantities of forms present. Lower left, the spread of sherd-datings of the Samian; lower right, spread of sherd-datings modified to allow survival of one-third of each decade's Samian into the next decade.

17 Much of roughcast cornice-rimmed beaker, smooth orange fabric, patchy brown slip; likely to date between *c.* AD 70-150; not imported. Period 6, gully (4.16).

18 Small colour-coated 'Pompeian Red' platter, imported. Period 6, flat-bottomed trench (4.18).

23 Fine rim in 'Belgic' tradition, fine pinkish brown micaceous fabric fired black on surface, well burnished, black slip applied to exterior and rim sherds join from period 6, disturbed rubble (7.2, 9.5) and Period 7, shallow trench (0.2).

The Samian Ware Kevin Greene BA PhD (see microfiche M3)
143 sherds were recovered, and after the exclusion of joining sherds, non-joining sherds from single vessels, and indeterminate fragments, 103 identifications were made. 63 were from Gaulish vessels, and 40 from Central Gaulish: no East Gaulish material was present.

The samian is presented in three ways. Decorated sherds are illustrated (fig. 17) where the context requires their dating evidence or where they are of interest in their own right. The plain ware is

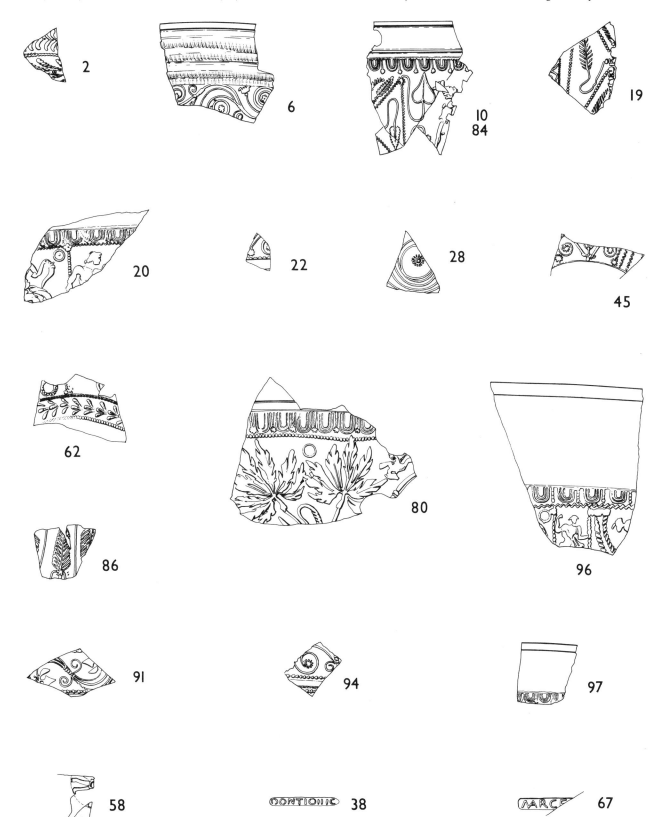

Figure 17. *The Samian Ware: decorated sherds scale 1:2, stamps scale 1:1.*

represented in graphic form to show the forms present (fig. 16) and the spread of the individual sherd datings (fig. 16 left). The former (fig. 16) is a simple histogram showing total numbers of sherds of each form, rims and body sherds being separately indicated. The block-diagram of sherd datings is constructed as explained in Greene (1974, 66), so that each sherd had the same value whether closely or loosely dated. As a comparatively objective control, decorated sherds (more easily and accurately dated) are shown within the diagram. It can be seen that the patterns agree well.

Some overall conclusions can be drawn. If the sherds reflect density of occupation, its heaviest concentration falls between *c.* AD 43 and 120. Experience of other sites indicates that these diagrams usually have a depression in the early second century, and then rise again to a peak in the mid-Antonine period. The absence of the latter is noticeable, and is independently observable from the small numbers of later second century forms on fig. 16. Forms 18/31 and 18/31R greatly outnumber 31 and 31R, 27 outnumbers 33, and 47 and 79 are the only distinctively late Antonine forms present.

At the earlier end of the occupation, material goes from the Conquest through to the end of the importation of South Gaulish ware, and the presence of 15/17, 18 and 18/31, together with 24/25, 27 and 33, and 29 and 37 all bear out the full range of pre-Flavian, Flavian and Flavian-Trajanic types.

Figure 17 Decorated Samian

2 Dr 37, wall, South Gaulish. Vespasianic. Period 1, primary scorched earth.
6 Dr 29, rim, South Gaulish. *c.* AD 65-80. Period 2, turf layers.
10 Dr 30 rim, wall, South Gaulish. Claudio-Neronian. Period 2 ploughsoil.
19 Dr 30, wall, Central Gaulish. *c.* AD 110-130. Period 3, chalk rubble.
20 Dr 37, rim, Central Gaulish. *c.* AD 125-150. Period 4 road (?).
22 Dr 29, rim, South Gaulish. Claudio-Neronian. Period 4 road (?).
28 Dr 30, wall, Central Gaulish. *c.* AD 100-130. Period 5, foundations walls.
38 Dr? 27, base, Central Gaulish. ?Trajanic. Period 5 rubble.
45 Déch. 67, base, South Gaulish. *c.* AD 80-110. Period 6, soil accumulation.
58 ?Walters 79 or 80, base, Central Gaulish. Late Antonine. Period 6 disturbed rubble.
62 Dr 37, wall, Central Gaulish. *c.* AD 100-120. Period 6, disturbed rubble.
67 Base indeterminate form, Central Gaulish. Mid-second century. Period 6 gully.
80 Dr 37, wall, Central Gaulish. *c.* AD 125-150. Period 7, pit (2.21).
86 Dr 30, wall, South Gaulish. ?Neronian. South of field boundary, pit (3.2).
91 Dr 29, wall, South Gaulish. Probably Neronian. South of field boundary, brown-red sandy soil (12.5).
94 Dr 29, South Gaulish. Probably Claudian. Unstratified.
95 Dr 37, Central Gaulish. *c.* AD 150-170. Unstratified.
87 Dr 37, Central Gaulish. *c.* AD 100-120. Unstratified.

The Worked Stone Clare Thomas BA FSA(Scot) (with notes on evidence for tools by N. J. Sunter BArch RIBA)
(for a complete catalogue see microfiche M4)

The worked stone belongs to the two main Romano-British Purbeck Industries, Kimmeridge Shale and Purbeck Marble, and to three subsidiary ventures, the production of tesserae and inlay elements of chalk and mudstone, and the working of various Purbeck limestones.

Many of the objects listed and described in the catalogue (microfiche M3) are unfinished or waste fragments, indicating that the working of these materials took place on or near the site. Earlier evidence had already suggested the manufacture of Kimmeridge shale decorated tablets and table-legs in the Norden area; the evidence from this site confirms this, and indicates that vessels were also made here. Similarly, the working of Purbeck Marble has been postulated, on the evidence of such finds as the disc of marble in the Stilwell collection. (R.C.H.M., 1970, 598; Beavis, 1970, 203).

The large number of articles discarded whilst still unfinished and the considerable quantity of waste industrial material found on the site provide evidence for the tools and the methods used in the various branches of the industry.

KIMMERIDGE SHALE

The shale used on this site is a highly bituminous oil-shale, fine-grained, and dark brown or black in colour, it has a definite grain, and has a tendency to laminate, especially when dry, it is very hard, and takes a good polish, giving it a black and shiny appearance. It forms part of the Kimmeridge Clay, and occurs in two coastal sections east and west of Kimmeridge. The eastern section is about three quarters of a mile long, and rises from the beach about 182.9m (200 yds) east of the headland known as Clavell's Hard. There the shale is about 86.4cm thick. The section in Brandy Bay to the west is thinner and shorter. (Arkell, 1947, 68-70, Calkin, 1953, 47; information also from Mr R. W. Sanderson, of the Institute of Geological Sciences, London).

The objects of Kimmeridge Shale are of several types: bracelets; vessels, decorated tablets, table-legs, waste material and miscellaneous articles. These can be broadly divided into two groups according to whether they were manufactured on a lathe or not.

The lathe was used largely for turning bracelets (whose waste products were the characteristic cores which more recently were otherwise known as 'coal-money'). The twelve bracelets (fig. 18) are typical of their kind. Ten had oval sections, flattened on one or two sides. Five had internal ribs or bevelling (fig. 18 nos. 3, 5, 6, 11, 12), indicating where they had been severed from the core using a chisel. Of these three (fig. 18 nos. 5, 11, 12) are probably unfinished. Henrietta Davies suggested that internal ribs like these were often developed into ornamental features; but on these examples, the rib has been left rough (Wheeler, 1943, 319). The lathe marks on the interior suggest chisel blades were either approximately 3mm wide (fig. 18 no. 4) or that a narrower blade or sharp point was used (fig. 18 no. 3). The process of manufacturing shale bracelets has been fully discussed by Calkin (1953, 54-64). He recognised a specialized industry, which produced flint lathe-tools

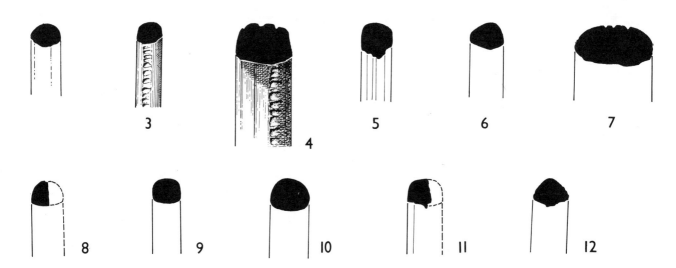

Figure 18. The worked stone, Kimmeridge Shale bracelets scale 1:1.

for the manufacture of shale bracelets. The tools were made from middle sections of flakes. Chisels with blades between 1 and 5mm wide were probably used for the initial heavy work, while the more delicate trimming was done with square-ended or oblique tools (*ibid*, 1953, 60-4). It is not clear what part if any the majority of the worked flints found at Norden played in the technology of the industry (see microfiche M8). The unfinished bracelets from Norden suggest that production took place on or near the site.

Three of the bracelets are decorated with grooves and ribs on the exterior (fig. 18 nos. 4, 7, 12), but none are notched. The internal diameters are mainly larger than the average sizes found by Calkin (1.8in/45.5mm; 2.3in/58.76mm, average internal diameters of bracelets from Gaulter, Colliton Park, Fordington and Woodcuts; Calkin 1953, 59-61), and larger than the two commonest sizes found in a recent study. (60mm and 50mm; Thomas, forthcoming.) Nine belong to the third most frequent size, 70 to 90mm, and two are even bigger, 110 and 147mm. It is probable that two or three bracelets were cut off the same core; these large examples may be the outer rings, which possibly broke during the final stages of production.

Four of the bracelets were found in first century layers, six belonged to the second century, while another probably dates from *c.* AD 175 to the late third century.

The vessels, like the bracelets, were also lathe turned, again with flint tools. Long class B cores, approximating to truncated cones, such as the ones found at Rempstone, Corfe Castle (SY 995820), and in the general Norden area, are probably waste from the manufacture of bowls (R.C.H.M., 1970, 598 (228); Dorset County Museum Catalogue (D.C.M.), 1908, 28.1 and D.C.M. unnumbered). The methods involved are probably similar to those used to produce wooden bowls on a pole-lathe at the Welsh Folk Museum,

St Fagans, Cardiff (Jenkins and Davies, undated). A block of wood of suitable size is set on the lathe, and is reduced to a round disc, then shaped on the outside, with a 25mm gouge. The inside is then removed, with smaller gouges and chisels, until the centre is smooth. The bowl is polished with beeswax, then removed from the lathe. The core, by this time a thin pillar of wood, is cut away, and the centre of the bowl is smoothed. In the case of the shallow dishes and plates at Norden, the cores must have been very small. It is possible that the stone base found against the east wall of the Period 5 building was designed to support a lathe. At Gallows Gore five stone blocks were associated with concentrations of shale-workers' debris, and it is suggested that these might have been bases for individual lathes (R.C.H.M. 1970, 621). The Norden base had two holes set 50cm apart in its upper surface which could have been used to locate the legs of a lathe. The lathe-bed would clearly in addition have had to be fixed securely to the wall. A lathe whose legs were only 50cm apart would have had only a short lathe-bed (cf. Singer *et al.*, 1957, 645, figs. 585-86 and Edlin, 1949, plates 21 and 82), but there are a number of precedents for such a design in several recorded pole-lathes, the principle of which is adequately described by Calkin (1953, 55). However, assuming that at Norden we have a base for a pole-lathe, it would be expected that the top surface of the stone block would have shown some signs of wear caused by the constant foot movement on the treadle, but no particular sign of concentrated wear was evident. Furthermore, Mr P. A. Brown, who excavated the area around the base, reports that no shale waste was discovered in association with it. It is of course possible that wood and not shale was being turned, as this would have left no trace. Alternatively a rotary whetstone would have left no recognisable waste (F. L. Wheble, Messrs Vokes and Beck, pers. comm.), and this could either have been operated as a pole-lathe or

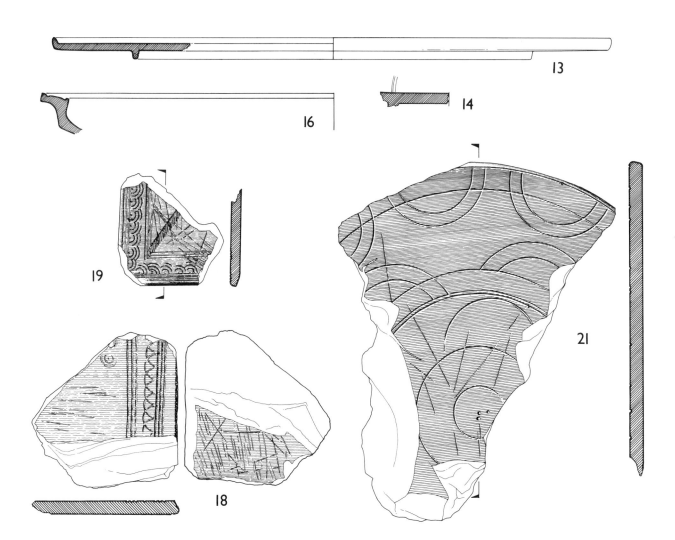

Figure 19. The worked stone, Kimmeridge Shale scale 1:3.

rotated by hand (as illustrated in Edlin, 1949, plate 39).

The vessels consist of fragments of several shallow plates (fig. 19, nos 13, 14) an open bowl (fig. 19, no. 16) and a small cup (fig. 20, no. 27). The flat plates are of a type common elsewhere; as, for instance, at Colliton Park, Dorchester (Calkin, 1972, 44-48) with footrings and short raised rims. The bowl has a wide, ribbed rim and carination. The sixth vessel is probably a small cup, possibly a child's toy. All the vessels were found in layers of the mid-second to fourth centuries.

This is a very important group, as few vessels have been found in the Isle of Purbeck. None of them appear to be unfinished, but they might have been broken in the final stages of production.

Fragments of three rectangular and two circular decorated tablets were found. The rectangular examples are of the type defined by Biddle (1967, 248-50) as trenchers, that is, rectangular plaques circa 7.5-10mm thick, and circa 500 x 400mm, or 320 x 250mm, with smooth upper and lower surfaces, and sometimes with bevelled edges. The upper surfaces are decorated with geometric motifs, and

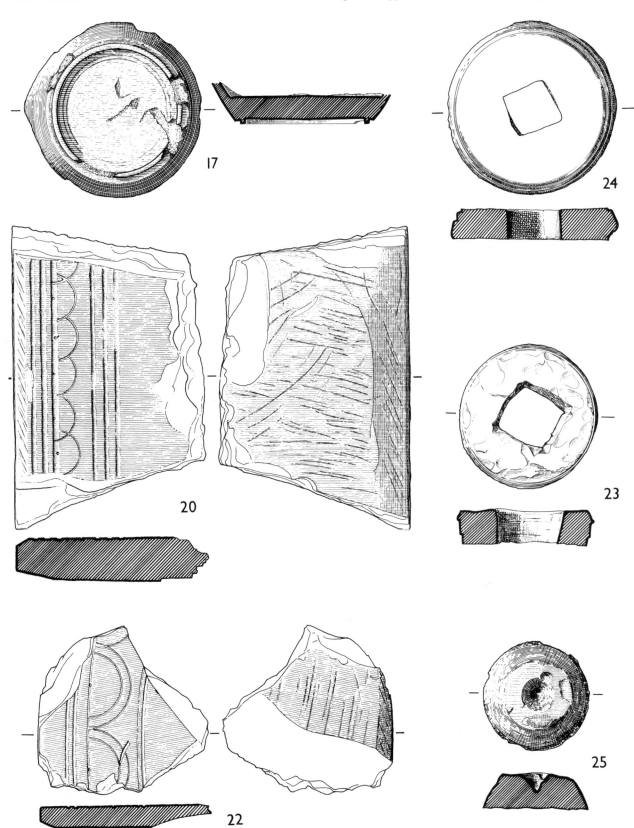

Figure 20. The worked stone, Kimmeridge Shale scale 1:1.

are sometimes scratched, as are the reverses occasionally. One such plaque from Grange Road, Winchester, which had vessels, a spoon and knives, and two pork joints on it, suggested that these might have been trenchers. However, this need not necessarily apply to all such plaques. Some may have been used as wall plaques, perhaps held in place by clamps, while others might have served as small table-tops. It is suprising that, if they were intended for eating off, they were not designed with some slight rim.

Having been cut roughly to size, both surfaces appear to have been rubbed smooth, and, on the underside which was generally less well-finished, the marks caused by the abrasion are still clearly visible. The scratch-marks on the upper surfaces are assumed to have been produced after the tablet had been discarded.

Around the perimeter of the tablet the lower edge (and in one case, fig. 20, no. 20, also the upper edge) was chamfered back using a rasp or file. This technique was commonly used around the

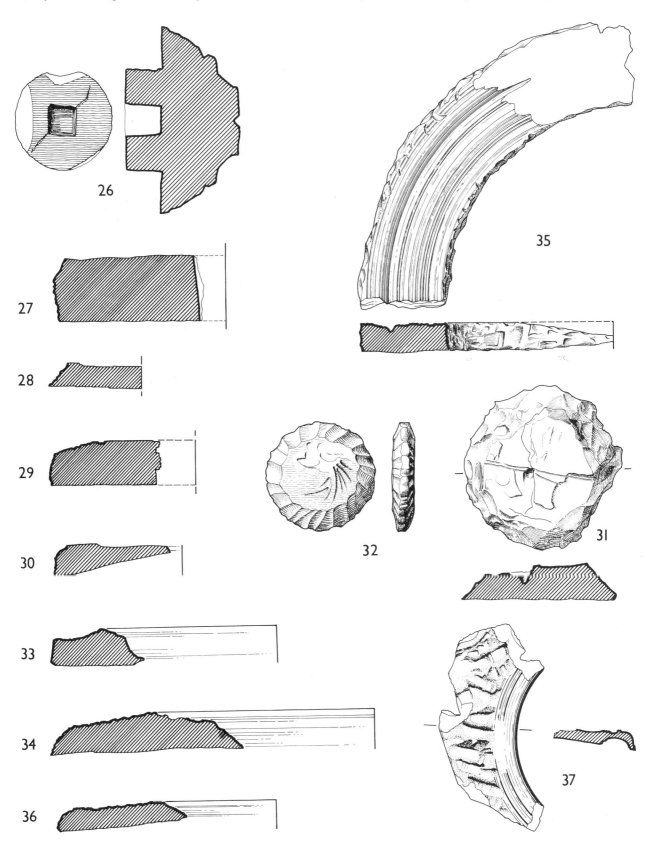

Figure 21. The worked stone; Kimmeridge Shale; 27-36, scale 1:1; 26 and 37, scale 1:2.

perimeters of tables made before the introduction of modern machine tools to avoid the difficulty of having to produce two absolutely true surfaces (Mr M. Legg, pers. comm.).

All five plaques (fig. 19 nos. 18, 19, 21; fig. 20, no. 22) are decorated with incised parallel lines and bands of hatching, scribed using a pointed instrument; interlocking arcs and two or three concentric circles, scribed using a pair of dividers, although the straight lines on one (fig. 20, no. 20) were produced by some sort of narrow flat-ended chisel. The large circular plaque (fig. 19, no. 21) is probably unfinished, as the diagonal band of hatching is bordered

by a line on one side only, not on both as on other fragments, as, for instance, on the tablets from Rotherley, Grange Road, Winchester, and from Jordan Hill, Weymouth. (Pitt-Rivers, 1888, 174-6, pl. CXVIII; Biddle 1967, 230-234). It is probable that these plaques were made on or near the site; four others have been found in the vicinity, including another circular fragment. A pair of bronze compasses were found near Corfe Castle (Austen, 1859-60, pl. XXVI, facing p. 226; Moule, 1900, 102; R.C.H.M. 1970, 598).

One of the tablets (fig. 20 no. 20), was found in a second century layer; this agrees with the dating evidence for other trenchers and

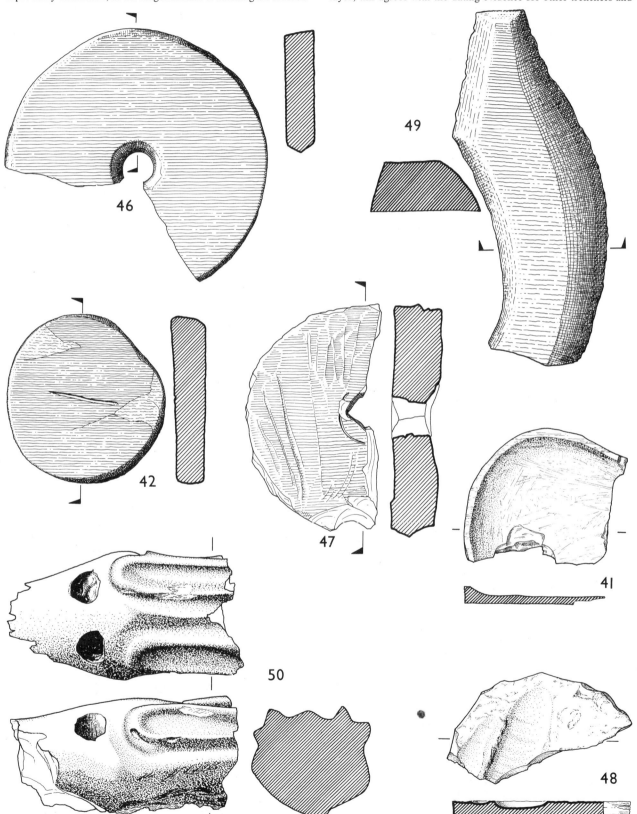

Figure 22. The worked stone, Kimmeridge Shale; 42, 46, 47 and 49, scale 1:2; 41, 48 and 50, scale 1:1.

plaques, most of which belong to the first and second centuries AD (Biddle, 1967, 248-259; Thomas forthcoming). Three of the tablets (fig. 19 nos. 18, 21; fig. 20 no. 22); however, come from late second to fourth century layers, but these could be debris from earlier periods.

One fragment of a table-leg (fig. 22 no. 49) was found; it is a section of the lower part of a leg, and is undecorated. In shape it corresponds to the lion or griffin type leg described by Liversidge, of which over twenty examples are now known (Liversidge, 1969, 166-7; 1955, 37-53; Liversidge and Peers, 1960, 72-3; Thomas, forthcoming). It is unusual in having no decoration at all on any part of that section of the leg. This fragment was found in a late ditch or gully, dated to circa AD 275 and later, but containing pottery from the first century. A late date is in accord with the evidence for most table-legs, which assigns them to the late third and fourth centuries (Thomas, forthcoming).

A carved object of shale (fig. 22 no. 50), with what appears to be a pair of eyes and a pair of ears, may be part of the head of a secondary animal; the legs and heads of such animals have been found on several table-legs, and may represent a dog chasing the griffin or lion. (Liversidge, 1955, 37-53; Liversidge and Peers, 1960; 272-3; Liversidge, 1969, 166-7). This object is probably unfinished, as the eyes and the 'chin' are rough. This suggests that table-legs, or other carved objects, were made on or near the site. This object is of the same date as the table-leg fragment.

Waste Fragments

Very few cores of the types classified by Calkin were found (Calkin, 1953, 56-58, fig. 4). Two Class A cores (fig. 20 nos. 23, 24), with a square hole through the core, which Calkin considered in early, clumsy and unwieldy form, were found in a first century layer. A large Class B core (fig. 21, no. 26), with a large square hole which does not perforate the core, has probably had several rings cut off it. A fragment of another core (fig. 21, no. 25) was recognized by the 'pin' hole on the reverse, where the core turned on the pivot (Calkin, 1953, 56-58). Several discs bore lathe-marks (fig. 21, nos. 27-31) but none of the usual peg-holes; these could be the rounds cut off the ends of couch legs (Farrar, 1970, 156-7), or else fragments of cores which have lost their peg holes by being split and broken. Several flat, wide rings (fig. 21, no. 33-37), with lathe-marks and sometimes with unworked shale attached, were also found. These are too big and flat to be unfinished bracelets; it is possible, on the other hand, that they may be waste material from the manufacture of vessels.

Other waste material included a small, roughly finished hand-cut disc with bevelled edges (fig. 21, no. 33), found in a dump of industrial material deposited after AD 296. Many other similar discs have been found by P. A. Brown (pers. comm.) in the immediate vicinity of the site. These discs are very similar to cores from hand-cut bracelets found on working sites of the early Pre-Roman Iron Age, as at Gaulter Gap, Kimmeridge (Calkin, 1948, 30-54).

The waste material, the table-legs, vessels and decorated tablets indicate that shale was worked on or near the site. The scarcity of the usual cores suggests that bracelets were not made here, but, on the other hand, many cores have been found in the surrounding area, especially at the Norden Well site, (R.C.H.M. 1970, 598, and information from P. A. Brown), and it is probable that production took place in the immediate neighbourhood.

The evidence from the flints (see Bradley microfiche M8) demonstrates that the flints from Norden do not belong to the specialized Roman industries of the region; but are more characteristic of the late prehistoric industries of the area. The flints and hand-cut cores perhaps point to a late revival of an earlier technique or else to a disturbance of earlier material. The former seems very unlikely.

MUDSTONE (fig. 23a)

The mudstone used for tesserae and inlay slabs is a more heavy and massive stone than the Kimmeridge shale, and has no pronounced grain; when dry it tends to split cubically (hence the manufacturing technique of tesserae), rather than to laminate, although lamination also occurs. It was probably originally black; its brown appearance is due to rusting (information Mr R. W. Sanderson, Institute of Geological Sciences, London). It might possibly come

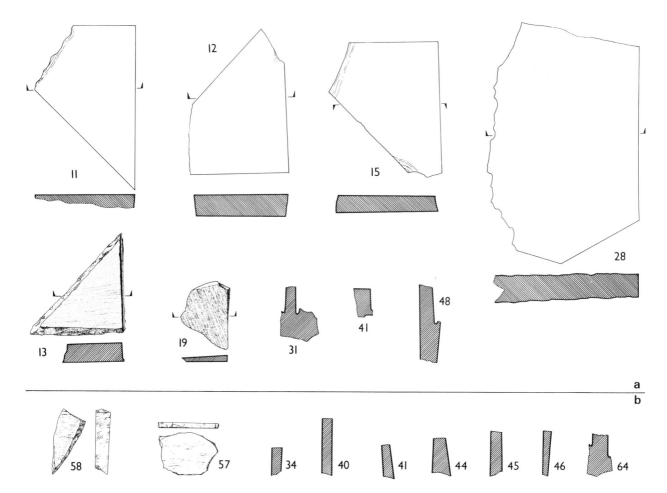

Figure 23. The worked stone; a – Mudstone, b – Chalk; scale 1:4.

from the Purbeck Beds (Arkell, 1947, 123, 142).

Eight tesserae, plus several unstratified examples, were found in layers dating from the second to the fourth century. Nineteen fragments (fig. 23a, 11-13, 15, 19, 28) of sawn slabs, varying in thickness between 3mm and 40mm, were probably intended for use as inlay elements in decorative schemes for walls and floors. The thicker slabs, 24mm, 27mm and 40mm, were probably meant for floor tiles. Six slabs are right-angled triangles, one is square, one is probably rectangular, another is lozenge-shaped, two are probably trapezoidal, while one is semi-circular, two are curved strips, and three have a slightly curved edge. Another nineteen worked fragments, mostly partially sawn (cf. fig. 23a nos. 13, 19) slabs were found.

One of these slabs was found in a late first to early second century layer, thirteen in second century deposits, seven in late second to late third century contexts, and eight in late third to fourth century layers. Accordingly, it appears that this brown or black mudstone was worked on or near the site, from the late first or second century, possibly until the fourth century.

CHALK (fig. 23b)

The chalk used is hard and white, similar to Beerstone, but not from that source, and is most probably of very local provenance (information Mr R. W. Sanderson of the Institute of Geological Sciences, London).

About 1,500 to 2,000 tesserae, and numerous chips from their manufacture, were found in a layer (1.57) dating to the late first century. This was evidently a workfloor. Sixteen other tesserae were found in layers of the second to fourth centuries. They could be survivals from the first century workfloor, or else later products.

Forty sawn (fig. 23b, nos. 57, 58) slabs of chalk were found, varying in thickness between 8mm and 30mm. It is possible that they were all intended for wall decoration, but some of the thicker examples, especially the 30mm thick fragment (fig. 5), were probably for floors. Eleven slabs were roughly triangular, two rectangular, one trapezoidal and two had curved edges. One fragment was marked with two incised interesecting arcs, possibly guidelines for cutting.

Five fragments were found in layers belonging to the third quarter of the second century, one in a late second to late third century deposit, and thirty-four in layers dating to the late third and fourth centuries; twenty-seven of the latter came from the dump of industrial rubbish.

Six other worked fragments of chalk includes a parallelogram, 42mm thick, and a cube, 32mm thick, with a domed surface. These objects date from the second to the fourth century.

The evidence clearly demonstrates that tesserae were manufactured here in the first century, and slabs for inlaid decoration from the second to third or fourth centuries.

Purbeck Marble

Purbeck Marble is a partly metamorphosed limestone which occurs in the top of the Upper Purbeck Beds; it is found only in a few places, chiefly in the Isle of Purbeck. It is bluish-grey, but sometimes has green or red shades, caused by mineral impurities. Between Durlston Bay and Peverill Point, for instance, the lower

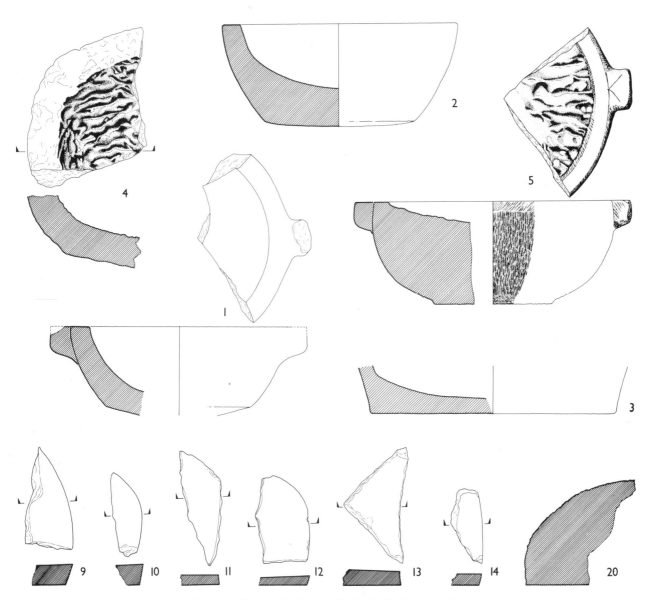

Figure 24. The worked stone, Purbeck Marble, scale 1:4.

band of marble is red, and the upper is grey-green (Arkell, 1947, 137). It is characterized by the freshwater pond small, Viviparus cariniferus (formerly called Paludina). It is hard, and takes a good polish. (Arkell, 1947, 134, 137; Arkell, 1933, Ch. XXVI; Andrews and Jukes-Browne, 1894, 44-71; Beavis, 1970, 183). The Purbeck-Portland limestones are at the hard end of the spectrum of English building stones, and up until the seventeenth century they were relatively neglected for ashlar work, presumably because of the slow and tedious task of sawing with the simple mediaeval toothed saw (Purcell, 1967, 46), such as that illustrated in an eleventh century manuscript (Singer, 1957, 385, fig. 348), which would no doubt have been somewhat more efficient on a softer stone such as, perhaps, mud-stone, chalk and Kimmeridge Shale. The cutting and surfacing of the much harder Purbeck Marble must have presented the mediaeval mason with considerable problems. It is unlikely that a toothed blade of iron would have stood up to the rigours involved in sawing large quantities of such tough stone. Nevertheless, it has already been established that a saw (producing grooves between 3mm and 5mm wide) was used commonly at Norden for slicing the larger varieties of stones. Cunliffe (1963, 7) experimented at Fishbourne using a saw comprising six strands of copper wire held in a hacksaw frame, with sand and water as an abrasive. However, Pliny (XXXVI, ix) described a technique employing iron with sand to cut blocks of Italian marble. Two types of framed saw depicted at Ostia (Meiggs, 1960, pl. XXVII) had very wide saw blades but no teeth. It is probable that these were also designed for cutting stone. Such saws have been used in more recent times, and one for use in cutting large blocks of stone is described and illustrated in a handbook of practical masonry published at the turn of the century (Purchase, 1904, 4 and Plate II; F. L. Wheble pers. comm). Hodges (1964, 105-6) points out the advantages of a wire blade over plate metal whose greater surface area increases the friction on the sides of the groove. However, one point worth noting about the sawn sections of stone from Norden is that although the two planes may not always have been sawn parallel to one another, no surface was produced which was not absolutely straight. The angle of the iron sawplate could be adjusted in the frame so that once set in a vertical plane it would cut a true and straight groove (Purchase, *ibid*). Wire could more easily waver to produce a crooked surface unless it was very carefully guided. Moreover, if the saw-plate was wrongly adjusted it would be expected to cut a straight groove but at an angle, like the Norden examples.

Sand was no doubt used as an abrasive for rubbing smooth the surfaces of sawn or otherwise tooled stone in just the way it was used in combination with the saw. Ideally a rubber should be formed of a material harder than the surface being abraded. At Fishbourne sandstone rubbers were found together with sand which had no doubt been used in this way (Cunliffe, 1962, 18). Two roughly cylindrical stones with rounded ends, one of fine-grained limestone and one of tufaceous burr-stone, were discovered by Mr P. A. Brown at Norden (see microfiche M7 nos. 19 and 20). It seems likely that these were used in combination with sand for smoothing the inner surfaces of stone mortars (see below).

From Norden also came a roughly square bar of Carstone which has a number of grooves worn into its surfaces (see microfiche M7 no. 18). Carstone is normally considered too sharply abrasive to have been used for honing metal tools where cutting edges would have been damaged by the coarse grits (R. W. Sanderson, Institute of Geological Sciences, London, pers. comm.). It could have been used without abrasive sand as a rasp (F. L. Wheble pers. comm.), although the grooves in its surfaces do not look as if they have been worn by a stone, rather by a narrow or pointed instrument. However, this find was not securely stratified and may be post-Roman in date.

The methods described above of rubbing the surfaces of stone with sand would have produced a smooth surface but not a polished finish. Beavis (1970, 189) points out that to achieve a good polish on Purbeck Marble abrasive grains must be combined with softer material, such as beeswax, so that they slide rather than roll over the surface. He suggests the use of successively finer grades of abrasives.

Fragments of five mortars were found (fig. 24, nos. 1-5), including several unfinished examples. One (fig. 24, no. 59; plates XII, XIII) is of particular interest in the sequence of manufacturing stages which can be detected. First, the top surface of a slab of marble, c. 11cm thick, was levelled, smoothed and polished. Then, the inner and outer limits of the rim were scribed onto the polished surface, presumably using a pair of dividers, in the form of two concentric circles. The lugs were then positioned in relation to the outer circle by a roughly scratched 'V'. From these guidelines the

top of the rim was cut into the polished area using a fine point (as opposed to a punch which would have been used for heavier work). The craftsman was apparently right-handed judging by the general direction of the tooling. The outer profile of the mortar was then tooled, the surface being left with the vertical scoring of a coarser point or punch. Towards the base a fine point was again used where greater precision was required. After completing the tooling of the exterior, which might have been followed by abrasion and polishing, the craftsman had started to hollow out the centre of the mortar using a heavy punch. It was presumably during this stage that the vessel cracked and was discarded. A slightly different technique was noted in another unfinished Purbeck Marble mortar, (fig. 24, no. 4; plate XIV), where both the outer and inner surfaces were roughly shaped using a coarse punch. Another mortar (fig. 24, no. 2), though badly pitted by subsequent deterioration of the stone, had apparently been completed but for the base where coarse tooling is still visible. It is most probable that these mortars were manufactured on or near the site.

Plate 12. Unfinished Purbeck Marble mortar no. 5 showing interior tooling; from Period 6, 9.5 (W. G. Putnam).

Plate 13. Unfinished Purbeck Marble mortar no. 5 showing exterior tooling. (W. G. Putnam).

Three of the mortars (fig. 24, nos. 1, 2, 5) have curved profiles, while one (fig. 24, no. 3) has straight, nearly vertical sides. Dunning (1968) believed that the first type dated to before *c.* AD 150, and the second after *c.* AD 350. Two (fig. 24, nos. 1, 5), however, were found in late second to late third century contexts. Dunning's typology stressed date and size, but a recent re-examination of all mortaria of Purbeck limestones (including marble) has indicated that it is shape that is significant, as there are large and small and early and late examples of curved and straight sided mortars (Thomas, forthcoming). Of the other mortars, two (fig. 24, nos. 2, 3) were unstratified, and one (fig. 24, no. 4) dated to *c.* AD 125-50.

Ten fragments of sawn slabs, 10-25mm thick, were probably intended for use as inlay elements in composite wall or floor decorations (fig. 24, nos. 9-14). Four were roughly triangular, while three had curved edges. Two (fig. 24, no. 12) retained clear saw marks. Only one fragment had a polished surface, but five had smooth partially polished surfaces. Two other slabs had smooth surfaces, while another had been only roughly smoothed.

Two fragments came from second century layers, six from late second to late third century deposits, and two from the dump of industrial waste which dates from after AD 296.

Five other fragments of Purbeck Marble consist of unfinished slabs and a block with several worked edges. Two slabs, 80 and 90mm thick respectively, and curved edges. All date from *c.* AD 175

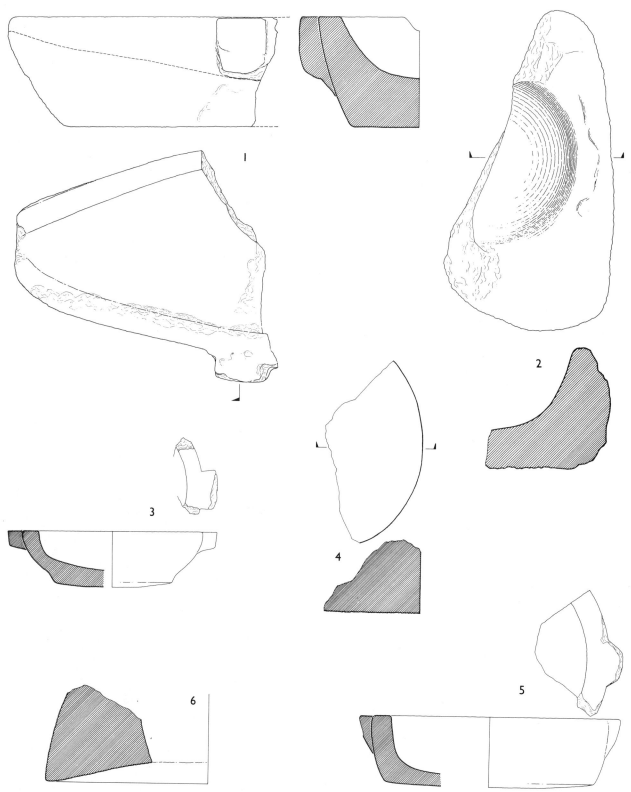

Figure 25. The worked stone, other Purbeck Limestones; scale 1:4.

to the late third century.

The mortars, inlay and other worked fragments indicate that Purbeck Marble was worked on or near the site from the second to the late third or fourth centuries. Dunning restricted the use of Purbeck Marble for inlay slabs to the first and second centuries (Dunning, 1949, 15; Beavis, 1970, 181-204). Opus sectile schemes also appear to belong more to the first century, as at Fishbourne and Angmering (Cunliffe, 1971, 24-30; Scott, 1938, 43). The amount of material in the late dump suggests that such decorative schemes either remained in use longer, or else were revived.

OTHER PURBECK LIMESTONE

Other Purbeck Limestones used on the site include fine-grained and coarser shelly limestones, and tufaceous limestone, or Purbeck Burr Stone, which originated as the boles of tree trunks (information from Mr R. W. Sanderson, Institute of Geological Sciences; Arkell, 1947, 125-6, 143-7). Three mortars (fig. 25, 1-3) were made of this stone, dating to the second and third centuries AD. One of these is very unusual, being oval, or boat-shaped (fig. 25, no. 1).

About thirty other mortars of various Purbeck limestones (excluding Purbeck Marble) are known. The stones used include fine-grained and tufaceous limestone, and Broken Shell Limestone, which is not present at this site. Their distribution is more restricted than that of Purbeck Marble mortars; it is concentrated mostly in Dorset, West Hampshire and South Wiltshire for example at Maiden Castle (Wheeler, 1943, 250-4, fig. 80, no. 57), Woodyates, Woodcuts, Rotherly (Pitt-Rivers, 1892, 150; 1887, 143, fig. 143; 1888, 180, pl. CXX, fig. 6), Poundbury (Dorset County Museum). Such mortars are also found further afield at Sketchley, Leicestershire (Jewry Wall Museum), London, Lullingstone, Orpington Caerwent, Aldborough (information G. C. Dunning, Col. Meates; Dunning 1968, 112; Baily, 1851, 442-3). The use of Purbeck stone for building purposes was mostly confined to Dorset and West Hampshire.

Two mortars, both of tufaceous burr-stone, are worthy of note. The unusual boat-shaped mortar (fig. 25, no. 1) appears to have been finished internally, but had an unfinished and uneven base, and still retained coarse tool-marks around the outside of the body. The other (fig. 25, no. 2), was essentially an irregular lump of stone into which a circular depression, presumably the inside surface of a mortar, had been formed. Traces of the beginnings of tooling around the outside of the rim can just be recognised.

Conclusions

A workfloor for shale may have existed inside the Period 5 building, where a stone block with two rectangular holes may have been a base for a lathe. Workfloors for other materials do not seem to have been found. Similar unfinished and scrap material has been found elsewhere in the Norden area – at the Well, at Artfleet Bridge and in clay workings, all indicating that the working of these materials covered a considerable area. The workfloors which produced the waste material on this site may lie on adjacent unexcavated ground. (Information from P. A. Brown; R.C.H.M., 1970; Hughes, 1973, 91.)

The dates available for the mortars of marble and other stones suggest that production took place in the first half of the second century, and in the second half of the third century. This is contrary to Dunning's dating of the industry to the first century and the first half of the second century, and to the second half of the fourth century. The evidence for the date of the working of Purbeck Marble at Norden confirms Beavis's suggestion that Dunning's dating of the Purbeck Marble industry, as outlined in 1949 and reiterated in 1968, requires revision (Beavis, 1970, 203-4). Beavis quoted the evidence from Norden, which was then only tentatively dated, and a third century inscription from Silchester; the Norden

Plate 14. Unfinished Purbeck Marble mortar no. 4, showing interior tooling; from Period 4 road make-up 1.25 (W. G. Putnam).

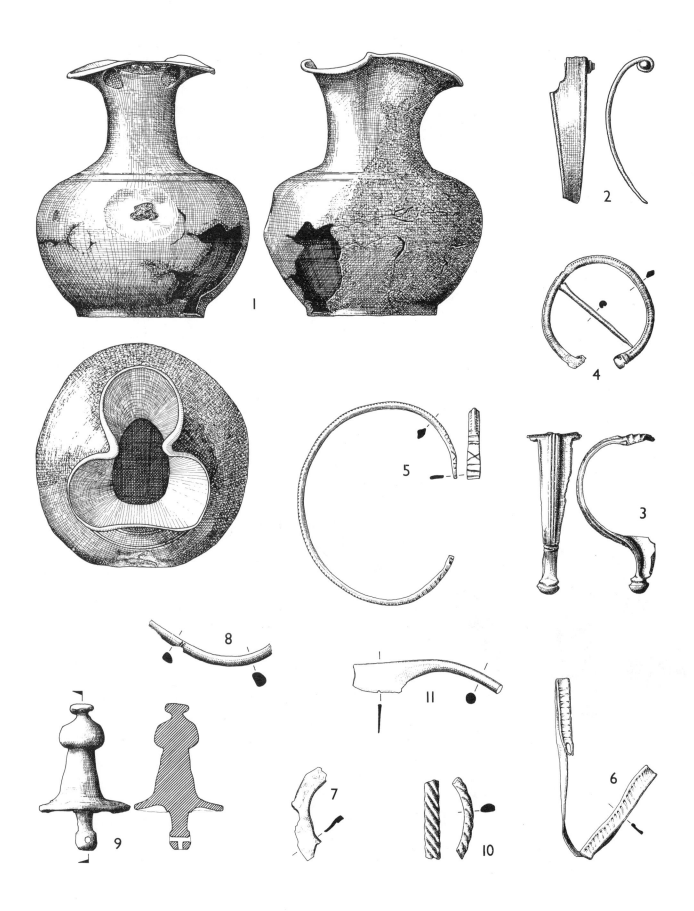

Figure 26. Small finds, copper alloy, no. 1 scale 1:2; 2-11, scale 1:1, see microfiche M7.

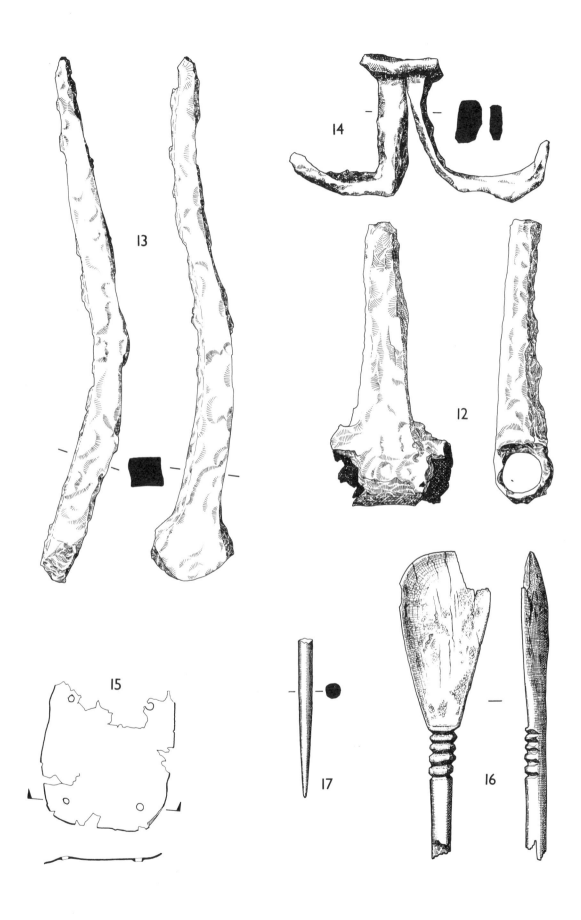

Figure 27. Small finds, iron, lead and bone; 12-14, 16 and 17 scale 1:1; 15, scale 1:2, see microfiche M7.

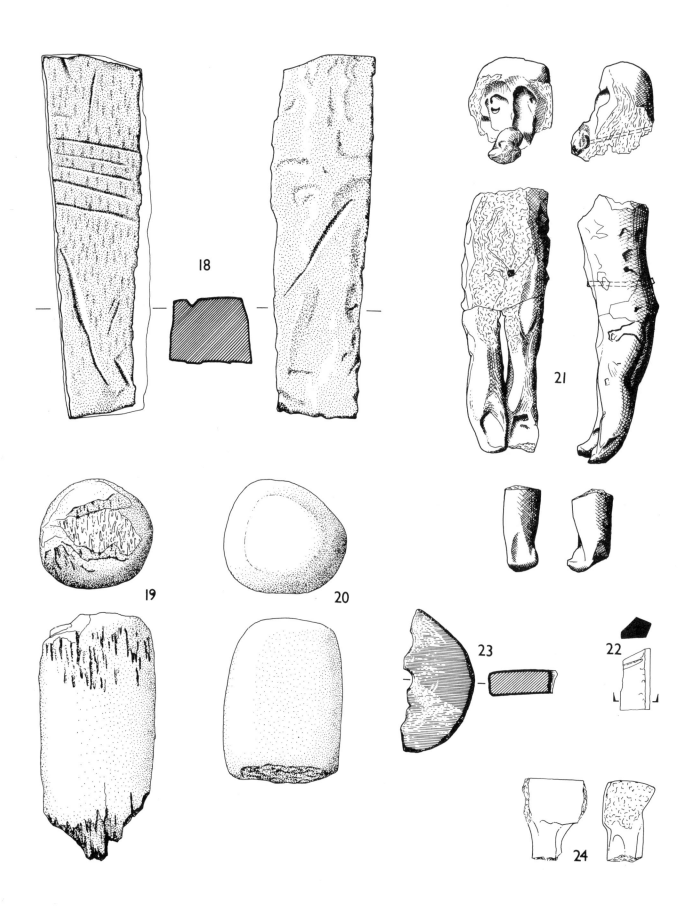

Figure 28. Small finds, stone and clay; 18-22 and 24, scale 1:2; 23, scale 1:1, see microfiche M7.

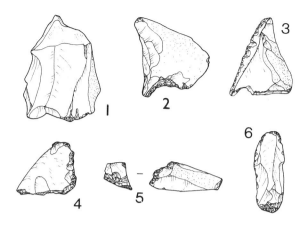

Figure 29. The worked flints, scale 1:2, see microfiche M8.

material has now been positively dated, and new evidence is available from elsewhere, for example slabs of third and fourth century date from Verulamium and a pilaster, possibly of fourth century date, from Pound Lane, Caerwent (Thomas, in Dunning and Evans, forthcoming). Overall, the evidence still indicates a decline in the industry in the second century AD, but it also suggests that manufacture continued, albeit intermittently, in the third and fourth centuries. Although the scale of production was substantially reduced, the industry was still capable of producing architectural fragments and high quality mortaria.

DISCUSSION

The excavated evidence from Norden and from other find-sites in the immediate vicinity (see fig. 1 and Gazetteer) point to the existence of a substantial Roman settlement north of present day Corfe Castle whose economy was based upon the mineral deposits extracted within the Isle of Purbeck. Direct evidence from the excavations at Norden that manufacturing processes were being carried out at a particular date were found in three instances.

Chalk tesserae appear to have been manufactured soon after AD 70. Very few mosaic pavements have been found in Britain which are known to date from the first century AD. White and coloured tesserae have been found at Eccles (Detsicas 1963, 128; Detsicas 1965, 74), at Angmering (Scott, 1938, 17) and at Caerlon (Rainey, 1973, 32), but in this context the most interesting first century mosaics were found in the Flavian villa at Fishbourne (Cunliffe, 1971, 11, 41) for whose construction other stones from the Isle of Purbeck were certainly being transported around AD 75. Perhaps the tesserae from Norden were also manufactured for use in that villa.

The dump of refuse which was deposited after AD 296-7 is a clear indication that industrial activities, the working of chalk, mud-stone and Purbeck Marble as inlays and possibly chalk as tesserae, together with the manufacture of objects of shale, were being carried out at or near the site. It is suggested above (p. 16) that there may also have been a pottery industry at Norden around the end of the third century.

By far the largest number of finds of an industrial nature came from layers which were not themselves a direct result of the manufacturing process, and the artifacts from these layers provide evidence only that industry of a particular type was active on or near the site by a certain date. Of these finds, which are more fully described elsewhere (microfiche M4), the triangular opus sectile

inlays of mud-stone, which were being made by the early second century AD, are worthy of comment. They are only rarely found in Britain, and the two nearest find-sites are Fishbourne (Cunliffe, 1971, I, 67) and Angmering (Scott, 1938, 15ff).

Dunning suggests that there was a decline in the Purbeck Marble industry after the mid-second century AD (Dunning, 1949, 15), and it is perhaps this which is reflected by the shortage of later samian. He also notes a revival of the industry in the second half of the fourth century. Certainly the evidence at Norden would suggest that there was renewed activity, but here dating to the last quarter of the third century and continuing into the fourth century. It is perhaps worth noting that comparatively few 'fine' wares from the New Forest and Oxford kilns were found, and this may be a reflection of the poorer and more locally-based industry which Dunning suggests may have been characteristic of this late phase. However, bearing in mind the abundant evidence in Britain for the construction of late villas and mosaics which presuppose a relatively healthy industry (C. Thomas pers. comm.), and also the lack of securely stratified and dated evidence from the excavation at Norden for industrial activity between the last quarter of the first century and the last quarter of the third century it is well to note the caution expressed about Dunning's interpretation by both Beavis, (1970, 204) and Thomas (see p. 39), and suffice it to say here that the evidence tends on balance to add weight to Dunning's theory of a prosperous and wealthy industry operating up to the mid-second century, and a later phase in which the industry was revived on an altogether different scale.

It remains to discuss the function of the Roman settlement at Norden in relation to Purbeck which it clearly served as a manufacturing centre. The Isle of Purbeck seems to have been intensively cultivated and industrialised during the Roman period (Calkin, 1968, 6; Ordnance Survey, 1956, fig. 5), but despite this apparent source of wealth no evidence has come to light that such local wealth was vested, as might be expected, in villa estates. The only possible remains of a villa site south of the chalk ridge so far known is at Bucknowle (Farrar, 1975). This pattern has been noted in other areas of the country, notably in the Fenlands and in North Dorset (Liversidge, 1968, 229), and it is suggested that these were imperial estates worked by tenant smallholders. It is known that mineral extraction was controlled in a similar way (Liversidge, 1968, 203), and it is possible that both the agriculture and the industry of the Isle of Purbeck were under state ownership and management. The two villas at East Creech (R.C.H.M., 1970, 595-6) and Brenscombe (Farrar, 1963b, 103; Farrar, 1967a, 144) lie immediately to the north of the chalk ridge and for this reason they may have been outside the imperial estate. However, it is unlikely that agriculturally the Isle of Purbeck was of sufficient importance of itself to justify state management, and the sparcity of villas may simply represent ownership of the farming land by outsiders. Indeed, the villas north of the ridge may have been built for managers of the local stone industries based at Norden and Povington (C. Thomas pers. comm.).

Norden is ideally situated, at the gap through the chalk ridge, as a centre for the assembly of raw materials, as a manufactory for converting the raw materials into consumer goods, and as a distribution centre from which the finished articles would have been sent northwards by road or eastwards to the southern shore of Poole Harbour where they would have been shipped around the coast. It has long been the tradition for the village of Corfe Castle to be the centre for Purbeck's stone carving industry. Here most of the masons lived and had their yards, and from Corfe Castle the stone was transported to the quays (which still exist) on the southern shore of Poole Harbour (Clifton-Taylor, 1972, 179-80). It is tempting to suggest that this tradition has its roots back in the Roman industry established before AD 70 at Norden.

The Excavation of a Late Iron-Age settlement and Romano-British Industrial site at Ower, Dorset

PETER J. WOODWARD

Field Officer for the Wessex Archaeological Committee, Salisbury, now Trust for Wessex Archaeology

SUMMARY

Excavation, geophysical survey, and fieldwalking defined an extensive settlement of at least 10 hectares on the Ower Peninsula. The complex of small, ditched and interconnected enclosures was apparently systematically planned, was of 'village-like' proportions, had no defined nor 'ditched' circuit and was of Late Iron Age date. The occurrence of pottery vessels imported from Continental Europe in the earliest ditches demonstrated that trade links with northern Spain and south-west France were well established in the period before AD 43.

Changes were apparent in the later first, and second centuries AD; the Late Iron Age ditches were infilled, and there was an accumulation of soils across the Late Iron Age earthworks. Little second-century material was deposited.

Across the accumulated soils and infilled earthworks a number of buildings and 'industrial' structures were recorded. These disregarded the former site layout, and were associated with the production of BB1 pottery in the late second to fourth centuries AD. Geophysical and field-walking surveys indicated that these buildings were located as a settlement to the south of an area of intensive industrial activity: for firing pottery, and crystallising salt from sea-water.

Post-Roman settlement and occupation was indicated by the presence of two glass beads which can be no earlier than the late 6th to early 7th century AD. These were found in association with post-built structure utilising earlier building stone for post-wedges.

This industrial area and the settlement as a whole, is now much eroded and reduced in area, owing to tidal movements within Poole Harbour. The site was also damaged by medieval and post-medieval strip cultivation, which reduced the latest settlement levels to 'islands of survival' within the open fields of Ower Quay.

INTRODUCTION AND SITE DESCRIPTION

The site located at Ower is one of those described by Farrar (1977), and Williams (1977), where there is some evidence for the manufacture of BB1 pottery. The site had been identified by H. P. Smith in 1940, and trial excavations were carried out by N. H. Field in 1951 (Farrar 1977). In these excavations soil-accumulations of up to 0.6m were re-corded, above the cap of what was interpreted as a kiln dome (fig. 31A, trial trench A). Excavation of this and other trenches (fig. 31A, A-1) identified both briquetage and oxidised BB1 products of the 2nd to 4th centuries AD. The site was taken in for permanent pasture from rough heath in stages from the late 1940s; during this process the final phase of occupation earthworks was probably reduced.

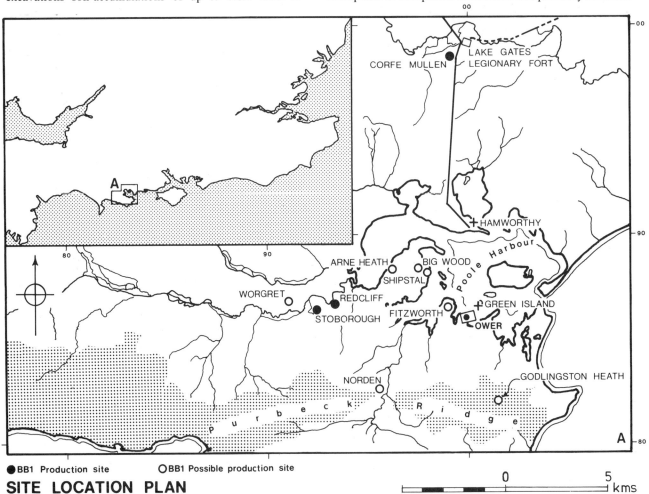

● BB1 Production site   ○ BB1 Possible production site

SITE LOCATION PLAN

0   5 kms

Figure 30. Site Location Plan 1 showing BB1 pottery production sites.

Aerial photographs of 1946 do indicate some banked enclosures (CPE/UK 1821.6392); however these probably all relate to the medieval settlement. The deep ploughing of the site in 1975 was halted when the plough hit the walls of a burial cyst (fig. 31A, J), recorded by John Beavis (this volume).

However the full extent of the site was not realised until the present investigations.

In 1978 a series of pipelines was planned to connect the well-heads of the developing Purbeck Oilfield by British Gas. A pipe supplying water from the harbour and a pumping station were to be located across the southern part of the peninsula (fig. 30 and fig. 31A). Since it was likely that the settlement would occur in this part of the field, excavations were undertaken in June 1978, prior to construction in July. However it was not possible to organise field-walking (the fields were down to ley pasture) nor to undertake a geophysical survey before excavations began.

Initial exploratory excavations were therefore designed to determine the extent and intensity of settlement on the basis of $1m^2$ trial pits on a 20m grid, aligned along the construction route (fig. 3A and B). From these a rapid determination of the distribution of Romano-British pottery (fig. 32), soil accumulations (fig. 32), the distribution of other occupational debris and identified features, and phosphate concentration (fig. 64) were generated. The

other objectives were to clarify the relationship between the land-limit of the peninsula and the present-day water regime in the Harbour, and in turn to identify the possible functional relationship to the site and history of the 'Causeway' (Plate 15) described by Farrar (1977), Taylor (1959) and Bugler (1966). Some of the distributional results are shown in fig. 32A and B. From these it was clear where the focus of settlement lay in this area, and the initial area excavation (20m by 15m) was opened by machine on the basis of the trial pit results, together with 1m machine trenches along the route of the pipe to relate the stratigraphy of this focus to areas of lower soil accumulation and Romano-British pottery concentrations. Subsequent trenches were opened as a result of these machine trials and geophysical survey, which was carried out while excavation was in progress. The results of these excavations should be viewed in conjunction with subsequent geophysical survey, field-walking and soil analysis which were carried out following the excavations between 1978 and 1981. The overall settlement pattern deduced is shown in figs 31 and 32.

Magnetic surveys by the Ancient Monuments laboratory on the three fields of the Ower Peninsula to the south-west of Ower quay and to the north and west of Newton Bay have progressively identified an extensive and organised complex of village-like proportions (*Microfiche M11*). The basic interpretation is shown in fig. 31A. The configuration of

Plate 15. Aerial view of Cleavel Point, showing the Causeway at low tide, connecting across to Green Island.

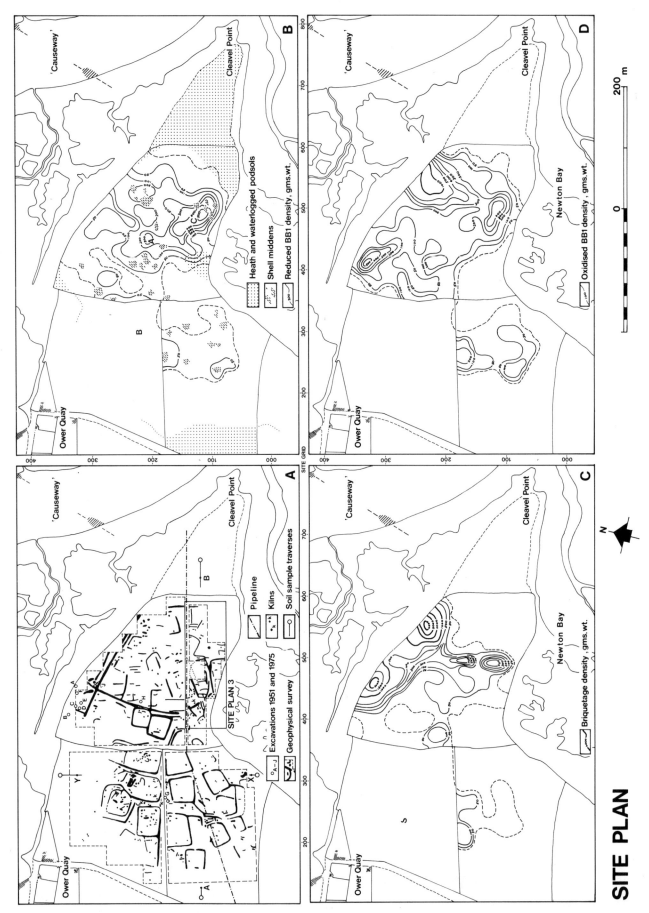

Figure 31. Site Plan 2, the Ower Peninsula settlement showing: A. The 1st century AD settlement enclosures identified by geophysical survey; B. The distribution of reduced BB1 and shell middens (the 3rd-4th c. AD settlement) from fieldwalking; C. The distribution of Briquetage (the industrial areas of 3rd-4th c. AD) from fieldwalking. D. The distribution of oxidised BB1 (the industrial areas of 3rd-4th c. AD) from fieldwalking.

magnetic anomalies, mostly representing ditches, in the most southerly field clearly indicates that the settlement continues around the west margin of Newton Bay. Briquetage and deep soil accumulation on the west and south sides of Newton Bay, to the west of Ower Farm and north of Game Copse, suggest that the settlement may well cover a much larger area. Evidence for continuing erosion is clear on all boundaries of Ower and Newton Bay; present-day boundary hedges and trees are root-exposed due to the wide range of tidal movement. It is also probable that some areas are being progressively silted. This combination of tidal movement and silt deposition has resulted in a much reduced site area.

It has been suggested that marine transgressions is south-west England in the Roman period (Hawkins 1971) had the effect of creating an expanse of water in the Poole Basin, which would otherwise have been little more than salt-marsh (Farrar 1977). The 'connecting causeway' from the peninsula to Green Island can perhaps be associated directly with the site (Plate 15). Subsequent changes in the tidal regime would have since cut the roadway, and progressive silting buried the approach to the settlement. However it would be necessary to obtain a radiocarbon date from the timbers of the causeway to substantiate a Romano-British date for this structure. The timber construction of the causeway is described in Taylor (1959) and Bugler (1966).

Trial pits cut close to the harbour edge showed no evidence for sealed land surfaces below the present-day High Water Mark. Testing the area below the High Water Mark immediately to the north of the settlement with the fluxgate gradiometer showed some indication of settlement features continuing, but with greatly reduced magnetic intensity. This could have been brought about by either erosion or the sealing of the earlier land surface by harbour silting, but the profile of the ground suggested that erosion was the more probable. Evidence for a post-Roman marine transgression may be found in the further examination and dating of the timbers in the submerged 'causeway'.

Shoreline change in Poole Harbour has been extensively discussed and depicted by May (May, 1968). However he has not suggested any shoreline change for the northern shore of Ower, nor Fitzworth (May, 1968; figs. 2 and 4a), but has shown the accretion of harbour silts at these two locations post-1807 (fig. 31b). The archaeological evidence from Ower does suggest that the northern shore of Ower, at least, should be included as an additional point of erosion on May's maps, and that the shoreline of Poole Harbour (6,000 b.p.) would then contain the possibility for a closer link between Ower and Green Island, and, indeed to Furzey. The excavation of truncated 1st century BC/AD field boundaries on Furzey, confirms May's observation of erosion of its southern and western fringes (Cox 1985). The possibility of the creation of deeper water channels between Ower-Green Island-Furzey Island-Brownsea Island, in the Romano-British/Post-Roman period which may have fundamentally altered the water regime in the harbour must be considered as a serious possibility. Those water channels may be the result of a marine transgression, together with a deliberate cutting and dredging of water channels by man.

The main magnetic survey was carried out with the Ancient Monuments Laboratory's fluxgate gradiometer trace recording system, based on a 30m grid. The survey was undertaken in four parts: in the eastern field to the north and south of the projected pipeline (*Microfiche M17, G27/78*), in the north-west field (*Microfiche M17, G6/79*), and the south-west field (*Microfiche M11, G6/81*). The normal traverse spacing was 1m, but in the northern part of the eastern field a spacing of 2m had to be used for economy in time, causing some loss of definition of small features.

On the northern shore of the site, to the south-east of the earlier trial pits A-F, an extremely strong magnetic disturb-ance was recorded. The activity was enclosed by a large and very magnetic ditch which ran roughly parallel to the hedge and the edge of the salt-marsh. It formed a corner to the north, although the magnetic enhancement was relatively slight there. From this point it ran south-eastwards for some 180m before running out of the survey area and being cut away by tidal erosion. There was a marked contrast in the character of the magnetic disturbance to either side of it. The anomalies to the north were so strong that a pattern was impossible to distinguish, although dense archaeological activity, probably kiln firing can be suggested. Such disturbance spreads south of the main ditch at two points, which suggests that the ditch ceased to function at some stage during intense industrial activity. This area is coincident with the main concentrations of oxidised BB1 and briquetage and also the kiln cap (trial pit A). This area can therefore be associated with the firing and production of BB1 pottery and salt.

To the south of this industrial zone, in the area of the main excavation trench, two alignments of enclosures can be identified from the geophysical survey; excavation confirmed the presence of two ditched enclosures, which totally ignore each other's alignment. Thus two phases of site organisation, at least, are evident.

In the north-west field area some kilns were identified by survey and confirmed by auger. One lay in the middle of the access to the double-ditched central enclosure. This again suggests two separate periods of activity. A large number of kiln type anomalies were noted over the site as a whole, but only some of these were further substantiated by auger (marked 'K' in fig. 31A).

The distribution of material was defined by field collection after ploughing in September 1980 (Maynard 1981), complemented and supported the basic interpretation of the geophysical survey in that the distribution of the briquetage and oxidised BB1 were coincident with high levels of magnetic enhancement; thus further defining the industrial focus (fig. 31, C and D). In addition the reduced BB1 wares, which can be interpreted as representing domestic locations (fig. 31B) could perhaps be seen to be grouping into three foci (A-C) with associated marine-shell middens. Focus C is probably over-accentuated due to excavation disturbance and machine stripping. It is also clear from the field-walking that no significant quantities of earlier material (1st century) were collected on the surface, suggesting that these levels were sealed below accumulated soils (see soil report and section, fig. 33) and beyond the reach of the plough. The field-walking results can therefore be taken as defining the settlement arrangement at the latest phase of the site's development, i.e. the pottery production complex of the 3rd to 4th centuries AD.

In the third geophysical report (*Microfiche M11, G6/81*), the intensity of magnetic enhancement in the south-west field was stated to be noticeably less, although the settlement enclosures were still extensively recorded. Exploratory magnetic scanning in the field to the north suggested that the enclosures spread yet further in this direction, but also with the corresponding decline in intensity. This, when considered with the evidence from a bore-hole, suggests that the area of the pottery production complex of the 3rd to 4th centuries AD, with its associated enhancement of soil magnetism, was probably limited to the northern and eastern parts of the peninsula.

There was an extremely close correlation between the boundary of the heath-soils, recognised and recorded as part of the field-walking survey, and the beginning of geophysical anomalies. The soil across the settlement area was darker in colour and had a humic and clay fraction. Soil samples were also taken at 10m intervals on two traverses across the site (fig. 31A), and measured for magnetic susceptibility values. These clearly defined the areas where industrial and occupational activities were at a maximum

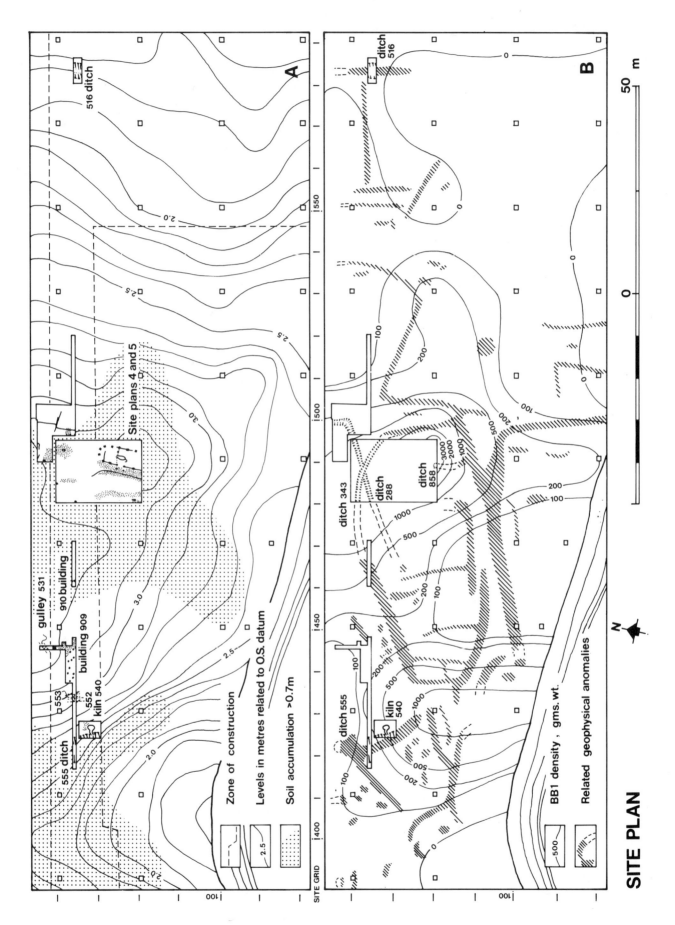

Figure 32. Site Plan 3, the Excavation Areas of 1978 showing: A. The main 3rd-4th c. AD settlement features, together with the levels of soil accumulation, contours, and the zone of destruction; B. The excavated features, which relate to geophysical anomalies, and the distribution of BB1 pottery as recorded from the test pits.

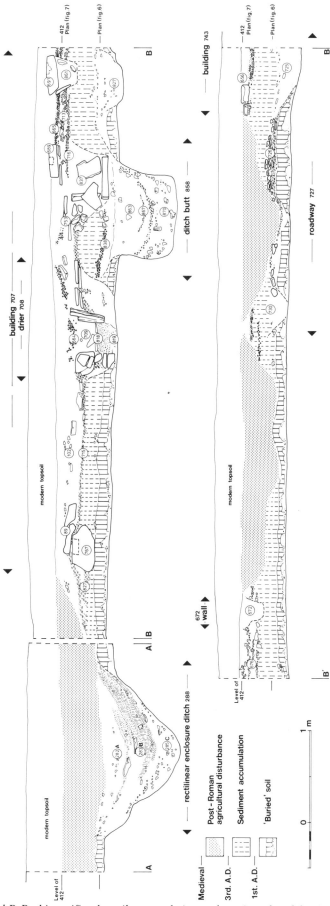

Figure 33. Site Section A-A and B-B: this typifies the soil accumulation and stratigraphy of the site as a whole, showing the 1st c. AD settlement horizon (SP4, fig. 35), the 3rd-4th c. AD occupation horizon (SP5, fig. 36), and the post-Roman agricultural disturbance, medieval (SP5 (inset), fig. 36). The section is a composite one but located along section lines A-A and B-B specified on SP4 and SP5.

(see fig. 65). Phosphate determinations were also used to define the settlement focus across the area of Site Plan B (fig. 64, soil report).

The phasing and occupational history of the site identified by survey was amplified by area excavation, and in general terms, it can be suggested that the two phases of planned 'village' enclosures can be placed into the Late Iron Age pre-conquest period and the 1st century AD. The industrial 'kiln' area on the northern shore is to some extent confined within a discrete unit of enclosures, but does eventually spill across them. It would seem likely that the site was highly organised in the first century with an industrial area sited away from settlement enclosures. However, later developments and continuing industrial activity began to ignore defined limits, and this may suggest reorganisation and growing specialisation in site function. Excavation in the southern area showed a clear stratigraphic division between 1st century levels and horizons which defined a pottery-making complex of the 3rd and 4th centuries AD (fig. 35, and following). Although this cannot be taken as a representative sample within 11 hectares, it would seem to at least correlate with the observation that some kilns are apparently located in droveways. Examination of the coinage evidence from this site and comparison with related sites within Purbeck, would also appear to confirm a lack of trading activity in the second century AD (Woodward 1980). A total reorganisation, or even reoccupation, of the site in the 3rd to 4th centuries is indicated.

The sequence of events in the Post-Roman period is not clear, but the site perhaps failed as an established industrial site in the early 4th century AD. The presence of two glass beads of 6th to 7th century AD date (see specialist report below) in association with a post-built structure (fig. 32A,

building 909), which utilised earlier building material points to a continuing occupation. Unfortunately subsequent agriculture developments have removed substantially the upper levels of the site.

The use of the site in the medieval period is clear from the excavations and documentary sources, although no evidence for the salt-panners mentioned in the Domesday Survey was found (Darby 1979). Excavation showed that the site had been cut by a series of 'trenches' which may represent the base of the furrows of strip cultivation within the open fields of Ower, which would have almost certainly existed across an area where the soils were deeper and more fertile. Traces of the medieval fields and enclosures across the site have now been totally removed by the modern ploughing, but field-walking and topographic observation suggests that the village focus was confined to the area around the Ower Quay.

THE EXCAVATIONS
As previously described the excavation areas were selected on the basis of the results of 1m[2] trial pits and the subsequent geophysical survey by the Ancient Monuments Lab. (D.o.E.). All areas were topsoil stripped with a JCB and toothless metre bucket to the base of the modern ploughsoil, 0.1-0.3m. All areas were otherwise excavated by hand. These excavations were carried out by Peter J. Woodward for the Dorset Archaeological Committee, with the permission of the landowners, Messrs. Ryder of Rempstone and were funded by the Department of the Environment and British Gas. The report was completed for the Wessex Archaeological Committee now Trust for Wessex Archaeology.

The Report and Archive
This report consists of a general site report referred to primary feature numbers and phasing. No detailed stratigraphic matrix has been published. The detailed stratigraphic analysis and phasing can

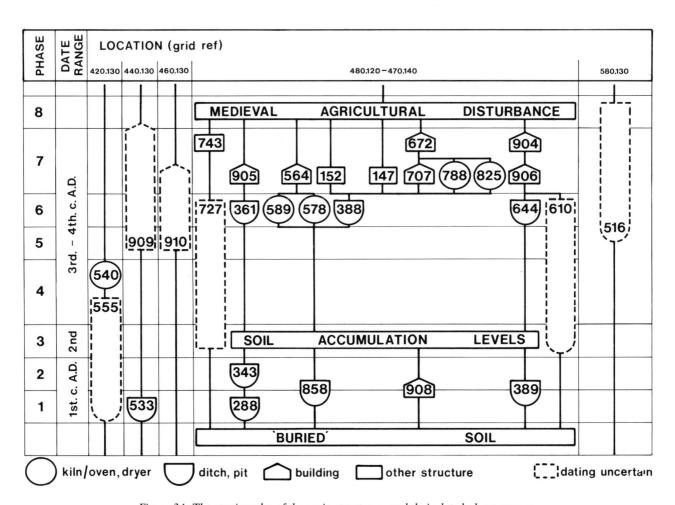

Figure 34. The stratigraphy of the main structures, and their dated phase groups.

be found in the Archive. The finds reports following the discussion also relate directly to detailed analyses stored in the Archive.

The Archive consists of two excavation records (OWR65, OWR78), and a fieldwalking survey record (OWR80). These are followed by post-excavation, field survey analysis in Archive files, and a Correspondence File. These two groups of record conform to the Level II and Level III archives as defined in *Principles of Publication in Rescue Archaeology – a Report by a working party of the Ancient Monuments Board for England* Committee for Rescue Archaeology (Department of the Environment, London, October 1975), and from which this Level IV publication report has been prepared. The details of this archive can be found in the Microfiche M10.

Microfiche copies of this archive can be found at: The National Monuments Record, The Trust for Wessex Archaeology (Salisbury), and Dorset County Museum. The original record Archive has been deposited at Poole Museum, together with the finds.

THE CHRONOLOGY AND PHASING

One of the primary sources of dating was the pottery which established the general date of two occupation horizons; early 1st century AD, and 3rd to 4th centuries AD.

The early 1st-century AD group contained an important series of pre-conquest fine wares and Amphorae, together with continental coarse wares and late Iron Age/early 1st-century AD BB1 pottery. The 3rd to 4th-century AD group contained late BB1 dishes, bowls and jars, together with New Forest and Oxford wares.

The coinage confirmed this broad dating, and the lack of trading activity in the 2nd century AD, although the latest coin from the site (Valens, A. D. 375-8), could not necessarily be used as a date for abandonment. The bronze brooches correspond with this interpretation of dating.

Two samples of marine molluscs from a midden infilling the 1st-century AD ditches, and infilling one of the 3rd to 4th-century AD buildings, were submitted for radio-carbon dating in order to establish a more certain and absolute date for abandonment. However the available carbon was too low from these samples to obtain reliable dates at the present time.

A composite drawing of a section through the main excavation area illustrates and typifies the soil accumulation process and the major occupation horizons across the site as a whole (fig. 33). The simplified phasing and corresponding structures are summarised in fig. 34. Some features have uncertain dating either due to the lack of stratigraphy, incomplete excavation, or the lack of diagnostic finds. The other major difficulty to dating was the problem of contamination of later levels with material from underlying occupation horizons. Thus post-building (909) could be later and also ditch (516) if one assumes that no dateable material survived or was deposited from the period of construction and use. Conversely, Roadway (727) may be earlier. This uncertainty is recorded in fig. 34 by a discontinuous line. The 3rd and 4th-century AD complex is described by four phases. Two of these phases, 4 and 5, were artificially designated for groups of features in differing locational positions; it is possible and likely that these could be contemporary with phases 6 and 7 or even later. All the finds have been tabulated according to the phases described following:

PHASES 1 and 2:
The first major occupation of this site occurred in the Later Iron Age, and probably in the first years of the first century AD, when a series of ditched enclosures was laid out. A second series of enclosures replaced the first, and both had their ditches substantially infilled during the first century occupation, but were never apparently recut.

PHASE 3:
Accumulation of soils over these ditches and in their upper levels could have resulted from a number of agencies induced by continued occupation and intensive industrial activity. Wind-blow of light sandy soils might be one such process (see soil report and discussion). The lack of material finds and coinage of the 2nd century AD (notably 2nd century BB1 forms and post in 1st century Amphora) suggests a lack of trading activity and break in occupation, although all activity may not have ceased on the site as a whole.

PHASES 4 to 7:
The building phases above this accumulative phase represent a complex of huts and workshops, perhaps primarily used for the manufacture of BB1 pottery, prior to firing. The firing was probably undertaken at a distance from the buildings and in the main on the northern shore, although the presence of a small oven or kiln may suggest experimental firing closer to hand (fig. 33A, kiln (540), and fig. 34, kilns (589), (578)). This complex exhibits evidence for continuous use through phases of building adaptation

Plate 16. Sections through the 1st century AD rectilinear enclosure (288) (refer also fig. 33), below the pitched clay box (152) (Phase 7).

and reconstruction (figs 36 and 37, building 707), and reuse of previous architectural and building fragments; Building 906 includes the reuse of a cylindrical marker stone (fig. 36 and fig. 56, 256), the posts of what is presumably a building (fig. 32A, 909) used a variety of stone (Purbeck Marble heathstone, and limestone derived from previous buidings) for post-packing. The use of a large number of constructional techniques for the buildings also points to multiple phasing; post-pads, sill walls, herringbone sills, and conventional wedged posts. The beginnings of this complex can be dated to the Late second/Early third centuries AD, and it is likely to have continued well into the fourth century and probably later.

PHASE 8:
Although no definite horizon can be attributed to any immediate post-Roman occupation, there were two glass beads of 6th to 7th-century date which can be associated with building 909. The Medieval agricultural disturbance which reduced the earlier site to a number of islands of survival, together with the modern plough disturbance have been attributed to Phase 8.

The First-Century Ditches and associated occupation features
(Phases 1 and 2), Excavation area 480.120-500.140.
Fig. 35 (Plan), Fig. 33 (section), Plates 16 and 17.
In terms of stratigraphy the earliest feature recorded on the site was a shallow 'scoop' (618) cut by the rectilinear enclosure ditch

(288) and overlain by its internal bank, the base of which survived in certain areas as a gravelly and coarse sandy spread above an old soil. This scoop was roughly rectangular with dimensions of about 5m × 4m and cut 0.1m into natural. It survived to a depth of 0.3m as a cut through the buried soil. Few finds were recovered in the infilling but the lenses of burnt reddish-brown soils and marine shells were very similar to the sediments infilling the adjacent enclosure ditch (288).

The portion of ditch (288) excavated was the south-east corner of a probable rectilinear enclosure only partly identified by geophysical survey (fig. 31A). The ditch in this area survived to a depth of 1.0m, was 2.0m wide and 'U' shaped in section (fig. 33). For much of its length it was cut through a 'buried soil' which varied in depth from 0.1 to 0.2m (fig. 33 and Plate 16). There was a primary silting (C) of light-grey coarse loam with small and medium stones, to a depth of 0.3m in the base and slightly thicker on the northern side (285). Above this was a series of alternating lenses of 'burnt' soils varying from dark grey through light-brown to bright reddish-brown (fig. 33, 388B) together with tips of marine molluscs (B). At certain points lenses of raw white ball clay and mottled muddy clays occurred. These lenses were tipped from various points both internal and external to the enclosure and represent a deliberate infilling with waste from occupation. The points from which the waste was tipped were spaced at intervals of about 3 to 5m along the length of the ditch (fig. 35, a-f). A notable layer of crushed/

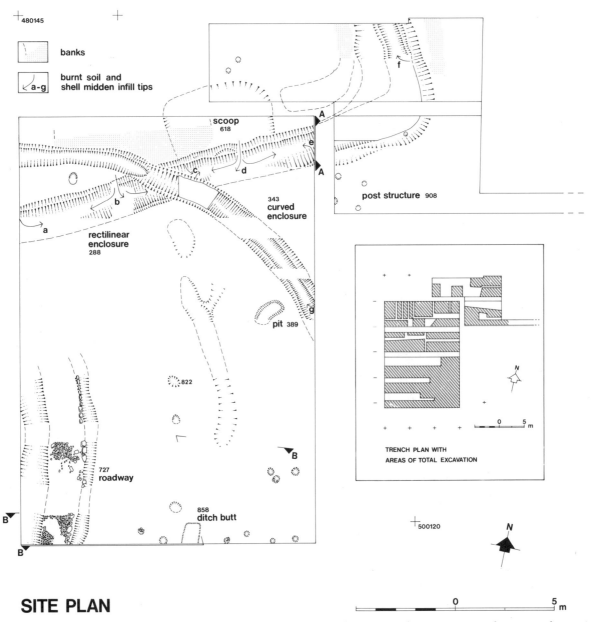

SITE PLAN

Figure 35. Site Plan 4, the excavation area 4812-5014 which shows the excavated 1st century enclosures and associated structures.

trampled pot occurred towards the base of tips d and e (323).

Above this deliberate infilling was a sediment (A) scarcely distinguishable from those covering the site above the old soil. It was a dark grey-brown sandy loam containing charcoal and occasional clay flecks; some medium – small stone lenses were present (282). In certain areas of the ditch later 3rd to 4th-century occupation debris had accumulated in the upper levels.

The second phase of the first-century occupation was represented by a curved ditch (343) which cut across and through the lower ditch sediments (B and C) of (288), and bank of the rectilinear enclosure. This ditch varied greatly in depth which may have been a result of the undulating ground through which it was cut, since it was shallowest (0.4m) at points where it cut across the earlier bank, and deepest (up to 1.2m) in the portion to the south and outside the earlier enclosure. Where the surviving profile is deeper, it is clear that it was cut as a 'U'-sectioned ditch, but had a steeper slope to its sides and more extensive erosion on its upper edges (depth: 0.9m, width: 1.5m), than that of the earlier ditch (288). The primary silting was also deeper (0.3-0.5m). Where the ditch cut enclosure (288), it was subsequently filled with broken shell and soil derived from the earlier deposit through which it cut. For much of its length the ditch is apparently infilled by gradually silting soils and 'natural' processes, and its upper fill is indistinguishable from the upper fill of (288) A, (235). However at the southernmost point a series of lensed soils and marine shell deposits, similar to those in (288) were tipped into the enclosure from the outside (tip 'g').

Associated with these two enclosure ditches were a pit (389) and what may be the butt end of a ditch (858).

Pit (389) 1.6m by 0.8m and with 'U' shaped profile was cut to 0.35m below its surviving cut line in the buried soil. The lower infill of this pit included burnt animal bone, shale and a lens of red-brown oxidised ('burnt') soil reminiscent of the infill tips previously mentioned.

Feature (858) may possibly be the butt-end of a ditch located on the geophysical survey (fig. 32B). The feature has near vertical sides and was flat bottomed with a shallow depression at its northern end filled with some 'ball-clay' lumps. This can perhaps be interpreted as a post impression. Sandy loam tips and occupation debris filled the basal third of the feature (870), including a broken iron sickle with flanged tang (fig. 54, 242).

This was sealed by thin lenses of clay and sand (867-9). The top of

the pit was infilled with the ubiquitous grey sandy loam similar to that in the upper levels of the ditches (863). Occupation levels relating to the 3rd and 4th centuries filled the upper level (838). The pit was apparently cut from a level slightly above the buried soil, which suggests that some soil accumulation was already taking place.

The occupation debris deposited in these four features comprised metalwork (iron, bronze), animal bone, marine molluscs and first-century pottery (imported fine and coarse ware, Amphora (Pascual 1) and local Black Burnished coarse ware). The datable range of material firmly places both phases of ditches in the pre-conquest period. The occupation characteristics of this settlement are discussed after the site descriptions.

In association with these datable features were a number of post-holes and ill-defined gullies and scoops (fig. 35). None of these were visible until all soils had been removed, as their fill was virtually indistinguishable from the buried soil. One group of posts formed a square outside the south-east corner of enclosure (288), and may represent a four-post structure for storage of fodder or grain (post-structure 908, Plate 17). The posts varied in diameter from 0.25 to 0.4m and were cut into 'natural' up to a depth of 0.4m. Small paired and single posts which otherwise occurred were of similar dimensions.

In area 440.130 to the west was another early feature. This was a small pit (533) on the eastern side of the trench at 446.138 and sealed below yard (441), which was associated with building (909) of phase 7. This pit was 'U'-shaped with a diameter of 0.5m and 0.4m deep. It continued by a quantity of amphora and charcoal. The amphora (Pascual 1) was not apparently residual, since it was present in some quantity, was not badly abraded, and occurred with no later material. The fragments were however, pitched and may have been used for post wedging.

Early features and Soil Accumulation, (Phase 3)
Excavation area 480. 120-470. 140
Fig. 35 (Plan), Fig. 33 (Section)

Across all the first-century features in the central excavation trench, a fairly uniform accumulation of soil occurred. This varied in depth from 0.1-0.3m, and was a light-dark grey brown sandy loam soil with occasional medium – small stones randomly distributed but sometimes occurring in undulating lenses. Frequent

Plate 17. Four-post structure (908) cut through old soil (removed), and below accumulation (Phase 3). Building (904) and the pathway show in the section (Phase 7).

occurrence of briquetage, oxidised ('burnt') deposits and marine shell was noted. Occupation debris was clearly churned up and apparently deposited in this horizon, and some features were cut from levels within this accumulation including (858) previously mentioned. Some reddish-brown deposits in this horizon may be derived from the 1st-century occupation.

Although the accumulation succeeded in sealing an old soil profile it did not apparently result in the preservation of a clear first-century occupation horizon. This horizon seems to have been severely disturbed by a process of churning into succeeding occupation levels; probably a result of the friable nature of these sandy soils, and also because the accumulation began as a process directly associated with occupation.

The mechanisms by which this accumulation occurred are not obvious, although it is clear that it was in part built up from occupation deposits. However it perhaps also owes something to natural causes such as wind-blow during intense exploitation of the surrounding landscape by de-forestation (see discussion and soil report).

Below and within this soil build-up are a numer of features whose dating is uncertain either due to the lack of diagnostic finds or as a result of later disturbance which has introduced later cultural material.

One of these features is the roadway (727). This has been truncated as a result of later occupation disturbance and the presence of a medieval furrow running along its length (fig. 36 and inset). Its relationship to the enclosures is therefore not clear. The metalling (726) is little more than 2 metres wide with a shallow ditch cut on each side. The western ditch (725) cuts 0.1m into 'natural', but otherwise survives as a cut through the 'old soil' to a depth of 0.4m, and a width of perhaps 2 metres in places. The eastern ditch (730) is slighter and does not cut into 'natural', 0.5m wide and 0.2m deep. The infill of the ditches is as described for the general soil accumulation. The metalling itself is composed of two levels. The lower layer, compressed onto the surviving 'old soil', is composed of a reddish brown burnt clay and briquetage fragments. This is somewhat discontinuous and crushed charcoal was noticeably present. The overlying road surface had surviving patches of what can best be described as roughly deposited hardcore (heathstone 'cobbles' and flint and broken limestone). This was edged with a kerb of roughly squared heathstone, marble and limestone pieces on the east side. However the foreign stone was probably imported to the site for some use other than track-hardcore. The presence of marble and limestone suggests a post-conquest date. The pottery contained in the road-surface would therefore be residual from the earlier 1st-century occupation. The road surface was heavily cut and robbed by later occupation which in turn introduced 3rd and 4th century pottery to the lowest levels. The roadway was

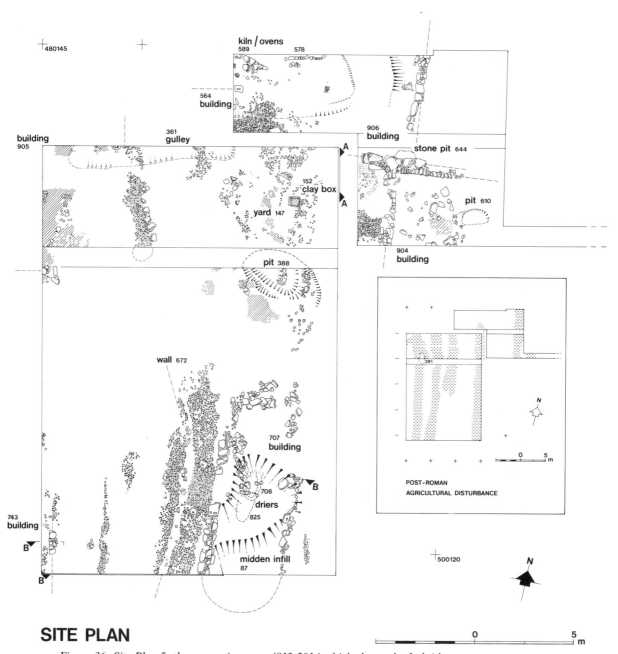

SITE PLAN

Figure 36. Site Plan 5, the excavation area 4812-5014 which shows the 3rd-4th century AD structures.

overlain by building (743), and was subsequently damaged by medieval furrows (fig. 36 and inset).

The other feature was a small pit (610) on the eastern side of the main excavation area (fig. 36). The upper levels had been substantially removed by a medieval furrow, but enough stratigraphy survived to suggest that it lay below the 3rd-4th century occupation levels. It was also cut from a level above the old soil.

The pit was ovate (1.5m x 1.0m), and 0.4m in depth. The infill was nearly indistinguishable from the surrounding soil accumulation. At its base were pieces of burnt limestone and heathstone, clay and briquetage fragments were present throughout the fill. Shale, ironwork, bone and pottery were also present.

The precise dating of this accumulation is uncertain. It contained a large quantity of occupation material from the preconquest

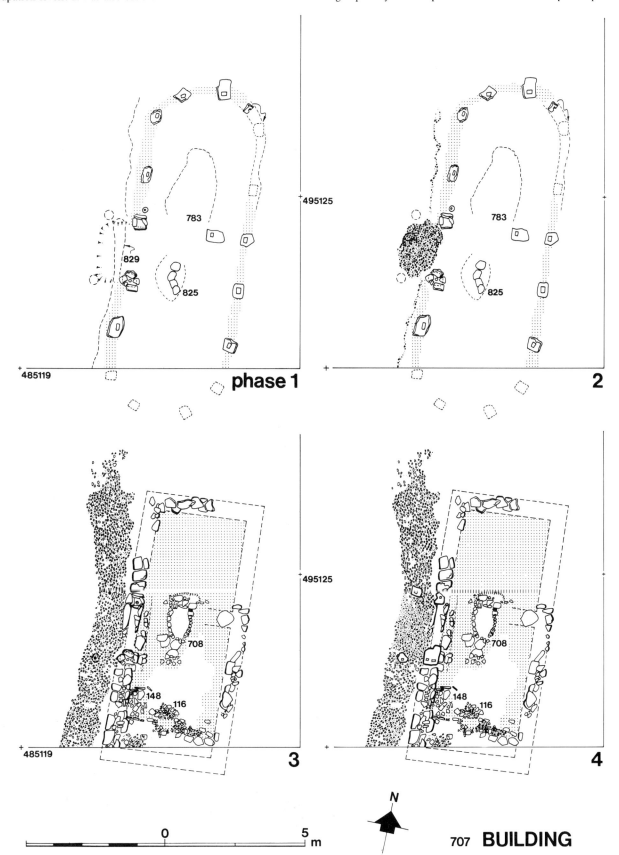

Figure 37. Building 707 with dryers 825 and 708 in area 4912, showing its development phases (1-4).

occupation. However, in contrast to the 1st-century AD ditches, it did in addition contain mudstone and ceramic tile. The mudstone (refer specialist report and Table 7) occurred in some quantity and could be identified as being tesserae pieces and waste. This points to some activity in the later 1st-century AD, but no extensive occupation can yet be suggested in the 2nd-century AD at Ower (see following discussion).

The Third-Fourth century AD occupation levels and structures
(Phases 4-7)
Plans: Figs. 36-38, and Section Fig. 33

The main sequence which can be placed in the 3rd-4th century AD was excavated in area 480.120-470.140 (figs 33 and 36), and grouped as phases 6 and 7. In other areas (fig. 32) less firmly dated structures and features could be associated with this central structural sequence, these were categorised as phases 4 and 5. The ditch (516) on the eastern boundary of the site (Location 580.130) was not given a phase number, and was not precisely datable (see post-Roman disturbance). The only chronological sequence implied by phase numbers is between phases 6 and 7:

Phase 6: Those features sealed below buildings;

Phase 7: Buildings and their subsequent alterations, extensions, renovation and replacement, and their associated occupation levels and structures.

The phase 6/7 occupation horizon was defined by a series of layers typified by (142); coarse sand and clay lenses within a grey brown sandy loam matrix. A general view of this occupation horizon prior to excavation can be seen in Plate 18. Within phase 7 there is clearly a sequence of buildings, but unfortunately a full understanding of their relationship to one another has been lost as a result of the nature of the soils and ill-defined structural and occupational horizon, the continual process of robbing and rebuilding within the site's occupational history; the medieval furrows which separated the site into islands of survival; and the removal of the upper levels of the site by medieval and modern ploughing.

PHASE 6: The features and structures sealed below the main building phase in area 480.120-470.140.

Two of these features, (727) and (610) have already been described in Phase 3, since they have some stratigraphy which could associate them with the soil accumulation and the lack of 3rd-4th century finds.

On the northern edge of the site, cut through the earlier bank of enclosure (288) were the remnants of a possible gully (361) running east-west across the site. This gully had dimensions of roughly 1.0m wide and 0.3m deep and had a shallow 'U' profile. It was filled with a soil indistinguishable from those of the phase 3 accumulation. This gully was cut from a high level below a severely disturbed building (905), and also cut through the bank to the ditch (288). The other edge of this feature was not found, but the tipping of the infilling silts suggested that it was a gully.

A pit (644) was similarly cut at a very high level below building (906) in the north-east corner of the site. This pit contained 3rd-4th century pottery types together with residual first-century material, which is not surprising since it cut through the silts of ditch (288). The pit was roughly ovate and had dimensions of 2.7m × 1.5m, had a regular 'U' profile, and was 0.9m deep. At the base of the pit was a thick (3cm) lens of pinkish ball-clay, but otherwise contained grey loamy sand. In the centre of the pit was a mass of carefully laid heathstone blocks, the tops of which protruded from the pit. These varied in size from small infilling pieces up to 0.3m. No tool marks were apparent. The plan shape of this central setting was roughly ovate, 1.1m x 0.9m, and was set to a depth of about 0.5m with up to about 4 layers of stones, wedged together to a very close fit, it is possible that this was what remained of a foundation setting. A cylindrical marker stone of some importance (fig. 56, 256) was reused in the wall of building (906) above, and may have originally been associated with this stone packing.

To the north of and below building (707), and below yard (147), was an ill-defined and irregularly cut pit (388) centred on a compacted area of baked clay and heathstone blocks. This contained a large quantity of broken briquetage, and concentrations of ball clay lumps and lenses. Deposited at the base of this pit was a large semi-circular limestone slab (dimensions: 0.75m diam., 0.1m thick). This stone showed very little sign of having been used as a rotary grindstone and may have originally been a column or post-base, (see specialist report). The activities involved with the production of a depression of this type are not identifiable from the surviving evidence, but the preponderance of briquetage and clay in the material recovered might suggest an association with salt production. The rough dimensions of the pit were: 3.5m × 2.5m and up to 0.4m deep. It was cut through the fill of ditch (343), the soil accumulation, and the old soil, but was not cut into natural. Limestone (including roof tile) shale and marble were also present in the fill.

Two kilns or ovens were part excavated on the northern edge of

Plate 18. *The 3rd to 4th century AD occupation horizon in area 4812.5014 from the north (Phase 7). This also shows the strips of post-Roman agricultural disturbance (Phase 8).*

the site, (589) and (578), Plate 24. These were not half sectioned nor emptied but carefully preserved for a time when they could be more fully examined in relationship to their surrounding deposits.

Kiln/oven (578) had a bowl of horizontal heathstone blocks (up to 0.2m x 0.4m and 0.1m thick), generally dry bedded but sometimes with clay. This bowl was at least three courses high and up to 0.2m thick, and only a single stone thickness. It was approximately 1 metre diameter with a slightly cranked flue composed of pitched limestone and heathstone blocks, running west (see Fig. 36 and Plate 24). It probably has close similarities with kiln/oven (540), phase 7, and contained burnt clay lenses. The interior of this feature was not fully excavated.

Structure (589) is less easily defined, and comprises of a single stretch of limestone walling (3 courses) with pitched heathstone blocks to south and west. Burnt clay and briquetage packing occur in the northern side which is reminiscent of the material in the oven-bowl of (578). Its function as an oven cannot be confirmed.

Both these structures occur in an area where the 'old soil' had been cut away by a sharply cut depression with an angled south-east corner (fig. 36). The extent of this cut was not determined. The deposits within this depression butted the 'kiln' structures. This cut depression was therefore contemporary with the use of the 'kilns'. These deposits contained 3rd-4th century pottery. Across the top of this cut depression the pottery was trampled horizontally and one pot had been crushed base down into this level. It is perhaps valid to suggest that this was the yard-level contemporary with the kiln/ovens. There were also a number of instances where limestone tiles had been deliberately pitched vertically into this level. These were often broken and may have been used as post-wedges. On this site it was impossible to identify post-holes unless post-wedges were present or the post penetrated through into the natural bedrock. This was primarily a result of the uniform colour of the soils and its extreme friability.

All these features were sealed immediately below the collapse of a post-pad building which was not well-defined and probably only partially complete: Building (564).

PHASE 7: The main building phases in area 480.120-470.140.
None of the buildings in this phase were excavated in their entirety, most were badly disturbed and only survived in part, and all were cut and separated by the later medieval disturbance furrows, so that it was virtually impossible to relate properly the buildings to one another. The stratigraphy was also such that different phases of buildings could not be easily separated, and there were no clearly defined occupation horizons, most of which had been disturbed and shifted by medieval and modern ploughing.

However despite these problems it was possible to interpret these buildings as a cohesive group in which the occupation was continuous and intense and where the buildings were continually adapted, extended and rebuilt, presumably as a result of changing requirements or the impermanent nature of the construction. This group of buildings, arranged around a yard (147), probably functioned as a BB1 pottery-making settlement. The material associations and the occupational characteristics of these buildings are described in a later section.

The sequence and preservation of building (707) enabled an overall interpretation to be made of the constructional techniques used in this group of buildings. A series of constructional techniques could be recognised:

Stone post-pad construction for timber post-structures (possibly cruck?); Building (707) phases 1 and 2, Building (564).

Cut post-holes for wedged timber uprights; Building (707) phases 1-3.

Stone sill-walls (herringbone, and horizontally bedded) for timber box-frame construction; Building (707) phases 3 and 4, Building (904) and (906), Building (743), Building (906).

All these structures were of drystone and/or timber construction, no mortar was apparently used. The walls were either of 'cob' or 'wattle and daub' construction. Slumped clay across the floor and walls of (707) phases 1 and 2, was probably derived from cob construction. Wattle impressions in burnt-clay in the later phases of (707) suggests the use of a wattle and daub technique. It is likely that the roofs were thatched. None of the lozenge-shaped limestone and shale tiles occurring on the site had been hung (no holes cut), and their use on the site probably relates to their use for the construction of structures related to the activities on the site, 'clay-box' (162), and 'trough' (148) within building (707) and related 'flooring'; and wedges to posts. The shale tiles were probably imported as raw material for shale-turning. The use of roofing-tiles for alternative purposes suggests that this commodity was surplus to requirements elsewhere (off-site), and arrived as a by-product of trade.

Plate 19. Building (707) post-pad phase, partly exposed from the north.

BUILDING 707, AND ASSOCIATED PATHS AND YARDS (Phase 7): (Section: Fig. 33, plans: Fig. 36-38)

This was by far the best preserved building on the site, showing a clear sequence of rebuilding and adaptation, and some indication of internal arrangements and function. Only the northern part of the building was excavated, but on the assumption of a central doorway, this would have been the substantial portion (fig. 37). Resistivity survey across the southern end of the site showed no indication of a continuance of the sill-wall building. The upper levels of this building sometimes survived little more than 0.2m below the ground surface (fig. 33). Plough-shares had often scored the top of the heathstone blocks of the entrance pad-stones and the sill-walls.

The first building (fig. 37.1, and Plate 19) was planned as a long rectangle with bay divisions, and with rounded ends. If it is assumed that the doorway was central it would have been 5 bays in length. The external dimensions would have been about 12.6m x 4.6m, with a bay width of about 2m, widened to 3m in the 'apsed' ends (fig. 37.1 *et seq.*). This building was a post-structure with the posts set on padstones, placed within the accumulated soils; the upper surface of the padstone being on the old-ground surface (fig. 33) Each of these padtsones was socketed (or morticed) with the socket varying in size from 0.15-0.18m (length) x 0.10-0.15m (breadth) x 0.6-0.1m (deep), for the insertion of a squared tenon on the base of the upright. The stones themselves varied in size but had a bulk and dimensions roughly comparable to that of padstone (770) depicted in fig. 33.

That it was possible to identify a 'doorway' in this building was a result of a different setting for two of the posts, which were coincident with the double socketed padstone and the external porch stones of the later building (fig. 37). These two post settings were composed of vertically pitched limestone slabs and a base-pad to form a squared box for the insertion of a large squared timber perhaps 0.3m square. The square base slabs had dimensions of about 0.5m square; that at the base of the southern socket (816) was broken, but had a central hole bored through it (0.1m diameter). The northern setting is shown in Plate 20. The particular nature of these two post-settings is further accentuated by the complete vessel set adjacent to the northern post-setting below the level of the post pads, and below the clay walls (715) (Plate 20). This pot (fig. 44, 64) is presumably *in situ* and placed deliberately as a 'foundation' vessel. A similar pot (fig. 44, 62) is set in association with building (905), adjacent to a sill wall and on the northern section of the site (fig. 36).

It is difficult to suggest a reason for this change in system for the base fixing of posts. However one suggestion which may be near the truth can be made; on the basis of the following points:

(i)   The reason for a tenon socket in the padstone is to prevent horizontal movement, which means that the base of the timbers were *not* tied across the building *nor* along the line of the walls.

(ii) The sunk posts can be suggested as the entrance posts which can be taken as *vertical* for door fixing.

(iii) In contrast to the door posts (ii) those located on the slabs may have been prefabricated units (crucks?), or perhaps of a lesser height (following from (ii)), and slighter in dimension.

From this at least a heightened doorway with a gable facing west can be suggested, running into a slighter and lower structure. The curved ends to the building suggest a ring-beam tying the heads of studs with a light thatched roof-structure, although the possibility of crucks should not be ruled out. The lack of used (i.e. holed and pegged/nailed) roof tiles in the collapse of this and all buildings also confirms the use of thatch (probably reed) for the roofing material.

Only one internal division within the building was noted, and was represented by a single additional padstone. This division presumably separated different functional areas related to the remains of a dryer (825) (fig. 37 and 38), located opposite the entrance and central to the building. The division coincided with the neck of the flue to the dryer and was a division perpetuated throughout the life of the building (fig. 37, 1-4). To the north of the partition was an area of burning (783), which was presumably rake-out from the dryer.

Outside the entrance and running along the western edge of the building was a gully (829) cut through the build-up and lying across the depressed ground in front of the doorway. The gully was not easily defined within the accumulated soils but it is interesting to note that its line was perpetuated by the space between the external yards and the wall in later phases. It is possible that it may relate in some way to the construction and wall-structure, otherwise a gully across an entrance is inexplicable. Posts for an external porch were not apparent for the post-pad building until external yards had been built up (fig. 37.3), and where pitched limestone pieces identified post positions. These post-holes would have accommodated an upright about 0.2m diameter. The depth of the post could not be ascertained, the soils being indistinguishable. Outside the entrance to the building was a worn hollow. The ground level outside the hut always seems to have been slightly higher than the internal floor level (fig. 33).

Plate 20. Door post-socket and 'foundation' jar (Phase 7).

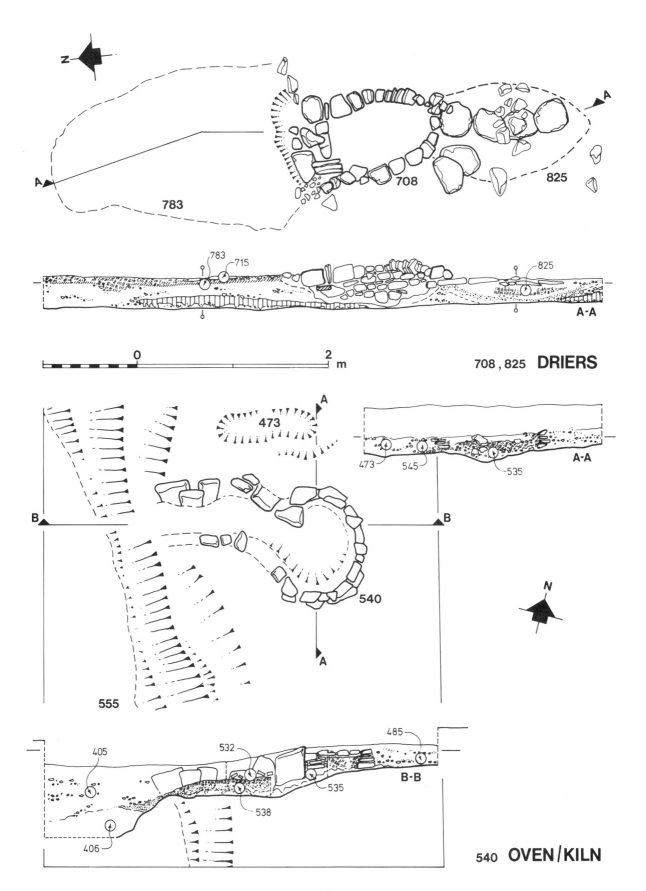

Figure 38. The Driers 825 and 708 in building 707 in area 4912, and oven/kiln 540 and ditch 555 in area 4213.

Plate 21. The sill-wall building (707 from the south (Phase 7).

Plate 22. Post building (909) cut into natural sands and stony gravels. The yard (441) can be seen surviving in the eastern end of the trench. Area 440.130.

The material of the walls between the posts is not certain but it is likely that it was of cob and not wattle and daub; from the quantity of clay (215) compacted between the padstones and across the floor and the lack of wattle impressions on the clay, or the presence of wattle impressed daub. If this building is considered to be used for the 'drying' of pottery prior to firing, some consideration should also be given to the possibility that the walls were semi-open and only constructed to be sufficient to protect the pots from weathering prior to large scale firing. The use of the building for smoking, curing and storage of fish should also not be ruled out although the presence of fishbones was minimal perhaps due to low pH of soil.

During the use of the building, external yards built up by about 0.15m at the entrance along the western side of the hut. These were often composed almost entirely of crushed briquetage and some oxidised BB1 pottery (713). Other levels were mainly composed of small – medium pebbles and gravels. The lowest yard was notably of heathstone fragments (construction debris?) (fig. 37.2). During the process of this yard accumulation a series of three steps (753) (composed of lines of limestone tiles), were inserted to accommodate the change in level. They were laid across the top of a layer of clay (715), which has been interpreted as the decomposed and dismantled walls of phase 2 (fig. 37). The removal of these walls coincided with a complete restructuring of the building, phases 3 and 4. This building (Plate 21) followed the basic lines of the previous post structure (Plate 19) apart from the curved ends. However the posts were certainly removed and a stone sill, to take a horizontal timber plate, inserted. The door-posts may have remained in use since the limestone tiles used to construct the steps respect their position, but lie beneath the new door post-pads that eventually replaced them, phase 4 (fig. 37.4). Through the upper yard two wedged porch posts were cut, possibly replacing earlier

Plate 23. Marker stone (fig. 27, 256) reused in foundation wall of building (906), above rectilinear enclosure ditch (288).

ones not identified (see previous). These were replaced by small socketed post-pads at the same time as the original door-posts were replaced by double-socketed and single-socketed post-pads (fig. 37.4). It was possible to replace the two large door-posts which were structured by smaller posts of a door frame because of the changed wall structure to a more rigid wall box frame (see above).

The internal division of the building also seems to have been perpetuated with the change of structure (fig. 37). The central dryer (825) survived as little more than an ovate dish-shaped cut which in proportion and infill resembled that of dryer (708). (708) can be inferred as a replacement to (825) in phase 3 of the building (fig. 37, plate 25). The structure of dryer (825) could not be defined but is likely to have had similar character of (708). A layer of burnt clay including crushed and oxidised pottery and briquetage (783) to the north of the dryers was sealed below a layer of trampled grey clay (715). (715) was interpreted as the disintegrated and spread wall material from the first building (fig. 38, section). The level (783) can perhaps be associated with the first dryer, and perhaps represent a spread 'rake-out' area.

The second dryer (708) (Plate 25 and 26) was well preserved, apart from the superstructure collapsed into the bowl and the upper wall levels which had probably been removed. This dryer was sausage-shaped with a slightly constricted flue. Three courses of horizontally laid heathstone blocks composed the bowl of the dryer with pitched heathstone for the upper course which had in part been removed on the eastern side. These walls were dry-bedded with some clay. The constricted flue was composed of a block and pitched slabs of limestone. The width of the flue was 0.3m, the bowl was 0.6m wide, 1.0m long and 0.4m deep. The bottom 0.2m of the bowl was filled with a finely sorted dark grey sandy loam with a large quantity of crushed charcoal (819). This lay below a layer containing broken briquetage fragments and burnt clay (818), probably derived from the lining and walling of the dryer. Above this was a layer of rubbish deposited when the hut was abandoned; this included a quern-stone fragment and large broken pieces of oxidised BB1 vessels (vessel types 2, 3, 28, 32, rolled rim jars with obtuse lattice decoration and countersunk handles, and flat rim and dropped flange bowls, pottery report). A large quantity of nails and bent iron binding in all infill layers of the dryer were probably derived from the dismantled or collapsed superstructure above the dryer (refer finds report). In the base of the dryer were three circular impressions in the sandy subsoil. These could be interpreted as possible stake-holes with dimensions of 5cm diameter and 0.2-0.6m in depth, and were filled with a finely sorted dark grey sandy loam with a large quantity of crushed charcoal. These may relate to the structure or use of the dryer.

Across the mouth of the dryer was a long 'tongue' shaped piece of briquetage/kiln furniture (finds report, fig. 51, 207, and plate 26). This may pehaps be a surviving piece of the dryer's floor. No rake-out for this dryer was present.

Apart from the dryer in the centre of the building there were a number of other elements cut into and laid across the floor. One of these was an area delineated by a 'box' of pitched limestone slabs (148). The slabs were pitched to enclose a rectangular area, about 1.0m x 1.1m, assuming that some upright tiles had been removed. Limestone tiles were laid across the inside. The pitched tiles cut through the collapsed clay level (149) derived from the walls of the previous building. To the east an area of burnt heathstone lumps (116) was noted on the floor level, and to the south-east of these what appears to be a deliberately laid area of lozenge-shaped roofing tiles. The floor of the sill-wall building (3 and 4) could be defined by these elements and the collapsed clay/cob walls of the post-pad structure. Accumulation of debris within the hut during occupation was not marked, it would appear that the hut was kept remarkably 'clean'. Briquetage debris was concentrated outside the hut in the accumulating yards; a lower level of debris was recorded within the hut.

The debris within the abandoned building included a quern stone and large pieces of pottery, including some nearly complete vessels. That this was the debris from a domestic area is clear but none of the huts examined in the surrounding area could have a domestic function attributed to them, apart from by implication. The lack of carbonised grain both in the dryer (708) and on the floor of this hut pointed to activities unrelated to an arable economy. It is possible that the querns recovered from the site were used for grinding imported grain or other materials. The repeated presence of marine shell-midden tips does however confirm the importance of Poole Harbour as a source of food, and that an economy and occupation is likely to have continued after the abandonment of this hut; *c.f.* the marine-mollusc midden (87), and antler bone points tipped into

Plate 24. Kiln (578) in area 480.140 (Phase 6), part excavated.

Plate 25. Section through driers (708) and (825), Phase 7.

Plate 26. Drier (708) from north, Phase 7.

and across the rubble collapse (fig. 36).

That the building was abandoned whilst occupation continued is also confirmed by a curving and square-cut gully (672), cutting through the yard accumulation to the west of building (707). This gully varied in width from 0.3m to 0.5m and was filled with a grey soil which could not be visibly distinguished from the accumulation levels below the yards into which it presumably cut. The base of the gully did not however cut the old soil (fig. 33). A number of large heathstone blocks and limestone pieces were pitched into this gully. It would seem likely that this was a post-trench or robbed footing for a fence line, defining a boundary division within the site, which may relate to the partially surviving remains of building (743) to the east. Its line continuing northwards was not distinguished as a result of the similar soils and later disturbance, but it can perhaps be seen to survive in the edging stones along the pathway or yard (175) which is associated with the remains of building (905) which was partly uncovered in the north-west corner of the site.

BUILDING (743) (Phase 7): Fig. 36 and plate 18

In the south-west corner of the site was a small fragment of dry-stone wall; a single course of squared heathstone blocks (656), the tops of which were little more than 0.2m below the present ground level. West and adjacent to the sill wall was a deposit of briquetage, and oxidised BB1 fragments. An oxidised and mis-shapen small flanged (BB1) bowl (fig. 48, 152) was found in association to the north. These elements were interpreted as belonging to building (743). The line of briquetage east of this wall and spreading as a north-south line can perhaps be best described as the surviving remnants of the yards to building (707), which were not affected by the linear medieval disturbance hollows (fig. 34, inset).

BUILDINGS (905), (564), AND YARD (147) (Phase 7): fig 36

In the north-west corner of the site were the ends of two sill walls, spreads of mixed and trampled clays, a line of yard or path, and a complete undecorated jar (fig. 44, 62) placed upright, behind, and adjacent to one of the sill walls. These were interpreted as parts of a building (905). This building was heavily disturbed by the medieval furrows and a pit (261) (fig. 36, inset) containing some larger pieces of masonry, including a quarter-segment of a semi-circular lime-stone block with centre hole (fig. 56, 257), and a limestone block with a fissured and worn hole in the centre (possibly used as a net or thatch weight). Perhaps this pit was cut so that larger pieces of building masonry could be removed below ground away from an arable furrow where they had presumably caught the plough. All these structural remains and the foundation vessel in combination are comparable with the more complete building (707) to the south-east.

To the east of building (905) were a number of other elements which again in combination suggest a building; designated (564). These elements (a large socketed heathstone post-pad, a large quantity of broken limestone tiles, burnt sandstone blocks) overlie a trampled area of pottery clay and medium gravels which have been interpreted as a yard (147). These elements probably represent the corner of a post and sill-wall building; collapsed or dismantled across a 'yard'.

This 'yard' (147) can be taken as being contemporary with the buildings surrounding it, although much of the material found in this trampled level relates to the first-century AD, which is mainly due to this area being directly over the earlier enclosure ditches. Some 3rd-4th century AD material was found within the upper fills (A) of the enclosure ditches which suggests that these earth-works were in part infilled when this yard-area and associated buildings were in operation. The 'yard' area was not metalled or surfaced as such. In the centre of the yard was a rectangular box (152) of squared and vertically pitched limestone tiles with a similar tile placed in its base (plate 16). This box was 0.35m square (internal), and was cut into the 'yard' to a depth of about 0.15m. The box was upstanding above the yard surface by 0.2m. At the base of the box was a deposit of clay, the chemical composition of which was analysed (refer specialist report). It was thought that this box was possibly a potter's clay store, with clay ready for use in making pottery vessels, this can be paralleled in the Oxfordshire Pottery production sites, Young (1977). However the clay in the base of the box did not conform to that of the finished BB1 vessels. Its function if it lies within a pottery making sequence is therefore obscure.

BUILDINGS (904) and (906) (Phase 7): Fig. 36

To the west of the yard was a sequence of a gravel pathway and two buildings (904) and (906). The pathway, the end of which lay below one of the walls of building (904), was very similar in composition to that associated with building (905), both paths were up to 1m wide with gravels up to 0.1m thick. A single course of horizontally bedded heathstone lay across the eastern end of this pathway, reminiscent of the other sill-walls previously described. This wall could be taken as the western wall of a rectangular building (904). This building was the latest in the sequence, the northern wall (of pitched herringbone construction, 3 courses) being laid above but aligned with a row of large reused heathstone slabs, which were interpreted as the sill wall of an adjacent building, (906), to the north. This was the only instance of herringbone construction used on site (other than in dryer 708), but as in all walls on this site no mortar was used. The eastern end of this building had been removed by a medieval furrow. The floor level of (904) was not well defined although some spreads of clay were noted. The large quantity of tumble within the building suggests that the sill walls were of at least 3 courses. These walls collapsed directly onto the floor surface, and no earlier infilling was recorded. Again unperforated limestone tiles were recorded on the floor surface, these could *not* be interpreted as the roofing material. A series of six coins (318-378 AD) were found in the floor levels and below the collapse of this building. The wall below the herringbone (plate 23) was composed of four extremely large monolithic heathstone pieces, with smaller infilling stones to square the sides. This was a single course. The western-most of these stones was a carefully chiselled, cylindrical marker stone (fig. 34 and fig. 56, 256). This probably weighed perhaps 50-100kg. It was obviously a stone of some importance and may at one time have stood nearby, perhaps with its base set into the stone pit (644). This wall was laid at right angles to one running down to it from the north to form a 'T' shape. A shallow gully ran to the west of the north-south wall. No floor levels which might have been expected to the east were found. Building (906) might therefore be better interpreted as a walled enclosure to which building (904) was abutted.

PHASE 5:
The buildings in area 440.130-460.130

These buildings to the west of the main complex were only partially identified and have not been depicted other than on the excavation site plan (fig. 32), and in plate 22.

Building (910) at 460.130 was only identified on the basis of a single heathstone wall and comparison should be made with more complex buildings excavated in area 480.120-740.140. This was two courses, including some fragments of broken marble. Little occupation material and no intact floor levels were found in association with this wall or within the trial trench running east; probably a result of post-Roman agricultural activities. It is probable that this was an outlier to the group of buildings to the east. Erosion of the land surface is very apparent in this area (contours, soil accumulation and pottery distribution, fig. 32A and B), and much had presumably moved downslope.

Building (909) was the only recognised post building identified in these excavations. This area was heavily eroded by modern ploughing and as a result the occupation levels associated with this building had been removed, apart from a 'cobbled yard' area (441) at the eastern end of the trench. A single north-south feature across building (909) was taken as a surviving medieval furrow. The original limits of this yard area are not known and parts of it may have been removed by ploughing, but the surviving portion is confined to an area with few posts, i.e. perhaps outside and to the east of the post-building (909). The post-holes vary in diameter from 0.2m to 0.5m, and in depth from 0.6m to 0.2m and where enough survived they were vertical sided with 'V' shaped bottoms, and all cut into 'natural'. Post-packing was present in all post-holes, although some post-holes were no longer 'complete', and erosion had removed packing material, which often protruded into the modern ploughsoil (plate 23). Pitched heathstone blocks were common in all post-holes, and limestone slabs or broken tiles in five. It is likely that this was reused building material. On the northern edge of the yard was a linear accumulation (0.6m wide) of small-medium heathstone blocks and medium flints (523) which may mark a boundary, and beyond this in the northern end of the

trench a shallow steep-sided and flat-bottomed gully (531) (0.4m wide and 0.2m deep). Two glass beads, which can be no earlier than 6th-7th century, were recovered from this area (see specialist report), one from the gully (531) and the other from disturbed material above the yard (441). To the west of this area two more parallel gullies (552) and (553) ran north-south across the machine trial trench at 443.135. The western gully (552) was ill-defined with irregular sides and bottom and survived only 0.1m into natural, and was 0.5m wide. To the east, gully (553) was more sharply cut with a 'V' profile, 0.6m wide, and cut 0.3m into natural. The dating of these is uncertain, but (553) did not closely resemble agricultural disturbance (medieval furrows) and may be a boundary gully with (531) to the building (909). The bulk of the finds recovered from this area of buildings was comparable with settlement material further to the east; BB1 pottery (3rd-4th century AD). The material included a quantity of briquetage with a number of vessel legs or 'kiln' bars.

PHASE 4:
Ditch (555) and Kiln (540) in area 42.13 (figs. 32 and 38)

To the west in area 42.13 the machine trial trench identified a boundary ditch (555) located in the geophysical survey, and one of the geophysical kiln anomalies (540). The upper levels of the ditch were excavated by hand, but the lower levels were below the water-table. The presence of Oxfordshire ware pottery in the upper fill suggested a late date for the infilling but it is possible that the cutting of the ditch could belong earlier in the first century AD. An earlier date is suggested in that the kiln/oven utilises the ditch for a rake-out area, and may be located in the area of a bank, i.e. it ignores the ditch as a boundary. The kiln is certainly of 3rd-4th century AD date, and would be contemporary with the other settlement features to the east. The upper filling of the excavated ditch sealed the flue and rake-out of the kiln/oven. The ditch was about 6m across with a possible recut on the eastern edge where the primary collapse of the ditch was thickest, indicating a possible bank to this side. The ditch was excavated to a depth of 1.2m below ground level. This material was well distributed pebble, and stone with pea grit lenses and silt lines. The derivation of these silts was uncertain, (see soil report).

Plate 27. Kiln (540) and ditch (555) (part excavated) from the north, Phase 4.

The oven/kiln (540), located on the eastern lip of boundary ditch (555), was very much eroded by modern ploughing (plate 27). The bowl of the kiln was 0.2m below ground surface and only 3 courses of a heathstone wall survived (fig. 38, section). Pieces of limestone were also occasionally used in the construction of the bowl. The stone was bedded horizontally with clay. The shape of the bowl was ovate with a cranked flue constructed of larger pieces of pitched heathstone which ran westwards into the open ditch (555). However it is likely that this ditch had already substantially filled since the 'rake-out' (538) runs across the top of the primary fill (406). The material in the ditch sealing the flue (405) contained Oxford ware. The bowl of the kiln was filled with baked clay, which can be taken as a collapsed lining, and fragments of partly burnt ball clay and heathstone fragments (535). The sand natural below the oven bowl had, as a result of heating oxidised to a reddish colouration. In the fire of the kiln was a concentration of charcoal and burnt clay, 'rake-out' (538), overlain by a trodden layer of ball-clay with large broken unabraded vessels (532) lying on and at the neck of the flue above this level. These vessels in (532) were reduced finished products with some oxidised surfaces and bodies and were not typical of waste debris from the kiln firing of pottery; although these may represent accidental breakage or perhaps rejects, no marked warping was noted. The vessel forms present were flanged and upright rim bowls with hoop decoration and overhanging rim jars (forms 4, 27, 29 and 32), pottery report), which suggests a 3rd-4th century AD date, and can be compared directly with material on the main settlement focus to the east. Outside the kiln there were areas of trampled gravels and grits (485), and the sand levels above natural were notably more loose and granular than elsewhere. This might be a result of kiln firing and 'yard' trample. Layers to the north of the kiln contained noticeable quantities of burnt clay, and pea grit and sandy lenses. One area had a concentration of compacted white clay, as well as briquetage/burnt clay (473). This may represent the dismantled roof and body of the kiln. No evidence for internal structure, floor support or raised oven flooring survived, and the lack of waste-debris made it difficult to attribute a function for this kiln/oven. Its association with a settlement which can be taken to be a pottery production site for BB1 suggests that this structure was a pottery kiln. However this is not proven. Also the small size and scale of the upstanding remains, and the insubstantial nature of the oven walls, would point to a small kiln load, and low productive capacity.

Its status as an 'experimental' pottery kiln, can perhaps be suggested within the context of a large scale industry, which was otherwise probably using a simple 'bonfire-kiln' technique, Farrar (1977).

The Post-Roman Agricultural Disturbance (Phase 8)

The abandonment of the Romano-British complex is ill defined, owing to the damage done to the site in the medieval period and by the onset of modern ploughing. It is possible that the earthworks of the Roman-British settlement survived into the modern period, but any that may have survived are now invisible, apart from where careful contour levelling could identify heightening of ground, e.g. building (707) (introduction). The survival of this one intact building, (707) outside the medieval disturbance was important in that its final phases of abandonment could to some extent be understood. However, the date of abandonment is elusive, since coin circulation probably ceased before the settlement's demise. The latest coin on the site was one of *Valens* (375-378 AD) deposited on the floor levels of building (904). The presence of two beads, dated to the 6th-7th century AD, in association with building (909) may suggest a very late occupation of the site. However the pottery types present on the site could not confirm this possibility.

The first disturbance of this abandoned settlement probaby occurred in the Medieval period when the area was taken in for the arable fields of Ower Quay. This medieval site was primarily concerned with salt extraction at Domesday, Darby (1979), and probably developed its own small arable fields during the succeeding centuries. Evidence for the medieval cultivation of this area can be found in the strip disturbance which was most notable across the central excavation area (fig. 30, inset; fig. 33, section Plates 18 and 28). These strips of disturbance were not well defined in width and depth, but were extremely consistent in direction. Late Iron Age and Romano-British pottery and other occupation materials were recovered from them. This was abraded and broken, and large pieces had sometimes been removed and deposited in deeper 'pits' cut down through the Romano-British levels (261). The soils infilling them were friable and uniform in colour (grey brown sandy loam). The most likely explanation of this type of disturbance is agricultural, the linear disturbances being the furrows of developed furlongs. The closeness of the three furrows on the western side of the site suggests that there was some rearrangement, probably as a result of the failure to remove

Plate 28. Post-Roman agricultural disturbance in area 480.130.

building (707) (fig. 34, inset). It is these furrows that have been defined as phase 8. The finds recovered from these furrows consisted of much disturbed Romano-British material, but the occurrence of two medieval buckles of the 15th-century AD suggest that the fields were in operation at this time. Clay pipe stems and glazed post-medieval pottery fragments were also present in the furrows, which suggest that the arable fields may have continued to be used and manured in the 18th-century AD.

Modern ploughing has continued to severely erode the site. Deep ploughing attempted in 1975 on the northern side of the peninsula disturbed a Romano-British burial in a stone burial cyst (fig. 63). As a result no further attempt was made to deep-plough. Surface ploughing has however continued to erode the soils from all areas of the site with considerable movement of soil downslope; e.g. from building (909). Further ploughing will result in erosion that will eventually see the total loss of 3rd-4th century AD occupational levels.

The Eastern Boundary Ditch (516), 580.130

A single trench (6m x 2m) was cut across a geophysical anomaly on the eastern boundary of the site at 580.130. This proved to be a substantial ditch 4m wide with shallowly sloping sides. It was cut in a low lying area, and it was only possible to excavate the top 0.2m of the ditch fill before touching the water table. The plough-soil above the ditch was only 0.2m thick and no stratigraphy survived on either side to suggest bank, or to identify associated structures, e.g. fence. The upper level of the ditch was filled with a sticky clay and large quantities of broken shale waste. Romano-British pottery (BB1) also occurred. No 1st-century AD material was recovered in the ditch nor in this area. The dating of the ditch is uncertain, apart from the shale dump which probably belongs to the 3rd-4th century AD complex. The date at which it found its way into the ditch is uncertain. It is possible that this is a medieval drainage boundary ditch cutting through waste deposits on the periphery of the Romano-British site (see fig. 32). Fuller excavation in this area with proper pumping facilities may perhaps give more certainty to the dating and function.

SITE INDUSTRIES AND OCCUPATION CHARACTERISTICS: AS DEFINED BY THE MATERIAL REMAINS AND STRUCTURES

The material finds which define the character of the occupation, and building functions, have been noted in the foregoing site description where their association with various buildings or structures has been particularly apposite to their function and dating. However a discussion of the site activities, building functions, and dating, as interpreted from the recovered finds and their structural associations will be given here.

The occurrence of few intact and well sealed occupation levels within the site's accumulated stratigraphy has been described in the previous section. The distribution of 1st-century fine wares and amphorae through all levels of the site (Table 1) showed that there was considerable disturbance of the earliest levels into the succeeding occupation horizons. Despite this problem of residuality some functional contrasts between 'contemporary' structures could be established in the 3rd-4th-century AD complex on the basis of the associated artefacts. It was also possible to contrast the activities and character of the two main occupation horizons; the 1st-century settlement enclosures, and the 3rd-4th-century building complex. The phased location of artefacts from the site have been substantially summarised in Tables 1-9. Additional description and discussion can be found within the individual finds reports.

It is evident from the pottery, and in particular the amphorae, that the 1st-century settlement had trading contacts with continental Europe prior to the Roman conquest. The consumption of wine, the use of imported fine wares and the scale and sophistication of the enclosure arrangements suggest that the economy of the settlement provided a surplus from which the occupants benefited, and that the settlement was permanent and established. The location of the settlement close to easily navigable waterways and access to the sea would have been a primary reason for its development into a successful trading emporium. However it is not entirely clear what the settlement was trading. Neither briquetage nor oxidised BB1 wasters occur in significant numbers in the excavated enclosure ditches.

In contrast the 3rd-4th-century AD settlement was open and ignored the previous ditched enclosures, which had been backfilled, and kilns frequently blocked the earlier trackways. Although the settlement buildings were systematically laid out, perhaps on a grid basis, the plan entirely broke with the development of the earlier rectilinear system of enclosures. The buildings were simple in

structure, were continuously modified, and reused stone from earlier phases for building material. The footings of one building incorporated an important markerstone, a copy of an Amorican stele type (1st century). This settlement would appear to be primarily concerned with the manufacture of BB1 pottery and salt, but was also concerned with manufacture of articles from other Purbeck materials such as marble, limestone, shale and mudstone. The lack of 2nd-century amphora and later types suggests that the pattern of trade in the 1st-century was disrupted, and that the site no longer commanded long-range wine or oil supplies. This disruption may suggest a decline in the wealth of the settlement. It is interesting to note that no villa development occurred on the site. If the site was used as a manufacturing base for an export industry then it is apparent that the profits from BB1 and salt production went elsewhere. The use of coinage on the site may perhaps be seen as a mechanism of trade rather than profits to enrich the life of the settlement. Comparison of this coin assemblage with that from other 'industrial' sites and villas in Purbeck has been taken to indicate trading at a later date, Woodward (1980). On the basis of foregoing evidence it is best concluded that this 3rd-4th-century industrial site is that of a small supply industry, run on a seasonal basis within an 'estate', with the workers and organisers living elsewhere for much of the year, but direct evidence for seasonal occupation is lacking. However the continuous adaptation of buildings, often on the same plan and alignment, e.g. (707), points to permanent occupation, but may also hint at some sort of short-term discontinuity, since the building quality and extent did not improve nor expand.

The developmental links between two such contrasting occupations is somewhat uncertain, but that both were located as a result of topography and local resources is undoubtedly the case. The 1st-century AD site can be seen as a coastal trading settlement using the sheltered and navigable estuaries of Poole Harbour, and taking advantage of its marine resources, minerals and mature woodland. The subsequent demise of the 1st-century trading settlement was perhaps due to Roman military incursions and reorganisation after the conquest. However at the end of the 1st-century AD activity continued with the introduction of new materials to the site; mudstone tesserae, limestone, ceramic tile (Phase 3). An increased quantity of briquetage was also recovered from the site in the soil accumulation levels. From field survey no substantial building was identified for this period, and so it follows that these materials were brought to the site for purposes other than building. The focus of activity from which this material derives was not located. The manufacture of chalk tesserae at Norden was also noted in the 1st century AD (Sunter, this volume). Perhaps the manufacture of tesserae represents the final activity of a now redundant trading settlement. The continued use of shale for producing armlets was also recorded, and the occurrence of a lathe shale core in the primary fill of the enclosure ditch (288) points very firmly to the introduction of a lathe at this date. The occurrence of only a few flint tools may indicate that the flint industry for the production of chisel tools (Calkin, 1953) was a post-conquest development, as were the developments in lathe fixing and the range of shale products (shale report).

At an archaeological level the distinction between a cottage or domestic producer of goods and a larger scale industry is sometimes not at all clear. At Ower from the finds alone and their associated structures in the areas excavated, nothing other than a small scale domestic occupation and indusry could be identified with certainty. However, taking evidence from survey and other sources it could be postulated that the site was a large scale producer of salt and pottery in the 3rd-4th-century AD. In the 1st-century AD salt extraction on a large scale was not indicated (very low quantities of briquetage), although the tipping of burnt soils and ash into the ditches together with marine molluscs was on such a large uniform scale that this was apparently the waste from a specific and universal activity.

The set of 3rd-4th-century AD buildings, and the associated kilns driers and clay-box, can be interpreted as a nucleus of a settlement concerned with the making of BB1 pottery on the basis of parallels with the type of structure found on other pottery-making sites (e.g. Oxfordshire, Young 1977), the fabric analysis (Williams 1977), and the kiln and oxidised pottery (wasters) evidence on the northern shore (Farrar 1977). However the lack of 'pottery-wasters' in association with the kilns, perhaps points to a more domestic function. The location of the two kilns, (589) and (578), close to buildings which were evidently thatched and of timber (although contemporenity cannot be proved), perhaps suggests their use as domestic ovens. The concentration of oxidised pottery and briquetage at the entrance to building (707), and to the north in feature (388), does confirm to some extent the association of this building with pottery-making and salt-extraction. The reduced BB1 pottery was probably used in the domestic arrangements of the settlement. The distributions of oxidised BB1, reduced BB1, and briquetage across the site as a whole suggests that the centre for pottery-firing and salt extraction was on the northern shore. This was also suggested by geophysical survey. It is probable that much of the BB1 production, certainly in the 1st-2nd century was produced in clamps or bonfires (Farrar 1977), and that the occurrence of kilns, e.g. kiln (540), may have been a late experimental introduction, as a result of influence from other pottery-production centres such as Oxfordshire and New Forest.

The circular limestone slabs with off-centre pivot holes, from (388), and the post-Roman robbing pit (261), may have been used a *tournettes*. Some quernstones may also have been used for the grinding of material for inclusion with the clay prepared for the construction of pots, apart from the normal use for domestic purposes. Although the clay-box has structural association with pottery-making, an analysis of the clay found in its base did not match the composition of the BB1 fabric. Its function therefore remains to some extent enigmatic. The function of building (707) was probably composite (see following) but its primary association with pottery-making and salt-production is likely. A drier was always a constant element in the centre of the building, and this would provide the heat for pottery drying, or the evaporation of water from brine. The lack of carbonised grain in the drier is interesting, and supports the argument that the site had no arable function. The occurrence of a quantity of iron nails and binding in the drier was probably part of a burnt wooden superstructure of 'racking'. Within the shed was also a pitched limestone structure and flooring (148), this can be paralleled on a pottery-making site (Wild, 1973) at Stibbington, in the Nene Valley, where stone-lined tanks were set on the inside face of the south wall of a workshop. The best preserved still contained about two cubic feet of clay, mixed with ground-up freshwater mussel. By implication an interpretation as a clay store was likely.

The occurrence of briquetage was primarily concentrated in the 3rd-4th-century horizons; 1st-century ditches (1%), 1st-2nd-century accumulation (8%), 3rd-4th-century AD horizons (50%). This perhaps indicates a change in the character of the settlement in terms of salt-production, or perhaps a change in location; c.f. northern shore. The concentration outside building (707) and its association with oxidised BB1 has been noted previously. It is probable that salt was an important product of the settlement, and was traded along with BB1 pottery. However it is likely that the pottery was not traded for itself, but for its contents. The marine and salt association suggests that the contents could have been cured and salted fish, or other marine delicacy, renowned perhaps for its concentrated food value, long life, or efficacious and medicinal qualities.

The tools and implements recovered from the site, included spindle whorls (bone, shale and pottery), loom weights (stone, lead), quernstones, reaping hooks and a scythe (iron), hone stones (heathstones), pestle (limestone), nails hinges and plates (iron), lathe chisels (flint); all these indicate domestic and perhaps 'cottage' industries. Only spindle whorls, a reaping hook and a few flint trimming tools were present in the 1st-century AD levels. None of these would be out of place on any Late Iron Age or Romano-British settlement. The range of imported materials to the site (limestone, mudstone, shale and marble), and also waste (slag/cinder, latheshale waste, flint lathe tools and waste) show that number of activities in addition to pottery-making and salt production occurred. These probably represent small scale domestic industry. Apart from the use of mudstone in the manufacture of tesserae, many of the items manufactured need not necessarily have been made on a commercial basis, but used by the occupants.

The occurrence of lathe shale waste and a flint-lathe-tool industry demonstrated the manufacture of turned-shale objects on site. Pieces of finished armlet occurred in all phases and statistical measurement suggests that this was the main product, and in the 1st-century-2nd-century AD the only product. In the 1st-century AD both lathe (see above) and hand chisel techniques were used. A change in the core fixing technique, and the cutting technique with flint-lathe-chisels in the 3rd-4th-century AD clear from the assemblage recovered from this occupation horizon. The occurrence of the base of a small beaker, part of a tray/table top (hand chiselled), and a bead indicated an increased range of products (fig. 58, 278, 279 and 277). One core was probably reused and turned for a spindle whorl or loom weight (fig. 58, 265). The presence of an unused lozenge-shaped shale roof-tile suggests that surplus tiles from another site were perhaps one source of the raw material. The scale of this industry was not large and is probably best described as a 'cottage' industry, and may have been purely domestic. There was no direct evidence for the turning of wood but this would not seem unlikely.

The reason for the import of limestone (also in the form of unused roof tiles), and marble to the site is not clear, but it was widely used in building construction (see above) and in the kilns/ovens. One squared bar of marble was considerably burnt. No limestone or marble were found in secure 1st-century contexts.

There is some evidence for smithing on the site, hearth buns were found in the upper levels of the enclosure ditch (288) and below yard (147), and the smelting of iron may have taken place somewhere on the site; slag runs were recovered from all levels. However no smelting furnaces were found. Fuel ash slag on the site may be derived from the burning of shale.

Iron objects were frequent in all levels of the site but were not well preserved, were of a general occupational type, and none could be associated with a particular industry. Nails occurred in all phases but hobnails were only recovered from the 3rd-4th-century AD levels. One broken iron reaping hook was recovered from 1st-century AD levels in ditch (858). The majority of ironwork came from 3rd-4th-century AD occupation phases, where most could be associated with timber construction; bolts, hinge plate, plank binding, tangs and nails. In addition a number of implements were recovered; a curved piece of ironwork which may be from tongs from yard (147), a scythe/sickle blade from the rubble collapse of (707), and two tangs of reaping hooks.

Personal possessions and clothing items were found on the site in all levels, fine vessel glass, bronze brooches, bronze spoon, bronze bracelets, shale bracelets, bronze rings, bone pins and glass beads. The two buckles recovered were medieval.

Fragments of fine blue vessel glass, including a handle were found residual in post-Roman agricultural levels, these were of 1st-century AD date on typological grounds. Light green vessel glass found in phases 4-7 (three pieces in building (707)), may be of the later 3rd-4th century AD.

The copper alloy brooches were well dated types and all were datable to the 1st-century AD. The 'Colchester' brooch, although residual in a later level, would have been derived from the pre-conquest horizon. Three iron spring brooches of 1st-century AD were recovered from ditch (288) and pit (644), and two copper alloy strip brooches from (288). All others were recovered from later contexts which again suggests that there were acute problems of disturbed stratigraphy. The copper alloy spoon was found on the floor level of building (904) in the 3rd-4th-century building complex. Bronze armlets appear to be the preferred personal ornament in the 3rd-4th-century AD levels. Copper alloy bracelets recovered from the upper levels of the site were of common forms. Shale bracelets would also have been common at this time. Two copper alloy rims, one of the 3rd-century AD and the other possibly Roman were found in the post-Roman agricultural disturbance. Two bone pins of later Roman date were recovered from the rubbish tip (87), infilling building (707).

Glass beads were recovered from late contexts, and two polychrome examples (one cylindrical and spirally decorated, the other part of a millefiori bead) were found in association with building (909), and can be no earlier than 6th-7th century AD in date. The other biconical beads found in late contexts are probably residual from 3rd-4th-century AD contexts, and two counters from the 1st-century AD; an opaque blue counter, was recovered from enclosure ditch (288).

Two metal buckles in the post-Roman agricultural disturbance were of medieval types (14th-15th-century AD).

The domestic arrangements in the period settlements cannot be fully defined from the excavated structure nor from the associated material finds. That divisions existed between domestic habitation, industrial and livestock areas is understood, see below. However no domestic structures were uncovered from the 1st-century AD levels. In the 3rd-4th-century occupation a nucleus of buildings survived, and were of timber, wattle and/or cob construction, on stone post-pad and/or sill/wall footings. The structures were continually adapted and reused. No building had a well laid floor, and the slight timber structures varied from post-hole or post-pad with ring-beam, to sill-beam and timber box-frame. The buildings were probably thatched and were not substantial. That one of the buildings, (707), was not domestic is certain, and that others by implication were also not domestic is also probable. The probability that most were workshops used periodically, and possibly seasonally by estate workers has been suggested and described. That some of these provided temporary accommodation is therefore the case. One building, (904), was not generally associated with briquetage nor oxidised BB1, and therefore industrial activity. In addition six coins were recovered from the internal floor levels; a higher level of coin loss than within (707). A spoon was also recovered from this building. A domestic function can be implied. Other structures were not sufficiently well preserved, or not fully excavated for functions to be suggested.

The exploitation of marine resources can be demonstrated in all levels of the site. Midden tips of marine molluscs are particularly notable in the 1st-century AD ditches, and contained primarily cockles, which would have been obtained from the nearby mudflats; winkles and mussels which would have been obtained from a rocky foreshore. A natural rocky shore would not have been found nearby, but a suitable environment may have been consolidated locally with heathstone, flint and gravels; otherwise these must have been obtained from further afield. Oysters were never a significant part of the occupants' diet but were numerically more frequent in the midden that infills the abandoned building (707) of the 3rd-4th-century occupation horizon. It is apparent that in the 1st-century ditches the marine-molluscs were shelled in their collected batches, since the shell waste occurred in definite bands prominent in a single species. Occasional eel bones were found in these 1st-century middens, but otherwise fish bones were absent. Localised less acid conditions in the shell-middens would have allowed the survival of fish bones had they been present. Elsewhere on the site only larger fish bones were recovered, and the general lack of fish bones from the site may be a result of the acid soil where small bones would not be preserved. However fish may have been collected at a different time (?seasonal) or place. The two lead weights in the phase 3 soil accumulation, and in the floor level of building (707) may have served as fishing (net) weights, although the well-formed circular cast should also be considered as a loom weight. A larger holed limestone lump recovered from the post-Roman agricultural disturbance (261) may be a fishing-net weight, but its use as a thatch weight would be just as likely. Although there is little direct evidence, it is conceivable that fish would have been exploited from nearby marine sources. It can be suggested that building (707) with its floor drier could have been used for smoke-curing fish, but perhaps its association with pottery or salt-extraction industries should be more seriously considered. However a composite function is quite possible.

The agricultural strategies of both the 1st-century and the 3rd-4th-century settlements are by no means certain. Systematic and extensive arable fields outside the settlements are unknown. That the landscape in the area had been progressively modified by man since the Mesolithic is well understood, from peat cores and pollen analysis (Haskins 1978). In the later Bronze Age the area around Ower was certainly the most wooded of what is now the lowland heath on the Eocene Sands and gravels of South-East Dorset; up to 75% trees (at Rempstone SY 983845) as compared to only 25%-40% trees in areas closer to the chalk (e.g. East Stoke, Dorset SY 864 866). Unfortunately the pollen diagrams at later datable horizons is less certain as a result of a 'rogue' carbon date. Analysis of the buried soil horizon (fig. 33) indicates that it was not a fully developed 'podsol', athough the development and characteristics of this soil is not fully understood (see soil report). This evidence suggests therefore that the soils on the site in the 1st century were not the sandy heath soils that are prevalent in the area today. Taken together with the pollen evidence, it can be suggested the full woodland clearance had not taken place by the 1st century in this area of Poole Harbour. Indeed this is probably the reason why a regional pottery industry was located in the area; a good quality fuel resource in association with good quality clays and temper, and navigable waterways for ease of transport. The farming strategy in such an area is likely to be very different from that of chalkland Wessex, and this may be indicated in the comparison of the faunal remains (see specialist report). At Ower there is an apparent concentration on pig-keeping in the 1st-century occupation phase, and this later declined in relation to the keeping of cattle and sheep. A tightly knit trading settlement, which was not primarily concerned with the arabilisation or extensive farming of the hinterland, would have had a preferred interest in the problems and resources of the salt-marsh, and access to the sea for transport and food resources. The keeping of pigs in this situation perhaps had distinct advantages (see specialist report for more detailed discussion). The settlement would have also had a vested interest in good woodland management; for the conservation of its fuel resources for the firing of its pottery kilns and for the salt-extraction

processes. However the lesser number of pigs on the settlement in the 3rd-4th-century AD may suggest that increasing areas of grazing had been developed for cattle and sheep. Indeed the proportion of pigs kept in the later settlement may have been very low, since there is a problem of residuality.

Although domestic and farming attributes can be suggested for both 3rd and 4th-century settlements, an alternative case associating them primarily with trade and industry has been made out. No doubt small scale 'farming' took place on any settlement; but at Ower it was probably not the *raison d'être* for its existence; mixed farming was not pursued on a large organised scale in either of the period settlements.

In conclusion; that the two main occupation horizons on this site are separate in time is clear; and also that they contrast in terms of their wealth and character. However no clear developmental links between them have been found in terms of the excavated finds, but these links may be found elsewhere on the site. The mechanisms by which the Romanised BB1 pottery industry developed from this 1st-century AD settlement are not obvious from the area excavated here, and the contrast in the character and relative wealth of the 1st-century AD settlement and the 3rd-4th-century AD pottery making focus are marked; especially if one takes the later settlement focus as one concerned with the large scale production of BB1 pottery and salt. The buildings of this later Roman settlement then take on the character of low status peasant accommodation, and it is clear that the wealth and profits were taken elsewhere. In these circumstances seasonal occupation by estate workers is the best interpretation.

The reason for the demise of the 1st-century AD trading settlement and its extensive enclosures is not certain but the Roman military occupation may have been one of the contributory factors for changes in trading patterns. The production of mudstone tesserae in the 1st-2nd-century AD is interesting, but may simply reflect the product of a season's casual work from a local outcrop. No building of any quality existed on the site. The eventual failure of Roman markets in the 4th-century AD clearly led to the end of pottery production on the site for export. However, the presence of two late beads in association with building (909), and late midden tips inside industrial buildings, e.g. (707), does suggest subsequent continuity. The extensive use of marine molluscs from Poole Harbour in the post-Roman period can be demonstrated; extensive middens up to 6 metres deep have been located at Hamworthy and Poole, and these have carbon dates ranging from 530 ± 70 AD to 980 ± 70 AD. (Ian Horsey, forthcoming, see also Carbon Dates below.) Poole Harbour continued to be the focus of continued activity on a large scale after the demise of Roman markets for pottery and other man-made products. However permanent occupation at the Ower site is not necessarily implied until the inception of arable activity across the site. Although salt-panning undoubtedly continued and was evident on a large scale in the Domesday Survey (Darby, 1979).

DISCUSSION

The evidence of Late Iron Age trade and contact between Northern France and Central Southern Britain has been discussed and described by Professor Cunliffe. He describes a Wessex Contact-Zone centred on Christchurch Harbour and Hengistbury Head, which can be considered as the port-of-trade, and that Poole Harbour provided subsidiary bases, Hamworthy and Green Island. From Poole Harbour the rivers Frome and Piddle would have provided trade access routes to West Dorset; salt from harbour fringes, and shale from the Isle of Purbeck would have been traded back to Hengistbury for wider distribution. These Poole Harbour trading links with Hengistbury and Northern France have been identified by the presence of Dressel 1a amphora and a range of coarse wares from Northern France at Hamworthy, Green Island and Hengistbury. This pottery was current in the period c. 129-c. 150 BC. He further suggests that the Caesarian conquest of Amorica in 56 BC disrupted and dispersed these established trading patterns, and that a certain level of overseas trade continued. The evidence for this can be found in the distribution of Pascual 1 (Late 1st-century BC and 1st-century AD) amphora found at both Hengistbury and Ower (Cleavel Point), Cunliffe 1983.

The intensity and duration of the later trade is uncertain, but at Ower (Cleavel Point) the association of the Pascual 1 amphora with other fine ware imports from Aquitaine (etc.), coarse wares from Northern France, and a cohesive series of settlement enclosures, point to an established 'trading' settlement, that had replaced those at Hamworthy and Green Island.

Cunliffe has pointed out that it is not unlikely that Amorican refugees may have reached Britain as a result of Caesar's Gallic conquest (Cunliffe, 1983). The presence of a sophisticated marker stone which resembles 1st-century Amorican Stele (albeit re-used in the footings of a 3rd-4th century AD building) reaffirms a close Amorican connection with the site. It is not inconceivable that the settlement at Ower was established by Amorican refugees, and that trade links were continued and perhaps expanded as a result of their entrepreneurial activity. However it is apparent that the older established settlements at Green Island and Hamworthy in Poole Harbour ceased to benefit from this continued link.

Williams has suggested that the presence in the Durotrigian area of late first century BC – early first century AD Roman Amphora (Pascual 1) at Ower (Cleavel Point) and Hengistbury Head, indicate that the Durotriges may not have been anti-Roman at this time, whatever the position may have been in the immediate pre-Conquest period (Williams, 1981). However although this may well be the case it is unlikely that the trade link with the Roman world was limited to and only continued through an Amorican intermediary. Political complicity with Rome is not necessarily implied.

The arrival of the Roman army and the establishment of port facilities at Hamworthy (Smith, 1930) and a legionary fortress at Lake Gates (Horsey, 1980) would have had a great impact on the socio-economic patterns of the inhabitants. That surviving trade links were again disrupted is evidenced by the differences in the fine wares from the two sites (Timby, following). The dislocation of activity at Ower can also be demonstrated from the structural evidence described here.

The subsequent development and expansion of the BB1 pottery industry perhaps should in some way be explained by mechanisms induced by a military presence in the region. It has been suggested that the lack of Roman villas in Purbeck south of the Purbeck Ridge may indicate that this area was an Imperial estate, (Sunter, pers comm.), although a single small Roman villa has been identified at Bucknowle. This suggests that the profits from mineral extraction went elsewhere, and it is known that mineral extraction was controlled by imperial management system (Liversidge, 1968, p. 203). It is possible that both the agriculture and the industry of the Isle of Purbeck were under state ownership and management. The two villas north of the ridge at East Creech (*RCHM*, 1970, 595-6) and Brenscombe (Farrar, 1963; Farrar, 1967A) may have had a closer relationship to the pottery industries, although Sunter also suggests that these may have been closely related to the stone industries at Norden and Povington (Sunter, this volume). The development of the pottery industry under Imperial or State management is perhaps possible, but the pottery itself should perhaps be regarded as little more than the containers for efficiency in shipment of other products.

Kevin Greene has discussed the various mechanisms by which the native potters in Britain may have responded to the conditions prevalent after the conquest. He points out that although the new and wider range of products were sold in large quantities to the army, they were never exclusively made for military use. The export of BB1 to the military frontier areas in the north of England can only have been a small proportion of the output. The greater bulk of the output would have found its way into the new civilian towns and the countryside near to the kiln sites. The military market was only a minor part of the 'romanised' demand for new forms alongside traditional vessels, and it is probable

that the pottery was only an incidental part of a much wider trade in ordnance via sea routes and the Irish Sea (Greene, 1979).

What other materials were being traded north from Dorset and the Southwest is not known, but that the coastal position and the sheltered waters of Poole Harbour were one of the principal reasons for the trade of BB1 northwards is clear. Greene suggests that grain and textiles may have been supplied to the army by a *negotiator* (Greene, *op. cit.*). Is it possible that the Amorican traders already operating in the harbour at the conquest would have been best placed to sign a contract and implement the transhipment of the agreed supplies?

Such suggestions are perhaps beyond the scope of the present evidence. However further excavations on Poole Harbour sites would also answer peripheral questions, of contact, status, and development which through inter-site comparisons would in turn give a more certain data base from which it would be possible to express archaeology at a historic-interpretative level. The excavations at Ower are little more than a small sampling exercise, and the interpretation and conclusions presented here are little more than surmise.

Certain answers to the questions relating to status function and settlement environment can only be obtained by large area excavation, which is beyond the brief of opportunist Rescue Archaeology.

THE FINDS

The finds from the site are described under the series of material headings and analyses, following. An exhaustive list of exact stratigraphic locations has not been published here. These can be found in the Level III archive. The finds have however always been given a phase, and sometimes a feature location, where this is particularly apposite, e.g. in the dating of occupation/phase horizons.

No overall correlation table has been published for the finds by phase or feature. These can be found summarised in Tables 1-9 and fig. 59. The detailed analysis of the horizontal distribution of material was not attempted for most material types, and where it was the results were not definitive because of the small areas excavated and the partial survival of the occupation horizons (refer to site report). Where distribution/location of finds was thought important, e.g. in building associations, the interpretation has been published with reference to the Level III archive.

All specialist reports have been stored in the Level III archive; some of these have been published in full, and in some cases only a summary of the main conclusions. This has been noted in the text where necessary. Unless otherwise indicated, reports are by P. J. W.

All finds have been deposited in Poole Museum, together with the original site record and Level III Archive. A microfiche copy of this record has been copied for the Wessex Archaeological Committee and the Department of the Environment, and a copy maintained in the National Monuments Record. The thin sections of the pottery have been retained in the reference collections by the Department of Archaeology, Southampton University.

THE SAMIAN

HEDLEY PENGELLY

This small group contains elements of marked importance and interest. First and foremost, both from the aspect of pre-Conquest trade with the Continent, and geographical distribution within Britain, it includes a small quantity of Arretine forms and wares (fig. 39, 1-8, together with a few pieces not illustrated). This signal addition to the Arretine distribution map, marks out the Ower Peninsular as just about the most south by south-westerly location in the Province to which such material can as yet be assigned, with the neighbouring Iron Age site at Gussage All Saints, near Cranborne, coming a close second. (Wainwright, 1979, 88).

This Arretine material from Ower has yet to be firmly placed. However, the results of David William's thin section analysis of a sample batch of sherds from seven different vessels (Section see following) indicates an interesting Italian/provincial mix, including a plate or dish, possibly from Puteoli, and assorted vessels from at least one Gaulish source, possibly Lyon (fig. 39, 3-8). None of these finds is large, though most are remarkably well preserved and there are quite excellent pieces such as, the 'Service' I plate form,

Loeschcke 1 (fig. 10, 4) and the 'Service' II cup form, Loeschcke 8 (fig. 39, 7): both vessels are conceivably of late Augustan to Tiberian date. The majority of pieces, including material stratified in phases 1 and 2 (fig. 39, 1-3) seem more firmly Tiberian, and on general grounds of content and appearance, one suspects that these Arretine wares were most likely starting to arrive from around AD 15-20.

The remarkable vessel found in Arretine-bearing phase 1 ditch contexts (fig. 39, 9 and Table 1) further confirms the belief of a very early date for trade with the Auvergne, perhaps via the Allier and Loire. Obviously, this vessel is of high intrinsic interest not least because it may reasonably be seen as a product of the early (Tiberian) days of transitional and developmental changes in indigenous samian manufacture from which emerged the true Gaulish samian tradition with its now familiar standardized forms.

The South Gaulish samian appears to be an entirely standard range from La Graufesenque and dates from the Tiberio-Claudian period to the Flavian-Trajanic inclusive. The quantities of pre-Flavian vessels (including fig. 40, 10 and 12), and those of later date (e.g. fig. 40, 11, 16, 19 and 22) are about the same. As with the Arretine wares, the majority of the earlier South Gaulish material

is, also unfortunately, residual in nature, though its very presence is pleasing enough.

In the early second-century, there is a little Central Gaulish samian including two or three pieces in Les Martres-de-Veyre/Lezoux overlap fabrics (e.g. fig. 40, 17).

From about the middle of Hadrian's reign, Lezoux becomes the main source of supply, as usually in Britain, with a preponderance of firmly Antonine pieces, tending towards the middle and later parts of the range and including three stylistically assignable decorated bowls of that date (fig. 40, 14, 15 and 21). Two bowls (fig. 40, 18 and 20) are somewhat earlier.

Of probable East Gaulish origin and late second- or early third-century date, is the enclosed vessel with 'cut-glass' facets (fig. 40, 13) from phase 7. This vessel provides a welcome addition to our record of the more unusual of the later provincial samian types.

There were no potters' stamps present from the area of the 1978 excavations. However, a stamp giving F·PRIM on form 27g was recovered from the burial excavated in 1975 (fig. 31A, J. fig. 63). This stamp, now lost, is by Primus of La Graufesenque (judging by its form) and presumably pre- or early-Flavian.

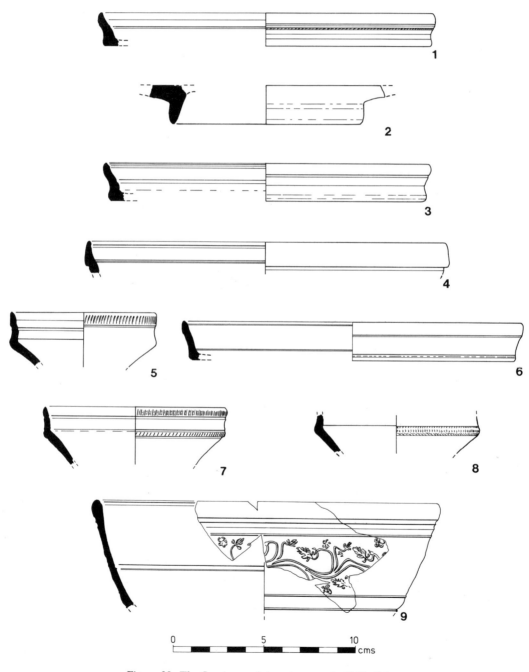

Figure 39. The Samian and Arretine vessels (1-9), 1:2.

Of the 113 sherds of samian recovered from the site a minimum total of 64 different vessels could be identified by form. The totals of each recognizable vessel form, according to source of supply, may be summarized as follows:

1. **Arretine Wares:**
   a. *? Puteoli*: plates or dishes (1)
   b. *?Lyon*: Loeschcke 1 (1), Loeschcke 2 (2), Loeschcke 8 (2), Ritterling 5 var (1)
   c. *?Source*: Dragendorff 17 (1), Loeschcke 2 (1), plates or dishes (1)
   Total vessels: 10
   The following sherds are described in the catalogue: A51, A52, A53, A89, A31, A1, A27, A84, A36, A37 and A78
2. **Early Lezoux Ware:** moulded vessels (1)
   The following sherds are described in the catalogue: A54, A32, A44 and A49
3. **Pre-Flavian South Gaulish Ware:** Drag 29 (3), Drag 15/17 (1), Drag 18 (1), Drag 18R (1), Drag 15/17R or 18R (2), Ritterling 9 (1)
   Total vessels: 9
   The following sherds are described in the catalogue: A2, A86, A55, A88, A92, A40, A46, A97 and A80
4. **Flavian and Later South Gaulish Ware:** Drag 29 (2), Drag 30 (1), Drag 37 (1), Drag 15/17 or 18 (3), Drag 18 (2), Drag 18/31 (1)
   Total vessels: 10
   The following sherds are described in the catalogue: A38, A57, A3 and A96
5. **Second-Century Central Gaulish Wares:**
   a. *Les Martres-de-Veyre*: Drag 18/31 (1)
   b. *Les Martres-de-Veyre or Lezoux:* Drag 37 (1), Drag 27 (2)
   c. *Lezoux:* Drag 37 (8), Drag 30 (2), Drag 30 or 37 (1), Drag 31 (1), Drag 33 (3), Drag 27 (2), Drag 18/31 (2), Drag 18/31 (1), Drag 36 (1), Walters 79R etc. (1). Curle 21 (1), enclosed jars or flagons (1)
   d. *?Lezoux:* Drag 36 (1)
   Total vessels: 34
   The following sherds are described in the catalogue: A11, A58, A19, A72, A6 and A17
6. **East Gaulish Ware:** enclosed vessels (1)
   Sherd A77 is described in the catalogue

The distribution of this material within the site phasing has been summarized in Table 1. Whilst a detailed description of each sherd of samian can be found in the Level III archive, this report confines itself to a detailed description of the pre-Flavian material and three much later vessels of particular intrinsic interest (fig. 40, 13, 14 and 15), together with a brief depiction of all remaining (drawable) decorated ware.

The archive reference of each published sherd is denoted by number with prefix A. The phase and the layer in brackets follows the description. Nine sherds from eight vessels were thin sectioned by David Williams (Southampton University); A53, A89, A31, A1, A27, A84, A54 (Fig. 10, 3-9) and A36 (not illustrated). These results are summarized under 'Petrological Analysis of the Pottery and Clays'.

The site references used in this text are as follows:

Bolsena	Goudineau, 1968
Camulodunum	Hawkes and Hull, 1947
Fishbourne	Cunliffe, 1971
Haltern	Loeschcke, 1909
Magdalensberg	Schindler and Scheffenegger, 1977

Acknowledgements: I am indebted to Dr Grace Simpson for some initial discussion on the Arretine pottery and, through the kind offices of Mrs A. C. Brown, in arranging access to the Arretine collections in the Ashmolean Museum, Oxford, for comparison study. Thanks are due to Mr G. B. Dannell for kindly arranging for the thin section analysis (Appendix I) to be carried out, and to Mr D. C. Mynard for access to a binocular microscope.

1. **The Arretine Wares** (fig. 39)
   1 (A51) Form Loeschcke 2; Arretine or provincial Arretine. Slip, very smooth; scorched. Fabric, pale; scorched. The dishes of *Camulodunum*, fig. 42, 12 [s4B] and *Fishbourne*, fig. 121, 23 are similar, though a little deeper and without the 'token' band of notched rouletting round the base of the rim. On the Continent, similar profiles are particularly plentiful at the Magdalensberg, Southern Austria, where the basic form is commonest in Complex 4 and 5 (*c.* AD 0-20/25).

Magdalensberg, Taf. 165 gives the general idea. Date Tiberian. From phase 1 (288A). (268).

2 (A52) Fragment of a dish or plate; Arretine or provincial Arretine. Slip, well-fired, bright red, good glossy finish, slightly 'silky' to the eye. Fabric, pale, slightly pink. Profile of footring somewhat rounded like an example from Bolsena, to the south of Arezzo, (*Bolsena,* 241, (C-2A-5). Date Tiberian. From phase 1 (288B) (306). Possibly same as A53.

3 (A53) Form Loeschcke 2; Arretine or provincial Arretine; very slightly burnt. Slip, pale and 'silky' like A52. Fabric, pale. Profile basically similar to *Magdalensberg*, Taf. 37, 7. Date Tiberian. From phase 2 (343IIC). (335). One other piece residual in phase 8 (261).

4 (A89) Form Loeschcke 1; Arretine or provincial Arretine. Slip, red, mirror bright; extremely smooth, but flaky. Fabric, pale buff to light 'dirty' yellow. For the profile, cf. *Camulodunum*. Fig. 42, 8 [s2A]. Date probably Tiberian; possibly late-Augustan to Tiberian. From phase 3. (792).

5 (A31) Form Ritterling 5 var., probably provincial Arretine. Slip, thin and washy, very variable through dull red-brown to orange-brown tones. Fabric, pale pink, with plentiful mica – clearly visible as such to the naked eye. The upper rim moulding only is rouletted (cf. *Camulodunum*, Fig. 43, 5 [s11B], though externally it is not flattened like this one). Such profiles appear not very common: one from Bolsena is similar (*Bolsena*, 171, 60) and Martin, 1974, Fig. 9, 2, shows a close match from the Tiberian kilns at Montans. Date Tiberian. From phase 7 (905). (162).

6 (A1) Form Loeschcke 2; Arretine or provincial Arretine. Slip, red-brown, slightly 'silky' to the eye. Fabric, pale. Profile similar to *Magdalensberg*, Taf. 35, 12 – Complex 5 (*c.* AD 20-25). Date Tiberian. From phase 8. (76), and (696).

7 (A27) Form Loeschcke 8; Arretine or provincial Arretine. Slip, thin, light orange-brown; somewhat pitted and worn. Fabric, pale orange-pink, fine; very light weight. Profile similar to *Camulodunum*, Fig. 43, 3 [s12]. Common Arretine type at Haltern (*Haltern*, 147), and now at the Magdalensberg, first appearing in Complex 3 (*c.* 10-0 BC), commonest in Complex 4 and 5 (*c.* AD 0-20/25), rapidly dying out through Complex 6 and 7 (*c.* AD 25 to close of occupation, *c.* AD 45). Date probably Tiberian; possibly late Augustan to Tiberian. From phase 8. (133).

8 (A84) Form Loeschcke 8; Arretine or provincial Arretine. Slip, palish brown, matt to slightly lustrous; interior smoother than exterior, though thin and washy, with orange-red streaks at the junction of the rim and wall. Fabric, pale salmony-pink. Date Tiberian. From phase 8. (730) and (751).

Not illustrated (A36) Fragment from the base of a dish or plate; ? true Arretine. Slip, thick dark red-brown, smooth. Fabric, pale, somewhat coarse; very slightly burnt. One rivet hole. Date ? Tiberian. From phase 7. (178).

Not illustrated (A37) Tiny fragment, burnt; Arretine or provincial Arretine. Slip, very smooth. Fabric, somewhat coarse; thin. Date ? Tiberian. From phase 7. (180).

Not illustrated (A78) Form Dragendorff 17; Arretine or provincial Arretine. Slip, orange tinted light brown, very smooth and glossy. Fabric, light orange-brown and a little coarse, with some calcareous matter, occasional black and red specks, quartz grains and flecks of mica. Date Tiberian. From phase 8. (681).

2. **The Early Lezoux Ware:**
   9 (A54), (A32), (A44), (A49) Three adjoining pieces and two others from the same moulded vessel; variably burnt. This signally important find embodies characteristics of both the crater series, form Drag. 11, and the carinated bowl, form Drag. 29. The upper rim moulding is basically like form 11, types B and C, and form 29, but lacks the small lip or chamfer generally found in these types. The corresponding interior grooving recalls the well-known early Lezoux 29 at Silchester stamped, after moulding, by Vitlus (see now Boon, 1967, 32ff) and some work of slightly date, by the Atepomarus school (Oswald, 1937, fig. 13). This vessel exemplifies well the infinite variety of unusual early Lezoux rim treatment, broadly resembling such 29 rims as Vertet, 1963, 111, fig. 5 and Vertet, 1968, 33, pl. IV, 1, but inclining markedly outwards – in much the same way as an Arretine *crater* in the Louvre (Oswald and Pryce, 1920, pl. XXVI, 2), but more simplified. The flatness of the exterior wall is like form 29, but the way in which the clay has been drawn up and thickened to form the rim makes for an

overall appearance that is slightly unusual. The exterior wall moulding, between raised lines instead of bead-rows, occurs early at Lezoux and its use there on forms 11 and 29 alike is well-illustrated in the large collections of early Lezoux sigillata at Roanne (cf. Vertet, 1962, 364, Fig. 14; 361, Fig. 11); the interior wall grooving recalls *ibid.*, 370, Fig. 23. The slip on this vessel is vermilion, and has an unusual, burnished-like quality, very smooth to the touch, with scant pitting and scaling and little sign of rubbing. The fabric is brownish-buff; coarse, with plentiful mica; fresh fracture shows occasional quartz-like inclusions (one or more of *c.* 1.05mm dia.) and some dark ferruginous matter. The surviving decoration comprises separate, detached stalks or tendrils, poorly scribed in the mould. The stalks diverge and end in small leaves and trifid buds. The upper margin carries poor impressions of a five-petalled rosette in imitation of the use of 'free' rosettes and flowers on Italian sigillata. This rosette, probably from a partially blocked die, is closely matched, in outline, on a form 29 at Lezoux (cf. Martin, 1942, 201, fig. 37) and is clear-cut on a mould for a skyphos there (Vertet, 1967, 277, fig. 17). The intricate leaf has not been paralleled, but cf. *ibid.*, 265, fig. 3, 29 and 30 and *Gallia* XIX (1961), 62, fig. 21. The bud recalls Martin, *op. cit.*, 202, figs. 52, 57, etc. and Curle, 1917, 150, fig. 17, 1. This ensemble is most unusual, and the closest parallel located in the more easily accessible published literature is the 29 mould of *Gallia* XXIX (1971), 332, fig. 21, but that is a running scroll of acanthus-derivatives, with added vegetation, and the stalks are firmly attatched. This vessel is possibly either a transitional variety between the *crater* and the carinated bowl, or a hybrid, and the likelihood of a pedestal base is high.

Two pieces from phase 1 (288), 171, and 236; three pieces, two adjoining, from phase 3 (203) and (390).

3.   The Pre-Flavian South Gaulish Ware:

10 (A2)   Drag 29 with brilliant slip. Fine scroll in lower zone. Date Claudio-Neronian. From phase 8. (76).

12 (A86)   Drag 29. Upper zone: traces of a very fine winding scroll, probably. Lower zone: a winding scroll with tendril-bindings composed of a bifid leaf and flattish beads; in the upper cavity, a thin stalk, with rudimentary multi-lobed head or small cluster of grapes (blurred), between two identical seven-lobed palm leaves; in the lower cavity, a triple plant with 'twist' tendrils. The palm leaves are reasonably close to a bowl ascribed to the work of Aquitanus (cf. *Fishbourne*, fig. 126, 4), and to the bowls of Knorr, 1952, Taf. 38D and 65D-G. The plant is like Hermet, 1934, pl. 35, 7, whilst a similar motif, together with the stalk, is shown for Aquitanus at Kempten (Knorr, 1919, Taf. 9K). A Nijmegen bowl stamped, after moulding, by Aquitanus has both the stalk and a similar scroll-binding (cf. *ibid.*, Taf. 8A). Other resemblances are: *Camulodunum*, pl. XXV, 22, and pl. XXXII, 12 which, for what it is worth, is possibly from the same mould as an Old Winteringham bowl (Stead, 1976, Fig. 49, 13). Date *c.* AD 45-60. From phase 3. (748).

Not illustrated (A55) Drag 15/17. Slip, matt brown-red, very smooth 'soapy'. Fabric, pale, fine. Date Claudian. From phase 3. (424).

Not illustrated (A88)   Drag 15/17R or 18R base. Slip, extremely smooth, though rather matt, brown-red. Fabric, slightly purplish brown-pink, very fine. Date Claudian or early Neronian. From phase 3. (791).

Not illustrated (A92)   Drag 29. Fragment, slightly burnt, from below the decoration. Slip, partially crackled. Date probably not later than mid first-century. From phase 3. (817).

Not illustrated (A40)   Ritterling 9. Slightly burnt. Slip, matt, very smooth slightly 'soapy'. Fabric, pale, with plentiful filler. Date probably late Tiberian or Claudian. From phase 8. (198). One other piece (adjoins) from phase 2 (343).

Not illustrated (A46)   Fragment, burnt, from a cup with low-slung curving base, very thin (*c.* 1mm towards the centre), and low footring. The angle of the wall suggests form Ritterling 9, and it is quite possibly the same cup as A40. From phase 8. (228).

Not illustrated (A97)   Drag 18. Two joining pieces; very slightly burnt. Slip, smooth, though patchy. Fabric, pale pink with slightly orange-brown hue, very fine. Light exterior wall rilling. Date Neronian. From phase 8. (849).

Not illustrated (A80)   Drag 18R. Two fragments. Slip, smooth brown-red, bright. Fabric, red-pink, fine. Date Neronian. From phase 8. (696).

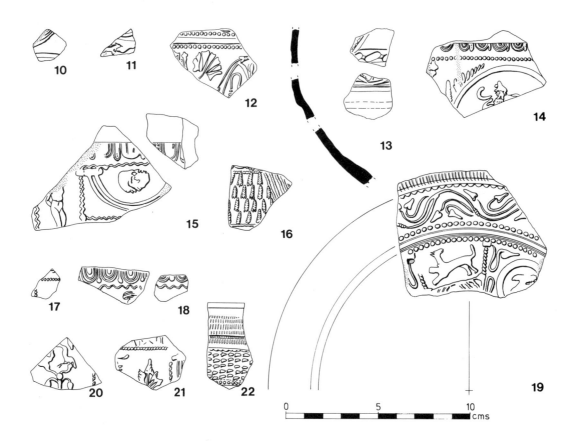

Figure 40. The Samian and Arretine vessels (10-22), 1:2.

4. The Flavian and Later South Gaulish Decorated Ware:

11 (A38) Drag 37. The illustrated sherd is from the bottom of the decoration and shows part of a poorly-impressed dog with collar (Hermet, 1934, pl. 26, 18 or the like). Date *c.* AD 85-105. From phase 3 (191). In addition two other pieces, base and footring, from phases 3 (195) and 8 (228).

16 (A57) Drag 30. Part of a panel with leaf-tips and diagonal wavy-lines below a trident-tongued ovolo. Date Flavian. From phase 5 (441).

19 (A3) Drag 29. The design is like that on a bowl of C. Valarius Albanus (cf. Knorr, 1919, Taf. 87D). There are also links with potters such as Censor, Crispus, and Vitalis. Date *c.* AD 65-85. From phase 8. (76)

22 (A96) Drag 29. One fragment of a small bowl with poorly-moulded leaf-tips. The workmanship is poor throughout. Date: Flavian. From phase 8. (849)

5. The Second-Century Central Gaulish Decorated Wares:

14 (A11) Drag 37. This piece belongs to a large, well attested class of decorated wares involving mid-to late Antonine potters such as Severus iv, Caletus, Servus ii and Iullinus ii. Its main interest lies in the ovolo, partially destroyed by the bowl-finisher when he formed the rim. This ovolo is the one on a bowl at York with mould-signature of Severus iv (cf. Stanfield and Simpson 1958, pl. 128, 1 and fig. 37, 1). There, the ovolo is described and illustrated as having a single border, but examination of a rubbing, kindly made available by Dr Grace Simpson, shows that it in fact has two and, Stanfield and Simpson 1958 and Roger's inventory (Rogers B183) should be re-interpreted accordingly. For the Pan (Déchelette 1904 412, Oswald 1936-, 710) and 'twist' on bowls by Severus iv, cf Stanfield and Simpson 1958, pl. 128, 6. The partially-impressed leaf (Rogers H93?) is known on at least two unpublished sherds with the large bead-row shown here. The Chichester bowl (Down, 1978, fig. 10, 12, 48) presumably belongs to the same area. Date *c.* AD 160-195. From phase 8. (80)

15 (A58) Drag 30. The ovolo (Rogers B153) was used by a number of mid- to late Antonine potters including, Servus II. Neither the Bacchus (Oswald 1936-7, 577 Déchelette 1904, 326) nor the mask (Déchelette 1904, 694, 0. 1341) seem to be known on signed bowls of Servus, but the general arrangement suggests him. For a broadly similar piece by Servus (or close associate) with the same ovolo and different figure-types, cf. Sauvaget, 1970, pl. I, 4. For Servus's (rare) use of form 30, cf. Vauthey, *et al.*, 1967, pl. XV. Date *c.* AD 160-195. From phase 8. (495), and (80).

17 (A19) Drag 37. Small fragment of a bowl by one of the early potters working at Les Martres-de-Veyre and Lezoux under Trajan and Hadrian. From phase 7 (187). (102).

18 (A72) Drag 37. The ovolo (Rogers B107), wavy-line and acanthus (Rogers K16) were used by Sissus ii of Lezoux. Date *c.* AD 135-160. From phase 7 (Lower yard 707) (3)). (663).

20 (A6) Drag 37. The ornament (Rogers Q6) and diagonal bead-row were used jointly by potters such as Laxtucissa and the Ianuaris ii – Paternus i association. Date Mid second-century AD. From phase 8. (76), and (222).

21 (A17) Drag 37. Fragment in the manner of the Lezoux potter Iullinus ii (or associate), with leaf (Rogers H70). Cf. Stanfield and Simpson 1958, pl. 126, 18 which also gives the festoon in the adjacent panel and the diagonal bead-row. Date *c.* AD 165-200. From phase 8. (97).

6. The East Gaulish Decorated Ware:

13 (A77) Four fragments of an enclosed vessel with 'cut glass' facets; slightly burnt. This appears to be a large globular jar, though the precise form is uncertain. The coarse fabric and somewhat 'soapy' slip suggest East Gaulish origin. Date probably late second- or early third-century AD. From phase 7 (collapse 707). (135), (661), and (669).

FIRST CENTURY IMPORTS AND NATIVE FINE WARES

JANE TIMBY BA (Southampton University), with a contribution on the Imported Coarse Wares by D. F. Williams (D.o.E. Ceramic Petrology Project, Southampton University)

In addition to the samian (above; H. Pengelly), amphorae (following; D. Williams) and mortaria, a quantity of other first-century imported wares were recovered from the excavations at Ower. The majority of these were finewares (460 sherds); together with some coarsewares (8 sherds). Native finewares of this period were also identified (17 sherds), and have been described with this group of imports, which provides an important contribution to our knowledge of early Roman pottery in Britain.

Of this material (485 sherds), only 40%, could be ascribed to recognisable forms or identifiable fabric types, and these are discussed below. The remaining 60% comprised mainly body sherds belonging to beakers or flagons in undistinguisable sandy fabrics, many of which may be later than 1st-century date. The distribution of the material within the site phasing is summarised in table 1. With the exception of material from the earliest enclosure ditches and pits (Phases 1 and 2, fig. 33), the pottery did not come from closed stratigraphic contexts, and many of the sherds were probably residual (also for the samain and amphora, see previous and following). This was also reflected in the differential preservation of the sherds.

The material has been divided into four main groups based on macroscopic examination:

1. Gallo-Belgic Wares; in particular *terra nigra* and *terra rubra*.
2. Other fine ware imports: flagons, beakers, bowls, and miscellaneous.
3. Coarse ware imports: jars, bowls, platters.
4. Native fine wares: butt beakers.

A detailed descriptive catalogue, together with petrological descriptions of 21 selected sherds can be found in the level III archive. The thin section reference numbers are recorded as (R000). For ease of reference the classification of vessel forms follow that of Hawkes and Hull in their report on the pottery from *Camulodunum* (i.e. *Cam.* – –), (Hawkes and Hull 1947) but is supplemented by other references where necessary. The vessels selected for illustration do not represent all the forms present on the site, but have been chosen to show the range, and present those pieces previously unpublished in this country. A list of those vessels illustrated and their feature location has been listed after the group descriptions.

Despite small sample size, the first century fine ware assemblage from Ower allows a fascinating and informative insight into early Roman trade. It raises many questions, however, not least of which is why is it at the site at all? Many of the vessel types have previously not been recognised in Britain and it is difficult to assess whether the Ower sherds represent traded items or arrived at the site by some other mechanism, perhaps accidental loss of property belonging to travellers, or even traders in other commodities? Most of the earlier material comes from the rectilinear enclosure (288) (Table 1). This includes those vessels considered to have come from the Saintes region, i.e. the carinated bowl and platter (fig. 41, 32 and 34), and the Central Gaulish micaceous flagon. Gallo-Belgic wares are scarce from this context and are limited mainly to *terra rubra* sherds, for example the pedestal beaker, girth beaker and butt beaker. All these vessels probably date to the Tiberian-early Claudian period. The remaining Gallo-Belgic wares, including most of the *terra nigra*, comes from other deposits, none of which can be closely dated, although a single piece of TN was sealed in the primary fill of enclosure 288 below shell midden dumps 'd', a single sherd of acute lattice BB1 was also present at the base of 288. Possible contamination (?).

The ring ditch similarly contained the first century material but on balance this seems to be slightly later than that of the rectilinear enclosure.

When the variety of wares present is considered in relation to their postulated sources, at least two routes of 'trade' can be suggested. The first, via the western seaways from the coast of western France and across the Channel, would account for those wares from Saintes together perhaps with the Spanish amphorae also present at Ower (see Williams, this report). This route was evidently used during the earlier period, i.e. the late first century BC and early first century AD. The second route, suggested by the vessel types present, is that via the Rhône-Saône-Rhine waterways. The use of this route by Roman traders is well documented by epigraphic evidence and the distribution of material. The Lyons ware, Roanne ware and much of the Gallo-Belgic wares probably arrived directly, or indirectly via other sites on the south coast such as Chichester, by this route.

It has traditionally been thought that the Durotriges as a tribe were anti-Roman, particularly in the immediate pre-conquest period (Wheeler 1943: 63, Bugler and Drew 1973) and were thus unlikely to have been involved in trade with Roman merchants at this time. On the basis of the Ower fine wares the provisional hypothesis can be suggested that pre-Roman 'trading' connections between Poole Harbour and south-west France were established at least by the end of the 1st-century BC, and that these were later accompanied and eventually replaced by alternative 'trade' connections via the Rhine and eastern seaways. The presence of the

TABLE 1: The stratigraphic location by phase of the pottery fine wares and continental imports

Phase Description	PHASE NO.	MAIN FEATURES	1 SAMIAN PRE-FLAVIAN							2 TERRA NIGRA		3 TERRA RUBRA				
			ARRETINE	EARLY LEZOUX	EARLY S. GAUL	SOUTH GAUL	CENTRAL GAUL	EAST GAUL	UNASSIGNED	I	II	IA	IC	2	3	UNASSIGNED
First c. Ditches and pits	1	288	·2·	·2·							1	1			3	
		858													1	
	2	389 343	·1·		1					1	·9·	1		2	1	5
First/second c. soil accumulation	3		·1·	·3·	5	2	6			1	·15·	1		8	5	3
Disturbed and infilled lower horizons	4	555 540								1	3				1	
and third/ fourth c.	5	441 909			1	·2					2			1		
occupation levels	6	644 727 388								1	9			6	1	6
Third/fourth c. occupation and structural levels	7	147 564 707 904 905 906	·3			1	···21	···4			3	1		1	1	1
Post-roman agricultural disturbance	8		···8		··8	··9	···28		5		15		1	2	5	2
Total Sherd Count			15	5	15	14	55	4	5	4	57	4	1	20	18	17
Total Sherd Count			113							61		60				

· ILLUSTRATED SHERDS

Roman army in Dorset shortly after AD 43 does not seem to have had any effect on the material at Ower. This conclusion is further supported by a comparison with the first century material from the large fort complex recently excavated at Lake Farm, near Wimborne, Dorset, (Wilson (ed.) 1973; 1974). *Terra rubra* appears to be absent among the assemblage at Lake Farm and the range of *terra nigra* very limited and of a different fabric type to that found at Ower. There is also Lyons ware and Pompeian Red wares at Lake which are respectively scarce and absent at Ower, suggesting perhaps that there were different supply systems operating at the two sites. If fine wares were imported into Poole harbour for further distribution, it is not yet apparent where they went.

1. The Gallo-Belgic Wares (*Terra nigra and terra rubra*)

Gallo-Belgic imports constitute 20% of the total fine ware assemblage. The ratio of *terra nigra* to *terra rubra* platter fragments is approximately 2:1, which is suggestive of an early date for the assemblage (Rigby 1978: 200). The incidence of forms and fabric is shown in Table 2, and the fabrics described following. Since the sample is small and mainly unstratified it would be inappropriate to discuss the presence or absence of certain forms. Indeed, most of the forms that are present are difficult to date, especially in the virtual absence of potters' stamps. Platter forms *Cam.* 2 and *Cam.* 5, for example, were standardised during the later Augustan period and features in both pre-and post-conquest groups. Micaceous *terra nigra* on the other hand is often associated with pre-conquest groups and is relatively scarce in Britain. It is undoubtedly Central Gaulish in origin and was probably made at a number of sites within that region. Unfortunately it is not yet possible to identify individual workshops from their products alone, but platters were certainly being produced at Roanne (Poncet 1974), St. Rémy-en-Rollat (Vertet 1961), and other centres in the Allier region from the Augustan period. In Britain, comparable material has been found at Canterbury (Timby n.d.), at Blackfriars, Leicester; at Skeleton Green, Puckeridge (Partridge 1975); at the cemetery at Baldock, Hertfordshire; and at the recent excavations at Colchester (1970 excavations) (Rigby 1985, 77).

Terra nigra platters of *Cam.* 16 types are among the commonest to be found in Britain, and the form survives from the Augustan period up until the end of the first century AD. During the second half of the first century it is frequently found in military contexts, usually in a fabric analagous to fabric IIa (see below). The *Cam.* 16 platter may form a 'set' with the cup (*Cam.* 58), whilst the platter (*Cam.* 7/8) may go with the cup (*Cam.* 56), all of which are present here (Rigby 1978).

Terra rubra sherds, although fewer in number, demonstrate the presence of platters (*Cam.* 5 and *Cam.* 8), three types of beaker; pedestal, girth and butt, as well as a globular jar (*Cam.* 91) (Fig. 12, 27) and an unclassified platter (Fig. 41, 26), all of which date to the Tiberio-Claudian period, and are fairly restricted in occurrence in Britain, especially the latter (fig. 41, 26). As on many other sites in Britain, the commonest fabric here is TR2. TR1A and C are present, but TR1B is apparently absent. Both TR1A and TR1B are pre-Claudian in date, the latter featuring among the fabrics at Reims from the Augustan period. Since this fabric features at other sites on the south coast, notably Chichester, Fishbourne and Hayling Island it might have been expected here as well. The incidence of forms and fabric are summarised in table 1.

Terra nigra: On the basis of macroscopic examination, the *terra nigra* was divided into two main fabric groups: I, micaceous *terra nigra* and II, non-micaceous *terra nigra*. The latter group is further sub-divided into seven sub-groups on the basis of finish colour and texture. No standard fabric classification has been defined for *terra nigra* owing to the considerable diversity which exists. The divisions used here are therefore subjective but consistent within this group of material. It does not necessarily imply differing production sources for the vessels concerned.

Fabric I: Micaceous *terra nigra*.

Thin section R874

Dark grey to mid-blue-grey in colour with smooth surfaces.

Hard fine sandy fabric, generally light grey in colour and containing frequent flecks of mica. Three *Cam* 2 platter basesherds; and a single basesherd with a pronounced footstand which demonstrates close affinities with a Campanian or Arretine prototype. This latter vessel *Cam* 1 or 2.

4 1st c. GALLIC IMPORTS						5	6	7 AMPHORAE												8 MORTARIA			9	10	11	
FLAGONS	BEAKERS	BOWLS	BOWLS/CUPS	PLATTERS	UNASSIGNED	1st. c. Coarse Imports	1st. c. Native Fine Ware	PASCUAL 1		DRESSEL 2-4		DRESSEL 20		PÉLICHET 47		AMPHORA/JUG CAMPAGNIAN		UNASSIGNED		1st. c.	NEW FOREST	OXFORD	NEW FOREST	OXFORD	B.B.1.	
								wt. g	no.	wt. g	no.	wt. g	no.	wt. g	no.	wt. g	no.	wt. g	no.							
2	1	1		1	12	1	3	2648	43							15	1	105	4							TABLE 3
1					24			486	4			233	2	38	1	45	3	7	1							
9	2		2		86	4	3	1315	37	109	2	7	1	175	6	14	1	20	1	1						
1					11	2		191	4	82	1							16	2				1	1		
1					5			5215	96							83	1					1				
8		2			33	1	3	1817	46					35	1	61	2	30	1							TABLE 4
2	1		2		9		1	1612	24					51	1	101	3	57	2	2		3	20	3		
9	3				111		7	2071	42			243	3	181	15	68	2	183	8		1	4	31	12		
33	5	3	5	2	291	8	17	296		3		6		24		13		19		3	1	8	52	16	1039	
339						8	17	361												12			68		1039	

Fabric II: Non-Micaceous *terra nigra*. (Fig. 12, 23-25).

A hard, fine, sandy fabric, generally light grey in colour. Occasionally grey ironstone grits are visible. This can be further subdivided into groups a-g.

a: Thin section R779.
Vessels with a glossy, highly polished dark grey to blue-grey interior. Exterior surface generally smooth but matt.
Cam 2, 5, 7/8, 12, 13, 16 (Fig. 12, 23), 16/17 (platters); *Cam* 56, 58 (cups).

b: Thin section R787.
Fabric indistinguishable from IIa (above), but the highly polished surface was absent, possibly as a result of the acid soil conditions. *Cam* 2, 7 (fig. 41, 24), 16, (platters); *Cam* 58 (cup).

c: Thin section R785.
Pale to dark blue-grey, smooth surfaces, the interior generally polished. Hard, fine sandy fabric, again similar to a/b, but slightly coarser in texture.
Cam 2, 16 (platters).

d: Thin sections R786, R782.
Very black polished interior surfaces with a black/grey-black matt or polished exterior. Light grey to greenish-grey fine, sandy fabric with occasional ironstone.
Cam 12, 13, 16, (fig.41, 25), 4 base sherds with footrings and incised concentric lines including one with the interior surface decorated with at least one rouletted wreath (platters).

e: Pale, smooth polished grey interior surface, dark grey, matt exterior. Hard, fine sandy fabric, almost white in colour. Distinguished by the presence of a small amount of white mica within the fabric. A single base sherd with a narrow footring (platter).

f: Hard, fine sandy, light-grey fabric with occasional ironstone grits. The surface was originally smooth with a black, polished finish but this has since worn to a speckled dark grey. *Cam.* 14 or 16 (platter). A single basesherd with a domed centre and a well formed footring. The centre is marked by a broken potter's stamp which is surrounded by two incised concentric circles. Little of the stamp survives but is possibly that of the potter *Casso*, 'a stamp found in Nijmegan, *Holwerda* No. 40, on a platter *Cam.* 14' (Valerie Rigby *Pers. Comm.*)

g: Hard, fine sandy and light grey in colour with occasional ironstone grits. The exterior is lightly burnished, the interior a matt grey. This fabric type probably originates in the Rhineland and although it occurs in abundance in that region has only been very rarely recognised in Britain. It generally occurs in contexts dating to the end of the 1st-century AD, usually military sites, *e.g.* Chester (Timby in Ward 1981)
Holwerda type 128-140, from the cemeteries at Nijmegan (Holwerda 1941; pl. iv), a single body sherd of a jar.

Terra rubra: The fabric classification summarised below is based on that by Hawkes and Hull (1947; 204), and modified by Rigby (1973; 11-12). Two vessels have been illustrated (fig. 41, 26 and 27). The vessel illustrated from fabric *TR2* (fig. 41, 26) is one of the three platters recovered, which are typologically identical to one another. The form is unusual for *terra rubra* and is not found in *Camulodunum* sequence. The closest parallel appears to be *Arretine* service 1c (Loeschcke 1909, 137), which is distinguished by an overhanging rim and in internal tripartite division. The internal wall moulding can be paralleled for example at Haltern (Loeschcke 1909; Abb. 1; 1-5), but not the slight concavity of the external rim face. The internal surfaces and the rim exteriors are a self-coloured dark orange matt, but originally displayed a highly polished finish. The fabric is hard, fine and sandy. The absence of mica and calcareous inclusions in the hand specimen would strongly suggest that they are neither Central Gaulish or South Gaulish samian as discussed by Dannell (Dannell 1977) or Williams (Williams 1978), but belong to the Gallo-Belgic tradition. Similar platters have been found at Nijmegan stamped by the potter *Arantedus* who was based at Reims for at least part of his working life (Holwerda 1941; form 76). The vessel illustrated from Fabric *TR3* (fig. 41, 27) is a globular jar, *Cam* 91. Similar vessels occur at Colchester, Chichester (Down 1978; fig. 10.7.47) and Haltern (Loeschcke 1909; Abb. 42; 6) in the last Augustan to Claudian period. Here several sherds occur which are probably from the same vessel. The date of this vessel is probably Claudian.

Fabric TR1A: Fine sandy fabric cream/pale pink in colour with occasional red ironstone grits. Dark red polished slip on the upper surfaces and rim. The exterior surface is self coloured matt.
Cam 73/74 (pedestalled cups)

Fabric TR1C: Fine sandy fabric, red-orange in colour with occasional red ironstone grits. Dark red slip on the upper visible surfaces. The exterior surface is self coloured and smoothed but not polished. Basesherd with a footring (platter). The interior is covered with a polished slip.

Fabric TR2:   Thin sections R809 (fig. 41, 26), R781
Dark orange-red sandy ware with occasional red ironstone grits. The surfaces are self-coloured with a highly polished finish on the upper surface. In some cases the exterior surface has a similar polished finish but is more generally left matt.
Cam 5, 8, and form illustrated in fig. 41, 26, basesherd with footring and interior surface decorated with at least one rouletted circle, two conjoining base sherds decorated with at least one ring

of single rouletting (platters); *Cam* 56 (cup).

Fabric TR3: (Fig. 12, 27)
Hard, fine sandy orange-red fabric. Bright orange well polished exterior surface, frequently fumed to a chocolate brown with the exception of the base which remains orange.
Cam 82/84 (Girth beakers);
Cam 91 (fig. 41, 26, Globular jar);
Cam 112 (Butt beakers).

2. Other Fine Ware Imports (flagons, beakers, bowls, cups and platters).

A number of other Gallic imports were recovered from the site. The fabrics vary from a hard sandy matrix to a very fine paste, with a wide variety of inclusions and finishes. Whilst the majority of this material was probably of Continental origin, the provenance of some vessel types could not be determined. It is possible that one of the ring-necked flagons was made at Corfe Mullen (fig. 41, 28)

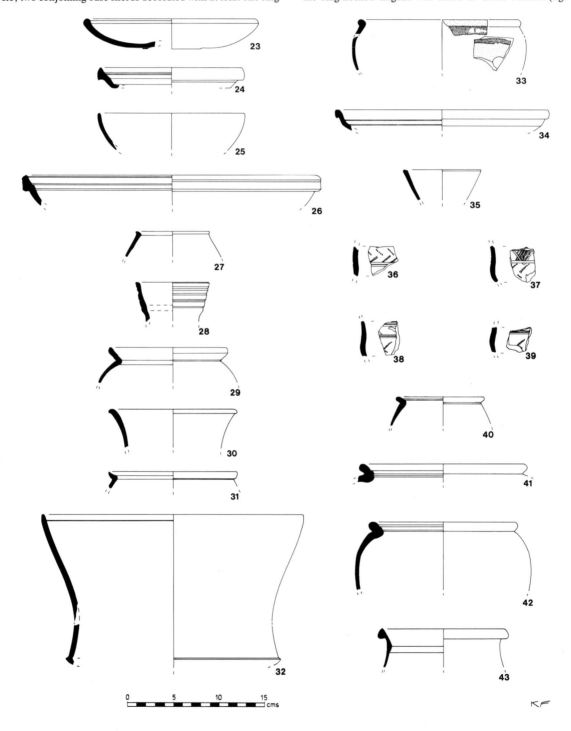

Figure 41. The 1st century fine and coarse ware imports, and native fine wares (23-43) at ¼.

(David Williams pers. comm.). The material has therefore been arranged by vessel type, and sub-divided under these headings into fabric type, form type or where possible centre of production (e.g. Lyons ware) as appropriate.

Flagons: A number of flagon types were recovered from the site.

Central French: Thin section R775, hard orange-brown sandy matrix with abundant flecks of golden mica. Exterior has a creamy white slip. Body sherds, rim and a four-ribbed handle occurred, and all probably came from the same vessel. Similar vessels were know in central France, e.g. the *oppidum* site at Chateaumeillant (*Mediolanum*), Cher, (Gourvest and Hugoniot 1957), and it is likely that they originate in this area. Probably Tiberio-Claudian in date.

White wares: Thin section R777

A hard, fine, sandy fabric. A rim sherd *Cam* 161, and base sherds with a slightly squared footring, probably from the same vessel. Flagons of this type were produced at the kiln complex in Reims (Marne), in the province of *Gallia Belgica* during the Tiberio-Claudian period. A body sherd with a strap handle attachment and two unfeatured body sherds were also recovered.

Ring necked: Thin section R780

A hard sandy fabric varying from pink-orange to buff, occasionally with a grey core. Red ironstone and mica inclusions present. Three vessels were recovered; one with at least three rings, one with four rings (*Cam* 154 type and possibly a product of Corfe Mullen, Calkin 1935), and one internally cupped with multiple rings. (Fig. 41, 28). Multiple ring necked flagons are a fairly common type with many variations in the first-century AD. They are well represented at Fishbourne where they predominantly occur in contexts dating to before AD 75 (Cunliffe 1971, type 109).

Orange ware: Dark orange sandy fabric with light orange surfaces, frequent grains of quartz and iron, occurs with a white slip on the first example. Body sherd with handle attachment. Strap handle.

Beakers: A number of beaker types were recovered from the site, one of which could be identified as Lyons Ware. Of the other pieces, one was probably from Central Gaul and the others probably imported but unprovenanced.

Lyons ware: Two sherds probably of the same vessel. Glossy brown colour coated surfaces with a pale cream, hard, fine sandy fabric. The exterior had a rough-cast sand finish.

Lyons form 20 (Greene 1979; fig. 8, 25).

This type of beaker was imported into Britain during the period AD 40-70, and is already well represented in the Dorset area (Kevin Greene *Pers. Comm.*)

Central Gaul: Thin section R778. (fig. 41, 30)

A hard grey-brown, finely micaceous ware. Exterior has a smooth, polished, black finish. The interior dark grey and matt. A single rim sherd from a beaker, although the slight flaring might suggest a bowl. Probably of Central Gaulish origin.

White ware: Thin section R789. (fig. 41, 29).

A hard pale brown to cream sandy fabric with a gold mica slip. Three rim sherds of small beakers, probably imported. *Cam* 114.

Other: A fine, sandy, light brown fabric with frequent flakes of white mica. Externally grey, interior reddish brown. Probably burnt. One rim sherd of beaker/small jar. (fig. 42, 31).

Bowls: Three identifiable bowl types were recovered from the site, two of which could be provenanced; Saintes and Roanne.

Saintes: Thin section R776. (fig. 41, 32)

A fine, hard textured fabric, brown in colour with a dark grey core. Fine quartz and occasional mica are present. Both surfaces have a smooth, black, polished finish. Four sherds of the same vessel were recovered. The form is probably a hybrid of the more commonly known '*vase bobine*', *Cam* 51. Such forms are characteristic of the products from Saintes in the Charente, South-West France (Santrot 1979; *cf.* type 171). Production here apparently took place in the last two decades of the 1st-century BC (Santrot 1979). The form is seemingly unknown in Britain.

Roanne: Thin section R788. (fig. 41, 33)

Fine fabric with mica present. Exterior surface is white in colour, considered to be a natural result of firing, with a band of orange paint just below the rim. The interior surface and core are a very pale brown in colour. A single rim and conjoining body sherd from a painted bowl of *Périchon type* 16 (Périchon 1974; 26).

TABLE 2: Incidence of Forms in Terra Nigra and Terra Rubra (Rimsherds only)

FORM	PLATTERS											CUPS		BEAKERS								JARS			TOTAL
	Cam 2	Cam 5	Cam 7	Cam 8	Cam 12	Cam 13	Cam 16	Cam 16/17	Unclassified	Unassigned	Total	Cam 56	Cam 58	Cam 73/74 rim	Cam 73/74 body	Cam 82/84 rim	Cam 82/84 body	Cam 112 rim	Cam 112 body	Unassigned rim	Unassigned body	Holwerda 128/140	Cam 91 rim	Cam 91 body	TOTAL
FABRIC		(24)						(23)	(25)	(26)												(27)			
TR1A										0	0			1	3										4
TR1C										1	1														1
TR2 (26)		2		1					3	20	26	1													27
TR3 (27)										0	0					1	2	1	3	3	4		6	4	24
TR TOTAL		2		1					3	21	27	1		4		3		4		7			10		56
TN 1										4	4														4
TN II (23)–(25)	4	1	1		2	2	4	2		27	43	1	2									1			47
TN TOTAL	4	1	1		2	2	4	2		31	47	1	2									1			51
TOTAL	4	3	1	1	2	2	4	2	3	52	74	2	2	4		3		4		7		1	10		107

· ILLUSTRATED PIECES
(00) Nos in brackets are illustration nos.

These bowls occur in large quantities at Roanne and were undoubtedly produced there, although none have yet been found associated with a kiln. (P. C. Poncet *Pers. Comm.*) Production seems to have begun during the early Augustan period and continued through until the beginning of the 2nd century AD. Generally speaking the paint used on the earlier vessels is dull red but this later becomes progressively lighter and more orange. The remainder of the vessel is frequently decorated with intricate geometric designs. The vessel here probably belongs to the second half of the 1st-century AD or slightly later. Although bowls of this type are found on a large number of sites in Central Gaul, examples in Britain are rare. A similar vessel to the one here was found in the 'late Celtic rubbish heap' near Oare, Wiltshire excavated earlier this century and more recently reassessed by Swan (1975, fig. 5, 57).

Mica Slipped ware: A hard, very fine sandy orange fabric, with a mica gilt slip on the exterior surface. A single body sherd from a bowl with fairly straight walls, carinated towards the base, possibly an imitation of a *sigillata form* 29 or 30.

Bowls/Cups: Three fragments of bowl/cup types and the rim of a small cup were recovered, but no reconstruction of form types was possible. However, the thin sectioning of one body sherd suggested that it originated from Campania. The origin of the other vessel was uncertain, but all were of a similar fabric; a hard dark orange sandy fabric, sometimes with a reduced core, colour coat surfaces, and mica grits.

Campanian ware: Thin section R791.

An orange, fine textured fabric with volcanic glass fragments. The interior and exterior surfaces show the remains of a black slip with a highly polished finish on the exterior. The form was indeterminable, but a slight curvature on the sherd suggests a bowl or a cup. The presence of volcanic glass fragments within the fabric adds to the probability that this sherd belongs to the Campanian industry. Campanian ware was produced from the 5th or 4th centuries BC until the 1st century BC when it became eclipsed by Arretine ware. Towards the end of this period a few products were imported into Gaul with other luxury goods, but hitherto none have been positively identified in Britain. Unfortunately this sherd comes from a residual context and was probably brought to the site during the latter years of the 1st century BC or early 1st century AD.

Other: Three cup or bowl vessels in a variety of fine orange fabrics.

a. Very hard, fine sandy fabric with orange-brown to grey-matt margins and brown core.
Rim sherd from a small cup (fig. 41, 35).

b. Orange sandy fabric with a worn matt colour coat. Base sherd from a small cup or bowl with a slight foot stand.

c. Moderately hard, fine dark grey sandy fabric with dark orange matt surfaces. Occasional fine mica flecks are visible on the surface. Rim sherd from a cup/small bowl.

Platters: A single fragment of a platter (fig. 41, 34) was recovered from the site, which was identified (with the bowl, see previous fig. 41, 32) as coming from Saintes.

Saintes: A rim sherd from a small platter. The exterior and interior surfaces are covered in a black slip, which originally displayed a smooth polished finish, since worn. The fabric is brown in colour with a grey core and has a fine, hard, sandy texture with visible flecks of fine mica. This platter is probably related to a type found in the central and south-western regions of France. A typologically similar platter with a central double line potters stamp, for example is known from the *oppidum* site at Chateaumeillant, Cher. (Gourvest unpub.) Arretine influence is apparent from the shape of the rim and the internal tripartite division. Similar platters are known to have been produced at Saintes, in the Charente (Santrot 1979, form 62), and at St Rémy-en-Rollat in the Allier (Vertet 1961; fig. 2). Material from the Allier is generally characterised by frequent fine mica within the fabric. However, the sandwich effect in the core is more characteristic of the products from Saintes. Probably dates to the Augustan-Claudian period.

3. Imported Coarse Wares (Jars, bowls, and bowl/platters)

Three coarse ware vessel types were identified as having been imported from Northern and Central Gaul. These are described under the vessel type:

Jars: Those identified, (fig. 4, 40), closely resemble a range of Gallo-Roman forms that are found in some numbers in Central and north-west France, and are dated to the second half of the first century BC and the first half of the first century AD. (Ferdière 1972; fig. 1; and Alain Ferdière *Pers. Comm.*). There is probably

little doubt that the Ower vessels originated from northern or central France, though the actual centres of production are as yet difficult to pinpoint. The petrology of the fabrics suggests an origin in a granitic area, but granite formations occur in both regions. Three similar fabrics were present:

Fabric a: Thin section R822. (fig. 41, 40).

A hard, compact fabric, light orange-brown to grey in colour (the exterior surface being darker), with inclusions of felspar, mica (muscovite and biolite), quartz and iron. Faint traces of a mica gilt slip on the external surface were apparent.

Rim sherd and body sherd of small hand-made jar. Slightly everted rim with a lid seating.

Fabric b: A hard fairly sandy fabric, reddish-brown throughout, with thin coat of mica slip.

Rim sherd (fig. 41, 41) similar in form to vessel in fabric c, following.

Fabric c: Thin section R823. (fig. 41, 42)

A hard micaceous fabric, inclusions as Fabric a.

Sharply everted rim with two deep horizontal grooves on the inner side. The shoulder and rim have received a light burnishing together with a thin coat of mica dusting, while the girth has been left in a rough state.

Bowls: Four body sherds (fig. 41, 36-39) with comb impressed decoration were recovered with at least two vessels represented. The fabric is dark grey and sandy with some fine mica present. No direct parallels can be found for these sherds but the tradition is reminiscent of the early *Gallo-Roman* wares of Central Gaul. Bowls in a hard grey ware with wavy line decoration for example occur amongst the *Gallo-Roman* assemblages at Gergovia (Ward Perkins 1941). These sherds may belong to the same or similar tradition.

Bowl/Platters: A single base sherd from a coarse ware bowl or platter with a foot-ring was recovered. This was a coarse greenish-grey, finely micaceous sandy fabric with dark grey matt surfaces. Probably Central Gaulish.

4. Native Fine Wares (butt beakers)

Three fabric groups were recognised for native butt beakers, *Cam* 113. These were probably products of Chichester and/or Colchester.

a. Thin section R774.
A hard, fine sandy white ware. Rim sherds, body sherds with rouletted decoration and a base sherd. White ware beakers of this type are probably Colchester products but no kilns have been identified at present.

b. Thin section R790. (fig. 41, 43)
Pale brown to grey-brown, hard, fine sandy ware. The exterior undecorated zones are lightly burnished and occasional inclusions of quartz and red ironstone are visible. The rim sherds and body sherds present in this fabric may have been produced at either Colchester or Chichester (Down 1978).

c. A fairly coarse, grey, very sandy fabric.
A single body sherd, decorated with fine vertical rouletting. Very thin walled (2mm).

Acknowledgements: I would like to thank all those who have shown me material from other sites prior to publication, and those who have commented on particular sherds from Ower: *Lake Farm, Wimborne*; M. Darling, *Chateaumeillant*; J. Gourvest, *Reims*; R., Neiss, *Lyons ware*; K. Greene, *Coarse ware Imports*; A. Ferdière, J. Collis, *Roanne ware*; J. Poncet.

I would also like to thank Tim Darvill, David Peacock, Val Rigby and David Williams for their help in the preparation of this report.

The Illustrated 1st-century AD imports and native fine wares (fig. 41)

23. *Cam* 16 platter (TNIIa), from phase 3.
24. *Cam* 7 platter (TNIIb), from phase 3.
25. *Cam* 16 platter (TNIId), from phase 2 (343IB).
26. Platter (TR2), from phase 3.
27. Cam 91 Globular jar (TR3), from phase 3.
28. Multiple ring necked flagon internally cupped, from phase 8.
29. *Cam* 114 small beaker (white ware with mica slip), from phase 8.
30. Beaker/bowl (Central Gaul), from phase 1 (288B).
31. Beaker/jar (from phase 8 (261).
32. *Cam* 51 'vase bobine' (Saintes), from phase 1 (288B).
33. *Périchon* 16 painted bowl (Roanne), from phase 6 (727).
34. *Santrot* 62 platter (Saintes), from phase 1 (288C).
35. Cup/bowl, from phase 1 (618).
36. Decorated bowl (Central Gaul), from phase 3.
37. Decorated bowl (Central Gaul), from phase 8.

38. Decorated bowl (Central Gaul), from phase 3.
39. Decorated bowl (Central Gaul), from phase 3.
40. Everted rim jar with lid seating (N.W. or Central France), from phase 4 (540).
41. Everted rim jar with internal grooves (N.W. or Central France), from phase 4 (540).
42. Everted rim jar with internal grooves (N.W. or Central France), from phase 1 (288B).
43. *Cam* 113 butt beaker (native), from phase 8.

THE AMPHORAE

D. F. WILLIAMS, PhD (D.o.E. Ceramic Petrology Project, Dept. of Archaeology, University of Southampton)

The amphorae sherds were classified by fabric and form and then weighed and counted. The proportion of the types represented by weight and number, together with the location by phase is summarised in the Table 1. The proportion of the types present by weight and count are; Dressel 1 – Pascual 1 (87%, 81%), Dressel 2-4 (2%, 1 %), Dressel 20 (3%, 2%) Pélichet 47 (3%, 7%), a probable Campanian amphora/jug fabric (2%, 4%), and a small number of unassigned types (3%, 5%). The origin and dates of these amphorae are summarised below.

The presence of quantities of Dressel 1 – Pascual 1 (fig. 13, 44 and 45, 47-52) and the Campanian amphora/jug (fig. 42, 46), together with the other 1st-century AD imports point to early (pre-conquest) trade in the 1st-century AD. Much of the Dressel 1 – Pascual 1 material is therefore in residual contexts (about 80%, see Table 1). The amphora trade in the 1st-century AD is discussed in detail under Dressel 1 – Pascual 1 below. In the succeeding centuries the amphora trade to the site appears to have declined. It is somewhat surprising that only six sherds of the most common amphora of the second century, Dressel 20, occur in the later levels (two in the upper levels of phase 2 features, one in soil accumulation levels, and three in the post-Roman disturbance).

DRESSEL 1 – PASCUAL 1 (fig. 42, 44 and 45, 47-52)
This is the first identification in Britain of this distinctive Catalan amphora type. Based on the Italian Dressel 1B form, it is characterised by a high vertical rim, cylindrical neck, ovoid body, straight rounded handles with a narrow longitudinal groove and a chunky conical spike (see Tchernia (1971) for illustrations of the complete form). Two fabrics are represented at Ower:
Fabric a: A hard rough, dark red to reddish-brown fabric, with large white inclusions of quartz and felspar, golden mica, and fragments of granite scattered throughout (fig. 13, 49 and 50).
Fabric b: A slightly softer, smoother creamy-white fabric, lacking the mica but containing the quartz and felspar present in the previous fabric (fig. 42, 44, 45, 47, 51, 52).

Both fabrics appear to have been produced in the Barcelona region (Pascual, 1977), but the lighter coloured one may also have been made a little further down the Spanish coast. These amphorae probably held wine, as the Layetanian area was praised by Martial as having a quality of wine second only to that of Campania (xiii, 118). A single kiln producing similar types is known at Aspiran in south-west France (Tchernia, 1971, 85), but its products do not seem to be represented at Ower.

Dressel 1 – Pascual 1 types are present on the continent in contexts ranging from late Republican/early Augustan at Vieille-Toulouse to AD 79 at Pompeii (Tchernia, 1971, 52-54). At Ower, Pascual 1 sherds are found in the securely stratified early first century AD levels (see below). A late Augustan or Tiberian date for the northern export of this amphora type at Ower would broadly agree with the dating of a similar find from the east Rhineland fort of Westphalie, near Holsterhausen, which should be dated to the last decade of the first century BC – early first century AD (Tchernia, 1971, 56-57). As far as is known, Dressel 1 – Pascual 1 amphora are rarely found in post-Conquest contexts in Britain (see below), and the occurrence of sherds of this form in the later levels at Ower no doubt represents residual material from the early first-century levels.

Outside Spain, the main distribution area for Dressel 1 – Pascual 1 amphorae was Narbonensis and Aquitania, and these types appear less frequently in northern Gaul and the Rhineland. In Britain, besides Ower, sherds from likely Pascual 1 vessels have recently been recognised at Hengistbury Head (stratification detail awaited), Bagendon, Gloucestershire (site dated AD 20-50) and Knighton, Isle of Wight (unstratified), while single sherds have been found at Colchester (unstratified) and Thaxted, Essex (associated with a Dressel 1B amphora-burial) (Chris Going *Pers. Comm.*). On present evidence, the distribution of the Dressel 1 – Pascual 1 form in Britain shows a distinct southerly bias, more especially towards the territory of the Durotriges, and seems likely to have arrived in late Augustan or Tiberian times. Given the paucity of finds in northern Gaul and the Rhineland, the only one certain pre-Conquest find in eastern Britain, it seems probable that the Pascual 1 amphorae from Ower came from northern Spain via the Narbonensis-Garonne route around the coast of Brittany. This would also help to explain the presence of early Augustan pottery from Aquitania in the early levels of the site (see Timby, previous).

It seems significant that no southern Spanish or Italian Dressel 2-4 types of amphorae appear in the early first-century levels at Ower, although both of these types are to be found in some numbers in the eastern part of the country at this date (Peacock, 1971). The answer may lie in some form of regional differentiation of amphorae deliveries to the late Iron Age tribes of pre-Conquest Britain, whereby the south-eastern tribes received southern Spanish fish products and Italian wine via the Rhone-Rhine route, while the Durotrigian region and surrounds were receiving Catalan wine by way of the Garonne waterway.

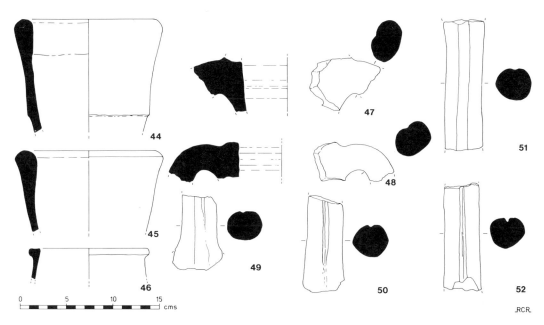

Figure 42. The 1st century Amphorae (44-52), 1:4.

Table 3: The Stratigraphic location by Phase of BB1 Vessel Types from the First Century Features and subsequent

PHASE	FEATURE		COOK-POTS		JAR-BOWLS							OPEN BOWLS						LIDS	BEAKERS	
			1	6	7	8	9	10	11	12	13	14	15	16	17	18	19	20	34	35
1	288B	+	45		2	39	8		2	12	5	7		4	1		23	1	2	3
1	288C	+	2	1		8	2			1	4	2	1	1	4		1		2	
1/2	858	+	2			3								3						
1/2	389	+				5	1	1				2		1		1			1	
2	343 I		17	1		9	3	1	6	3	7	8	1	2	1		1		2	1
2	343 II A		7			7	1					2		2					4	
2	343 IIB	+	2	3		6	1		2		2	4		1	4	1	1	1	2	
3	Soil accumulation	*	44	3		41	14		14	10	2	8		9	6	1	2	1		
6	288A		17	6	2	29	3		2	1	4	13		1	4		8		4	
Vessel Type Totals			158		263							131						3	21	
Vessel Percentages			26%		42%							22%						1%	3%	

·Illustrated vessels. +Well sealed groups with little contamination. *Sampled from deposits: (i) above all old soil and sealed by building 707; (ii) above accumulation below (142). Vessel numbers by diagnostic sherd count.

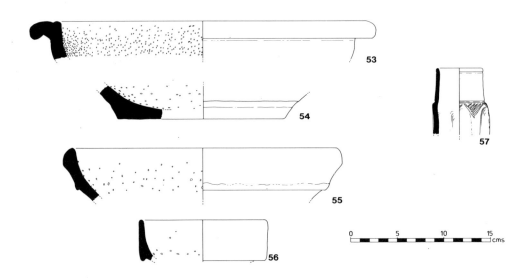

Figure 43. The Mortaria (53-56), and New Forest wares (57), at ¹/₄.

This amphora trade is discussed more fully in Williams (1981).

Dressel 2-4
This type of amphora was made in a variety of places during the first and second centuries AD, e.g. Italy, southern France and Spain as well as the Aegean and was probably used for carrying wine.

Dressel 20
Dressel 20 amphorae came from the Guadalquivir region of Spain, between Seville and Cordoba, where they were used primarily for the transportation of olive-oil. This type of amphorae has a wide date-range from the pre-Roman Period I levels at Camulodunum to the third/fourth centuries AD.

Pélichet 47
Wine-amphora, probably from southern Gaul, in particular the area around the mouth of the Rhone and the Gulf of Lyons. In Britain, these vessels date from the latter half of the first century AD to the beginning of the third century, with the main concentration occurring during the second half of the second century.

Campanian Amphora/Jug (Fig. 42, 46)
This fabric is particularly distinctive in the hand-specimen as it appears to contain numerous inclusions of 'black sand' set against a white to light grey clay background. Thin sections were made of four of the eighteen sherds represented in this group, and study under the petrological microscope revealed grains of green or colourless

soil accumulation (Phases 1-3)

OTHER	BASES				HANDLES			BODY DECORATION							VESSEL FORMS MORE TYPICAL OF LATER OCCUPATION (POSSIBLE CONTAMINATION)					VESSEL TYPE
37	38	39	40	42	43	44	47	48	52	53	54	56	57	61	2/3	24, 25	29-32	36	55	FORM/GROUP
i	1		7	3	8					3	2			1	1					
		3				2		2		1										
				1																
	6	1	2															1		
	5		9		1										1		2			
			1			1		1					i							
	2		4				i								3					
	30	2	25		6	1	i	10	5			1	1				2			
	17	2	7		1			5	3					i	10	2	7	i	i	Vessel Total
1																		31		608
1%																		5%		100%

and with old soil; and (iii) single vessel (124), type 20, from

augite scattered throughout the clay matrix, together with sanidine felspar, a little basaltic hornblende and fragments of volcanic rock. Both in the hand-specimen and in thin section, these sherds recall the 'black sand' fabrics of certain Dressel 1 amphora types and Pompeian red slipped wares convincingly shown by Peacock (1971, 1977) to have been made in Campania, more especially the area around Pompeii and Herculaneum. A similar origin for the Ower material is highly likely.

Only one of the Ower sherds is other than a featureless body sherd. The exception is a small flat-topped rim from second/third century layers (fig. 42, 46). A similar type, though in a red fabric, has recently been found at Mushroom Farm, Braughing in first-century contexts. One sherd of this fabric at Ower, identical in the hand-specimen to the above amphora/jug rim, was found in early first-century contexts. This implies that the material found in the later levels is residual.

The Illustrated Amphorae (fig. 42)
44. Rim and neck of amphora (Dressel 1 – Pascual 1b), from phase 6 (727).
45. Rim of amphora (Dressel 1 – Pascual 1b), from phase 3.
46. Rim of amphora/jug (Campanian), from phase 6 (644).
47. Handle/neck of amphora (Dressel 1 – Pascual 1b), from phase 1 (288C).
48. Handle/neck of amphora (Dressel 1 – Pascual Ib), from phase 1 (533).
49. Slit handle of amphora (Dressel 1 – Pascual Ia), unstratified.
50. Slit handle of amphora (Dressel 1 – Pascual Ia), from phase 6 (727).
51. Slit handle of amphora (Dressel 1 – Pascual Ib), from phase 1 (288B).
52. Slit handle of amphora (Dressel 1 – Pascual Ib), from phase 6 (858A).

THE MORTARIA

Three groups of Mortaria were recognised on the site, on the basis of form and fabric: First-century AD forms, Oxfordshire forms, and a local coarse-ware mortarium. One sherd was unassigned.

1. The First-Century AD Mortaria:
These are almost certainly derived from 1st-century AD contexts, although they were recovered from the later phases of the site (Table 1). They are therefore residual, as was much of the 1st-century AD material as a whole (see above). No obvious source was identified from the macroscopic fabric descriptions (provided by D. F. Williams), but parallels for the two rim forms present could be found in 1st-century AD contexts at Hod Hill (Richmond 1968), Fishbourne (Cunliffe 1971), and Camulodunum (Hawkes and Hull 1947).
53. Flange fragment of mortarium in a very hard creamy-buff fabric. The trituration grits are composed mainly of quartz and quartzite. Common before AD 75; Fishbourne type 141 (Cunliffe 1971, 206-207, fig. 18); (Hawkes and Hull 1947, fig. 53, No. 23). Claudian-Neronian period.
54. Base of mortarium in a very similar fabric to above.
55. A wall-sided mortarium in a very hard light reddish-buff fabric. The trituration grits are composed mainly of quartz, quartzite and sandstone. Fishbourne type 144 (Cunliffe 1971), Augustan-Claudian, in this country: almost always confined to Claudian groups, although a later date is quoted at Camulodunum. Hod Hill, type 2C, 111 (Richmond 1968); mid-1st-century AD.

2. The Oxfordshire Mortaria
Seven sherds of Oxfordshire mortaria were identified on the site. These could be divided into two wares:
    Colour Coated; 2 rims, 1 base, 2 body.
    White Ware; 1 rim, 1 body.
These are fabrics described in detail in Young (1977), and the forms present correspond to Young's catalogue of material. All were recovered from contexts of phase 5 onwards (Table 1).
Colour Coated Ware: Two vessel types were identified from rims: *Young* C97, a wide date range AD 240-400+. *Young* C.100.2, fourth century AD 300-400+. One pedestal base and two body sherds were also recovered.
White Ware: A single vessel type was identified from a rim. One body sherd with trituration grits also occurred: *Young* M22, a wide date range AD 240-400+.

3. A Coarse Ware Mortarium
A single mortarium was characterised by a coarse grey sandy fabric with a dark red-brown core and oxidised surfaces (orange). The surfaces were smooth. Angular flint trituration grits. Probably produced locally, but not BB1 type fabric. The rim, illustrated (fig. 43, 56), derived from a wall-sided mortaria, *Dr. 45*.

TABLE 4: The Stratigraphic Location by Phase of the BB1 (Category 1) Vessel Types in the 3rd-4th century AD. Features and Occupation Horizons (Phases 4, 6 and 7)

		COOKING POTS/JARS					LIDS		BOWLS/DISHES											FLAGONS		BEAKERS	
PHASE	FEATURE	1	2	3	4	5	20	21	22	23	24	25	26	27	28	29	30	31	32	33	34	35	36
4	Kiln/oven 540				12									1		2			4				
4	Ditch silts of 555 above kiln 540		1	5	6		4	1								1		5	5				
6	Kilns 589 and 587 in depression 606	2	3	1	6			1															
6	Gulley 361	6																			3		
6	Pit 644	11		3	7		1	1								10		2	3	1			
7	Floor levels 707.1		9		1		7	2			1	5		2	1	3			3	1			
7	Floor levels 707.3		1	7	1		1	9				1			2	11		1	4				
7	Wall of drier 708; 707.3	2	1																				
7	Steps/Yards 707.3	6	7	7	11		2	3				2			5	4		2	2				
7	Sill wall 707.3			2	2		1	1			1					3			6				
7	Drier 708 infill; 707.4		1	2											1				2				
7	Rubble collapse 707.4	1	4	3	20		6	3			3			1		24	1	5	6	3		2	3
7	Shell Midden tip 87		6	6	52	2	5	4			1			2	1	37	2	5	13	2			
7	Robbed building 905		3	4	9		1	3						2									
7	Building 743			1	7									1		5		1					
7	Robbed Wall 672		2					2											3				
7	Yard 147		3	2	12			3							4	5		2					
7	Building 564	11	16	7	22		7	14							1	15		1	16	1	1		
7	Building 904	2	4	2	28		5	6						1	2	8		1	11	1	1		1
7	Building 906	3	4	1	7		1	1						1		8		1	2				
Vessel type totals			162		205		95						287									20	
Vessel percentages			18%		22%		10%						31%									2%	

· Illustrated Vessels   Vessel Numbers by Diagnostic Sherd Count

The Illustrated Mortaria (fig. 43)
53. Rim of flanged mortaria (1st-century AD), from phase 7 (floor 707).
54. Base of mortaria (1st-century AD), from phase 7 (floor 707).
55. Rim of wall-sided mortaria (1st-century AD), phase 3.
56. Rim of well-sided mortaria (local coarse ware), unstratified.

THE NEW FOREST WARE

Of the fifty-two pieces of New Forest ware recovered from the site, only nine were diagnostic. These were all fine wares in fabrics as described in Fulford (1975). The vessels represented were of the following forms as categorised by Fulford:

F4   Body sherd of flask with barrel body, ladder decoration AD 300-30

F8   Neck and rim of flagon with globular body, narrow neck and plain everted rim AD 300-30

F27-33   Two sherds of indented beaker 4th-century AD

F42   (Fig. 43, 57), Indented beaker with tall body and neck with narrow mouth, decoration not of type illustrated in Fulford 1975, but most similar to F42.4. AD 300-30/40

F63   Two sherds of flanged bowl resembling Dr 38, AD 300-70

F72   Small rim fragment of carinated bowl, AD 325-75

F89   Probably body of bowl with internal flange below rim, AD 270-400

The Illustrated New Forest Ware (fig. 43)
57. Rim of tall-bodied indented beaker with painted shoulder decoration (early 4th-century AD), from phase 7 (564).

The Oxfordshire Ware
Apart from the mortaria only seven other diagnostic sherds of Oxfordshire ware were identified from a total of twelve. These were all colour coated wares in a fabric as described in Young (1977). The six-sherds recovered were of moulded and decorated bowls. All were recovered from contexts of phase 4 onwards (Table 1). The form numbers are as in Young 1977.

c.45.3:   Body sherd of samian form, Dr 31, with rouletting on floor of vessel. AD 270-400+

c.51.2:   The rim of a flanged bowl, copying Dr 38. AD 240-400+

c. 75-84:   Body sherd of necked or carinated bowl with rouletting

c.77:   Body sherd of curved body bowl with white paint decoration. AD 340-400+

c.84:   wall-sided carinated bowl with cordon half-way down wall, and rouletting. AD 350-400+

c.84:   The base of a cordonned bowl with rouletting on either side

OTHER	BASES					HANDLES					DECORATION COOKING POTS/JARS						DECORATION BOWLS/DISHES		BASES	LIDS	WASTERS	(PROBABLE) RESIDUAL FORMS				FORM/GROUP
37	38	39	40	41	42	43	44	45	46	47	48	49	50	51	55	56	58	59	60	61	62	6,7,10-13	8,9	14-19	52-54	
	8		10				1				3	4														
	4		1	1		2	1				2		1				4	1				1	9	6		
	2	1	2					1			3	3							1				8	1	1	
	1	2	3				i																1	11	7	
	4	6	3			1		1			2							5	1				7			
i	6	5	3				1				9	1		4			2					i	3	2		
	9		8								3	12	3	2			1	8				2	2			
														1								i				
	1										1						1				4	1	1			
	1		2			1	1												1	1						
	2		1			1					4						1	1	1	1	2					
	10		6	1			1	1		2	20	8	2	i	1		2	3				2			1	
	26		23			2	5			i	1	21	14	4			1	13	8	8	7	3	4			
	10	3	2				1		1		1		2								3	16	4	5	
	2											1					4	2								
			4																				1			
	3	3	6							i	11	24	2		1		2	3				1	1	3		
i	23	3	13			1	1				3	23	9	6			2	7	5	1		5	14	5		
	6	1	i	3		2	2				1	5	4	2		2	2	6	2			2	5	1		
i	5		2			1	1					3	1				2		1			i	4	1		VESSEL TOTAL
3																								147		918
1%																								16%		100%

of a very low cordon just above a rounded carination to a Pedestalled base, AD 350-400+

THE BLACK BURNISHED COARSE WARES

The remaining coarse ware pottery was made locally, and was of a distinctive type; classified on the basis of fabric, finish and vessel form, and known as Black Burnished (Category 1).

The fabric, which showed a wide variation in terms of quartz grain size and impurities (chalk, limestone, shale and ironstone), was not analysed in detail and no attempt was made to assess any possible variations in the fabric through time. The fabric was in general terms taken to conform to that described by Farrar (1973 and 1977), and analysed by Williams (1977). A more detailed visual description of the fabric of each illustrated sherd can be found in the level III archive. A petrological comparison with the briquetage was carried out by David Williams (see following). Although it is likely that this pottery was made in the immediate vicinity of the excavation area (see site report) no waster tips were found and few waster pieces (Tables 3 and 4). Of the sherds illustrated perhaps vessels 68 and 109 may have been 'wasters' on the basis of their oxidised, cracked and warped bodies and surfaces. Vessels 65, 66, 76, 78, 109, 110, 113, 137, 161-163, 187, 189 and 193 (figs. 44-50) were substantially oxidised to a reddish-brown. Vessel 113 may have been deliberately finished to a red-brown colour. However in general terms the majority of the material conformed to a dark-grey reduced core with dark red-brown oxidised margins. Surfaces were in general black and burnished, but often had a variation in colour across them; from grey-white to buff and oxidised red-brown.

The surface treatment was also not analysed in detail, and has not been depicted in the illustration (figs. 44-50), unless it is an intrinsic part of a decorative motif, e.g. the burnished lines of hoop, or lattice decoration, or the treatment of whole surfaces (e.g. dish fig. 48, 146). The technique of burnishing has been described in detail by Farrar (1973), and so will not be discussed in full for this assemblage. However it is worth making the following observations:

i the material from the pre-conquest groups was more evenly and carefully burnished, in particular the imitations of Gallo-Belgic bowls (fig. 47, 108-116), than the later material.

ii the later material from phase 7 was frequently wiped or smoothed, both internally and externally, with a 'rag', a technique not noted in the pre-conquest assemblage.

iii wheel-finished material was only noted in phase 7, although one of the Gallo-Belgic imitations of the pre-conquest group (fig. 47,

113) is so finely made that it could well have been wheel-finished.

iv some of the later material was notably slipped or slurry-burnished. This technique could not always be distinguished, but was notable in vessels 65, 66, 68 and 69 (fig. 45), amongst others.

v internal burnishing on jars and closed vessels tended to be applied well below the rim in the pre-conquest groups. In the later groups burnishing sometimes ended between the lip and the base of the neck, although the interior was often better treated and more even, having been in part wiped when wheel-finished.

The vessel forms and types are summarised in tables 3 and 4, and described in the catalogue. They fall into two groups:

i Those derived from the pre-conquest occupation; sealed groups occurred in the ditches and pits of phases 1 and 2, and in the old occupation levels within the soil accumulation of phase 3. Large quantities of this pre-conquest material was residual in later phases (Table 3).

ii Those derived from the building complex of phases 4-7, the most clearly stratified group occurred in the phase 7 complex, and in particular the sequence in the development and abandonment of building (707) (Table 4).

The illustration of this type series are depicted in figs 44-50. The illustrations have been selected where possible from well stratified groups, and in particular from ditch (288) B and C, building (707), building (904), and kiln (540). Material which was very badly stratified or considerably disturbed – from levels across yard (441) and building (909), road levels (727), soil accumulation levels below (142), and post-Roman agricultural disturbance – was not analysed in detail since the groups were too mixed. No forms outside that of the type series were noted in these levels, apart from a single vessel 124. However a basic analysis and sherd count for all contexts was carried out, and this is stored in the Level III archive.

The Pre-Conquest Group:
This group of material was derived from the ditches and pits of phases 1 and 2, and the residual occupation levels sealed with and under the phase 3 soil accumulation. This group has been firmly placed in the pre-conquest period by a detailed examination of the associated fine-wares and amphorae. It was also associated with pre-conquest brooch types. This group of vessels is summarised with reference to the illustrated type series in Table 3, and can best be compared with the groups from *Tollard Royal* (Wainwright 1968), *Gussage All Saints* (Wainwright 1979), *Marnhull* (Williams 1950), *Maiden Castle* (Wheeler 1943), and *Hengistbury Head* (Bushe-Fox 1915). This group should also be viewed in a wider regional context (Cunliffe 1974), and in relation to local Purbeck pottery and other industries, (Farrar, 1977). Current excavations at Hengistbury Head, (Cunliffe 1980 and 1981), and subsequent research will also provide additional links with which it will be possible to trace the origins and development of the Ower assemblage and pottery industry, in particular its relationship to the Continental pottery types. The general description of the assemblage from Ower does not include exhaustive parallels. These should be sought by the reader within those assemblages cited above.

Within the stratified assemblage the division between cooking-pots, jars, and open bowls was roughly equal (Table 3), and in addition there were a few beakers, possible lids, and a straight rim to a dish (?) (vessel 181).

The cooking pots/jars were primarily of the upright bead-rim (type 1) with full rounded shoulders (fig. 44, 58). These vessels were probably in general undecorated, apart from one with zig-zag pattern on the neck (fig. 44, 59). However one type of body decoration can perhaps be associated with this vessel type; the hoop (fig. 50, 193). Some of these vessels probably had countersunk handles (as on vessel 96) and all had flat bases, although the lack of bases in the ditch silts of (288) is problematical, unless they all had a secondary use e.g. for spindlewhorls. Other decorative forms were probably confined to storage jars with bead and developed bead-rims. Cooking pots/jars with straight, slightly everted rims (type 6) also occurred in well-sealed pre-conquest levels, although they were few in number (fig. 45, 73-74). A residual vessel of this type (fig. 45, 76), all-over burnished with a squiggle and line decoration superimposed, was probably residual in a later context. Four examples of slightly everted or rolled-over rims (types 2 and 3) also occurred in 1st-century deposits, but these may be present as a result of later disturbance, possibly animal.

Jars/bowls were characterised by flat-top rims (type 7; fig. 44, 77 and 78) and a variety of bead-rims and developed bead-rim forms (types 8-13), sometimes with a double bead (type 10), and sometimes developed into a rolled-over rim and deep channel (type

12). Well stratified examples of all these are illustrated in; fig. 46, 77 and 78 (type 7); fig. 46, 80-82 and 84 (type 8); fig. 46, 85-86 (type 9); fig. 46, 87 (type 10); fig. 46, 89 and 90 (type 11); fig. 46, 93 and 94 (type 12); fig. 46, 95-97 (type 13). Most of these vessels were undecorated, but a variety of decorative types did occur. Two types of decoration could be directly associated with these well-stratified examples; irregular line on unburnished zone (fig. 46, 81), and complex squirl and zig-zag band on a remarkable unburnished vessel (fig. 46, 80), a decorative type which can perhaps be best described as a free interpretation of decorative motifs from the Glastonbury series, (Wheeler 1943). Other well-stratified decorative motifs which probably also belong to this type of vessel include; regular acute lattice on unburnished decorative zone (as on later vessel fig. 44, 64); squiggle and line decoration (as on residual vessel 76, fig. 44). Shell-impressed decoration may also perhaps derive from this period. Vessels of this type which occur residually in later contexts exhibit one other decorative variation; irregular lattice as on vessel 83. Countersunk handles occur with a well-stratified vessel 96, which also shows that these vessels had flat bases, but they probably also occurred with pedestal bases, particularly where the vessel was of bowl proportion (Wheeler 1943, 234).

Open bowl forms (types 14-19) were less common (26% of assemblage), but occurred in a profusion of forms, some of which may have been used as lids (types 18-20). The commonest was the bead rim form (type 14; fig. 47, 99). The remainder can be considered as Gallo-Belgic imitations (fig. 47, 100-124). These vessels do not occur in great numbers in the published assemblages of the type-sites mentioned above. *Maiden Castle* has bead-lipped (type 14) examples and groove-lipped (type 15) examples, and there are plain platter-types at *Gussage*. At *Hengistbury* a wider range is known. It is likely that some of these examples are copies of the contemporary continental imports, perhaps the arretine example (fig. 39, 6) and samian forms *Drag.* 18 (fig. 47, 14). Lids (type 19) can be found at *Maiden Castle*, where they are decorated (Wheeler 1943, 234). These small bowls/platters would have all had ring or pedestal bases and the lids a neat solid pedestal top (as in the later examples fig. 47, 120 and 121).

Good examples of well-stratified beakers or tankards are few, and those illustrated have been taken from contexts with later material. These have been placed under three headings based on available rim forms; lipped and straight-sided beakers/jars (type 34); straight-sided beakers/cups and tankards (type 35); and small round-bodied jars and butt-beakers (type 36). None of the latter category occurred in securely dated pre-conquest deposits. The examples of lipped and straight-sided beakers derived from pre-conquest levels, and are illustrated in fig. 49, 170-172, 174 and 176-179. Examples of the tankard can be found at *Maiden Castle*, together with a funnel shaped pot reminiscent of vessel rim 171. The butt-beaker (fig. 49, 170) is a plain copy of more sophisticated types. The pedestal cordoned beaker (fig. 49, 173) may be a loose copy of samian form *Ritterling* 9 (although there are no beads, there is an external groove half-way down the wall), and this is a form rare after AD 60, but may be a copy of a later Oxford-type coarse ware 042 (Young 1977), in which case it belongs to the 3rd-4th century AD.

The only other well-stratified vessel form was a crude straight-sided unburnished thumb-pot, (?) dish (fig., 49, 181).

It is possible that other vessels belong to this pre-conquest group, but have become inextricably mixed with the later occupation material. This particular group of stratified coarse wares in the phase 1 and 2 ditches can be securely dated to the period of perhaps 25 BC-43 AD. However it is clear that these types will have continued in use in the post-conquest period. It is also perhaps significant that there are none of the earlier Hengistbury vessel types or haematite-coated wares at Ower.

The Romano-British BB1 (3rd-4th century AD) Group:
At present it is difficult to give close date ranges to BB1 coarse wares in Dorset, since the main dating has been applied to stratified material in Northern Britain (Gillam 1976). It is likely that earlier dates, or at least different date ranges, could apply in Dorset which was the source of this pottery. However until well stratified sequences have been excavated in urban situations (e.g. Dorchester, *Durnovaria*), the dating based on Gillam must be treated with caution, although recource has been made to Gillam in the first instance.

The material from the later occupation complex is less securely dated than the earlier one because of the problem of residual material, and the lack of closed sequences. However the group of coarse wares as a whole can perhaps be best placed in the late 2nd-4th centuries AD. This has initially been founded on the basis that there was an almost complete absence of bead rim or flat top-flanged bowls with chamfered or carinated bases (Gillam (1976) types 50-52, types 34-41, and types 54-57), although the remains of a single chamfered vessel did survive from (809) in the soil accumulation below building (707) (Phase 3). There were a few of the incipient flanged bowl types with flat bases and hoop decoration (Gillam (1976) types 42-44), (fig. 48, 152 type 31), and also a number of early bowl and dish types with flat bases and acute lattice and irregular line decoration; straight rim type 24 (Gillam (1976) types 75 and 76), bead rim type 27 (Gillam (1976) types 68-74), flat flanged rim type 28 (Gillam (1976) types 58-66), straight rim type 29 (Gillam (1976) types 77, 79-81, 83-88). This paucity or near absence of 2nd century AD material was also noted by Farrar (1977, 212); but he suggests that this vessel type was simply not made in the kilns at Ower, and suggests that the jars and cook-pots

present could fill the apparent gap in occupation, and that occupation was in reality continuous. This might well be the case, and occupation of some sort in the 2nd century was apparent here and in other areas of the site. However the acute lattice jar (fig. 44, 64) which was found in the foundation of building (707) could be of any date to the mid-third century AD.

Within the pottery assemblage there are flanged bowls (Type 32; 153-157), and straight-walled dishes (type 29; fig. 48, 146-150); both with hoop decoration. The former are almost universally ascribed to the late second – early third century AD, Gillam (1976), although Dorset dates could well be earlier.

The frequent presence of New Forest and Oxford types in the building occupation horizon also lends weight to a building complex primarily dating to the 3rd-4th century AD. In addition the pedestal beaker (fig. 49, 173), although reminiscent of a 1st century AD

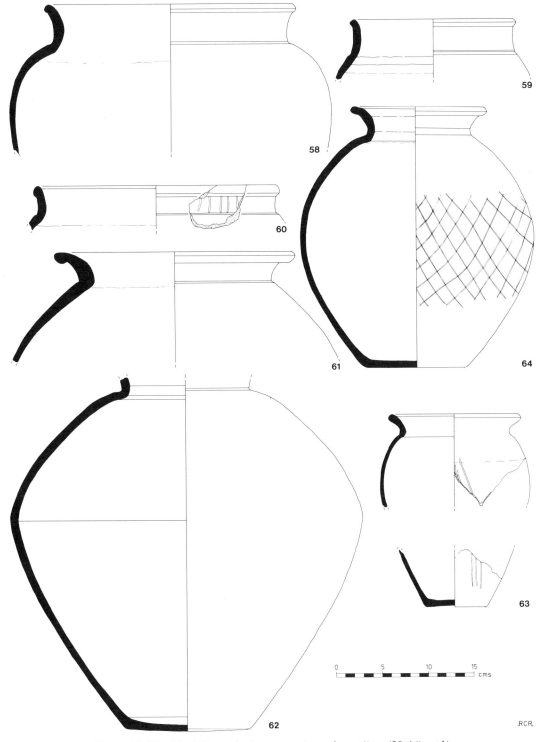

Figure 44. The Black Burnished category 1, cook pots/jars (58-64), at ¼.

samian type, could also be a plain copy of an Oxford pedestal bowl or New Forest pedestal cup (Oxford: Young (1977) 042.2, New Forest: Fulford (1975) 53.9). The flagon neck (fig. 49, 161) may also perhaps be taken as the base of a candlestick which can be found in the New Forest assemblage, (Fulford 1975, type 96), and also the droop flanged bowl *Drag* 38, (Fulford 1975, type 63). These and other vessel forms e.g. the skillet handles (fig. 51, 191 and 192) are not well known in BB1 fabric, and are at present unique, although exhaustive parallel searching has not been carried out.

The vessel types and forms present are summarised in Table 4, and the typical form types illustrated in figs. 44-50 in relationship to the vessel type catalogue.

To summarise: In general the preponderance of material suggests a 3rd-4th century AD date for the main habitation phase, although it is clear that this occupation has been superimposed on and into earlier horizons which owe their inception to the early 1st century AD settlement. The earliest building (post-pad phase of 707) with its acute lattice 'foundation vessel' may be of the 2nd century AD, but its continuous adaptation and the pottery associated with its use and infilling make a later date for this earliest building of phase 7 more likely.

The Illustrated Black-Burnished Coarse Wares
Type 1. Cooking pots/jars with upright or slightly everted rim, 1st century AD.
58.   From 870 in ditch 858, Phase 1/2.
59.   From 563 in P-Roman disturbance, Phase 8.
60.   From 178 in ditch 288A, Phase 6.

Type 2. Jars with everted rims, 2nd century AD onwards.
61.   From 87, 135 in tip 87, Phase 7.
62.   From 193, in sill wall building 905, Phase 7.
63.   From 261 in P-Roman disturbance pit, Phase 8.

Type 3. Jars with outward flaring rim from shoulder with beaded lip, 2nd century AD onwards.
64.   From 149 in foundation 707.1, Phase 7.
65.   From 709 in Dryer 708, Phase 7.

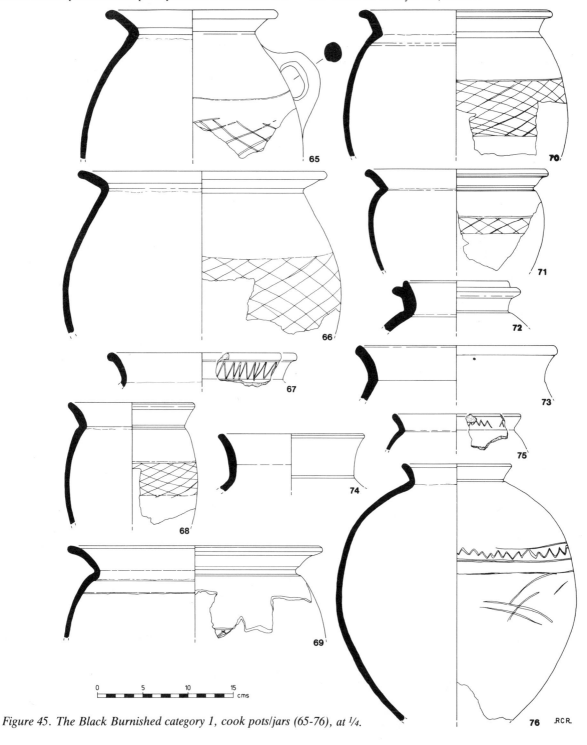

Figure 45. The Black Burnished category 1, cook pots/jars (65-76), at ¼.

66. From 819 in Dryer 708, Phase 7.
67. From 492 in Rubble collapse 904, Phase 7.

Type 4. Jars with outward flaring rim, with beaded lip nearly overhanging side of vessel, 3rd century AD onwards.
68. From 135 in tip 87, Phase 7.
69. From 123 in tip 87, Phase 7.
70. From 532 in kiln/oven 540, Phase 7.
71. From 606 with kiln/ovens 589 and 578, Phase 6.

Type 5. Jars with flanged neck, 3rd century AD onwards.
72. From 123 in tip 87, Phase 7.

Type 6. Jars with straight rim slightly everted, 1st century AD onwards.
73. From 794 in soil accumulation, Phase 3.

74. From 634 in ditch 288C, Phase 1.
75. From 709 in dryer 708, Phase 7.
76. From 89 in rubble collapse 707.4, Phase 7.

Type 7. Jars with flat top rim, 1st century AD.
77. From 374 in ditch 288B, Phase 7.
78. From 374 in ditch 288B, Phase 1.
79. From 521 in ditch 288A, Phase 6.

Type 8. Jars/bowls with bead rim and deep rounded shoulders, 1st century AD.
80. From 634 in ditch 288C, Phase 1.
81. From 631 in ditch 288B, Phase 1.
82. From 320 in ditch 288B, Phase 1.
83. From 255 in post-Roman robbing 261, Phase 8.

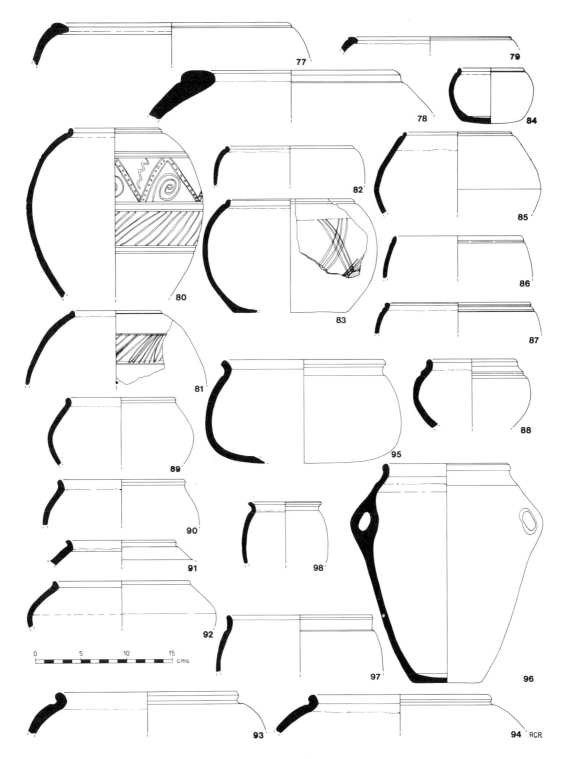

Figure 46. The Black Burnished category 1, cook pots/jars (77-79), jars and bowls with constricted mouths (80-98), at ¹/₄.

84.   From 316 in ditch 288B, Phase 1.

Type 9. Jars/bowls with bead rims with straight and 'carinated' shoulders, 1st century AD.
85.   From 330 in ditch 288B, Phase 1.
86.   From 773 in soil accumulation, Phase 3.

Type 10. Jars/bowls with double channelled bead, 1st century AD.
87.   From 349 in pit 389, Phase 1/2.
88.   From 295 in ditch 343I, Phase 2.

Type 11. Jars/bowls with developed bead rim and deep rounded shoulders, 1st century AD.
89.   From 214 in ditch 288B, Phase 1.
90.   From 648 in ditch 288B, Phase 1.
91.   From 80 in rubble collapse 707.4, Phase 7.
92.   From 817 in soil accumulation, Phase 3.

Type 12. Jars/bowls with rolled over rim and channel, and deep rounded shoulders, 1st century AD.
93.   From 634 in ditch 288C, Phase 1.
94.   From 283 in ditch 288B, Phase 1.

Type 13. Jars/bowls with developed bead or pulled up rim, and slight shoulders, 1st century AD.
95.   From 330 in ditch 288B, Phase 1.
96.   From 330 in ditch 288B, Phase 1.
97.   From 418 in ditch 288C, Phase 1.
98.   From 583 in building 906, Phase 7.

Type 14. Open bowls with bead rims, 1st century AD.
99.   From 648 in ditch 288B, Phase 1.

Type 15. Open bowls with flattened rims, Gallo-Belgic copy, 1st century AD.

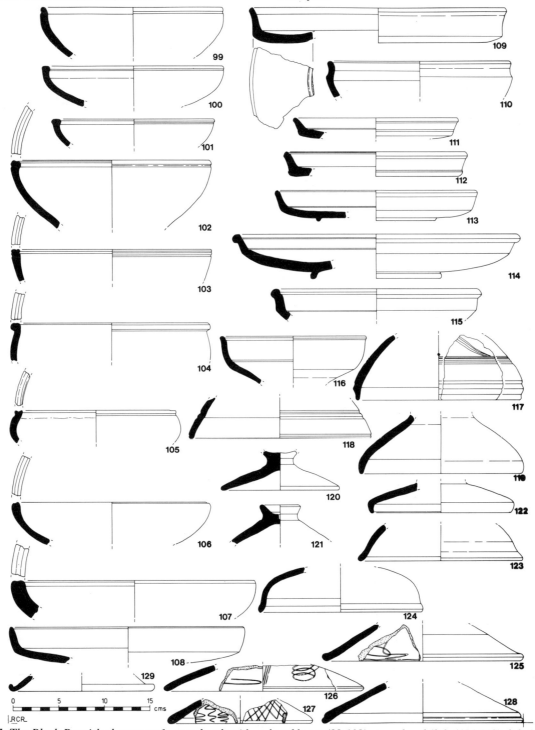

Figure 47. The Black Burnished category 1, open bowls with pedestal bases (99-108), open bowls/lids (116-118), lids (119-129), at ¼.

100. From 296 in ditch 343IC, Phase 1.
101. From 373 in ditch 288C, Phase 1.

Type 16. Open bowls with grooved lips, Gallo-Belgic copy, 1st century AD.
102. From 870, in pit 858, Phase 1.
103. From 831, soil accumulation, Phase 3.
104. From 521, in ditch 288A, Phase 6.
105. From 257, in soil accumulation, Phase 3.
106. From 263, in ditch 288B, Phase 1.
107. From 318, in ditch 288B, Phase 1.

Type 17. Open bowls with carinated body, Gallo-Belgic copy, 1st century AD.
108. From 283, in ditch 288C, Phase 1.
109. From 367, in ditch 288C, Phase 1.

110. From 335, in ditch 343 IIB, Phase 1.
111. From 521, in ditch 288A, Phase 6.
112. From 464, in ditch 343 IIB, Phase 1.
113. From 424, in soil accumulation, Phase 3.
114. From 289/230, in ditch 288B, Phase 1.
115. From 773, in soil accumulation, Phase 3.
116. From 834, in soil accumulation, Phase 3.

Type 18. Deep open bowls/lids with grooved and beaded sides, 1st century AD.
117. From 349, in ditch 343 IIB, Phase 2.
118. From 719, in soil accumulation, Phase 3.

Type 19. Deep open bowls/lids, no decoration, 1st century AD.
119. From 381, in ditch 288B, Phase 1.

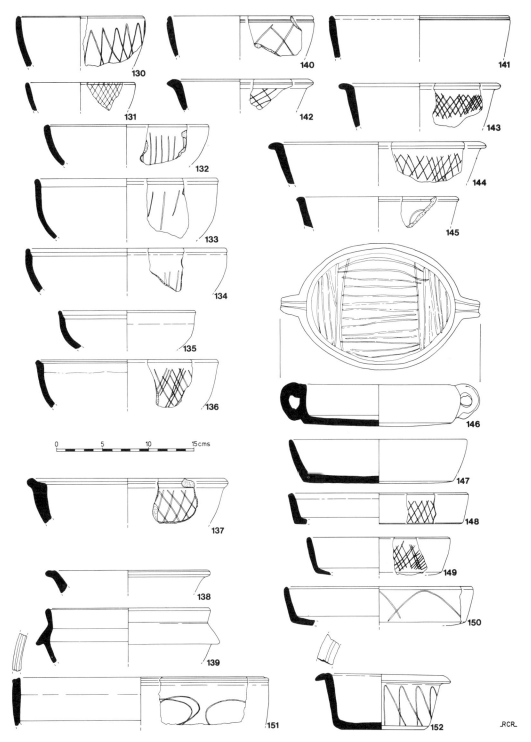

Figure 48. The Black Burnished category 1, Bowls/dishes (130-152), at ¹/₄.

Type 20. Deep lids with convex or straight sides and down turned lips, 1st century AD bowl/lid types, 3rd-4th century AD lid types.
120. From 155, in building 905, Phase 7.
121. From 661, in rubble collapse 707.4, Phase 7.
122. From 584, in rubble collapse 904, Phase 7.
123. From 460, in ditch 343 IIB, Phase 7.
124. From 603, in soil accumulation below 142, Phase 3.

Type 21. Plain lids with out-turned or up-turned lips. 3rd century AD onwards.
125. From 174, in robbed building 905, Phase 7.
126. From 664, in tip 87, Phase 7.
127. From 704, ditch (?) to west of roadway 727, Phase 6.
128. From 667, sill wall to 707.3, Phase 7.

129. From 559, building collapse 564, Phase 7.

Type 22. Upright bead rim bowls/dishes with chamfered or carinated base, Gillam (1976) types 50-52, 2nd century AD.
No certain examples.

Type 23. Upright flat top flanged bowls/dishes chamfered or 'carinated' at base, Gillam (1976) types 34-41, 54-57, 2nd century AD.
No certain examples.

Type 24. Bowls/dishes with straight plain upright rim, and slightly rounded bodies possible chamfered or carinated at base. Gillam (1976) types 75-76. Examples 132 and 133 may be lids. 2nd

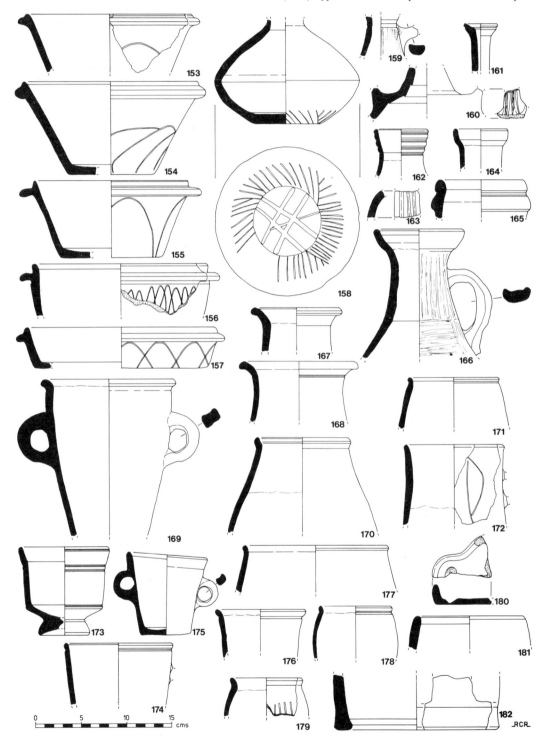

Figure 49. The Black Burnished category 1, Bowls/dishes (153-157), flagons (158-168), beakers/jars (169-172), beakers/cups, tankards (173-176), round-bodied beakers (177-179), Lamp cresset (180), plain inturned vessel (181), crenallated vessel (182), at ¹/₄.

century-3rd century AD.

130. From 734, in sill wall to 707.3, Phase 7.
131. From 674, in rubble collapse 707.4, Phase 7.
132. From 732, in soil accumulation below 707, Phase 3.
133. From 669, in tip 87, Phase 7.

Type 25. Bowls/dishes with internal groove, and slightly rounded bodies, possibly chamfered or carinated at base, possibly lids. 2nd century-3rd century AD.

134. From 753, steps/yards with 707.3, Phase 7.
135. From 792, soil accumulation below 707, Phase 7.
136. From 521, in ditch 288A, Phase 6.
137. From 692, steps/yards with 707.3, Phase 7.
138. From 715, floor level of 707.3, Phase 7.

Type 26. Round bodied bowl with dropped flange, *Drag* 38, 3rd-4th century AD.

139. From 575/492, in building collapse 904, Phase 7.

Type 27. Bowl/dish with straight side and bead lip or external groove(s). Gillam type (1976) 68-74, 2nd century–4th century AD.

140. From 656, with building 743 and yards, Phase 7.
141. From 669, infill tip 87, Phase 7.

Type 28. Bowl/dish with straight side and flat-flanged rim. Gillam (1976) types 58, 60-66, mid-late 2nd century AD.

142. From 492, in building 904, Phase 7.
143. From 160, in Yard 147, Phase 7.
144. From 812, in dryer 708, Phase 7.
145. From 664, infill tip 87, Phase 7.

Type 29. Bowl/dish straight side and rim, sometimes oval. Gillam (1976) type 77, 79-81, 83-88. 3rd century AD.

146. From 653/548, in pit 644A, Phase 6.
147. From 593, in building 906, Phase 7.
148. From 543, on Yard 147, Phase 7.
149. From 692, steps and yards to building 707.3, Phase 7.
150. From 149, floor to building 707.3, Phase 7.

Type 30. Bowl/dish with straight side and grooved lip or internal channel, probably 3rd-4th century AD.

151. From 664/123, infill tip 87, Phase 7.

Type 31. Bowl/dish with straight sides and incipient flange. Gillam (1976) type 42-44. Late 2nd century AD-3rd century AD.

152. From 403/655, with building 743, Phase 7.

Type 32. Bowl/dish with straight sides and dropped external flange. Gillam (1976) types 45-49, 3rd-4th century AD.

153. From 575, in collapse building 904, Phase 7.
154. From 575, in collapse building 904, Phase 7.
155. From 709, in drier 708, Phase 7.
156. From 149, on floor level building 707.3, Phase 7.
157. From 661, in rubble collapse 707.4, Phase 7.

Type 33. Flagons/Jugs (various), some can be related to New Forest and Oxfordshire forms, 3rd-4th century AD, whilst others, e.g. fig. 20, 162 are copies of 1st century AD ring necked flagons (refer Timby fig. 12, 28).

158. From 135, in infill tip 87, Phase 7.
159. From 548, in pit 644, Phase 6.
160. From 661, rubble collapse 707.4, Phase 7.
161. From 542, in building 904, Phase 7.
162. From 107, in Post-Roman disturbance, Phase 8.
163. From 107, in Post-Roman disturbance, Phase 8.
164. From 568, in Post-Roman disturbance, Phase 8.
165. From 678, in rubble collapse of 707.4, Phase 7.
166. From 661, in rubble collapse of 707.4, Phase 7.
167. From 97, in Post-Roman disturbance, Phase 8.
168. From 774, in infill tip 87, Phase 7.

Type 34. Lipped and straight sided beakers/jars. Examples 170-171 resemble butt beakers, 1st century AD. Example 169, 3rd century AD.

169. From 584/492, in rubble collapse 904, Phase 7.
170. From 464/307, in ditch 343 I, Phase 2.
171. From 627, in ditch 288A, Phase 6.
172. From 183, in building 564, Phase 7.

Type 35. Straight-sided beakers/cups, tankards. Example 173 may

be intrusive at this level and copy of New Forest/Oxfordshire type 042 (3rd-4th century AD), Example 174 tankard *Maiden Castle* (1st century AD), Example 175 probably 3rd-4th century AD, Example 176 1st century AD tankard type.

173. From 240, in ditch 343 I, Phase 2.
174. From 300, in ditch 288B, Phase 1.
175. From 734, in rubble of building 707.4, Phase 7.
176. From 661, in rubble of building 707.4, Phase 7.

Type 36. Small jars. Example 177 probably 1st century AD butt beaker type. Examples 178, 179 probably 3rd century-4th century AD.

177. From 627, in ditch 288A, Phase 6.
178. From 661, in rubble collapse 707.4, Phase 7.
179. From 584, in rubble collapse 904, Phase 7.

Type 37. Miscellaneous vessels. Example 180 small lamp crescent (probably 3rd-4th century AD), Example 181 small round bodied bowl unburnished (1st century AD), Example 182 crenellated vessel possibly a lantern (probably 3rd-4th century AD). Example 183 mixing bowl/mortaria (?) (probably 3rd-4th century AD). Example 184 perforated colander (possibly 3rd-4th century AD).

180. From 97, in Post-Roman disturbance, Phase 8.
181. From 318, in ditch 288B, Phase 1.
182. From 583, in building 906, Phase 7.
183. From 774, in accumulation levels below 707.4, Phase 3.
184. From 85, in rubble collapse 564, phase 7.

Type 38. Flat cooking pot/jar bases, unburnished and side of vessel slashed internally 1st-4th century AD. Refer 62-64, 83, 96.

Type 39. Moulded jar bases, 1st century AD.
185. From 521, in ditch 288A, Phase 6.

Type 40. Pedestal bases, Example 186 with (?) omphalos (possibly 1st century AD), Example 181, exaggerated 1st century AD type.

186. From 575 rubble collapse 904, Phase 7.
187. From 217, in ditch 343 I, Phase 3. Other examples 113 and 114; 173.

Type 41. Bowl/dish flat bases, burnished and/or wiped both sides. Refer 146-150, 152-155, 157.

Type 42. Secondary pierced bases including those reused as (?) spindle whorls.

Type 43. Applied and countersunk handles. Refer 65, Fig. 17, 96.

Type 44. Applied handle to body of vessel.
188. From 197, in gulley 361, Phase 6.
Refer also 166, 172 and 175.

Type 45. Applied handle to rim of vessel. Refer 146.

Type 46. Lid handles (refer also pedestal base eg. Fig. 20, 173). Refer 120 and 121.

Type 47. Other handle types, Example 189 cylinder handle (1st century AD). Example 190 dropped flange (4th century AD, refer also 139; 153-157). Examples 191-192 skillet handles ((?) 4th century AD).

189. From 464, in ditch 343 IIC, Phase 2.
190. From 719, in soil accumulation below 707, Phase 3.
191. From 147, in Yard 147, Phase 7.
192. From 21, in infill tip 87, Phase 7.

Type 48. Acute lattice decoration on cook pots/jars. Gillam (1976) types 1-6 (1st-2nd century AD). Refer 64.

Type 49. Obtuse lattice decoration on cook pots/jars. Gillam (1976) types 7 and 8 (3rd century AD). Refer 66.

Type 50. Obtuse lattice decoration with burnished border line on upper edge of decorative zone on cook pots/jars Gillam (1976) type 9-11 (4th century AD). Refer 65, and 66, 68-71.

Type 51. Irregular acute lattice on cook pots/jars Gillam (1976) types 30-32 (1st-2nd century AD). Refer 63; 83.

Type 52. Squiggle and/or line, irregular and regular decoration on cook pots/jars. (1st century AD). Refer 63; 76; 80 and 81.

Type 53. Triangle and stabbed decoration on cook pots/jars (1st century AD). Refer 80.

Type 54. Hoop decoration on cook pots/jars (1st century AD) 193. From 374, in ditch 288B, Phase 1.

Type 55. Regular ripple decoration on cook pots/jars (4th century AD).
194. From 661, in rubble collapse 707, Phase 7.
195. From 282, in ditch 288A, Phase 6.

Type 56. Decoration on neck of jars/cook pots (usually zig-zag or line (1st century-2nd century AD)). Refer 60; 75.

Type 57. Shell impressed decoration on cook pots/jars ((?) 1st century AD).
196. From 336, in ditch 343 IIA, Phase 2.
197. From 357, in ditch 288, Phase 6.

Type 58. Acute lattice decoration on bowls/dishes, Gillam (1976) types 53-59 (2nd century AD). Refer 131 and 136-137, 142-144, 148-149.

Type 59. Hoop decoration on bowls/dishes, Gillam (1976) types 42-49, 65, 71-81 (3rd-4th century AD). Refer 130, 140, 145, 150-152, 153-157.

Type 60. Decorated bases of dishes/bowls, Gillam (1976) type 73 and 79, and other example as illustrated. Refer 146.

Type 61. Decorated lids. Refer 117, and 125-127.

Type 62. Waster type sherds where the vessel is warped, overfired, oxidised and surface cracked. Refer Table 3 and Vessels 68 and 109.

THE BRIQUETAGE AND KILN MATERIAL

JOHN HAWKES

The stratigraphic distribution of the briquetage, kiln material and other burnt clay is summarised in Table 5. It is apparent that activities generally associated with this type of material, e.g. salt extraction and perhaps pottery production, are concentrated in the 3rd-4th century AD complex. The fragmentary nature of the briquetage and the lack of *in situ* kiln furniture from this site also

limits interpretation of this material. The lack of comparable material in primary contexts from other sites in the Isle of Purbeck also makes generalisation difficult.

Within the vessel briquetage there was a considerable range of fabric, varying from a tile-like untempered clay to heavily tempered examples reminiscent of BB1. The shale and mudstone noted in the petrological analysis (see following) were only rarely detectable, and the variation within individual large sherds was such that any distinction on the grounds of inclusions was likely to be invalid.

The material from Ower has therefore only been presented in two morphological typologies, on the basis of vessel rims and bases, and kiln furniture (bar) cross-sections.

Vessel Material: Most vessels appear to have been coil built and then finger smoothed, although the folding of the clay within the clean breaks suggests that some of the larger vessels may have been pulled or slab-built. Wire or knife marks are frequently seen on the exterior of sherds. The typology of the rims and bases present is summarised in the following, and the types are illustrated in fig. 51, 198-204.

Type 1 rims – plain but usually rounded, occasionally showing evidence of folding and consequently assumed to be hand finished. No evidence for wire or knife trimming (fig. 22, 198-200).

Type 2 rims – knife or wire trimmed, flat and often burnished (fig. 51, 201 and 202).

Type 1 bases – plain but usually slightly indented above the angle, so making them distinguishable in theory from non-rim corner sherds, of which no examples were noted (fig. 51, 203).

Type 2 bases – splayed or protruding (fig. 51, 204).

It was not possible to correlate rims to bases, by means of reconstruction or wall thickness measurements. However the latter measurements did indicate that type 2 rims were often associated with thinner vessels.

The relationship of this typology and that constructed for Dorset briquetage by Farrar (1975) was not readily apparent, although 'Fitzworth troughs' were certainly present, but other vessels may be pans, cut cylinders etc. Neither was it possible to understand any chronological developments.

Perhaps only one aspect of an industry was visible at Ower. Although the robust vessels were of a type suitable for brine boiling (Farrar 1962), they are equally well adapted to the rigours of transportation (although rather heavy compared to the better constructed and more useful BB1 jars etc). The fabric of some of these vessels is such that they would not attract attention amongst an inland assemblage of mid- to late Romano-British pot.

Kiln furniture: The 27 pieces of kiln furniture could all be classified as bars, but none were *in situ*. In addition quantities of undiagnostic burnt clay with no specific structure may be derived from kiln lining. The fabrics were either standard vessel fabric or

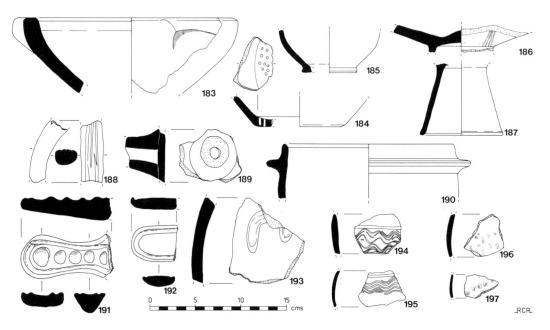

Figure 50. Black Burnished category 1, bowl/mortar (183), perforated vessel (184), bases (185-187), handles (188-192), decoration (193-197), 1:4.

untempered (refer Level III archive). The typology of the kiln-bars based on cross section is summarised following, and the types are illustrated in fig. 31, 205-208:

Type A – Circular or sub-circular in section, including hand moulded and irregular shapes. All complete examples have flattened bases, and are analogous to Farrar's 'kiln prop' group (Farrar 1975), (205).

Type B – Square or sub-square in section, often showing (?decorative) finger impressions along the angles, or stab marks along one of the surfaces. Function uncertain, possibly bars or vertical members (206).

Type C – Rectangular in section, often tapering to a rounded end. Almost certainly kiln-bars. The illustrated example was recovered from the neck of dryer (708), 207.

Type D – A single irregular 'socketted' lump of fired clay, apparently complete. Function uncertain, 208.

PETROLOGICAL ANALYSIS OF THE POTTERY AND CLAYS

JANE TIMBY AND D. F. WILLIAMS, Ph.D.

Thin sectioning and microscopic examination of three groups of material from the pottery assemblage were carried out at Southampton University, as part of a Ph.D. Thesis (J. Timby), and as part of the work programme of the Department of the Environment's Ceramic Petrology Project (D. F. Williams). The detailed descriptions of the thin sections can be found in the Level III Archive and in the Department of Archaeology, Southampton University. The conclusions from thin sectioning are summarised here.

The Early Samian (D. F. Williams):
Nine sherds from the samian assemblage were thin sectioned and

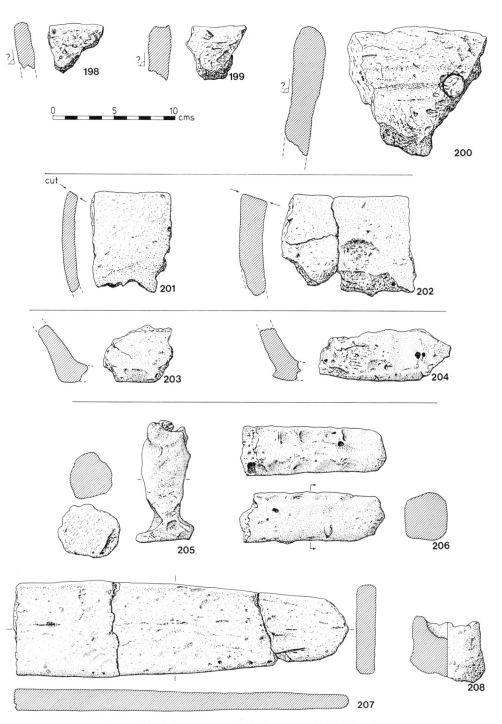

Figure 51. Briquetage and kiln furniture (198-208), 1:3.

BRIQUETAGE

KILN FURNITURE

DATED PHASE DESCRIPTION	PHASE Nos.	RIM SHERDS						BODY SHERDS		BASE SHERDS						TOTAL %				KILN FURNITURE							
		1		2		TOTAL				1		2		TOTAL		TOTAL				A	B	C	D	Unassigned	Totals		
		No.	Wt.	No.	Wt.	No.	Wt.	No.	Wt.	No.	Wt.	No.	Wt.	No.	Wt.	No.	Wt.	No.%	Wt.%							No.	Wt.
1st c. AD pits and ditches	1-2	–	–	–	–	–	–	44	234	2	22	–	–	2	22	46	256	2	1	–	–	–	–	–	–	21	142
1st c.-2nd c. AD soil accumulation	3	1	37	–	–	1	37	228	1754	1	45	–	–	1	45	230	1836	12	8	2	–	–	–	–	2	11	654
3rd c.-4th c. AD occupation and structures	4-7	18	596	29	879	47	1475	1079	10185	4	172	1	94	5	266	1131	11926	60	55	2	4	5	1	1	13	127	4025
Post-Roman agricultural disturbance	8	15	812	15	781	30	1593	446	559	6	544	2	84	8	628	484	7817	26	36	6	3	3	–	–	12	148	3802
Total		34	1445	44	1660	78	3105	1797	17769	13	783	3	178	16	961	1891	21835	100	100	10	7	8	1	1	27	307	8623

·ILLUSTRATED PIECES   weight (wt) in grams.

TABLE 5: The stratigraphic location by dated phase group of the briquetage and kiln furniture.

examined under a petrological microscope. The sherds examined (Level III Archieve reference) were: A1 (two pieces; one is fig. 39, 6), A27 (fig. 39, 7), A31 (fig. 39, 5), A36, A53 (fig. 39, 3), A54 (fig. 39, 9), A84, A89 (fig. 39, 4). Three sources of origin can be suggested:

Puteoli: A36, in thin section this sherd was quite different to the other samples, as it contained a small amount of volcanic material. This suggests an Italian centre, possibly Puteoli which is situated in a volcanic area on the Bay of Naples.

Lyons: A1 (two pieces), 27, 31, 53, 84, and 89. All these sherds contained numerous small grains of quartz and flecks of mica. Comparison with material attributable to the main arretine and early samian production centres (Williams, 1978), shows that texturally the Cleavel Point sherds are unlike samples attributed to Italy (Arezzo, Puteoli and Pisa), South Gaul (La Graufesenque and Montans) and Central Gaul (Lezoux). Instead, the Ower material compared fairly well with samian considered to have been made at Lyon. However, to date the amount of Lyon samian thin sectioned is small, and more sherds need to be analysed from this centre to check for any possible variation in the fabric. In view of this, the Ower sherds cannot as yet be confidently allocated to a likely production centre on the basis of the thin section results.

Lezoux: A54. This sherd has a highly micaceous fabric which compares favourably with early samian examples from Lezoux (Williams, 1978).

The First Century Fine Wares (Jane Timby):

Twenty-one sherds were selected for thin sectioning and microscopic examination from the main fabrics present. These thin sections are catalogued and stored at the Department of Archaeology, Southampton University by thin section number, e.g. R000. These have been noted in the foregoing text, and are cross-referenced here. The full microscopic descriptions can be found in the Level III Archive.

R774:   Native butt beaker, *Cam 113*, this sherd compares favourably with similar beakers sampled from Colchester, although none have yet been found in association with a kiln.

R775:   Flagon, the type of mineral assemblage identified was typical of those derived from regions which have been subjected to metamorphic activity, thus supporting the possibility that this vessel originated in Central France.

R776:   Saintes bowl (fig. 41, 32), refer vessel description previous.

R777:   White ware flagon, comparable to other white ware flagons. Probably produced at Reims in North-East France (R. Neiss *Pers. Comm.*).

R778:   Beaker (fig. 41, 30), a mineral assemblage typical of a metamorphic area, for example the Auvergne, Central France.

R779:   *Terra nigra* 11a, *Cam 16* (fig. 41, 23), textural analysis has demonstrated a close similarity between this vessel and similar platters from Winchester, amongst others.

R780:   Ring necked flagon, the mineral assemblage indicated that this vessel probably originated from a region of sedimentary geology, but insufficient work has been done on this type of

flagon to know whether this is a British product or an import.

R781:   *Terra rubra* 2, platter basesherd, fabric comparable to other sherds, and probably originates from a region of sedimentary geology (refer also R809).

R782:   *Terra nigra* IId (fig. 41, 25), comparable to R779.

R783:   Unassigned bodysherd, source unidentified, but probably an import.

R784:   *Terra nigra* I, basesherd from platter, the dominance of mica within the matrix suggested that the clay from this vessel was obtained from a metamorphic zone, like that found in Central France, where similar platters are known to have been produced. Unfortunately individual kilns cannot be characterised at present due to the similarity of the mineral assemblages found within the clays (refer also R778 and 788).

R785:   *Terra nigra* IIc, *Cam 2*, slightly coarser textured than is usual for *terra nigra*, but otherwise comparable to R782 . . . etc.

R786:   *Terra nigra* IId, platter basesherd.

R787:   *Terra nigra* IIb, (fig. 41, 24), textural analysis has demonstrated a close similarity between the three *Cam*. 16 platters sampled (R779, R782 and R787), despite their apparent macroscopic differences. This would suggest that they originated from the same source area of production.

R788:   Roanne bowl (fig. 41, 33), the petrology of this sherd was similar to R784 and R778; this is consistent with a source from the metamorphic rock zones of Central France.

R789:   White ware beaker, *Cam* 114 (Fig. 41, 29), source unidentified but probably imported.

R790:   Butt beaker, *Cam* 113 (fig. 41, 43), almost iron free, source unidentified, but probably native.

R791:   Black gloss cup/bowl, unidentified form. The presence of volcanic glass fragments within the matrix lends strong support for this sherd originating from a region of volcanic geology which would in turn be expected for vessels originating from Campania, in Southern Italy.

R809:   *Terra rubra* 2, platter (fig. 41, 26), this fabric was comparable to other *terra rubra* sherds (inc. R781), and probably originates from a reign of sedimentary geology.

The Imported Coarse Wares (D. F. Williams)

R822:   Fabric a, jar (fig. 41, 40).

R823:   Fabric c, jar (fig. 41, 42).

The Black-burnished Pottery, Briquetage and Clay
(D. F. Williams):

A small number of Romano-British black-burnished ware vessels associated with the 'potters yard' (147) were submitted for examination under the polarizing microscope, together with samples of briquetage and clay from the site. The object of the analysis was threefold: (1) to see if it is possible to characterize the black-burnished ware products associated with the Ower (?) kiln, (2) to see how the briquetage fabric compares with the pottery, and if local production is possible, and (3) to compare the clay samples submitted with both the pottery and the briquetage.

The sherds of black-burnished ware were firstly thin sectioned and then submitted to a heavy mineral separation. Thin sectioning showed a clay matrix containing frequent grains of quartz, average size 0.20-0.60mm, and a little shale. Inclusions of shale have previously been noted in black-burnished pottery found at Butcombe (Fowler, 1968), Exeter (Bidwell, 1977) and by the writer in 'waster' samples from a number of sites in the Wareham-Poole Harbour area of Dorset. The heavy mineral residue from the Ower sherds produced a tourmaline-rich assemblage characteristic of black-burnished pottery made in the above mentioned area (Williams, 1977). However, neither the proportion of the different minerals present nor the character of the grains, vary sufficiently from other black-burnished ware produced in this region to characterize the heavy mineral suite of the Ower material.

Heavy mineral separation on a sample of briquetage also produced a high tourmaline content similar to that obtained from the pottery. There were some differences in thin section though, the briquetage containing a higher percentage of shale, and mudstone also appears to be present. A local, or fairly local, source for the briquetage would be in keeping with the petrology.

Several samples of baked clay (Feature 388; Kiln oven and flue 540), and unbaked clay (Fill of clay box in potters yard and trample on yard; Post-pad building (707)); and natural seams of clay in the Ecocene deposits from various locations along the construction route of the pipe) were also studied in thin section and compared with the pottery and briquetage. None of the clay samples sectioned appeared to contain noticeable amounts of the shale/mudstone present in the pottery and briquetage, though a few fragments were noted. Instead the clay was found to contain a very high quartz content, especially the samples from the structure of the kiln, the latter possibly a deliberate addition for refractory purposes.

THE COINS
RICHARD REECE

The identifications of twenty coins recovered from the site are summarised below. The abbreviated references used in these identifications are:

RIC, 'Roman Imperial Coinage', H. Mattingly and E. A. Sydenham (Eds.) 1923 ff.

HK, 'Late Roman Bronze Coinage', R. A. G. Carson, P. V. Hill, J. P. C. Kent, 1960; part I

CK, as above part II

The condition of the coins vary from extremely corroded as to make recognition difficult (e.g.? Durotrigian coin from phase 3), to quite good (e.g. coin of Valens from building 904). Although the degree of wear is to a great extent entirely subjective, the two latest coins, of the house of Valentinian (Valens and Gratian, building 904), can be considered to be not particularly worn. These cannot therefore be used to date safely after about AD 380.

Coin loss comparison with neighbouring sites in Purbeck can be found in Woodward (1980), together with its implications.

Phase 1 Copper Alloy, Durotrigian, 1st. *c.* AD (288B).

Phase 3 Copper Alloy, Durotrigian, 1st *c.* AD, completely corroded.

Phase 5 HK 93, Constantine II, 335-337 AD (909).

Phase 6 CK 25 (copy), House of Constantine, 350-360 AD (288A).

Phase 7 RIC 7 Cyzicus 34, Constantine I, 324-326 AD (904)

HK 62 (Copy), Constantine I, 330-345 AD (904).

CK 537, Valens 375-378 AD (904).

CK 352, Gratian 367-378 AD (904).

RIC 7 Lyon 107, Constantine I, 318-322 AD (904).

HK 201, Constantinopolis, 330-335 AD (904).

HK 80, Constantine I, 333-335 AD (564).

Sestertius (reverse illegible), Severus Alexander, 228-235 AD (707 collapse).

Phase 8 RIC 34, Claudius II, 268-270 AD.

RIC 7 London 28, Constantine I, 313-317 AD.

HK 185 (Copy), Constantinopolis, 330-345 AD.

Barbarous Radiate (*Rev* Pax), 270-290 AD.

RIC 71, Victorinus, 268-270 AD.

RIC 56, Tetricus I, 270-273 AD.

HK 51 (copy), Urbs Roma, 330-345 AD.

THE BROOCHES
D. F. MACKRETH

The stratigraphic location of the seventeen brooch fragments recovered from these excavations is summarised in Table 6. All are 1st century types, and can be considered to be residual in the later contexts. The occurrence of five brooches well stratified in the pre-conquest levels of the rectilinear enclosure (288) (Fig. 52, 212, 213, 217 and 219), is important in that the copper-alloy strip brooches (212 and 213) have not otherwise been published in pre-conquest levels. The three fragments of Colchester derivative brooches (fig. 52, 210-211) from the Phase 3 soil accumulation are probably of the later 1st century AD. The occurrence of a Colchester brooch is of great interest (fig. 52, 209), although it is residual in post-Roman agricultural disturbance. The illustrated brooches are described in detail, following. All the brooches are made from a copper alloy, unless otherwise stated.

209: *Colchester type* from phase 8. Half of the eight – coil spring and the pin are missing. The end of the hook is broken. One wing survives in part and is plain. The bow is broad at the top and tapers to what may have been a pointed foot, but the tip is broken off. The bow is thin and the catch-plate, largely missing, was narrow and had two long piercings divided by a narrow bar. This is an example of a continental Colchester. The differences between such and British specimens are distinct: British hooks are long, continental ones being short and often very wide where they meet the top of the bow. On the present example there is a distinct widening on the fragment of hook. British bows tend to be thick with a round, oval or faceted section, continental ones are like that of the brooch from Ower. While bows of British brooches are mostly curved, it is possible that those with straight bows are typologically early and derive directly from their continental counterparts which have a straight profile. The catch-plates on British Colchesters are, unlike the Ower brooch, triangular rather than trapezoidal in shape. The continental type is dated by Ettlinger to *c.* 25 BC to *c.* 25 AD but lasting until the middle of the 1st century (Ettlinger 1973, 28, 188, Taf. 4, 8-10). This is supported by the stratified examples from Augst where the bulk of the material had been lost by *c.* 50 AD (Riha 1979, 65, Taf 1n, 4-6, 138-184). As far as the Ower brooch is concerned, while it could have been brought into Britain after the Roman Conquest, it is more likely to have arrived before and the continental dating should apply here, say *c.* 25 BC to *c.* 25-35 AD.

210: *Colchester Derivative* from phase 3, the axis bar of the hinged pin is housed in the short and plain wings. The plain bow is wide at the top and tapers to a pointed foot. On either side of the head of the bow is a short moulding separated from the bow by a groove. The added mouldings at the head of the bow place this brooch with a fairly wide-spread group which has the same decorative trait, although in varying forms. The most elaborate have sprung pins held in the Polden Hill manner and their distribution lies in the lower Severn Valley spreading into Oxfordshire and down towards the south-west of England.

Those brooches which belong to the same group, but have hinged pins like the present example, have a much more restricted core to their distribution being largely confined to Dorset and Somerset with a spread into Wiltshire. There are not enough recorded details of each group for it to be certain whether or not the hinged variety is the outcome of typological development or is a quirk of workshops operating in a small area. The only relatively detailed dating evidence comes from Camerton where one is dated *c.* 65-85 AD. (Wedlake 1958, 219, fig. 50, 10), one is 1st or 2nd century (ibid. 229, fig. 53, 40) and another two or before 180 AD (ibid. 219, fig. 50, 9) and 2nd century (ibid. 229, fig. 53, 39). The date range suggested by these specimens is from the second half of the 1st century into the second.

211 *Colchester Derivative* from phase 3, the wings housing the axis bar of the hinged pin are circular in section and each has a buried moulding at the end. The bow tapers with a rounded front to the pointed foot which has two cross-cuts on it. On either side of the head of the bow is a moulding lying in the junction with the wings. The catch-plate has, down its back, a groove marking the beginning of the return. The whole brooch is carefully finished.

The general ornament which distinguishes the groups to which brooch 210 belongs is, to some extent, repeated here in

the two mouldings at the head of the brooch. While there may
be a relationship, the present case belongs more to a line of
development from which the Dolphin (*cf.* Gould 1967, 17, fig.
7, 7) derives. There are several parallels for the present
brooch and all, save a doubtful one from Northamptonshire
(private collection), lie in Dorset and Wiltshire. The dating is
poorly fixed as so few come from satisfactory contexts.
However, one comes from Hod Hill and dates before *c.* 50 AD
(Brailsford 1962, 10, fig. 10, C96. For date: Richmond 1968,
117-9), but the type may have continued until the latter part of
the 1st century.

212: *Strip brooch* from 288B (phase 1), in very bad condition, the
details of the brooch can only dimly be seen. The hinged pin
had its axis bar housed in the expanded and rolled-under head
of the bow which is straight-sided and has only a very slight
taper to the squared-off foot. The front of the bow bears traces

of there having been a gently swelled face between bordering
ridges. The fragment of a spring bagged with this brooch
belongs to another. The distribution of Strip brooches is
mostly concentrated in Dorset, Wiltshire and Somerset. There
are a few spreading further north and into the Midlands. An
exception is the iron Strip brooch which is to be found over a
wider area running from East Anglia into the south-west of
England. The origin of the type is obscure except that one
particular variety may have derived from the Langton Down
(Brailsford 1962, 8, fig. 7, C30-1, C40-2). The dating seems to
be mid first century. Although the iron examples may have
come into being before the Conquest, no copper alloy brooch
has been published from a pre-Conquest context, and the
present brooch may have passed out of use by *c.* 75 AD.

213: *Strip brooch* from 288C (phase 1), Three fragments which
might make up the bow from a Strip brooch. There is no trace

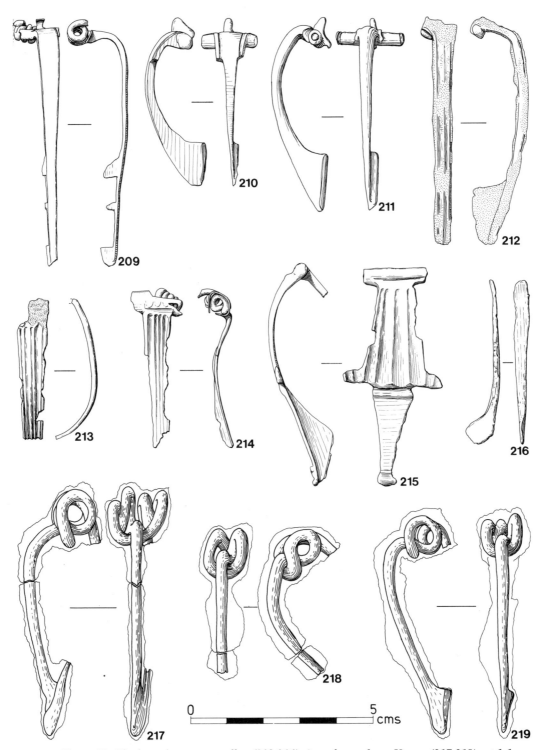

Figure 52. The brooches; copper alloy (209-216), iron drawn from X-rays (217-219), at 1:1.

TABLE 6: The stratigraphic location by phase of the metalwork.

PHASE DESCRIPTION	Phase Number	Main Features	BROOCHES: BRONZE/IRON							BRONZES					IRONWORK													LEAD	
															Nails															
			Colchester	Colch. derv.	Strip	Langton	Hod	Nauheim	Unclass.	Bracelets	Rings	Spoon	Buckles	Unclass.	A	B	C	D	E	Unident. bars/rods	Plank binding	Plain and pierced plates	Pierced pegs	Chainlink (?)	Scythe/sickle	Horseshoes	Link/ring	Weights	Unclass.
First c. ditches and pits	1	288 858	3				2							1	1					4					1				
	2	343 389						1							1					4									
First/second c. soil accumulation	3		3												3	1			1	10				1				1	1
Disturbed and Infilled lower horizons and 3rd-4th c. AD Occupation levels	4	555 540													2														
	5	441 909															1			1	1	1							
	6	upper fill 1st c. ditches 644 727 388												1	2	1				5									1
3rd-4th c. AD Occupation and Structures	7	147 564 706 904 707 906 905								2	1				25	1	1	4	1	33	21	1	1	1	2			1	
Post-Roman Agricultural Disturbance	8		1		1	1	1	1	3	2	2		2	1	13	1				35					1	1	1		
TOTAL			17							11					59					125								4	

· ILLUSTRATED OBJECTS

of either the pin fixing arrangement or the catch-plate. The front of the strip has two wide flutes alternating with three narrow grooves. On the edges of the central groove are incised chevrons. The dating which applies to brooch 212 should apply here as well, if this is a brooch.

214: *Langton type* from phase 8. The spring, now separate, was once housed between two flaps on the head of the brooch which were closed round it. Along the front of the case is what appears to be a line of rocker-arm ornament. The bow is bent and has lost nearly all its edges. Down the centre of the bow run three ridges separated from bordering ridges by flutes. Most of the catch-plate is missing, but there is a trace of a circular hole.

The brooch is of a poorer quality than most of the type and it is hard to be sure whether this is because it is the result of devolution, or because it was produced for those of slender means. The Langton Down was imported extensively into Britain before the Conquest as the examples from Camulodunum (Hawkes and Hull 1947, 318), Skeleton Green, Puckeridge, Herts. (Partridge 1981, 133-4, 139, 140, figs. 71, 43, 44 and 46) and the King Harrys. Lane cemetery, St. Albans, Herts., (excavations, Dr. I. M. Stead) show. Both of the latter collections contain 'cheap' versions and the dated examples from Augst (Riha 1979, 99, Taf. 19, 504-524) give a hint that the simplified design may be later than the more elaborate and definitely early specimens: late Augustan times to *c.* 50 AD.

215: *Hod Hill type* from phase 8, Now in two pieces, the axis bar for the hinged pin is housed in the rolled-over head. The upper bow consists of a panel with five ridges separated by flutes tapering outwards towards the bottom. The three internal ridges are beaded. Attached to the bottom corners of the panel are wings each of which is made up of two weak mouldings. The lower bow is a flat plate narrowing towards the bottom, with a line of square punch-marks down the middle, and finished top and bottom by a cross-moulding. There is a foot-knob and the brooch had once been tinned or silvered. No Hod Hill has been proved to have come from a pre-Conquest context and the great variety of the type, along with the small numbers belonging to the typological stage between it and its parent, the Aucissa, suggests that, when it

was introduced after the Conquest, it was near the end of its manufacturing life, if it was still being made. The type had decreased markedly in use by 60 AD and the very small number that were taken into the lands conquered under Cerialis suggests that it had effectively passed out of use by *c.* 70 AD.

216: *(?) Nauheim derivative* from phase 8, Whilst not demonstrably a Nauheim derivative, there is a sign that the top of the surviving bow was beginning to narrow to the start of the spring in the manner expected in the type. The bow is flat, thin and tapers to a pointed foot. The catch plate is small and is clumsily formed.

Post-conquest and could date to *c.* 80 AD (refer more detail discussion under the iron example, brooches 219).

217: *Nauheim derivative* from 288B (phase 1). This iron brooch is covered in corrosion products and the details have been taken from a X-radiograph. The number of coils in the spring appears to be four and the chord is internal. The bow may be bent, but there is a trace of a recurve in the lower part. For dating and discussion refer to brooch 219.

218: *Nauheim derivative* from 288A (phase 6). This iron brooch again is only visible from an X-ray photograph. The spring appears to have only two coils. The lower part of the bow, with the catch-plate is missing. For dating and discussion refer to brooch 219.

219: *Nauheim derivative* from 288C (phase 1). This iron brooch again is only visible from an X-radiograph. The chord is internal and there appear to be only two coils. There is a marked kink in the lower part of the bow at the top of the catch-plate.

Nauheim derivatives run from before the Roman Conquest to the latter part of the 1st century AD. In general, iron brooches tend to be early, and those which are large are more likely to be early than those of average size. Of brooches 217-219, none may be classed as large and none has any feature which helps to place it on one part of the general *floruit* rather than another. While the use of X-rays may establish the form and profile of the bow, it is difficult to disentangle complex structures such as spring arrangements. Brooch 217 appears to have normal four-coil internal cord springs, but 218 and 219 seem to have only two coils. This is very unusual, although it is clear that springs with three coils are reasonably common, and five coil springs are not unknown, indeed, some with eight coils are recorded (Down 1981, 256, fig. 10.1 and 12), it is unlikely that this may be taken as a dating criterion, unless more evidence becomes available.

There is nothing in brooch 216 to lead to any conclusion other than it is post-Conquest and could date up to c. 80 AD. (Nos 218 and 219 on fig. 52 show the coils from X-rays, and since these are damaged and corroded they may not conform to the undamaged brooch – P.J.W.)

Acknowledgements: I am grateful to Dr. I. M. Stead and Miss V. Rigby for information relating to the occurrence of Langton type brooch from the excavation at King Harrys Lane, St. Albans, prior to publication.

THE COPPER ALLOY OBJECTS

MARTIN HENIG

Copper alloy objects (other than brooches, see above) from the site include bracelets, rings, spoon fragments and buckles (figure 53). The stratigraphic location of these objects is summarised in Table 6. Apart from one unclassified piece, all occur in the 3rd-4th century AD occupation levels (phase 7), or the post-Roman agricultural disturbance (phase 8). The three stratified items from phase 7 were: the spoon (226) from the collapse of building (904), the bracelet (221) from the rubble collapse of building (707), and the bracelet (222) from the 'potters yard' (147).

The bracelets (220-224) were all of forms common in the 3rd and 4th centuries AD. Parallels can be cited in publications on the following sites: *Shakenoak* (Brodribb, Hands and Walker, 1971,

fig. 48; 73 and 77); *Lydney Park* (Wheeler and Wheeler 1932, fig. 17); and *Winchester Lankhills* (Clarke 1979, 304, *esp.* fig. 37, 141).

One of the two rings (224) possibly dates to the 3rd century AD. Similar examples were found at *Gadebridge Park* Hemel Hempstead (Neal 1974, fig. 60, 142), and *Chichester* (Down 1978, fig. 10.48 4). The simple octagonal ring (225) is also probably Roman (Charlesworth 1961, 26, Nos. 25 and 26, both from South Shields), and of the 3rd century date.

The spoon also dates to the 3rd or 4th century AD (Strong 1966, 177 Fig. 36b). A similar example was found at *Shakenoak* (Brodribb, Hands and Walker, 1973, fig. 53, 187).

The two spectacle buckles are medieval, probably of 15th century date (Fingerlin 1971, 184-187).

The grooved and 'V' shaped object (229) could not be classified nor dated, but may have been used as sheathing.

THE IRONWORK

PETER COX

A total of 184 iron objects were recovered from the site, most were badly corroded, broken and in general badly preserved. In conservation the objects were stabilised, but not cleaned down to the original object profile, which was only observed from X-ray photographs. Where the corrosion products obscured detail, this is shown in the illustration (fig. 54). The stratigraphic location of the ironwork is summarised in Table 6.

The nails were in a fragmentary state, and none were complete. These were classified in a series (A-E) on the basis of the type of head. The five types are illustrated in fig. 54, 230-236. The type classification can be summarised as follows:

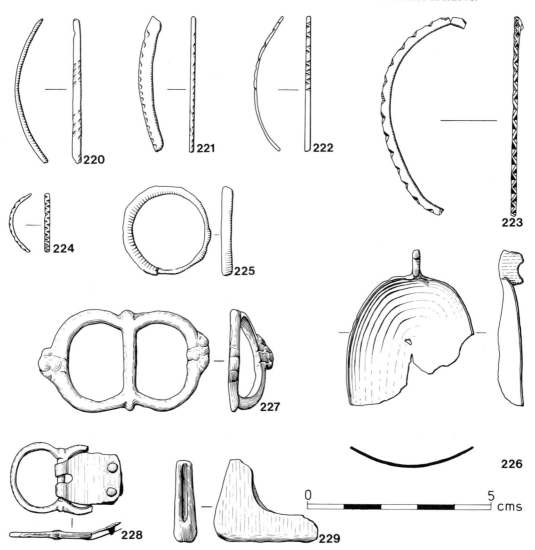

Figure 53. The bronze objects; bracelets (220-223), rings (224-225), spoon (226); spectacle buckles (medieval) (227-228), other (229), 1:1.

A: Sub-rectangular/round head in plan, flat in cross-section (230-232)

B: Narrow rectangular head in plan, flat in cross section (233)

C: Flanged head nail, rectangular head in plan, flat in cross-section, possible part-formed nail head prior to hammering out on a mandril (234)

D: Hobnail (235)

E: Heavy duty nail with domed cross-section (236)

The majority of nails recovered appear to derive from the 3rd to 4th century AD complex (Phase 7). The nails illustrated were from: drier 708 (230-232), pit 644 (233), 'potter's yard' 147 (234), building 564 (235) and yard 441 (236).

In addition to the ninety-two unidentifiable small bars and rods (many of which were probably the broken stems of nails), were twenty-one pieces of bent-angle irons, eighteen of which occurred in the drier 708 (237 is typical). It is thought that these belonged to a wooden superstructure, which ultimately collapsed on burning (?) into the drier. These pieces were recovered mainly from the

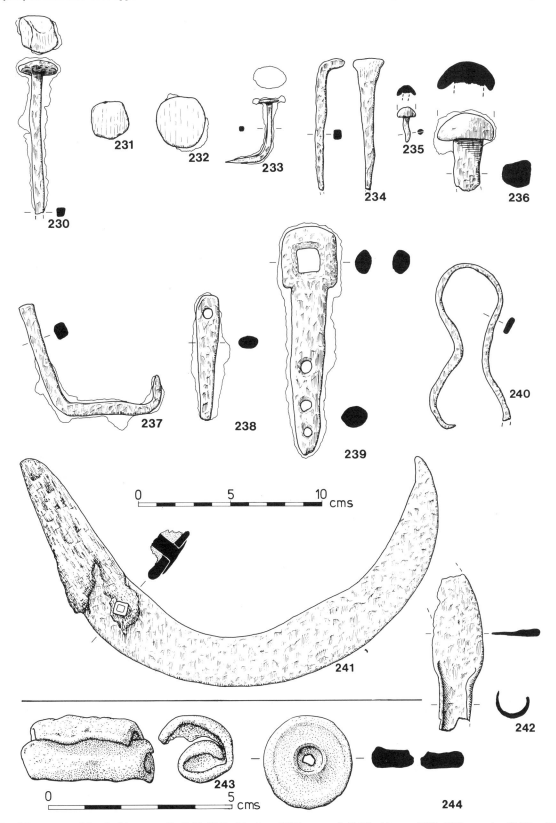

Figure 54. The iron and lead objects; nails (230-236), binding (237), tongs? (240), hinges (238, 239), scythe (241), all at 1:2; sickle (242), lead fish weights (243, 244), 1:1.

TABLE 7: The stratigraphic location by phase of the glass, bone pins, spindle whorls and loom weights, architectural fragments, portable stone objects, slag and cinder.

Phase Description	Phase No.	Main Features	Glass Beads: 'Frankish'	Biconical	Globular	Counters	Glass Vessels: Cast	Blown	Square Bottles	Bone pins	Spindle/Loom: Pottery	Bone	Shale	Sandstone	Post-Padstones	Roofing: Limestone (complete)	Shale (complete)	Ceramic (fragments)	Tessarae A	B	C	D	Markerstone	Net-Thatch wt	Circular Limestone blocks	Purbeck Marble	Querns	Pestle	Honestones/Polishers	Fuel Ash	Hearth buns
1st c. AD Ditches and Pits	1	288 858				1					4																				2	
	2	389 343									1																				
1st/2nd c. AD Soil Accumulation	3						1	1						1		5	3	14	3	1									1	7	1
Disturbed and Infilled lower horizons, and 3rd-4th c. AD Occupation Levels	4	555 540																		1		5				*					
	5	441 909	2																	2	1	3	2									
	6	361 644 727 388			1								1			15		6	1						1	*			1	1	1
3rd-4th c. AD Occupation and Structures	7	147 564 707 904 905 906							3	2	1	1			15	15	1		3	2	2	1	1		*	3		1		
Post-Roman Agricultural Disturbance	8		1	1	2	4	2	4	4		2	1				2		36	1	5	2	6			1	1	3		1	8	
TOTALS			6				15			2	12				15	17	1	56	63				1	1	3	*			10	27	

· ILLUSTRATED OBJECTS   * PRESENT

charcoal rich layer (818), where the charcoal identification suggested burnt structural timbers (some mature oak). This angle iron can perhaps be taken as 'plank-binding' and bent fixing nails for squared structural timbers. In addition three round-headed nails were recovered from this deposit (230-232). The 'plank-bindings' were characterised by their 3-sided J-shape, and were all of similar dimension.

It is probable that all these nails and bindings were made on site, *c.f.* evidence for smithing (refer specialist report, below.)

Pierced iron plates (two) occurred in 3rd-4th century AD levels (not illustrated).

Pierced iron pegs (three) occurred in a number of levels, two are illustrated (238 and 239). The smaller (238) was recovered from the phase 3 soil accumulation, and the larger (239) from yard 441.

The possible remains of a chainlink (240) were recovered from the 'potters' yard' 147.

A single curved scythe blade with the remains of a decomposed wood handle, and single rivet and hole was recovered from the collapse of building 707 (241).

Three broken socketed sickles or bill-hooks were recovered from: the 1st century AD ditch/pit 858, the 3rd-4th century AD 'potters' yard' 147, and post-roman agricultural disturbance. The most complete example is illustrated (242), but the hook itself is completely broken away. Hooks of this type are well known from Iron Age sites, e.g. *Maiden Castle* (Wheeler, 1943, 278 fig. 91, 3).

A horseshoe of late medieval or post-medieval date was recovered from the post-Roman agricultural disturbance.

THE LEAD OBJECTS

Four pieces of lead were recovered from the site, two of which were identifiable objects (Figure 54, 243 and 244). The stratigraphic location of the lead is summarised in Table 6.

243. Rolled sheet of lead, possibly used as a net weight. A similar object was recovered from a late Roman pit at *Portchester* (Cunliffe 1971; fig. 123, 167). From the phase 3 soil accumulation.

244. Pierced disc of lead with raised lip around central hole and outer edge. Probably a net weight, but could be a spindle whorl or loom weight. From the floor of building 707C.

THE COLOURED GLASS
MARGARET GUIDO
JUSTINE BAYLEY and LEO BIEK (Ancient Monuments Laboratory) with analyses by GORDON R. GILMORE (Universities Research Reactor, Risley, Lancs) and as a contribution from GEORGE C. BOON (National Museum of Wales)

The basic data have been collected in Table 8.

There are two beads which deserve particular attention, especially as the dating of their context rests on them, and thus they are of chronological as well as intrinsic significance.

One is the cylindrical bead no. 530 (fig. 55, 246). This has been made by winding a blue thread into a spiral round a preformed red tube. While one cannot cite another identical bead from Britain, the general type often made with green on yellow on terracotta red, blue on white, and so on, is common among Frankish beads. Three made of the same colours as our bead come from a well-dated Romano-Frankish grave (Grave 1996) belonging to about AD 525-600 from Krefeld-Gellep in the Rhineland (Pirling 1979) and this is also approximately the date of a number found at the big late 6th-early 7th century Merovingian site at Schretzheim near Dillingen, South Germany (Koch 1977). Related types are not uncommon in Britain.

The small globular millefiori bead no. 457 (fig. 55 no. 245 and below) can also be matched at Schretzheim, but the publication which specifically draws attention to these beads is an important paper, also by Koch (1974), dealing with the fur trade between Finland and the Mediterranean. Fortunately a precise description of our bead can be given despite its broken and battered appearance. The decorative outer layer was laid on a 'colourless' (turquoise) core which appears semi-opaque as the glass is very bubbly. The decoration is made up of a polychrome equatorial band bordered above and below by plain yellow-green, semi-opaque glass. The polychrome band consists of a number of slices from a millefiori rod set side by side around the bead, probably four in total. The unit which repeats has the design illustrated below:

R – red W – white
T – turquoise blue Y – yellow

All colours are opaque, in a 'black' ground. Nearly 1½ repeats survive on the bead fragment.

Koch points out that beads of this type are commonest in the Upper Rhine and Danube regions (Alemannic-Frankish territory) and may have been brought over the Alps by returning Frankish troops in the mid-6th century, having been acquired from some hitherto undiscovered, perhaps North Italian, bead-making centre which ceased work before AD 568. In Britain few millefiori beads of this date are known, and occurrences in the following cemeteries are cited by Koch (1974): Abingdon, Berks., (Leeds and Harden 1936 pl. 6 no. 5); Chessel Down, Isle of Wight and Faversham, Kent (Baldwin Brown 1915 436, 443, 733-7); Ipswich, Suffolk (Layard 1907a, pls 6 & 7; 1907b pls 32 & 33); Leighton Buzzard, Beds. (Hyslop 1963); Kenninghall, Norfolk (Clarke 1939); and Sarre, Kent (Brent 1868). All are mainly 6th-7th century in date.

The present evidence which, had only one of these beads been found, would have been inadequate (for either one alone might have been suspected as a stray), seems to point satisfactorily to a late 6th or early 7th century date for Building (909).

The recent revival of interest in the basic chemistry of coloured, and particularly opaque, glass (see Biek and Bayley 1979 for a general review) has shown that apart from time and place a third parameter – technological tradition – needs to be seen as an equally important and contributory but quite separate factor (Biek 1983). Briefly, glassworking was a highly conservative and jealously guarded 'hereditary' family occupation. Specialist knowledge travelled far but exclusively in the heads and hands of the

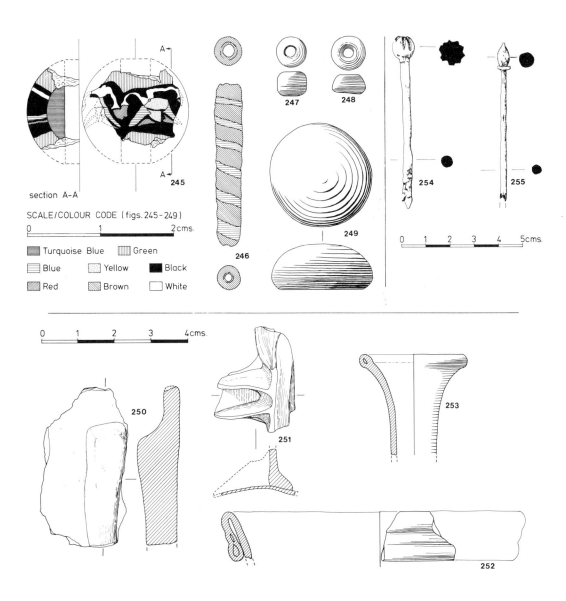

Figure 55. The glass beads at 2:1 (245-249), glass vessels at 1:1 (250-253), and bone pins at 2:3 (254-255).

TABLE 8
The Coloured Glass

SITE SMALL FIND NO.	ILLUSTRATION (Figure 26) No.	ANCIENT MONUMENTS LAB. NO.	COLOUR(S)	TRANSMISSION	SHAPE	CONTEXT		PHASE	TYPOLOGY
78	248	794663	med. blue	translucent	small biconical bead	machine clearance of trench 480.120-470.140		8	Guido 1978 Fig. 37 no. 12 p. 97
157	–	794664	mid-blue	transparent	bowl fragment	robbing of Late Roman Buildg. (905)	Late/post-Roman?	7	pillar moulded bowl
209	251	794665	dark blue	transparent	jug fragment	post-Roman agricult. disturb.		8	blown, ribbed globular jug
396	249	794666	pale blue	opaque	bun-shaped counter	primary fill of Ditch (288)	early 1st c., pre-conquest	1	reckoning or gaming piece, von Saldern 1974 (G. C. Boon)
457	245	794667	colourless (turquoise) yellow-green with polychrome millefiori (red, white, yellow, black, turquoise)	semi-opaque (bubbly) semi-opaque opaque	globular bead fragment	just below plough-soil above Late Roman Yard (441) post-Building (909)	with 1st-4th c. debris; some post-medieval contamination.	5	'Frankish' (see text below)
530	246	794668	red and blue	opaque	spiralled cylinder bead	fill of shallow Gulley (531) bounding Yard (441)	with 3rd/4th c. debris	5	'Frankish (see text below)
551	247	794669	dark turquoise green	translucent	small undecorated globular bead	Post-Roman agricult. disturb		8	Guido 1978 not a class, Gp. 7,p.70; not unusual
782	–	794670	yellow with swirls of pale amber	opaque clear	bun-shaped counter fragment	build-up below Bldg. (707): up. lev. rdy (727)	1st-4th c. debris	6	as for 396 above; also Curle 1911; Next below (G. C. Boon)
Wilderspool Fig. 82 no. 12		761115	yellow	opaque	bun-shaped counter	unstratified			Hinchliffe 1982 (unpub. results of analysis here given for comparison.)

Semi-quantitative results for Pb (by JB) using X-ray fluorescence analysis. Other data from neutron activation analysis (by GG); 5 min. irradiations at between 2 and 300 kw depending on specimen weight; measured on high resolution gamma spectrometer, after about 5 mins. decay, for 10 mins. at distance of 4cms. Mainly aimed at Sb and Sn; other elements referred to standards from other runs, so their values more significant in relative terms.

All specimens contained traces of Cl. Si, Ca, Fe etc. not measured but clearly present.

Standard deviations, largely due to counting uncertainties but including calibration, are <5% rising to > 25% for low contents in smaller specimens.

practitioners and tradition changed little in a thousand-year span. Yet the cross-currents of the Migration Period produced conflicts and confluences – as well as leaving backwaters – of technology which are as diagnostic as they are fascinating.

The elements antimony and tin are of special interest here. Both give very pronounced yellow opaque colours in lead glass and have also been used to produce white and other coloured opacity. It had been proposed that there was a general change from antimony to tin in Europe about AD 450 (Rooksby 1964). But it now seems that we need, rather, to think in terms of a Central European (tin) tradition as distinct from a 'Mediterranean' (antimony) tradition.

The latter originated with the earliest Assyrian glass and includes (? independent) Early British and 'Roman' practice. The tin tradition first appears in Britain (imported ?) and Gaul as early as the 2nd century BC (Henderson and Warren 1983) but certainly sweeps the board with the Saxon occupation, as recently shown again by Gilmore (1985) and Bayley (forthcoming).

What is of particular significance here is the preponderance of antimony in stratigraphically post-Roman and typologically 'Frankish' 6th-7th century opaque beads (nos. 457 and 530 in Table 8). This would be consistent with their production at a workshop which even at that late time was still operating in the Mediterranean tradition – i.e. possibly south of the general protection of the Alps. At the same time Koch (1974) suggests this production ceased soon after AD 565; and also, tin becomes conspicuous in no. 457 (c. 15% of the antimony content) possibly indicating a 'mixed technology',

highly likely in such a polychrome millefiori context. By contrast, all of the rather more 'prominent' tin (nearly 40% of the antimony) in translucent no. 551 could have entered the glass incidentally if a 7% tin bronze had been added instead of pure copper.

In another context, it is worth drawing attention to two very tight clusters of data in terms of Na:Al ratio and, hence, conceivably in terms of 'standard basis glass' (Biek et al 1980): nos. 78, 157 and 209 (Na: Al 6.25 ± 0.21, i.e. ca.3%), and the rest except 551 (Na: Al 5.51 ± 0.05, i.e. less than 1%).

THE ROMAN VESSEL GLASS

JENNIFER PRICE

Twenty-nine fragments of vessel glass were found during the excavations, of which twenty three were from Romano-British vessels, and the rest were post-Medieval and modern.

All of the Roman glass was most probably produced during the 1st and 2nd centuries AD, and the fragments of pillar moulded bowls (250), and the handle fragment of a dark blue blown jug (251) certainly belong to the mid-later 1st century. None of the pieces represent vessels of great rarity; three fragments come from coloured tablewares, and most of the rest belong to bluish green household wares and containers.

The stratigraphic location of the fragments from the three groups (cast, blown and square bottle glass) is summarised in Table 7.

					ELEMENTS PRESENT (weight % unless otherwise stated)									MAIN ELEMENT(S)/AGENT(S) IN	
														COLOURANT(S)	OPACIFIER (Solid except[+])
	Pb	Sb	Sn	Cu	Na	Al	Mn	V ppm	Co* ppm	As	Au	In	Mg	Ti		
Late Roman	w	2.5	<0.03	0.17	15.7	2.59	0.35	40	<300			×			Co, ?Cu	
mid- to later 1st c.	–	0.07	<0.02	<0.1	21.1	3.35	0.33	20	100			×			Co.	
ca. AD 60-125	–	0.05	<0.02	0.18	18.0	2.76	0.73	30	500		×	×			Co, ?Cu	
Early Roman	w	3.4	0.03	<0.2	13.5	2.45	0.35	16	100		×	×		×	Co	Sb, (Ca)
Late 6th/early 7th c.	s	2.0	0.36	0.63	12.3	2.25	0.92	30	<50						yellow-green: &/or Sn Pb→ / black: Mn (Fe)→ / red: Cu$_2$0, 0Pb→ / turq.: Cu, Pb/ / white: Sb, (Ca)→ / yellow: Sb &/or Sn, Pb→	?Cu+sB / +saturation effect / ?Sb, (Ca)
late 6th/early 7th c.	s	0.84	0.04	1.29	15.1	2.73	0.19	<30	100		×				red: Cu$_2$?, Pb→ / blue: Co, Cu?/ / blue: Co, Cu?/	Sb, (Ca)
period undefined, prob. Late Roman	–	0.37	0.14	2.0	19.2	2.59	0.12	<50	<50	×?					Cu (blue) / (?Fe) (yellow)	
Early Roman	vs	1.94	0.094	<0.08	10.3	1.85	0.155	<10	<50	×			×		Sb, Pb →	
Early Roman	(vs)	1.8	0.07	<0.1	13.0	1.65	0.37	<50	<50						Sb, Pb →	

ppm – parts per million
s – strong signal
v – very
w – weak signal
× – present
* – estimated order of magnitude, only
(Unconfirmed data in brackets)

A full description of each fragment can be found in the level III archive. The descriptions here are confined to the more complete diagnostic examples, illustrations fig. 55 (250-253).

Cast, Ground and Fire-Polished vessels

Two fragments from pillar moulded bowls were recovered from the excavations. Pillar moulded bowls were in common use throughout the Roman world during much of the 1st century AD (Isings, 1957, Form 3), and fragments are often found at sites in Roman Britain. Polychrome mosaic and opaque monochrome, as well as translucent monochrome, bowls were produced during the early and mid 1st century (Harden and Price 1971, 320-1, 329) but only the bluish green bowls occur in large numbers at late 1st century sites. Camulodunum (Harden 1947, nos. 8, 10-14, 16-18, 40, 61-67); Fishbourne (Harden and Price 1971, nos. 3, 17-21), and Verulamium (Charlesworth 1972, p. 198), are three Romano-British sites which have produced considerable numbers of these vessels.

The method of manufacture of these bowls has been the subject of much discussion and uncertainty; modern experiments have shown that they may have been produced in a closed mould (Schuler, 1959), or by forming a disc of glass, impressing this with a circular tool with slits corresponding to the ribs, and then sagging the ribbed disc over the mould (Cummings, 1980, 26-9), but a variety of other methods have also been suggested.

250. Pillar Moulded bowl, rim fragment from shell midden in Trial pit 450.099. Bluish green. Rim edge ground (now mostly missing), vertical shoulder, deep convex curved side, one prominent vertical rib bent to the right. Grinding marks visible on shoulder outside, and on inside surface. Outside surface dull. Some evidence for secondary use of fragment, edges roughly grozed. Ht. of fragment approx. 30mm.

Blown Vessels

Two fragments of a dark blue jug were recovered from the excavations. This jug most probably had a long narrow neck, an undecorated globular body with an open, pushed-in, base ring, and an angular handle with two or more central ridges which was applied to the upper body and attached to the neck below the rim (cf. Thorpe, 1953, Pl. IIIa – from Colchester), though too little has survived to be certain of many of these features. Jugs of this kind were in use in Italy and the western provinces during the second and third quarters of the 1st century AD, and dated examples are listed by Isings (1957, Form 52a). However, they are not very common at sites in Roman Britain, where the usual form of 1st century globular or discoid bodied jug has a thicker walled body which is nearly always decorated with raised ribs (Isings 1957, Form 52b), and it may be that this fragment comes from a jug of the latter type. The globular and discoid jug forms have been discussed in some detail recently in connexion with a nearly complete example from Enfield (Price, 1977, 155-8); it seems probable that they were produced in the lower Rhineland or northern France from about AD 60 to about AD 125.

251. Jug, dark blue; body and handle fragment from phase 8. Part of a thin walled convex curved body and handle attachment with one lateral and two central ridges surviving.

The other fragment which could be from the same vessel was recovered from the phase 3 soil accumulation, and was part of the convex curved lower body with slight evidence for a riased rib.

A fragment of a bluish-green collared jar was found residual in phase 8. Collar rims of this type are found on two later 1st/early 2nd century vessel forms in Britain, one being the square jar which occurs in Italy and elsewhere in the western provinces, and the other being the globular jar, which often has a ribbed body and is only found in the Rhineland, central and northern France and Britain (Isings, 1957, form 67c). The square jar has not often been recognised in Britain, perhaps because these vessels were only rarely included in burials and so do not survive intact, and the bodies are indistinguishable from those of square bottles, while the rims are similar to those of globular jars. However, a large specimen is known from Cirencester (Thorpe, 1935, pl. IIc) and others have been found at Lincoln, Richborough (Bushe Fox, 1949, pl. LXIX), and Chichester (Down and Rule, 1971, fig. 5.22). The globular jar, on the other hand, is known from very many Romano-British sites, and some have also been found in burials, as at Shefford, Bedfordshire (Liversidge, 1969, Pl. 34), Wroxeter (Haverfield and Taylor, 1908, fig. 32), and Thornborough, Buckinghamshire (Price, 1975A, fig. 10, 3). They were made in dark blue and yellow brown, as well as bluish-green glass, and were produced between about AD 60 and AD 125.

252. Fragment of double folded vertical rim, jar. Bluish-green, edge rolled inwards, then bent out and down to form collar. From phase 8.

The nine neck and rim fragments of a bluish-green unguent bottle or flask with folded rim were found residual in phase 8. Unguent bottles and flasks and this type of rim are found from the 2nd century AD onwards. It is not possible to identify this vessel type with certainty.

253. Reconstructed neck of unguent bottle. Folded rim, edge rolled inwards, funnel mouth, narrow cylindrical neck. From phase 8.

Square and Cylindrical Bottles

Eight fragments from vessels of this type were recovered from a number of phases (Table 5). One piece may have been deliberately shaped as a tessera in secondary use (from collapse of building 564 in phase 7). The remains were too fragmentary for illustration. Square and cylindrical bottles were in common use as containers for liquid and semi-liquid substances in the 1st and 2nd centuries AD, especially in the western provinces (Islings, 1957, Forms 50 and 51; Charlesworth, 1966; Charlesworth, nd). They are by far the commonest glass vessel forms found at sites in Roman Britain, and were also often re-used as cinerary urns, so many have been found complete. It seems that they were not produced after the end of the 2nd century AD, though individual examples may have survived for a considerable period after this time. The re-use of bottle glass to produce tesserae has not often been recorded, though the rather similar cubes were found at Bradwell (now Bancroft) Roman Villa, Milton Keynes (Price, 1975B, fig. 33, nos. 20-21).

THE BONE PINS, AND WORKED BONE

Two bone pins were recovered from the site (Figure 55), both from the shell midden and rubbish infilling tip (87), inside building 707 (fig. 7), and in association with cut and sawn antler fragments and a bone spindle whorl made from the ball-joint head of a femur (Fig. 26, 264). These two pins can be dated to the 3rd-5th century AD, Crummy (1979).

254. Pin with spherical head and incised star decoration, made from horn or antler. Pins with spherical heads from Colchester are classified in Crummy (1979) as type 3. A more highly decorated example with a similar incised head decoration was found in a late 4th century AD context at Chichester, (Down, 1978, 313. fig. 10.44 and no. 195).

255. Pin with a single reel below a conical head, made from bone, snapped point. Pins with 1-5 reels beneath a conical or ovoid head from Colchester are classified in Crummy (1979) as type 5. Similar examples can be seen from Portchester (Cunliffe 1975, 217. Fig. 116.84).

SPINDLE WHORLS AND LOOM-WEIGHTS

The spindle whorls and loom-weights (figure 58) were manufactured from broken pottery (not illustrated), stone (263), animal bone (264), and shale waste (265-266). The stratigraphic distribution by phase of this material is summarised in table 7.

The larger pieces of pottery base with secondary bored holes were probably either related to the complete vessel, or subsequent use as loom-weights, or perhaps both. The lead 'net' weight (fig. 54, 244, see above) might also be sufficiently heavy as a loom-weight, and perhaps the shale waste core (265). However the only obvious and purpose-made loom-weight example was made from local sandstone (263), otherwise some naturally holed and utilised pebbles may have made serviceable loom-weights.

The six pottery spindle whorl pieces were all manufactured from broken BB1 body sherds of large jars, two of which were oxidised. Five of these were derived from the 1st century AD levels. All were rough cut to a rounded shape of about 3cm diameter, and the 'centre' hole was about 0.5 - 0.6cm diameter.

The bone spindle whorl was formed from the cut head of an animal femur (264). This example was recovered from the shell midden and rubbish infilling pit (87) in building (707). These bun-shaped spindle whorls were only noted at Portchester in the Saxon levels (Cunliffe, 1976, 220), whilst spindle whorls in the Roman levels are turned (Cunliffe, 1975, 219-222, obj. 106-109).

The two shale whorls, one of which might be a loom-weight, were derived from shale lathe-waste cores (265-266), and are described in that section.

In all cases the hole cut into these objects was bored from both sides. One of the pottery pieces was only part bored with the incision forming a sharp core, which was more reminiscent of a metal 'bit' rather than flint, which would have been used for boring and lathe cutting the shale in later phases of the site.

THE BUILDING MATERIALS, ARCHITECTURAL FRAGMENTS, AND MISCELLANEOUS STONE OBJECTS
PETER COX and PETER J. WOODWARD

The building materials and architectural fragments have been described under the following headings:
The post-padstones, The roof tiles, The tesserae, The markerstone, The net/thatch weights, The circular slabs (bored) and Purbeck Marble.
The stratigraphic location of these objects is summarised in table 7.

Acknowledgments: We are indebted to Paul Ensom of Dorset County Museum, for the geological identification of the stone fragments, Quentin Palmer (geologist with English China Clays) for information relating to the mudstone tesserae, and to W. G. Putnam for comments on the cutting of tesserae and the laying of mosaics. We would also thank Patrick Galliou and Professor Pierre-Roland Giot for drawing our attention to Armorican steles.

The Post Padstones:
None of these are illustrated here, but have been recorded in detail in the Level III Archive. Their location can be seen in figs 36 and 37, and a section through three of the blocks (767), (689) and (691) in fig. 33. Amongst the general use of local heathstone in walling, fifteen heavy blocks had been used as socketed supports for structural uprights in building (707), and (564). These padstones were generally brick-shaped and varied in size from 65 × 72.5 × 22.5cm to 35 × 32.5 × 15cm. Most stones had only one socket while one example (the largest) had two.

The size of socket and support function were related, and may be divided into two classes:
A. Large sockets, up to 17.5 × 12.5 × 10cm. All stones of this group form the main wall lines of building (707), including the apsidal northern end. In general these are larger, heavier stones.
B. Small sockets, up to 15 × 7.5 × 5cm. These include one stone with two small sockets and one with a recut socket. In all cases these blocks are used in lighter, load-bearing situations, such as the porched entrance and internal partition wall in building (707).

Few stones exhibit working on their sides, although their upper and lower faces are generally flat. Tooling inside the sockets indicate that chisels were used for working the stone. Several blocks exhibit striations across the upper surfaces: a result of post-Roman ploughing.

If the timber posts were located in the sockets by means of mortice joints then it is unlikely that the cross-sectional area of the wood would have exceeded that of the block upon which it was resting. The large socketed padstone with the smallest surface area measures approximately 32 × 40cm. If all upright timbers were of the same dimension then this may approximate to the maximum preferred size throughout.

The use of socketed padstones for building construction elsewhere in Purbeck has been noted at the Romano-British settlement at Studland (Field, 1965), and at Bucknowle Villa, Corfe Castle (Field, 1978).

Post padstones of limestone also occur at Ower to bear building timbers. Two were used, set below the two main door jambs in the 1st phase of building (707), and later replaced by sandstone socketed stones (mentioned above). The two are of broadly similar dimensions, around 52 × 40 × 10cm. Both are flat without well finished edges. Only one, however had a circular hole (10cm diameter) cut through it. This might have been to allow drainage around the post, but the fact that the other had no such facility might indicate that the stone was being re-used in this context. Furthermore, the stone was badly cracked on excavation with fractures radiating from the hole, possibly resulting from the pressure of the structure it supported. If these stones were to have borne the posts, then the dimensions of the posts as they sat on the stones could have been no more than 52 × 40cm or 40cm in diameter.

The Roofing Tiles

Limestone, shale and ceramic roofing tiles occurred in small quantities in the excavated area, generally in association with the 3rd-4th century AD building complex. The total number of identifiable (complete) pieces, and their stratigraphic distribution are shown in Table 7. The paucity of material, and the lack of fixing holes in the complete limestone and shale examples suggests none of this material had actually been used for roofing. The provision of peg holes would have occurred immediately prior to the tiles being mounted in position. Furthermore, the limestone tiles possessed a larger variation in dimensions than has been used on villa sites in Dorset, where consistency in size enables neat and accurate cover of the roof area (Cook, 1980).

All the categories of tile from this site were therefore probably not used for roofing material. Roof covering was probably confined to reed thatch. The purpose to which the unused tiles were put were various. In several instances limetone tiles and slabs were used for post-packing and cist construction. The shale may have been brought to the site in the form of unused roofing tiles for raw material to be used for lathe turning armlets and other items (refer report below). It is not likely that roof tiles were manufactured at Ower for export since the site is at some distance from the source of the raw material. No doubt there was an occasional use for ceramic tile and no doubt the occurrence of these materials on site was a result of the occasional trade associated with BB1 pottery production.

The ceramic tile included 9 fragments with combing which were probably fragments of box tile.

The Tesserae (Mudstone)

The scant occurrence of mudstone inclusions in briquetage fabric on the site has already been noted (see above). A total of 63 larger pieces were also retrieved, most of which had apparently been shaped to form small tesserae or tesserae blanks.

The mudstone used for tesserae is a compacted fine clayey silt found in the upper Tertiary Bagshot Beds around Poole harbour. The deposits occur in thin bands, generally around 3cm thick and easily accessible without substantial quarrying. The material is massive, without any significant lamination except when dry, but sometimes quite friable. However, it may be easily worked by scoring and snapping. The material is brown in appearance, although this may be the result of oxidation either *in situ* or after quarrying and use. Sources of mudstone in the locality of the Ower peninsula are numerous owing to its rather widespread occurrence. Significant amounts are known between Rempstone and Goathorn. (*Pers. comm.* Quentin Palmer, English China Clays.)

Sixty three larger pieces of mudstone recovered may be classified in four size/shape groups. The stratigraphic distribution of these is shown in Table 7.
A. 'Flat': dimensions up to 3.5 × 3.5 × 1.0cm
B. 'Squat/long': dimensions up to 3.5 × 1.5 × 1.5cm
C. 'Small cubes': dimensions up to 1.2 × 1.2 × 1.2cm
D. Partly worked or unworked lumps: Maximum size 7.8 × 7.0 × 2.0cm

All types were found in contexts dating from 2nd century build up levels through to post-Roman, and from the upper of two 1st century features (858) and (359). Indeed, as much as 50% of type B tesserae come from phase 3 contexts. There appear to be no significant concentrations of worked mudstone on the site that

might indicate a working floor or workshop related specifically to this task. However, 20 pieces (32% of total by count) are from build-up deposits pre-dating the 3rd century 'potters' buildings and might be derived from an earlier, functionally different focus of the site outside the excavated area. Certainly, 14 (22%) are from post Roman disturbance, while the remaining 29 (46%) are from scattered 3rd century contexts, phases 4-7. This dating is consistent with the tesserae manufacture at Norden, Corfe Castle, Dorset (Sunter, this volume).

The occurrence of mudstone in tessellated pavements does not appear to be common, paticularly from the 2nd century AD. It has been suggested that dark grey tesserae from 2nd to 3rd period mosaics at Fishbourne are of Purbeck origin, Cunliffe (1971, 41-42). In Dorset, mudstone tesserae have been found in pavements at Dewlish villa dating to the late 3rd/4th century. Here, they measure approximately 1cm square and are only a few mms thick. The disparity between the large size of the Ower example and the ultimate size in pavements may be accounted for by the method of laying. The 'blanks' would be inserted into the pavement and then planed down (and subsequently worn) to a level (W.G. Putnam, *pers. comm.*). This fact and the early date of deposition would seem to discount the possibility that the mudstone tesserae blanks at Ower are derived from a villa or tessellated pavement elsewhere on the site.

The Markerstone (Stele):

The markerstone (fig. 56, 256) was reused in the sill wall footing of building (906), Plate 8 and fig. 36. The upper two-thirds of the stone were chiselled to a frustrum of a cone, the remainder being roughly rectangular in horizontal section and unfinished. The latter portion would have been embedded in the ground. The tooled part was 20cm in diameter at the top and 30cm at the base. The overall height was 90cm, of which nearly 55cms would have been above ground. The stone weighed perhaps as much as 5 cwt (254kg). It was carefully chiselled to give a pecked surface.

The markerstone was clearly an object of some importance. A similar object, but inscribed, is recorded from Thrapston, Northants (*Journal 4*, Northampton Museums and Art Gallery, December 1968 p. 3). Similar centuriation and boundary stones have been described (Dilke, 1971, 92 and 103). Elsewhere in the Roman empire, during the Gracchan period, centuriation stones were generally cylindrical with a slight taper, but of larger diameter (45cm). Augustus ruled that stones should be set 2.5ft (80cm) into the ground and protrude about 1.5ft (45cm). Under later emperors stones tended to be square and not circular.

However this stone has perhaps closer parallels with Armorican steles. These have a wide distribution in Brittany, and some have been found directly associated with Iron Age cemeteries (Briard *et al.*, 1979, 261-273). However most of these stones have now been displaced and in many cases reused and christianised. They are now frequently associated with later christian cemeteries.

Armorican steles, have a range of forms and have been classified and described by Briard *et al.* (*op. cit.*) The Ower stone is of a common type with circular cross-section. These circular steles are generally truncated cones, sometimes rounded at the top, and are usually undecorated. Their distribution is coastal and western, with high concentrations occurring in *Morbihan* and *Finistère*. These Breton stella are always made from granite and allied rocks.

If this parallel for the Ower stone is accepted, then it can at best be described as a copy, but would provide a direct cultural connection with Brittany, which when considered with suggested trading patterns (see above) is of great interest.

This markerstone has now been displayed at the centre of the (new) Rempstone stone circle (SY 98748240) in the grounds of Bushey House, Rempstone.

The Net/Thatch Weights:

A single rough hewn sub-rectangular block of limestone (27cm × 30cm × 7cm thick) with flat chiselled upper and lower faces and with an oval slot (in part a result of a natural fissure) worked into a central perforation 10cm × 5cm, was recovered from the post-Roman agricultural disturbance, pit (261). This was interpreted as a net or thatch weight. Circular slabs with holes could also have served this function, although one at least was used a a post base (fig. 37, and below).

The Circular Slabs:

Three circular and semicircular slabs of soft limestone were recovered from the later phases of the site (Table 7). One complete circular slab (32cm diameter, and about 8cm thick) was found at the south end of dryer (708), and above the remains of 'dryer' (825), fig. 38. Its function is uncertain. Another sawn semi-circular limestone slab with a well-rounded outer edge and pitted on one face was found in pit (388). This stone would have been originally of diameter 64cms and was about 10cm thick. The third was a segment of a circular limestone slab (fig. 56, 257). On this latter stone were the traces of a circular hole eccentrically placed; it was broken along natural fissures, had an estimated diameter of 80cm, and was recovered from the post-Roman disturbance pit (261).

None of these slabs had any sign of milling, and limestone of this type would be unsuitable for use in quernstones. However, they may have served as pivot stones for potters wheels (Swan, 1973). The fact that a similarly pierced limestone slab had been used as a padstone (see above) elsewhere on the site may suggest an alternative use. Large unmilled circular slabs of limestone were also noted at Rope Lake Hole, Kimmeridge, where lathe turning shale was the principal occupation (Woodward, this volume).

Purbeck Marble

The presence of Purbeck Marble as a material on the site was only noted in the 3rd-4th century AD levels, Table 7. It did occur as a building material, e.g. sill wall of building (910), and wall of kiln (540). However this was probably a secondary or casual use of this 'valuable' material. Its use for a pestle (see below) should be noted. The absence of this material from 1st century AD levels is of interest, although one of the querns was made from a hard limestone/marble, had late Iron Age affinities and may be residual (fig. 57, 258; see report on portable stone objects, below).

QUERNSTONES AND PORTABLE STONE OBJECTS

PETER COX

The stratigraphic distribution by phase of the querns and portable stone objects is summarised in Table 7. This material is described under the following headings; Querns, Pestle, Honestones.

The Querns:

Although all the querns were found in 3rd-4th century AD levels, they were of a type common in the Later Iron Age (Wheeler, 1943, 326). It is possible therefore that they would be residual, although not out of place in 4th century AD domestic sites. However in the contexts in which they were found it is possible that they were used for some purpose other than grinding cereals (see above). It has been suggested (Fulford, 1975, 16) that querns may have been used in the pottery manufacturing process to grind materials intended for tempering clay. No deposits containing grain have been identified on the site, but neither is there any evidence for quantities of ground tempering material (for pottery). The querns were made

from a hard Purbeck marble limestone (1), a large gritted Tertiary sandstone (3), and greensand (3). No upper or lower stones were paired, and only two complete examples were found (fig. 57, 258 and 260). The more complete examples are described following:

258 Complete topstone of Purbeck limestone/marble. A circular tapering handle socket on side with second (handle?) groove on top. Similar to example noted at *Maiden Castle* (Wheeler, 1943, fig. 115.16). From dryer (708), phase 7.

259 Topstone segment of local Tertiary large gritted sandstone. Rectangular handle socket on top. Coarsely tooled, shallow hopper around central socket. From phase 8.

260 Complete lower stone of local Tertiary sandstone. Sub-circular in shape. From rubble collapse of (707), phase 7.

Pestle

The base of a Purbeck Marble pestle (fig. 57, 261) was recovered from the infill (87) of building 707, phase 7. The handle was broken away, see complete example from *Silchester* (Boon, 1957, 166), and illustrated in Beavis (1971).

Honestones

Two honestones were recovered from the site, one of mudstone and the other of a fine sandstone. The mudstone piece may have been in part a natural pear shaped lump with traces of wear on the upper surface. The sandstone piece (fig. 57, 262) was in several fragments, with wear on the broad upper and lower surfaces.

THE KIMMERIDGE SHALE

Considerable quantities of Kimmeridge shale (waste and finished objects) were recovered from all levels of the site. This waste was derived from the working of slabs of the raw material brought to the site. One of the shale blocks found in the 3rd-4th century AD levels on the site had been cut into the outline of a lozenge-shaped roof tile, but not pierced for hanging. It is likely that in this period unused (waste) roof tiles from other sites (villas), or simply roof tile surplus, were brought to Ower for manufacturing small objects, rather than the site being concerned with the manufacture of roof tiles since the site is a long way from the raw material source (see also ceramic tile and limestone roof tile reports). The majority of the object types found at Ower were lathe-turned products; armlets, beads, vessels and trays. However some products were simply chiselled and then hand smoothed and polished: armlets and possibly a circular tray.

The assemblage was analysed on the basis of the following categories:

1. 'Unworked' raw material, exhibiting no identifiable working (saw/chisel marks, conchoidal type fracture).
   Often laminated and with rough edge fracture.

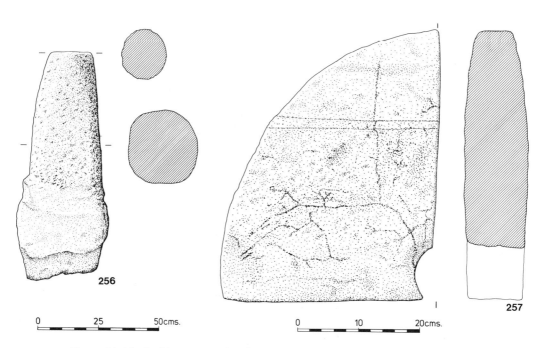

0   25   50cms.

0   10   20cms.

Figure 56. The building material and architectural fragments (25, 1:15; 257, ⅙).

2. Worked shale waste showing conchoidal fracture, chisel and saw marks.,
3. Circular prepared pieces (measurable) for armlet production (sawn, 3s), and chiselled waste from hand-made armlets (3ci-3ciii):
   3s: 'Sawn' circular blanks for lathe mounting.
   3ci: Shale sheets with punched or chiselled holes.
   3cii: Shale sheet with part removed chiselled disc.
   3ciii: Chiselled waste discs.
4. Calkin (1953) type lathe mountings on shale discs and lathe waste cores.
   A. With central square through hole.
   B. With central square part-through hole.
   C. With paired circular part-through bored holes.
   D. With three or more circular part-through bored holes.
5. Rough armlet products with little surface smoothing or polishing, unfinished.
   C. Hand chiselled.
   L. Lathe turned.
6. Finished armlet products.
   C. Hand chiselled.
   L. Lathe turned.
7. Other shale products and vessel core waste.
   C. Hand chiselled.
   L. Lathe turned.

The proportion of these various categories of material are shown on a percentage histogram (fig. 30). Comparison of the material from 1st-century AD contexts (A) and 3rd-4th-century AD contexts (C) shows marked contrasts. The material from the soil accumulation levels (B) also contrast strongly with the later levels. Interpretation of this contrast suggests that when the site was reorganised in the 3rd-4th-century AD, the technology of turning

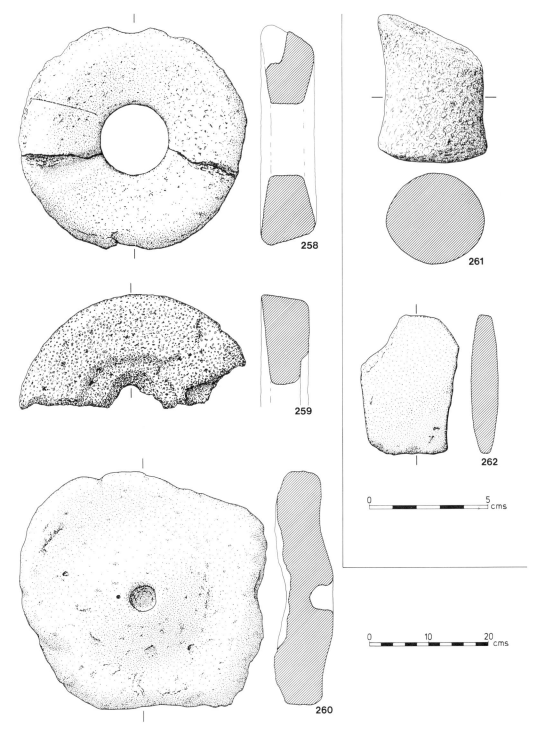

Figure 57. Querns and portable stone objects (258-262). 258-60 at 1:6; 261-262 at ⅔.

shale had changed and the range of products increased, a new lathe fixing technique had been introduced (4B-D), and an interest in a wider range of products had developed (vessels, beads, table tops, . . . etc., 7C and L). The lower proportion of chiselled waste (category 2) in the later levels is consistent with an increased use of lathe, bow drill and saw. The high percentage of chiselled waste in the earlier levels probably results from the hand-chiselling armlets, also indicated by the presence of 3ci waste and 3ciii waste (residual in phase 8, fig. 30D). These dated changes in technology can be paralleled on other shale working sites in Dorset (Calkin, 1953), and further discussion on lathe-fixing techniques can be found at Rope Lake Hole (Woodward, this volume).

The majority of lathe-cores, -discs and -armlets conformed to the types described in detail by Calkin (1953), and no exhaustive description has therefore been presented here, apart from the measurements of diameter. The measurement of all discs, lathe core-waste, and armlet diameters (fig. 60) show these diameters as a percentage frequency accumulation. This demonstrates a marked conformity of sizes, which suggests that the majority of lathe waste was derived from armlet production, and that single armlets were removed from each shale disc. This has also been demonstrated by Calkin on other Purbeck sites (Calkin, 1953). However a number of lathe cores did not correspond to the armlet core waste (fig. 60). These were much smaller in diameter and thicker (fig. 58, 267, 268), and were derived from turning vessels. The vessel core (fig. 58, 268) may perhaps be an unfinished vessel base subsequently abandoned. The size of some discs and lathe-core waste (fig. 60) was clearly much larger than the size of the armlet apparently produced on this site. The discs were perhaps prepared for the making of other object types, or perhaps the larger armlets were simply not recovered.

The flint industry described in a separate report (following) was directly related to the lathe-turning of shale. It was essentially similar to that industry described by Calkin, for the production of

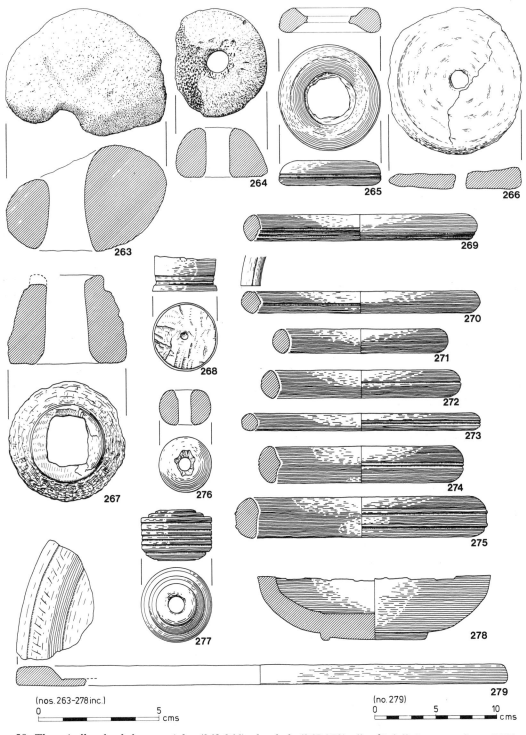

Figure 58. The spindle whorls loom weights (263-266), the shale (267-279) all at ⅔ full size apart from (279) at ⅓.

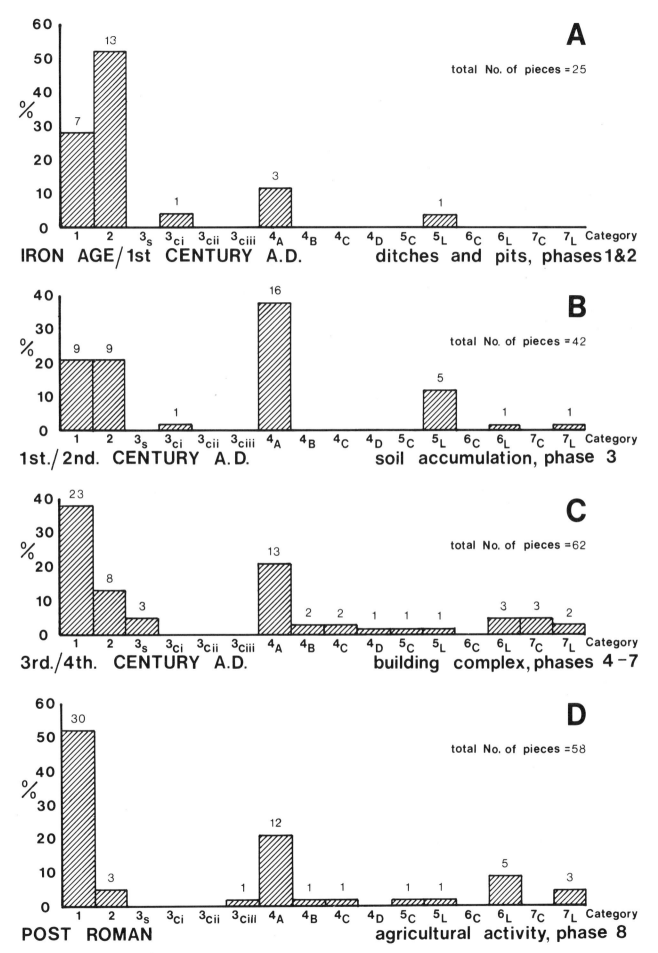

Figure 59. Histograms showing the distribution of the shale categories by dated phase.

small lathe-chisels, suitable for cutting rotating shale (see also Rope Lake Hole).

The range of shale objects made at Ower is shown in fig. 58. These are all common Romano-British types and well known on Dorset sites and further afield. No exhaustive list of parallels has therefore been sought. The objects illustrated are:

265. Core, reused as spindle whorl, Calkin type A with enlarged centre fixing hole. Phase 8.
266. Sub-circular disc, with small centre hole. Slight evidence for the lathe turning on edge, laminated and worn. Probably lathe disc reused as spindle whorl. Phase 8.
267. Core of Calkin type A, roughcut sides, possibly core from vessel production. Infill pit (87), Phase 7.
268. Small laminated core fragment. Neatly cut side and groove. Perhaps from vessel base. Phase 3.
269. Unfinished armlet from fragment with 'D' section Category 5L. From post-hole (822). (?) 1st. century AD, phase 1.
270. Reconstructed unfinished armlet from fragment with 'D' section. Category 5L. From occupation horizon (142), with phase 7.
271. Reconstructed armlet from fragment with 'D' section, undecorated. Category 6L, phase 8.
272. Reconstructed armlet from fragment with 'D' section, and single decorative groove. Category 6L, from yard (441) with building (909), phase 5.
273. Reconstructed armlet from fragment with 'O' section, and double decorative groove. Category 6L. From phase 8.
274. Reconstructed armlet from fragment with 'D' section, and double decorative groove. Category 6L. From yard 147, phase 7.
275. Reconstructed armlet from fragment with 'D' section, and wide groove with raised edge decoration. Category 6L. From yard 441 with building 909, phase 5.
276. Lathe turned bead, undecorated, Category 7L. From test-pit at 510.119, with marine shell midden, phase 8.
277. Lathe turned bead, with multiple grooves. Category 6L. From infill pit (87) to building (707). Phase 7.
278. Base of lathe-turned beaker, undecorated with small footring, Category 7L. From pit (644) with BB1 dish (fig. 19, 146). Phase 7.

279. Reconstructed circular tray/table top from fragment illustrated. Some cross-hatched decoration within concentric lines around wide rim. Possibly hand-made. Category 7C. From floor level of building (707)C. Phase 7.

THE FLINT

The flint varies in colour from a dark grey-white and most is patchy in appearance and faulted. A thin hard granular chalk cortex is present on some flint, but usually the cortex is much eroded to a thin granular and pitted surface. Most of the material probably originates from the nearby Eocene sands and gravels. The degree of similarity between many of the struck flint pieces, both in faulting, body colour and cortex, suggests that many came from the same nodules. However no fits were found.

The majority of the material was recovered from the upper levels of the site. Some materially similar pieces in the medieval agriculture disturbance could be related to pieces stratified in the later building phases of the site (3rd-4th century AD). The working techniques used were also uniform throughout the assemblage. The bulk of the material can therefore be considered to have been derived from the 3rd-4th century building phases of the site. Four flakes (three without retouch) came from upper silts of the curved enclosure (343), and the rectilinear enclosure (288) ditches, it is likely that these are derived from the upper levels of the site and few are associated with the 1st century occupation (Table 9). No specialised flint industry could be related to the lathe-turning of shale in the 1st-century AD, although a lathe turned shale core did occur in phase 1 ditch fill. (See above).

The industry represented here is characterised by:
i   Snapped flake segments (for use as lathe tools).
ii Retouch of segments, often along the snapped face, and retouch of bulbar ends (for hafting).
iii Burin, hinge fractures, and pressure flake retouch at angle between snapped face and flake edge (for chisel cutting edge of hafted lathe tools).

This industry can be usefully compared with that from a number of other sites in Purbeck described in Calkin (1953), from Norden (Bradley this volume) Rope Lake Hole (this volume) and can be directly associated with the lathe turning of shale.

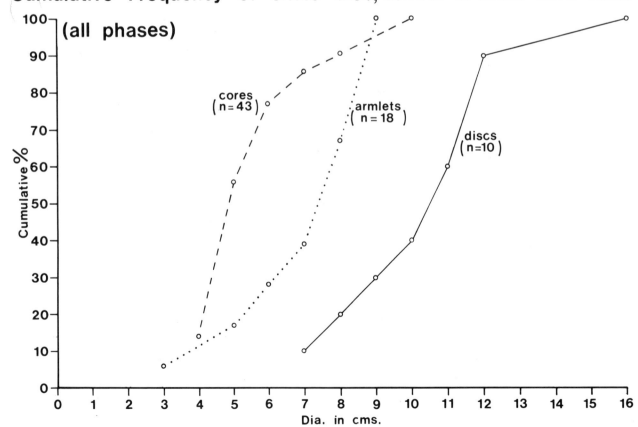

Cumulative Frequency of shale disc, armlet & lathe core dias.

(all phases)

cores (n = 43)

armlets (n = 18)

discs (n=10)

Cumulative %

Dia. in cms.

Figure 60. The Cumulative percentage frequency of shale cores, armlets and discs.

Calkin describes a technique which involved the production of long, deep and rigid flakes, with their subsequent snapping to produce parallel sided 'kite' shaped pieces. These were then usually retouched along the broken edges for hafting and subsequent use as a lathe tool for cutting shale. The angle between the original flake edge and the snapped face was often blunted by the removal of a burin-type flake or retouched. This could be due to deliberate sharpening, or a result of use.

The characteristics of this technique can be recognised at Ower, and it is only the limitations of the local material that evidently prevented the regular production of the ideal kite-shaped tools. Only two pieces roughly conformed to a 'kite tool'; one was so crudely made, that it was severely mis-shaped and faulted and probably never used (not illustrated), the other was produced from a thermal flake, and has near vertical edges and parallel sides (fig. 61, 280). This tool shows retouch only in one corner; it was also probably too square to cut rotating shale, and not therefore used.

Although it was not possible to produce 'kite' shaped pieces, tool points were still produced by the technique of snapping flakes (fig. 61, 281-284), the removal of a burin flake (fig. 61, 281, 282 and 287), and secondary retouch (fig. 61, 283-286, 288). In the illustration of these tools the sides around which they would have been hafted are indicated, and an arrow denotes the 'operating point' of the tool. The orientation of the arrow indicates the direction in which the burin flake has been removed where this occurs, otherwise it indicates the direction from which the rotating shale would have impinged on the cutting edge or point. The bulb, or putative bulb, of the flake lies at the base of the drawing.

The ratios of cores: waste: secondary worked (retouch) flakes (tools), is expressed in table 9. The high percentage of s/w material (46%) shows the intensive use of the available flint brought to the site. The s/w flakes can be divided into two categories:

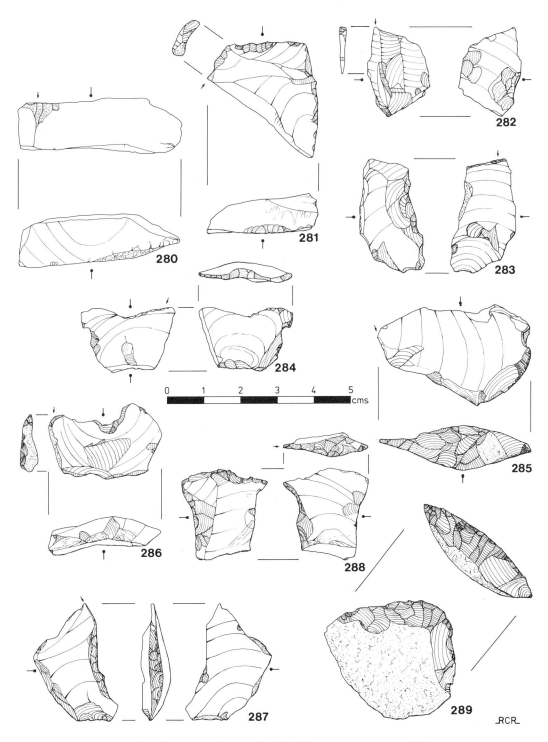

Figure 61. The flint; lathe chisel tools (280-288), trimming flakes (289), 1:1.

TABLE 9: The Stratigraphic Location of the Worked Flint by Dated Phase Group

Phase Nos.	Date range	Cores		S/W Flakes*		Non S/W Flakes		Total
		Systematic	Worked Lumps	A	B	Complete	Snapped	
1-3	1st. c. AD	–	–	–	1	2	1	4
4-7	3rd/4th c. AD	–	–	7	–	4	2	13
8	Post-Roman	1	2	13	7	5	16	44
	TOTAL	1	2	20	8	11	19	61
	%		5%		46%		49%	100%

*Secondary Worked Flakes
A: Snapped and trimmed flakes to produce chisel element for mounted tool (fig. 61, 280-288).
B: Unsnapped but retouched flakes to produce trimming/scraper type tools (fig. 61, 289 and fig. 62, 290-291)

TABLE 10: The Numerical Analysis of the Secondary Worked Flint Flake Tools (Lathe Chisels)

SECONDARY WORKED FLAKES	A		B		TOTAL	TOTAL
	No	%	No	%	No.	%
Position of retouch on flake:						
Number of retouched snapped edges	13	33	–	–	19	39
Number of retouched distal ends			6	67		
Number of retouched sides	19	47	3	33	22	45
Number of retouched butts	8	20	0	0	8	16
TOTAL	40	100	9	100	49	100
Number of flakes with:						
1 retouched/trimmed edge	6	30	7	88	13	46
2 retouched/trimmed edges	8	40	1	12	9	32
3 retouched/trimmed edges	6	30	0	0	6	22
4 retouched/trimmed edges	0	0	0	0	0	0
TOTAL	20	100	8	100	28	100

A those snapped and trimmed flakes to produce chisel type elements of a hafted tool. (fig. 61, 280-288).

B those unsnapped but retouched flakes to produce trimming/scraper type tools (fig. 61, 289 and fig. 33, 290-291).

Of the s/w tool flakes, type A (71%) occurs most frequently and therefore has more frequent and specific usage. It is notable that within this group A, all four edges of the flake are used equally in retouch including the butt (Table 10). It is interesting that the butt (thick end) of these flakes is frequently used to produce chisel tools (fig. 61, 283-288) and is frequently retouched (20%) (fig. 61, 285-286 and table 9). This use of the butt end is clearly a result of the flake size available. Only one clear case of a utilised intermediate flake segment was recovered (fig. 61, 283).

The simpler B type tool resembles the ubiquitous scraper (fig. 61, 289 and fig. 62, 290, and table 2), and finely retouched blades, (fig. 62, 291). These were presumably used for trimming and polishing, the larger pieces (fig. 61, 289, and fig. 62, 290) were undoubtedly hand-held. The retouch on these tools is confined to the sides and distal ends (Table 9).

The core technique for flake production on the available evidence is not clear, but was probably variable and unskilled. However it is clear that the platform on flakes was often deep, which created thicker bulbar end flakes (Bradley this volume) for retouch to form 'type A' tools (above).

The core evidence is confined to three pieces and only one of these can be used to characterise an intentional technique (fig. 62, 292). This core shows almost cone like fractures, and miss-hits are apparent. Deep platforms and positive bulbs occur on all faces. From this square-sided 'core' a single positive flake has been removed from one of the 'ventral' surfaces at right angles to the

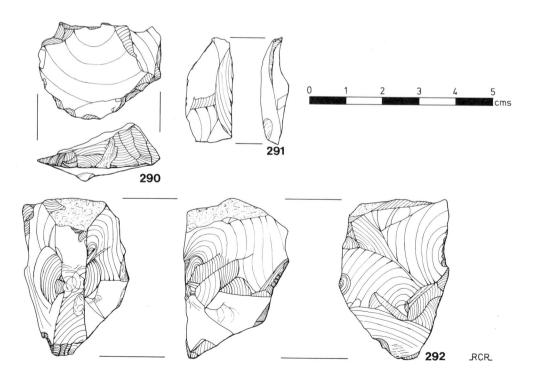

Figure 62. The flint; trimming flakes (290, 291), core (292), 1:1.

'core' platform. The squarish flake removed may have been suitable after trimming for a lathe tool. This technique of flake removal from the ventral surface of a deep flake is reminiscent of a gun-flint manufacturing technique in the 17th and 18th centuries AD (Clay, 1925). However no other flakes of this type were noted in the assemblage, nor manufactured tools.

A portion of a well-rolled blade with deep brown patina was recovered on the top surface of the undisturbed Eocene sand in trial trench (590.059), away from the focus of the Romano-British settlement. This piece bore no resemblance to the industry described above, and is likely to be of Palaeolithic origin. It has not been included in the above analysis.

Acknowledgement: I am grateful to Phil Harding for his comments and ideas whilst writing this report, P.J.W.

METALWORKING RESIDUES

LEO BIEK

Three categories of material were identified: 'fuel ash slag', a few iron 'slag runs', and some 'hearth buns'. The stratigraphic distribution of these types of material is summarised in table 7. The presence of run slag in the pre-conquest levels of ditch (288) may be important, since this could result from smelting. No material occurred in suggestive concentrations and there was no furnace lining. Smithing was clearly a nearby activity. Some of the 'fuel ash slag' might be derived from burning shale and not necessarily indicative of metalworking. A full catalogue of the stratified material can be found in the Level III archive. (See also Rope Lake Hole, this volume)

THE HUMAN SKELETAL REMAINS

This report summarises bone identifications by Jennie Coy from the 1978 excavations, and the description of the burial uncovered in 1975 by John Beavis, with the identification of the interred bones by Liz Cox.

Five fragments of human bone were recovered from the 1978 excavations: cranium fragment, and tibia fragment from the rubble collapse of building (707), a (?) humerus from wall trench (672), a humerus from ditch (288)B and one unidentifiable fragment from the Phase 3 accumulation.

The cist burial (fig. 31A.J., and fig. 63) was discovered as a result of deep ploughing and was rapidly recorded by John Beavis. The associated objects with the burial, and the bones themselves are now lost. A report on the bones and burial type was produced, with particular reference to lead levels in Romano-British burials by Liz Cox as part of a dissertation for the degree of B.Ed., (Cox 1980). This description is freely adapted from the original burial report which can be found in the Level III Archive, together with the site record drawings and survey.

The burial was placed in a cist of pitched limestone slabs; the burial being originally laid at the base of the cist at a depth of perhaps 0.3m. This would have originally been covered with a set of limestone slabs (fig. 63ii) to complete the box. Above the collapsed slabs were a number of disarticulated human bones which may have been a secondary burial, (Cox 1980), but were not otherwise examined. However it is perhaps possible that these were bones of the primary burial below the slabs which had subsequently been disturbed by animals.

The disturbed primary burial occurred with what were described as coffin nails, and what are clearly hob-nails around the feet. A

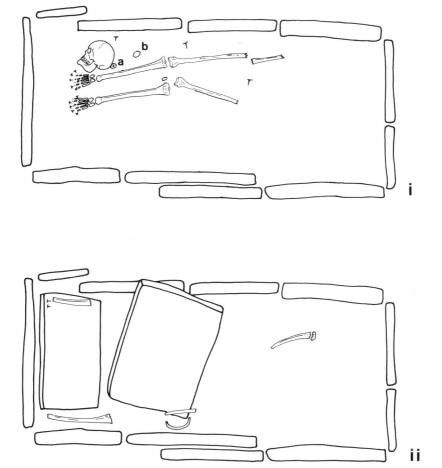

Figure 63. The Romano-British burial at Ower located at J (fig. 31A).

TABLE 11: Phase Divisions and Species Representation (no. of fragments)

	Phase 1+2	Phase 3	Phase 4/5/6	Phase 7	Total
MAMMALS					
horse	9	1	5	12	27
cattle	101	46	42	181	370
sheep	132	41	35	175	383
pig	238	44	45	79	406
red deer					
Cervus elaphus	–	–	–	6	6
roe deer					
Capreolus capreolus	1	–	–	–	1
fox					
Vulpes vulpes	5	–	–	–	5
cattle-sized	75	26	27	57	185
sheep-sized	135	82	26	68	311
BIRDS					
domestic fowl	1	–	–	16	17
swan					
Cygnus sp.	1	–	–	2	3
mallard/domestic duck					
Anas platyrhynchos	6	2	–	5	13
Duck, *Anas* sp.	1	–	–	1	2
white-tailed sea eagle					
Haliaetus albicilla	1	–	–	–	1
curlew					
Numenius arquata	1	–	–	1	2
guillemot					
Uria aalge	–	1	–	–	1
greenshank					
Tringa nebularia	–	1	–	–	1
unidentified bird	–	–	–	1	1
FISH					
*common eel					
Anguilla anguilla	–	1	–	–	1
gilthead sea bream					
Sparus aurata	–	–	2	–	2
unidentified fish	5	–	–	–	5
TOTAL	712	245	182	604	1,743

*There were also remains of small eels found in the shell deposits (See separate mollusc report)

small spindle whorl, a water-worn pebble and number of limpet shells may have been deliberately placed at burial (fig. 63 i; spindle whorl (a), water worn pebble (b)). The dating of the burial is difficult from the material recovered from the site, since the burial cyst was substantially damaged prior to a controlled examination. However briquetage, and 3rd/4th century AD pottery were recovered but these may derive from the topsoil. A single piece of samian from the burial cyst was of a pre-conquest type (Pengelly, see previous).

The skeletal remains were probably of a male of about 30 years.

What remained of the skeleton was extended with the skull laid to one side of the feet. This together with the possible secondary burial, spindle-whorl, and limpets has an almost exact parallel with a Romano-British (double female) burial at Kimmeridge (summarised in *R.C.H.M. (Dorset)* II, 609). This was dated by a coin of Carausius (286-93) in the grave-pit. This burial was cut through a shale working floor. It is possible that the burial at Ower could be of similar date.

A similar burial can also be found at Studland (*R.C.H.M. (Dorset)* II, 611), again with a small spindle whorl near the pelvis, and skull near left foot (female – 30-40 years old).

The lead levels in the bones were 60ppm (lower skeletal bones) and 70ppm (upper skeletal bones). These were rather higher than levels from other rural sites (Sutton Pyontz, Radipole, Came View and Wyke Regis) which were 30-40ppm, (Cox 1980).

THE ANIMAL BONES

JENNIE COY
Faunal Remains Project, University of Southampton

There were 1,743 animal bone fragments. Phases and species represented are given in Table 11. Information was recorded using the Ancient Monuments Laboratory's computer coding scheme (Jones n.d.) and is housed at the Faunal Remains Project. An earlier Level III Archive Report is also available (Coy n.d.). The present account mainly concentrates on the two collections of any size – one mostly from the 1st century AD ditches (Phase 1 + 2) and the second from more variable contexts of the 3rd and 4th centuries AD (Phase 7).

Species Represented:
Most common were bones of the three major domestic species – cattle, sheep, and pig. There was a small amount of horse bone. As all ovicaprid remains identifiable to species were definite sheep all 'sheep or goat' categories were included in the 'sheep' row in Table 11. As 'cattle-sized' fragments were mostly small fragments of unidentifiable long bone or fragmentary ribs there is a faint possibility that these contain a few fragmens from horse or red deer. Similarly the fragments from 'sheep-sized' animals may include pig fragments although the pig's distinctive anatomy makes this less likely.

The native red deer, *Cervus elaphus*, was represented in Phase 7 and roe deer, *Capreolus capreolus*, and red fox, *Vulpes vulpes*, in Phase 1+2.

Domestic fowl bones were mostly in Phase 7 and there were a few bones of other birds throughout. Fish appeared in few contexts and were probably not often preserved.

Specific Percentages of Cattle, Sheep and Pig:
On the basis of fragments identified to species (or to ovicaprid) there was a significantly different species representation in Phase 1 + 2 and Phase 7 (Table 12). Chi-squared testing of original frequencies showed them as highly unlikely to occur by chance (p=<0.001, chi-squared = 108 on 6 d.f.).

The most significant values contributing to this result were the high value for pig fragments in Phase 1 + 2 and the low value in Phase 7, where pig was replaced as major contributor to fragment counts by cattle.

Including 'C-size' and 'S-size' counts as well as specifically identified fragments it is clear that small ungulates (sheep, pig, 'S-size') always form the major fragment totals throughout the occupation (range 58.5-74.0%) but in Phase 7 the large ungulate representation is 42.5%, compared with 26% for Phase 1+2. This presumably mirrors the relative percentages of pig and cattle shown in Table 12 for the species identifiable bones.

Together these figures suggest a significant change in diet or husbandry between the earliest and latest phases with an enormous decrease in the significance of pig, some increase in cattle, and to a less significant extent an increase in sheep. The assumptions that must be made to come to such conclusions will be discussed after a brief diversion on the anatomical elements represented; a subject intricately related to any comparisons of specific percentages.

| | PHASES | | | |
	1+2	*3*	*4,5,6*	*7*
No. fragments	(471)	(131)	(122)	(435)
cattle	21%	35	34	42
sheep	28%	31	29	40
pig	51%	34	37	18
	100%	100	100	100

TABLE 12: Specific Percentage for the Three Major Species

Anatomical Elements of Cattle, Sheep and Pig:
The anatomical parts of the three major species are given for the two larger samples in Tables 13 and 14.

Bones identified to species were used to compare the number of fragments from heads and feet (including distal radius and distal tibia) with those from the rest of the body which carry the major meat masses. This rough index served to pinpoint the rather high values for head and foot bones for sheep in Phase 7 and for pig in Phase 1+2.

Discussion:
An individual bovine would provide several times the amount of meat provided by a pig. Estimates for meat yield of cattle compared with pig range from about 1:3 for Manching (Boessneck *et al* 1971, 9) to 1:6.6 for Gussage (Harcourt 1979, 155).

Even taking the latter the results suggest that in Phase 1+2 pork was a significant source of food, whereas in Phase 7 beef was overwhelmingly the most important mammalian food.

But this is to make a number of assumptions.
1. that these bones are the remains of animals used for food
2. that fragment counts relate directly to the number of animals, with no differential degrees of fragmentation or preservation for the different species, or for different phases
3. that collections are representative of the economy of the phase and are comparable.

To deal with the first assumption – it is beyond doubt that there were bones from butchered and processed carcases of the three major species, in all contexts. There was no butchery on any of the horse bones. There was no evidence for whole or partial skeletons of the three major species.

Burning was more common for Phase 1+2 than for Phase 7 and butchery very slightly so, although the last phase had a higher proportion of loose teeth which are unlikely to show butchery.

These criteria demonstrate that this is a typical domestic assemblage where the bones are likely to be remains of meals and carcase preparation. The degree of fragmentation of the deposits is also confirmation that carcases were heavily utilised.

Assumption two is more controversial as the amount of material from this site is too small for secure conclusions. King has suggested that overall fragment counts do relate in a rough way to the calculated minimum number of individuals (King 1978, 208). The relationship between calculated minima and actual number of animals represented is more obscure for such a small bone collection. King also confirmed that pig often showed a smaller number of bones per individual than sheep or cattle when minimum numbers are calculated, something already known from Wessex Iron Age settlements (e.g. Coy 1969, 47) and associated with differential loss of post-cranial elements. Pig at Ower certainly seemed to present a high proportion of non-meat bones (mostly jaws, head bones, and loose teeth) in Phase 1+2 (81%) and this may mean that it was *underestimated* in importance at least in that phase, if fragment counts were used.

The degree of fragmentation of the major bones was compared for the three major species. Only the Phase 1+2 sample was large

enough to be useable and this showed no significant differences in the fragmentation pattern of the different species. The fragmentation pattern in Phase 1+2 and Phase 7 was generally similar. Samples from the other phases were too small for valid analysis. The fragmentation pattern was not significantly influenced by excessive fragmentation, in either of these phases, to small unidentifiable fragments. There was, however, a slightly higher value for such unidentifiable fragments in Phase 1+2.

There is some evidence that Phase 7 contains a slightly higher proportion of eroded bone than Phase 1+2. The slightly acid nature of the soil could have been a factor in some contexts,. The pH of the soil would also vary with the amount of bone and mollusc waste deposited. Erosion may also explain why there were several associations of obviously related maxillary teeth with no sign of maxillary bone. It may also explain the large number of loose teeth in some of these collections.

Apart from the relative scarcity of pig post-cranials, which is not confined to acid sites, there is no suggestion that erosion has affected different species in different ways.

The problems raised in assumption 2 are very big ones and an important part of the overall studies of Wessex bones taking place. They can only be elucidated by the detailed study of large accumulations of carefully collected samples. Large Iron Age samples have certainly demonstrated that depositional and preservational factors as discussed here do influence results obtained for specific ratios, anatomical elements, and age groups (e.g. Maltby 1981, 166).

In order to test the third assumption a context by context analysis of the material took place and some points for this are highlighted in the following discussion.

Context by Context Discussion:
It is interesting to compare individual contexts with overall phase results.

In Phase 1+2 there are 525 mammal bones from the rectilinear enclosure and 166 which come from residual material from this and from the ring ditch. There are no significant differences between the two deposits in terms of species and anatomical elements represented.

Other criteria relating to preservation (eg. percentage of loose teeth, percentage of unidentifiable long bone fragments) were tested. The value for large ungulate unidentifiable fragments was noticeably higher in the rectilinear enclosure than for the phase as a whole but otherwise differences were minor.

Phase 3 contained too small a sample of study in depth but it was generally badly preserved with high values for loose teeth. It showed the highest proportion of small ungulate fragments, presumably linked with slow build-up of this deposit where bones may have been exposed over long periods.

There were 108 bones in Phase 4,5,6 contexts thought to be later contamination of earlier ditches. This small sample showed a higher proportion of pig bones than in the phase as a whole (47%) but this could be bias due to the small sample.

Material in the briquetage feature 388 and kiln/oven 540 was very fragmentary and probably highly residual.

The Phase 7 potter's yard, 147, produced 120 fragments which give specific percentages of cattle, sheep, and pig, respectively, of 39%, 32%, and 29%. This is rather higher for pig than the phase average but again sample size was very small (82 species-identified bones). Other Phase 7 values were not unlike the phase figures except that loose teeth formed 50% of total sheep fragments and 29% of pig fragments. The building collapse material in context 564 produced 192 bones, most of which were in O.P. 568. This particular collection was very interesting as it contained much of the highly fragmentary small ungulate material in this phase. Here 70% of all species-identified fragments were sheep, 87% of these being non-meat bones. In addition 91% of unidentified fragments were from small ungulates – a highly significant value. This shows how small deposits can vary and this one in particular with its concentration on sheep extremities is unrepresentative of the whole phase, where cattle form 42% of the total fragment count.

Quite different was the midden/rubbish material in context 706/707 in which 82% of the 184 fragments were from cattle – with a high proportion of cranial fragments and teeth.

Results for contexts within Phase 7 were thus remarkably variable and did not present the consistency of those forming Phase 1+2. It is therefore difficult to compare bones from the two phases with any sense of security in the data. The midden/rubbish collection with its concentration on cattle has a big effect on the Phase 7 figures. The very high sheep values in the building collapse

TABLE 13: Mamalian bones in Phases 1 and 2 (Numbers of fragments)

	horse	cattle	sheep	pig	roe	c-size	s-size	totals
horn core	–	1	3	–	–	–	–	4
cranium	–	11	11	42	–	1	2	67
maxilla	–	–	3	24	–	–	–	27
mandible	–	12	15	41	–	1	–	69
vertebra	–	6	7	5	–	8	11	37
ribs	–	5	1	1	–	20	40	67
scapula	–	–	6	7	1	4	3	21
humerus	–	4	8	4	–	2	2	20
radius	1	5	14	4	–	–	2	26
ulna	–	2	3	2	–	–	–	7
pelvis	–	8	7	4	–	–	1	20
femur	–	3	4	9	–	1	5	22
tibia	–	4	12	8	–	1	9	34
fibula	–	–	–	3	–	–	–	3
carpal/tarsal	–	10	2	6	–	1	1	20
metapodial	–	9	19	3	–	2	–	33
phalanx	–	5	1	4	–	–	–	10
loose teeth	8	15	14	70	–	–	–	107
other	–	1	2	1	–	34	59	97
TOTALS	9	101	132	238	1	75	135	691

TABLE 14: Mamalian Bones in Phase 7 (Numbers of fragments)

	horse	cattle	sheep	pig	red deer	c-size	s-size	totals
antler	–	–	–	–	2	–	–	2
horn core	–	4	4	–	–	–	–	8
cranium	2	28	23	11	–	3	–	67
maxilla	–	5	3	3	–	–	–	11
mandible	–	9	22	6	–	–	–	37
vertebra	–	10	2	7	–	4	2	25
rib	–	3	–	–	–	12	29	44
scapula	–	10	1	1	–	1	2	15
humerus	–	1	5	4	–	–	–	10
radius	–	7	8	2	1	1	2	21
ulna	–	2	1	3	–	–	–	6
pelvis	–	8	6	1	–	2	1	18
femur	–	5	1	3	–	1	5	15
tibia	–	4	4	9	–	1	4	22
carpal/tarsal	1	2	1	6	1	–	–	11
metapodial	4	13	12	5	–	1	–	35
phalanx	1	5	10	3	2	–	–	21
loose teeth	4	65	69	15	–	–	–	153
other	–	–	3	–	–	31	23	57
TOTALS	12	181	175	79	6	57	68	578

TABLE 15: Total Lengths of Pig Lower Molar (mm)

site	reference	period	no.	range	mean	s.d.	c.v.
Gussage	Harcourt 1979	I.A.	18	30 – 35	33	–	–
Ower		Rom	9	28 – 35	31	2.4	7.8
Puckeridge	Croft 1979	Rom	9	31 – 35	33	1.2	–
Shakenoake IV	Cram 1973	Rom	8	29 – 40	35	3.8	10.7
Shakenoak V	Cram 1978	Rom	16	30 – 38	34	2.4	7.1
London 1	{ Armitage	Rom	4	26 – 33	31	–	–
London 2	{ pers. comm.		12	27 – 37	31	3.0	9.5
Frocester	Noddle 1979	Rom	19	28 – 38*	33	–	–
Fishbourne	Grant 1971	Rom	c.50	29 – 38*	(modal group 30-32)		
Hamwic	Bourdillon & Coy 1980	Sax	51	25 – 34	31	2.0	6.3

*Not included in the statistics are suspect wild boar from Frocester and Fishbourne with length of M_3 respectively 43 and 44 mm.

material likewise contribute in large measure to the relatively high value for sheep.

The Phase 7 deposits may not therefore be so representative of the contemporary economy as those from Phase 1+2 as the high value of loose teeth for cattle and sheep and the two rather odd deposits discussed above suggest that this is poorly-preserved and biased material. There is also very slight evidence that the bones from Phase 1+2 provide better evidence of useage, such as charring and butchery, than 7, and there is slightly more erosion and dog-gnawing in Phase 7 which may militate against pig.

These deposits were not good ones for the preservation of animal bone and any conclusions drawn about the animal economy must be treated with caution for this reason and because of the small samples involved. Maltby's recent work on the Iron Age bone assemblages from Winnall Down, Hampshire, show how different results may be obtained for different context types, notably pits and ditches (Maltby n.d.).

Age and Sex of the Domestic Animals:

Pig jaws and canines gave a ratio of male to female of approximately 3:1. There could be some preservational bias to explain the high frequency of male lower canines as they are larger and stronger than all others. We must assume that preservation of young pigs has been poor as the breeding of pigs nearby would normally have produced a proportion of bones of new-born or very young pigs.

Using Grant's system for recording tooth wear (Grant 1975, 437) and including all estimates of age made from loose teeth the pigs represented included 22 older than Grant stage 30 and 18 younger than this. This gives a figure of 55% for the older group. Such animals would be at least 2 and more likely 2½ years old according to tooth eruption data from wild pigs. The material in Phase 1+2 produces a figure of 71% for pigs over stage 30.

Only 24 age estimations of cattle could be made for the whole site from jaws and loose teeth. The distribution of these was fitted to the provisional figures given by Maltby for Iron Age and Roman material (Maltby 1981, 181) and could easily fit into either pattern.

Grant wear stages could be estimated for 30 mandibles or loose teeth of sheep. This limited evidence fitted data given by Maltby for the Iron Age (Maltby 1981, 173). There were no really young mandibles.

The preservational aspect of the material casts some doubt on any conclusions relating to age structure. That very young or foetal material could survive in some layers is evident for all but Phase 3. There were parts of two sheep (or goat) foetal skeletons in both O.P. 249 and 269 in Phase 1+2 and occasional finds of porous and unfused long bone, mostly from animals skeletally immature but over one year. It is interesting that these have survived in this soil but it is likely that these immature finds are chance ones in a favourable context and that we should not attach too much importance to the age structure evidence for what is a small and biased sample. The good age reached by some of the animals was clear. There was some fairly mature pig jaw material in Phase 1+2 and the same for cattle in Phase 7. The butchery evidence suggests that these were eaten.

Ageable horses were 14 and 6-10 years respectively.

Size of the Domestic Mammals:

There were not many pig bone measurements, apart from a good sample of third molar teeth. Upper third molars (24) ranged from 25.4 to 32.8 with a mean of 29.3mm. This corresponds almost exactly with the figures for Saxon Hamwic. A more detailed comparison was possible for Ower lower third molars with other sites of the Roman Period; Iron Age Gussage All Saints, Dorset; and Saxon Hamwic. Table 15 gives a summary. The overall analysis suggested great similarity in modal groups and ranges between the three periods, with perhaps more odd larger individuals in the Roman Period. The Ower measurements fit better with the large samples from Gussage and Hamwic which are assumed from their low standard deviations and coefficients of variance to represent consistent and, probably domestic, populations. There is no suggestion at Ower, unlike Fishbourne and Frocester, that wild pig with its longer jaws and teeth is represented.

No attempt was made to compare Early and Late Roman material within these small samples. Other pig measurements from Ower were scarce but fitted the ranges of the Gussage Iron Age material.

The cattle were typical of the size found on Wessex Iron Age sites with withers' heights calculated from three metapodial bones at 107, 111, and 114cm respectively. There are some bones from stocky individuals and a number of individual bones were near the

Gussage maximum. Detailed comparison with other Wessex material of the Roman Period will be possible when more of this has been processed.

Sheep produced few useful measurements but withers' heights calculated fit the Gussage range. These were values for 62cm in Phase 1 (from metacarpus); and 52 (humerus), 54 (metacarpus), and 60 (metacarpus) in Phase 7. The Gussage range was 53-64cm.

A horse metacarpus in Phase 4, 5, 6 (O.P. 265) gave a withers' height of 122cm.

Birds and Fish:

Of the domestic fowl bones, two leg bones were by the evidence of their medullary bone, from hens in lay and the only tarsometatarsus found was also of a hen. There was no evidence from anatomy that the ducks were domestic but many of their bones were charred and presumably these represented food remains. The sea eagle bone came from O.P. 296 (Phase 1+2). This impressive bird was a breeding species in coastal and lake districts until the 19th century and is now only an occasional visitor.

The evidence for fishing at Ower was poor. Of the fish bones retrieved by normal excavation listed in Table 11, the eel dentary was larger than one in the Faunal Remains Project from a fish weighing 1kg and the two premaxillaries of gilthead sea bream, on the basis of the measurements described by Boessneck and von den Driesch (1979, 55), probably exceeded 40cm in length. The bulk samples examined for molluscan remains (see Mollusc report) produced a very few eel vertebrae from the rectilinear enclosure in Phase 1+2.

Conclusion:

This is a very small sample of bone from which to reconstruct diet or animal husbandry practices. Assuming, however, that these specific ratios reflect the real situation there is evidence that pig was of major importance in the earliest phase of occupation and that pigs were domestic and often mature.

The lack of pig post-cranials alluded to earlier may be more than outweighed by the increase in fragment numbers caused by the inclusion of loose teeth.

These problems of interpretation are symptomatic of the widely diverse methods used for assessing specific ratios by archaeozoologists. It was difficult to compare Ower results with those for the Dorset Iron Age at Gussage as there minimum numbers of individuals were used to calculate relative meat weights. Even so, pig was clearly relatively unimportant at Gussage. In the same way comparisons with Fishbourne, although syperficially useful (the early Roman pig there represents from 34 to 43% of the major domestic bones), were treated with caution as these fragment counts excluded shaft fragments and loose teeth. Counts from Puckeridge were more comparable (although ribs and vertebrae were not identified to species) and produced a figure of 35% for pig in Group 1 (AD 40-AD 70).

Results for Ower, Fishbourne, and Puckeridge therefore showed a far higher proportion of pig than the levels discussed by King (1978, 216) who used 10% pig as the cut off when contrasting 'Romanised' and 'native' settlement assemblages. King hypothesised a trend towards pig and cattle keeping and away from sheep in the latter half of the Roman Period, linked with increasing woodland usage and establishment of orchards. King also suggested that assemblages rich in pig were more likely to be 'Romanised' and to occur in the area of river valleys or heavier soils. Work on Roman London supports this trend towards beef and pork eating (Philip Armitage, personal communication).

Fishbourne and Puckeridge assemblages, being from 1st or 2nd centuries AD, do not really fit into this 'Romanisation' theory, although they could both be used as evidence for an environmentally influenced husbandry. The area of the South Coast around Fishbourne, for example, is currently graded 1 or 2 in the Agricultural Land Classification of England and Wales. Recent work at the Iron Age 'banjo' settlement at Groundwell Farm, Blunsdon St Andrew, Wiltshire, gave values for pig of up to 42% using an identical methodology to that for Ower (Coy 1982, 69). 'Native' sites can therefore produce high figures for pig and in this case there could have been nearby marshland.

Ower Phase 1+2 fits neither the cultural nor the environmental hypothesis. It is too early to fit any Late Roman trend towards pig and cattle keeping (which would involve some previous manipulation of the environment). It is also a heathy and apparently poor area for woodland with Grade 3 or 4 soils, although this does not necessarily mean that there was not extensive woodland or scrub cover in Roman times. The poor land may even have delayed the development of arable agriculture or the keeping of sheep and cattle until the later Roman Period.

Unless we are to assume that the pig carcases were brought to Ower cultural explanations related to the Roman taste for pork must be discarded. There is no real evidence at Ower for a concentration of butchery waste (heads and feet) other than normal domestic processing. The high value for teeth of all the major species in one deposit or another should rather be seen as an expression of exposure to air and soil water affecting subsequent preservation of bone.

The environmental and cultural factors leading to a choice of pig keeping are often too narrowly defined. Groundwell results show that there is no reason why native tastes for pork should not have developed. Access to marshy areas and, in the case of Ower, possibly to saltmarsh, may have been as important as to the woodland so often postulated. The present day surroundings at Ower are a mixture of grazing land with oak (this may well be the only tree species able to survive intensive cattle grazing – Oliver Rackham, personal communication) heathland; and a coastal area much influenced by recent changes in the topography of Poole Harbour.

Pigs are diversivores and can flourish in a variety of habitats, including farmyards. Their advantages are prolificity (a combination of short gestation, litter size, and rapid growth), adaptability, and intelligence. A pig can be kept in the house complex, is smaller than a cow, and certainly more sensible than a sheep. We can only assume that a combination of cultural and environmental factors led to a concentration on pig-keeping in the earliest phase of occupation at Ower, and that this later declined in relation to the keeping of cattle and sheep.

Acknowledgements:

Mr Graham Cowles of the British Museum (Natural History) identified the fragmentary coracoid bone of the sea eagle, Sarah Colley of the Faunal Remains Project identified the fish bones.

THE MARINE SHELLS

JENNIE COY (Faunal Remains Project, University of Southampton)

Although the soil was slightly acid, marine mollusc shells survived in shell midden tips in ditches, and in some other features.

Information on shells came from three sources – large bulk samples which had been kept in fertiliser bags and were still well-preserved and moist; small bulk samples of various sizes; and a small amount of shell kept from trowelling.

The large bulk samples were from 296, 299, 302, 316, 318, 322, 370, 628, 649, and 664. Each was tipped into a wheelbarrow and carefully mixed. A two litre sample was then taken at random. This was water sieved, using meshes as fine as 1mm, the products air-dried, and then sorted into 'whole' shells (i.e. those with an apex) and fragmentary, but species-identifiable, fragments. Fish remains were also sought. Results are shown in Table 16. The duplicates are cases where two bulk samples were available from a deposit.

Sample 296 was from the 1st century AD ring ditch with residual material from a rectilinear enclosure. Sample 664 came from midden material in Phase 7 in the infill of buildings 706/707 and dated to the late 3rd century AD. The other large bulk samples were from the 1st century rectilinear enclosure itself.

Results from smaller bulk samples of various sizes are summarised in Table 17. Those in Phase 1+2 (early 1st century AD) came from 309, 334, 339, 365, and 398. Those in Phase 7 (3rd and 4th century AD) were from 88, 95, 141, 178, 734, and 1010.

The additional hand-picked shell finds from the excavation are totalled in Table 18. Phase 3 represents 1st and 2nd century soil accumulations. Hand-picking of shells is likely to lead to under-estimation of those species that fragment easily, such as mussel, and those not easily recognised by the diggers, especially the small species. These are also fortuitous finds in that presumably not every common shell found by diggers was saved. They cannot therefore be used for estimations of relative abundance.

Shells from bulk samples shown in Table 17 are more reliable from this point of view as *all* shells are included. These samples were not treated in such depth as those summarised in Table 16 because they mainly contained cockles and the extra time which would have been required was thought not a productive investment. Again it would be misleading to compare the two Phases from this Table as the sample sizes for them are not comparable.

Species Present:

The following species were represented, those marked with an asterisk by a single or occasional specimen:

edible periwinkle (*Littorina littorea* (L.))
*auger or screw shell (*Turritella communis* Risso)
*rough tingle or sting winkle (*Ocenebra erinacea* (L.))
common mussel (*Mytilus edulis* L.)
edible cockle (*Cerastoderma edule* (L.))
*carpet-shell (*Venerupis decussata* (L.))
common oyster (*Ostrea edulis* L.)

The shells in this collection are reasonably well-preserved but with some signs of acid attack especially at the edges of the cockle shells. Although many winkles and cockle valves were almost whole, all the mussels and most carpet shells were in small fragments presumably because their shells are less rigid.

The extensive middens must have produced a localised higher pH than that of the surrounding soil but despite this fish were only represented by an occasional eel vertebra (in O.P. 649, 332, and 316). There was a little evidence of fishing from the bone collection (see separate bone report) where a few large bones were retrieved from trowelling. The eel vertebrae above were from much smaller fish than those represented by the other fish bones and were well-preserved which suggests that had fish bone been discarded in the midden deposits it would have survived. But fish may have been eaten at different times from shellfish and their remains deposited elsewhere.

The methods used in this shell analysis were constrained by lack of time and manpower and this has restricted the questions that can be asked of this material. To adequately probe the lateral and horizontal variability of such extensive shell middens it would have been necessary to sample by volume consistently in every deposit. As marine shell study is not yet generally recognised as a scientific study of value to archaeology this would have been regarded at the time as a foolhardy waste of resources.

As can be seen from the volumes and shell numbers in Table 16 the shell deposits were dense with very little soil between the shells.

The majority species is indisputably the edible cockle. This species can occur in very large numbers in some habitats where it can be dug out of the beach with ease as it only burrows to 2″ or less. It prefers clean sand, muddy sand, mud, or muddy gravel from mid-tidal level to just below low water mark (Tebble 1966, 105). Carpet-shells occupy a similar wide range of habitats and could be found when digging for cockles.

The cockle deposits seemed to consist of disassociated valves, although this is not certain as the deposits were not seen *in situ*. This suggests that the shellfish were eaten and that shells may even have been redeposited after the hinge ligament had rotted. Shells of all sizes were present indicating no selection prior to use, confirming that these were a local food source brought straight to the table.

There were notable collections of winkles in some of the large bulk samples, especially those from 275, 249, and 370 (Table 16). The edible winkle inhabits rocky, stony, or muddy beaches from high to low water mark. It feeds on detritus on rocks or mud (Graham 1971, 57-8). The common mussel, which needs a natural or artificial obstruction like rock, well-anchored nodules, or wooden jetties or posts, is more difficult to explain in this context. Mussels were especially noticeable in 628 (both samples) but were present in smaller quantities in most samples. Mussels would do best from mid-tidal level to a few fathoms.

Oysters were mainly in the Phase 7 samples but in such insignificant numbers that it is unlikely that they played any real rôle in the diet. The other shells are probably chance finds and cannot be used for ecological insight as they could have been collected as empty shells from the foreshore, inadvertently or by design.

Conclusions:

Limited time and resources make a detailed mollusc analysis impossible. The material available, however, does indicate that during both the early and late phases of the settlement there was some exploitation of an area of sand, mud, or sandy gravel nearby which was dug over for cockles. This could have been quite close to the settlement. Carpet shells were probably collected at the same time.

Similarly, somewhere in the vicinity, there was probably a shore with some rocky shore species – common mussel, periwinkles, and sea bream (*Sparus aurata*, the gilthead, was identified from the

TABLE 16: Numbers of 'whole' shells and volume of Broken Shell in bulk samples of 2 litres

Phase	Sample	Cockle*	edible winkle	mussel*	carpet-shell*	Other	broken shell in sample (ml)			
							mussel frags	cockle frags	winkle frags	other frags
2	296	45	4	+	2	3	–	100	–	–
1	299	80	313	1	–	1	50	100	250	–
1	302	62	79	–	3	1	100	250	50	–
1	302	18	275	1	–	1	+	50	400	–
1	316	4	1	9	–	2	250	100	–	–
1	318	50	3	1	–	–	–	400	–	–
1	332	243	1	–	2	–	100	750	–	–
1	370°	276	228	17	–	–	–	–	–	750
1	628°	69	5	260	–	35	900	–	–	100
1	628	29	3	125	+	23	600	100 (and carpet-shells)		850
1	649	319	52	13	17	9	100	–		850
7	664°	230	4	+	–	1 (oyster)	–	–	–	400
								–		

Notes:
*For these bevalves there are two shells per individuals   + Some fragmentary remains
°Samples submitted for carbon dates

TABLE 17: Shells from Small Bulk Samples of Different Sizes

	Phase 1+2	Phase 7
cockle	1,297	2,198
winkle	1	14
mussel	2	14
carpet-shell	11	24
oyster	1	14
other	–	2

TABLE 18: Shells found by Trowelling

	Phases 1+2	Phase 3	Phase 7
cockle	54	3	12
winkle	4	1	1
mussel	1	–	1
carpet-shell	1	–	1
oyster	3	2	17
other	–	–	–

bone collection – this species often feeds on mussels). A true rocky shore nearby is unlikely even though changes in the shoreline of Poole Harbour have been considerable (May 1969, 149). It is more likely that a beach consolidated with flints from the chalk or large pieces of gravel provided a suitable substrata for mussel beds and winkles.

This could have been less than an hour's walk away on the shore of Studland Bay, nearer than the sea is today because of the subsequent accretion in the Studland area (May, personal communication). These mussel beds might have been of considerable extent and the food collected a useful addition to the meat in the diet. Such trips could have been combined with fishing expeditions. Winkle collecting would have been more tedious but if the species were available they would add variety.

The extent of the middens, especially in the 1st century AD ditches indicates that shellfish were a significant part of the diet.

Acknowledgements:
I am grateful to Catherine Backway and Rod Fitzgerald for help with sample preparation and sorting and to Jessica Winder and V. J. May for discussion during the writing of this paper.

THE CHARCOAL IDENTIFICATIONS

RICHARD THOMAS

A total of 102 identifiable charcoal fragments were recovered from 20 separate layers; all pieces were small and fragmented.

Whilst the material derived from a number of different layers they could be generally grouped into a number of features from two broadly datable horizons; the early 1st-century AD rectilinear enclosure and associated pit, the 3rd/4th-century AD pottery production settlement complex. The charcoal derived from the

1st-century phase was probably derived from scrub growth within the ditch and possibly from clearance around it. The charcoal from the settlement complex was probably derived from structural timbers, and kiln/oven fuel.

The species present are summarised in table 19.

The 1st-century AD Rectilinear Enclosure Ditch
All the species identified were of types which would quickly colonise and readily establish themselves along the undisturbed edges of ditches (Rackham, 1978, 20, 23, 32-6). This may suggest that the charcoal was derived from scrub and brambles cleared and burnt during ditch cleaning, or from nearby hedging or field clearance. The absence of other identifiable timbers might suggest that this ditch was at some distance from settlement structures. Much of the charcoal occurred within deliberate tips of marine molluscs and burnt soils and clays which composed the fill of the ditch.

The 3rd/4th century AD Settlement Complex
Since the site had been previously cleared at some time prior to the 1st-century, and since the only identifications were of hazel and oak, it is likely that this charcoal was moved to the site from the surrounding area. The deliberate selection of one species (oak) perhaps suggests the exploitation of primary woodland in the vicinity for building material, and fuel.

A record was made during the identification of the approximate maturity and growth rate of each sample, by examining the curvature of the annual rings and measuring their width. The results

TABLE 19: The Charcoal identification by phase and feature

Phase	Feature	BRAMBLE (Rubus sp.)	GORSE (Ulex sp.)	HAWTHORN (Crataegus sp.)	WILLOW (Salix sp.)	HAZEL (Corylus avellana)	OAK (Quercus sp.)
1	Rectilinear enclosure 288	T	O	T			
2	'Horseshoe' pit 389		O				
2	'Ring-Ditch' enclosure 343				O		OM
4	Flue of kiln 540				O		
5	Timber post-building 909 and yards 441						O
6	Upper infill of Rectilinear enclosure, 288A				O		OM
7	Building 564						M
7	Building 906						M
7	Dryer 708						OM
7	Rubble Collapse of 707					O	OM

T: Twig   O: Large roundwood   M: Mature timber

showed that all samples from the building collapse levels were from large timbers with varying growth rates; annual ring widths from between 2-3mm, and occasionally 3-5mm. The varying widths (very narrow-wide) of the timbers suggests that they were derived from trees growing under dissimilar conditions (i.e. were slow and quick grown), and were subject to varying degrees of shade and overcrowding from other trees, perhaps indicative of primary woodland.

The hazel rods or poles were also fast grown perhaps up to 5cm diameter with annual rings 2mm wide.

Oak charcoal was also recovered from drier (708) within building (707), and was an even mixture of fast grown roundwood and slow grown timber. This was recovered with a quantity of ironwork and may partly represent the remains of a collapsed superstructure. However it is worth noting that a slow burning fuel such as oak would have been required to maintain an even temperature within a kiln/oven (Dimbleby 1978, 53-4). A second kiln (540) contained large roundwood charcoal of willow. The absence of other more suitable woods for fueling this kiln/oven makes interpretation difficult. The use of willow in a kiln/oven is perhaps unusual, although if fed into the fire in its 'green' state it may perhaps have provided a slow, hot burning fuel.

THE SOILS

The soils at Ower are typical gley podzols (Soil Survey of England and Wales, 1983, Soil sub-group 64lb), overlying the Tertiary Sands.

Analysis of these soils was limited to disturbed samples from ditch silts (555) and (343), accumulated soils (242) and putative buried soil (348) (fig. 33). The description of these soils can be found in Porter (1980). A more general discussion can be found in the level III Archive (Beavis J., and Porter G., 1981). However since no rigorous examination of the soils was undertaken on the site, and the sampling strategy was insufficient, 'no unambiguous conclusion is appropriate from these measurements, although some features of the buried profile are not inconsistent with a soil of reasonable base status in which some development towards a podzol has occurred' (Beavis and Porter 1981).

Soil samples were also taken from across the site on a grid basis, to test for phosphate. This was undertaken to test the significance of a phosphate distribution on low pH soils (5.9-6.5pH).

The phosphate levels were estimated by a simple chemical test described in Schwarz (1967). This test was applied to soil samples obtained from two levels within the trial pits:

A: Just below the modern ploughsoil
B: From the soil just above the subsoil, i.e. in places from the putative buried horizon (refer fig. 31A, for area of greatest soil accumulation).

The methods and results are recorded in the level III archive. The Phosphate level distribution is shown for soil sample A in fig. 64. These results show that there is a clear correlation between settlement focus and phosphate level, compared with other material distributions (fig. 32B for pottery). The phosphate distribution for soil sample B showed a similar distribution with high positive values in squares 380.110, 380.130, 440.110, 440.130, 480.130, 500.110, 500.130. This latter sample was less viable since some samples were taken from a putative buried soil and some not. However it is clear that on the settlement focus, high phosphate level and soil accumulation all coincide. The phosphate analysis was undertaken by Archaeology Diploma Students at the Dorset Institute of Higher Education (Weymouth) under the supervision of John Beavis.

THE GEOPHYSICAL SURVEY AND THE MAGNETIC SUSCEPTIBILITY OF THE SOILS

The reports by Andrew David are included in the *microfiche MII*.

The geophysical survey plan was generated from four units of survey, the results of which are discussed in the site report and depicted in fig. 31A.

Whilst the second unit of survey in the north-west field was being carried out, augered soil samples were taken, from a level (where possible) just below the modern ploughsoil, at ten metre intervals, on the 1978 site grid, and along two traverses AB and XY (fig. 31). These samples were tested for magnetic susceptibility, and the results plotted and discussed in the third report (*Microfile MII, G6/81*). The values are represented graphically in fig. 65, relative to the site grid.

In both traverses the high values, as would be expected, coincide with the thickest concentrations of buried features, and especially where industrial or occupation activity appears to have been at a maximum. Exceptional to this observation are the high values at either end of traverse XY, where there appear to be no archaeological features. The cause of this is not understood, but might relate to special conditions associated with waterlogging causing localised redistribution or alteration of magnetic constituents of the soil. Elsewhere along the traverse, high susceptibility values correspond with areas where magnetic anomalies are at their strongest.

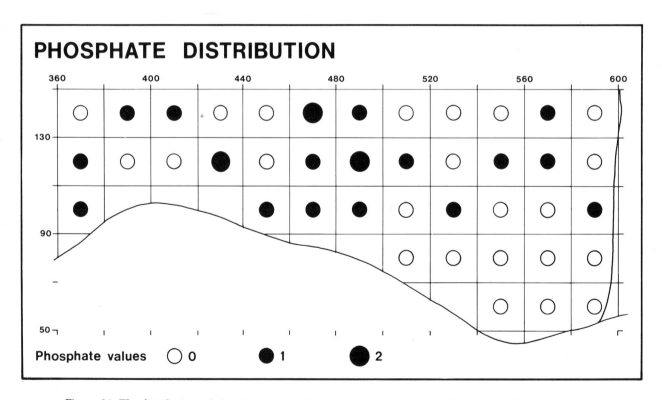

Figure 64. The distribution of phosphates across the site (compare with other distributions fig. 31A and B).

On traverse AB values are low to the west where there appears to be no human activity, but rise substantially over the dense remains in and around the excavation area where occupation and industrial activity have been shown to have taken place. Values fall off sharply at the eastern extremity of the traverse where features again become scarce.

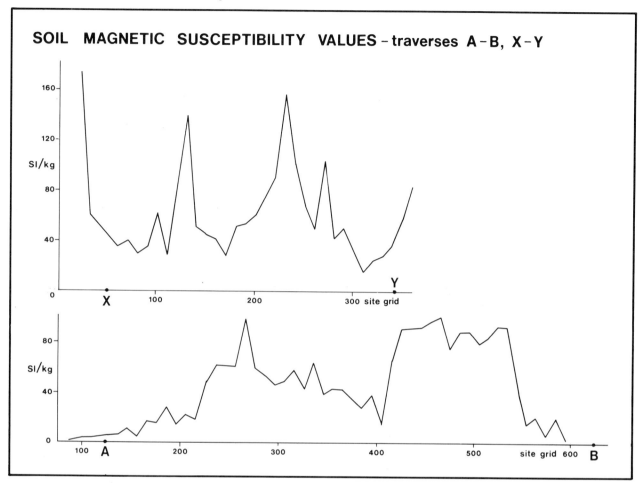

Figure 65. The distribution of soil magnetic susceptibility (fig. 31A).

TABLE 20: Element concentrations in parts per million.

sample No	La 1596kev	Sc(1) 889kev	Sc(II) 889kev	Co 1332kev	Rb 1077kev	Cs 795kev	Ce 141kev	Hf 482kev	Ta 1221kev	Pa 311kev	Cr 320kev	Fe 1092kev	Eu 1408kev	Tb 964kev
P7	26.74	12.10	12.26	12.01	70.6	9.36	37.8	3.80	0.95	8.81	78.7	38141	0.92	0.57
P8	35.94	16.78	16.99	14.13	92.8	10.83	50.1	3.35	1.18	11.52	102.5	36983	1.36	0.68
P9	29.95	12.00	12.19	11.28	65.6	8.47	39.8	4.05	1.01	8.67	75.9	36450	1.14	0.63
P10	31.12	15.46	15.57	10.80	86.5	10.11	44.0	3.32	0.94	10.27	97.6	34749	1.09	0.69
P11	26.68	13.12	13.13	7.28	81.6	10.36	37.0	2.64	0.64	7.88	78.5	30641	0.86	0.48
P12	25.53	12.95	13.05	9.03	70.5	9.62	34.7	2.84	0.74	8.57	81.2	30769	0.79	0.48
P13	31.98	12.69	12.72	7.97	86.0	9.14	39.5	3.95	0.87	9.24	81.0	32982	1.19	0.69
P14	19.20	12.28	12.19	9.36	93.5	10.47	24.5	2.22	0.56	5.96	79.0	37579	0.60	0.48
P15	27.29	12.09	23.14	9.41	47.9	8.03	39.2	3.13	0.77	6.90	78.4	27120	2.37	1.32
P16	29.38	14.64	11.94	9.28	40.7	8.08	40.8	2.52	0.66	6.72	78.9	26862	2.43	1.29
P17	28.95	13.66	13.99	10.70	100.7	13.43	40.0	3.85	1.01	9.55	82.8	32221	0.82	0.56
P18	26.08	13.45	13.18	9.58	70.5	8.11	39.1	3.78	0.77	7.22	90.7	34229	0.90	0.49
R6	26.44	14.71	14.86	10.57	70.9	12.04	29.8	4.97	0.66	9.00	97.5	39805	0.94	0.51
R8	00.53	19.99	20.03	16.51	116.7	17.30	64.2	5.32	0.98	14.04	122.8	38179	1.38	0.87
R9	12.49	12.81	12.29	8.77	83.2	10.37	N.D.	3.19	0.50	8.76	87.1	33482	0.30	0.34
R10	19.02	10.40	10.40	7.26	55.6	8.73	21.8	2.79	0.43	6.42	67.2	30120	0.54	0.34
R11	33.23	17.33	17.45	9.39	119.3	15.28	46.8	4.90	0.78	11.48	109.7	39259	0.64	0.44
R12	27.16	13.77	13.75	11.64	74.4	10.23	42.5	5.22	0.71	8.02	89.1	33828	1.08	0.66
R13	35.31	14.45	14.75	14.19	104.7	17.53	51.3	5.00	0.92	10.96	89.6	33136	1.05	0.72
R14	28.81	12.69	12.69	6.67	71.1	10.46	40.9	2.52	0.56	8.78	82.7	29165	0.85	0.44
R15	26.28	12.26	12.22	5.71	67.2	7.47	37.5	4.00	0.72	7.13	84.9	26258	0.74	0.52
R16	30.93	16.16	16.32	16.03	105.1	14.29	50.7	5.54	0.92	9.93	107.5	37463	1.12	0.62
R17	15.36	14.03	14.12	7.09	51.6	8.91	N.D.	4.98	0.81	10.46	99.4	34755	0.29	N.D.

N.D. – not detected

ARCHAEOMAGNETIC SAMPLES FROM KILN 540

This kiln was sampled for directional archaeomagnetic dating by David Haddon-Reece of the Ancient Monuments Laboratory. Nineteen samples were obtained by the disc method, and measured in the laboratory's Digico magnetometer, but the results were too scattered to give a mean value of any use for dating: the kiln had clearly been subject to considerable disturbance.

RADIOCARBON MATERIAL

Three samples of marine mollusc shell from layers (370), (628) and (664) were submitted to the Ancient Monuments Laboratory for radiocarbon dating at Harwell. It was hoped that these would provide an independent date for the abandonment of building (707) as a 'pot-drying' shed, and also provide a comparative sequence for the radiocarbon dates from the marine mollusc middens at Hamworthy and Poole, where uncalibrated dates of ad 530 +/− 70 (Har 3465) and ad 980 +/− 70 (Har 3462) have been obtained (Horsey, forthcoming). However, the Harwell Isotope Measurement Laboratory advised that shell is not a sufficiently reliable medium to give dates of the precision and accuracy required in the present context.

NEUTRON ACTIVATION OF SOME BB1 FROM OWER AND REDCLIFF

JEREMY EVANS

Some 12 sherds of BB1 from Ower and another 12 sherds from Redcliff (fig. 1.53) were subjected to Neutron Activation Analysis as a part of a program of research undertaken at the University of Bradford. The general method of sample preparation at Bradford has been described by Aspinall (1977). A powdered sample from each vessel was prepared by crushing a small chip from each sherd. The samples were then irradiated in the Herald reactor at A.W.R.E. Aldermaston together with two NPSI pottery standards. The resulting gamma radiation spectra were counted twice, on an Ortec 50cm² germanium – lithium detector and a Canberra 1024 channel analyser, immediately after return from irradiation and again one month after irradiation.

The results in parts per million (ppm) for the 13 most reliable elements detected are presented in table 20. These results were then standardised by the value of Scandium (at 889 Kev) to avoid a number of possible difficulties (Aspinall 1977). The 'normalised' results were then subject to further scrutiny using the Cluster analysis packages of Clustan Version 2 (Wishart 1977).

The sherds from Ower comprise two groups; samples P7-P10 are

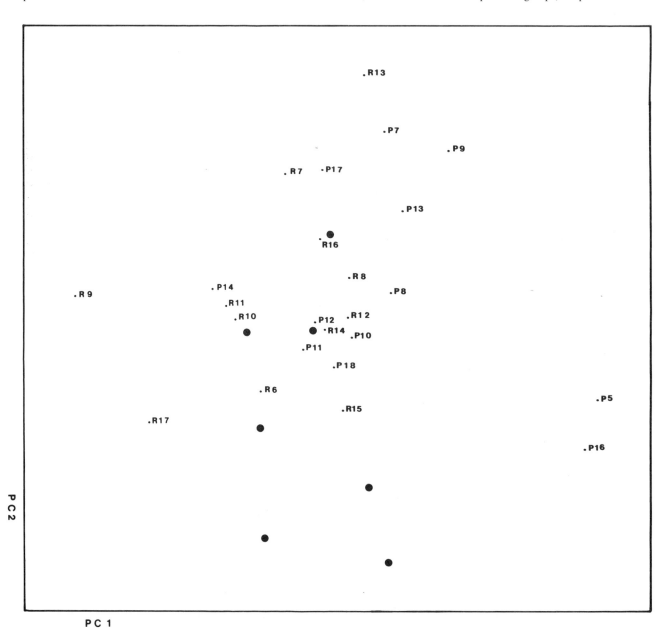

Figure 66. Principal components analysis plot of BB1 from Ower (P7-P18), Redcliffe (R6-R17) and Vindolanda (larger filled circles).

from feature 540 (kiln/oven) on the Cleavel Point site and P11-P14 from feature 708 (dryer) on the same site whilst sherds P15-18 were kindly provided by Mr R. A. H. Farrar from material excavated in 1951-8. The sherds from Redcliffe were all provided by Mr Farrar and are represented by sample numbers R6-R17.

These sherds, together with 7 sherds of BB1 from Mr P. Bidwell's excavations at Vindolanda, were subjected to cluster analysis and the principal components plot from this is presented as figure 66. The cluster analysis dendrogram shows very little evidence on differentation between Ower and Redcliff or the Vindolanda sherds and the cumulative variance accounted for by the principal components does not exceed 90% until the seventh component suggesing very little structure to the data.

The principal components analysis plot (figure 66) suggests some slight differentation between the Ower and Redcliff samples and the Vindolanda samples but this is far from clear and the clustan technique is so sensitive that it is possible that the slight trends can be accounted for by the fact that the 3 groups originate from three different irradiations.

Figure 67 shows the Ower and Redcliffe data, in a principal components plot, together with both BB1 and BB2 from Vindolanda. This figure demonstrates the clear discrimination between BB1 and BB2 and that the Dorset BB1 tends to give a single, fairly well defined, chemical 'fingerprint' in comparison with BB2.

I would like to acknowledge the support of the Science and Engineering Research Council and to thank Mr A. Aspinall and Mr J. Crummett for their encouragement and assistance; to thank Mr P. Woodward, Mr R. A. H. Farrar and Mr P. Bidwell for making samples available to me.

Acknowledgements

These excavations and fieldwork were carried out by the author for the Dorset Archaeological Committee, in his capacity of Archaeological Field Officer (implementation). The excavations were financed by the Department of the Environment through the implementation fund of the Wessex Archaeological Committee, and by British Gas. The excavations were undertaken prior to the construction of a water-pipeline across the peninsula. As a result of the excavations and survey, and in liaison with the Dorset County Council and British Gas, the construction works were greatly reduced and the disturbance to the site minimised; no topsoil was displaced across the site apart from where trenches were cut for the pipes and electricity cables, and where a pumping facility was constructed close to Cleavel Point. Much of the equipment used for the excavations was loaned by Poole Museums, the Dorset Natural History and Archaeological Society (Dorset County Museum), and the Dorset Institute of Higher Education (Weymouth).

Following construction work and reinstatement the fields were ploughed and put down to grass by the Rempstone Estates, who in consultation with the Department of the Environment have agreed to ensure that no further erosion of the site as a result of farming will occur.

Thanks are due to all these organisations, and in particular the officers who liaised on, and promoted the sites archaeology; Les Groube (Rural Survey Officer, Dorset Archaeological Committee), Tim Schadla-Hall (Field Officer, Wessex Archaeological Committee; Phil Catherall (British Gas Archaeologist); Laurence Keen (Archaeological Officer, Dorset County Council); Ian Horsey (Poole Museums Service); Roger Peers (Dorset County

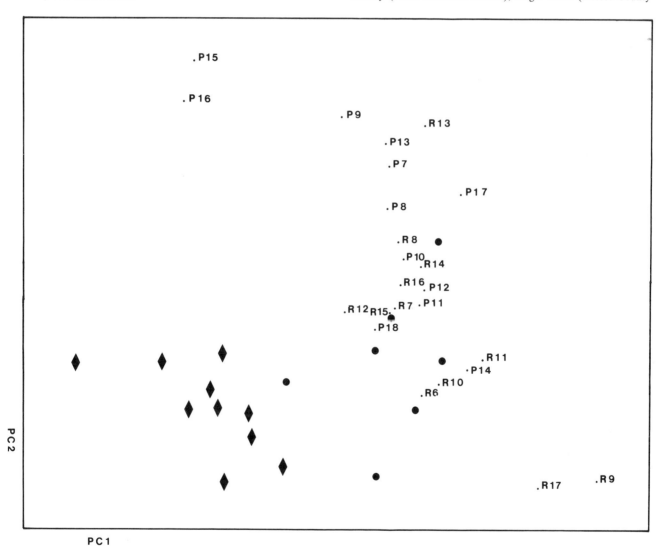

Figure 67. Principal components analysis plot of BB1 from Ower (P7-P18), Redcliffe (R6-R17), and Vindolanda (larger filled circles; and BB2 from Vindolanda (filled lozenges).

Museum); Bill Putnam, Alan Hunt, John Beavis and Pat Morris (Dorset Institute of Higher Education, Dept. of History and Archaeology); Stephen Dunmore and Chris Young (Dept. of Environment). Thanks are also given to all the members of the Dorset Archaeological Committee, and in particular George Wickham, who managed the finances and arranged banking facilities for the excavations; and Ian Horsey (Secretary of the Dorset Archaeology Committee) who arranged correspondence and a point of communication at Poole Museum during the excavations.

The excavations could not have taken place without the assistance of the landowner, Remptstone Estates, and the Ryder family. In particular, the author would like to thank Ben Ryder for allowing access to the site prior to construction, and for use of Cleaval Point as a camp site for the duration of the excavations; and to Major D. C. D. Ryder for providing historical and archaeological information on the site and the locality. The author also thanks the local residents of Ower for their interest and many kindnesses shown during the excavations; Miss Oliphant, Mr Whitney, and in particular Simon Trehane who provided hot baths for some ingrained and grubby volunteers.

The excavations were carried out during the months of June, July and August, and for much of the time in hot sunny weather. The excavations were planned and begun as a rapid three-week evaluation exercise with a group of final year post-examination students from the Archaeology Certificate Course of the Dorset Institute of Higher Education (Weymouth); Peter Cox, David Maynard, Dawn Eldridge, Derek Hall, Martin Papworth, and Karen Upton. This group provided a skilled supervisory unit throughout the excavations. Particular thanks are owed to; Peter Cox for his overall supervision and management of the excavations when the author was immobilised for two weeks with torn back muscles, for the photographic record, and for much of the subsequent post-excavation work; Karen Upton in her capacity as on-site finds assistant; and to Dawn Eldridge who supervised the off-site finds processing, the archive record of the pottery, and the conservation of the shale; David Maynard and others who provided additional transport to a remote site. Many volunteers came and worked on the site, and many camped in isolated and rough conditions. Most became hardened to the rigours of camping, and all (I hope) enjoyed the communal responsibility for cooking and all other necessities of an isolated campsite; the excavations would not have been possible without their hard work, energy, enthusiasm, and resourcefulness. Special thanks are due to Lizzie Brandon-Jones, Jeany Poulson, Verna Care, Phil Diment, Ruth Harding, Marcus Wardle, Ross Wallace, and Stephen Johnson.

After the excavations were completed further survey work was carried out by the Ancient Monuments Laboratory (Geophysical Section), and a field-walking survey team. Thanks are due to the fieldwalkers; Stephen Sherlock, Peter Norfolk, and David Maynard, and Peter Cox who organised the fieldwalking. The material archive was organised by Stephen Sherlock and David Maynard; and the latter analysed the distributions and discussed the results as part of his dissertation at Sheffield University (Specialist Report).

Many specialists provided advice both during and after excavations. Thanks are due to the many specialists who produced reports for publication, and for discussion and advice during the preparation of the report, comments and ideas also came from conservations with Mike Fulford, Bill Putnam, Christopher Sparey Green and Chris Young. General comments on the final text were received from Ray Farrar, Leo Biek, Peter Fasham and Anne Ellison. The author acknowledges all these sources, but takes responsibility for the published statements and ideas expressed in this published site report.

Pat Coulson and Sue Tovey typed the report through several retypes; grateful thanks.

The Excavation of an Iron Age and Romano-British Settlement at Rope Lake Hole, Corfe Castle, Dorset

PETER J. WOODWARD

SUMMARY

Trial excavations, aerial photography, and fieldwalking have defined the limits of an Iron Age and Romano-British settlement which survives on the cliff edge above Rope Lake Hole. The central area of habitation has now been reduced to 0.5 hectare due to cliff-edge erosion. The position of earlier shorelines could not be accurately computed, although the present rate of erosion in this particular location was perhaps 1m/8 years.

The Iron Age settlement was probably continuous, although buildings were replaced and relocated several times within a system of shifting terraces, huts and working areas. The settlement structures from the earliest period through to the 1st century AD were circular huts with dry-stone sill walls; these were terraced and probably 'unenclosed'. By the Later Iron Age terraces had been built up by soil movement and waste tipping (particularly as a result of shale-working), and were revetted by curved dry-stone walls which may have been in part integral with hut structures. The estimated width of the terrace excavated was perhaps 14m.

This pattern of shifting huts, accumulation of waste, and terrace development was broken in the 1st century AD, and in the 2nd and 3rd centuries AD a rectilinear building and yard were laid out at 45° across the earlier terraces. Analysis of the large quantity of lathe-shale waste and flint chisel tools recovered from the yard level outside the building suggests that this was a working area for the large scale production of the well-known shale armlet of the period.

The site was considerably damaged in the medieval period when new terraced fields were developed across the site, for the settlement now located in the coombe to the east; many of the Romano-British levels had been removed and considerably damaged. The construction of a military target range in World War II, the subsequent arable recovery, and the growth of a badger sett further damaged the site. However current ploughing probably only just touches archaeological levels on the crest of the hill.

INTRODUCTION AND SITE DESCRIPTION

This Iron Age and Romano-British settlement site lies midway between Kimmeridge and Chapmans Pool (SY 932777), on a gentle south-facing slope above the 200ft contour. The topographic location of the site on the cliff edge can be seen in plate 29 which was taken during the 1979 excavation. The processes of coastal erosion have now reduced the site to its present form (fig. 68). The present rate of cliff-edge erosion is variable in this area. However on the extremely 'active' area on the southern face of this site, the rate could be as much as 1m/year (Schadla-Hall, 1976), but more conservatively at 1m/8 years (Hall, 1983). The site was first recognised by John Beavis as a result of badger disturbance, and further detail of the sites stratification, development and extent was obtained from a series of trial pits by Rosemary Maw (Maw, 1975 and 1976), and by fieldwalking and documentary analysis (Maw, 1981).

The locations of the four trial trenches (2m x 1m) are shown in fig. 68. A diagram of the recorded stratification within these trial pits is shown in fig. 69. It is clear from these trial pits that much of the southern part of the site was sealed by an accumulation of soils. This accumulation was undoubtedly the result of post-Roman agricultural activity, and the area, part of a lynchetted field system associated with the medieval settlement in the coombe to the east. This settlement, *circa* 12th-17th century AD, has been defined by material distributions from fieldwalking (Maw, 1981). Below this accumulated lynchet the trial trenches presented a clear sequence from the Early Iron Age to the 3rd or 4th century AD, and it was possible to locate and identify structures (in some levels), waste tips, 'industrial' activities, horizons with derived occupation debris, and the location of 'agricultural' soils. From this information it was possible to define the foci of the period occupations (fig. 68).

An aerial photograph of the site, taken during the excavations of 1979 by Aly Aviation for Dorset County Council (Excavation Record, Colour Slides 206-208), further suggest the limits of the site; the colour of the green oats and grass was darker in some areas, presumably where the crop had been retarded on archaeological horizons and accumulated agricultural soils, i.e. where the sediments are deepest. The limits of the darker retarded crop are shown in fig. 68, and it is suggested that this was the limit of the main settlement area. No trace of associated field systems outside this focus can now be discerned, and as a result any visible relationship that existed in the Iron Age/Romano-British period between this site and that located 1km to the west of Eldon's Seat (Cunliffe, 1968) has now been lost. This loss of earthwork relationships is in part undoubtedly due to medieval farming developments. Search of existing aerial photographs has identified an earthwork or parchmark to the north west of the site focus; RAF aerial photograph 1946 (CPE/UK 1824, 4 Nov. 46/3249). Examination of the photograph suggests that this may be in part covered by soil slip movement and certainly predates the military trackways (fig. 68, B and C). No trace now survives on the ground and the date and function of this feature cannot be at present determined. Two additional habitation sites have also been located to the west of Rope Lake Hole (fig. 68, B, i and ii); Early-Middle Iron Age pottery scatters (R. Maw, *pers. comm.*). These latter two sites, and the sites at Rope Lake Hole and Eldon's Seat begin to give an impression of the occupation intensity along this 'coastal' strip, and although no earthwork relationships now survive to directly understand inter-site relationships the application of systematic fieldwalking and intensive survey techniques, such as those used at Cleavel Point (Woodward, this volume) to the area may be able to establish clearer patterns of land-use and settlement development.

The overall destruction of all settlement earthworks in the immediate area of the site took place in 1940 when a military target range was constructed. The layout of the target tracks was depicted on the 1:2500 maps (1953 revision), fig. 68C. The clearance of shells from the area and the target trackway in the post-war period led to high levels of disturbance.

The establishment and growth of a badger sett in the 1950s, in the softer areas of the stratified occupation (cliff-edge, and hill-crest (trench C, 1976)) has further damaged the site, but animal disturbance of this type has now ceased as a result of the badgers' demise in the late 1960s. Ploughing of the site now causes little damage to the

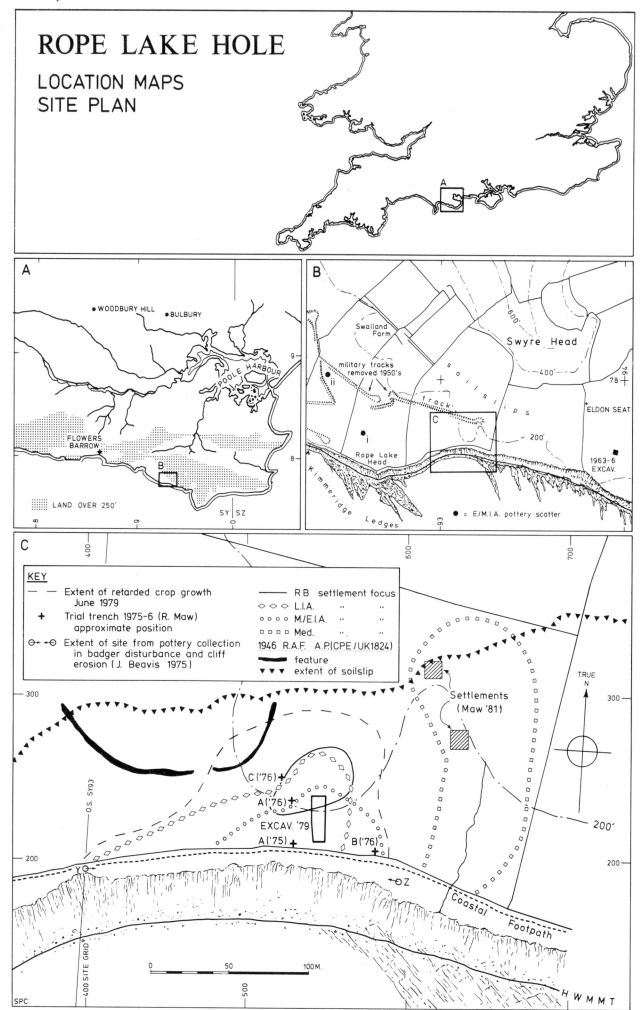

Figure 68. Rope Lake Hole. Site location and settlement plan, as defined by aerial survey, fieldwalking, and the results of the 1975-76 trial excavations.

well-sealed deposits up to 50m from the cliff-edge, although Romano-British material has been seen in the plough soil on the crest of the hill-slope. This field-surface material does not occur in great quantities and is probably derived from occupation levels peripheral to the main focus of activity.

As a result of these trial excavations and the acute problem of extremely active cliff-edge erosion on the southern face of the site, a more extensive excavation was carried out in 1979, in order to determine the character and development of the site, and delineate the industrial functions of the settlement. These excavations are described below.

The archives of both the 1975-76 and 1979 excavations have been stored and catalogued together. The original site records and all original archival material have been deposited with the finds in Dorset County Museum. Microfiche copies of these records and archive have been prepared for the National Monuments Record, and the Trust for Wessex Archaeology, Salisbury.

The Excavation Archive

This excavation report was prepared for publication in the form recommended in *Principles of Publication in Rescue Archaeology*, Department of the Environment, October, 1975, page 3 (Levels I-IV). The excavation data and analysis has been stored and indexed in the following order:

FILE 1:   Introduction, Contents and Drawings Register for RLH 75, RLH 76 and RLH 79. Interim and editing notes. Drawings 1-58.

FILE 2:   (A-B) Excavations 1975 and 1976 (R. Maw). Site record. (C) Synthesis (P. J. Woodward). (D) Photographs (R. Maw).

FILES 3-4: (A-E) RLH 79 Site record sheets 1-322.

FILE 5:   (A-D) RLH 79 Site record indeces and survey.

FILES 6-8: RLH 79 Photographic record (P. W. Cox).

FILES 9-11: (A-R) RLH 79 Pottery archive (S. Davies, D. Williams and P. J. Woodward).

FILES 12:   RLH 79: (A) Stratigraphy (P. J. Woodward), (B-T) Material analysis, specialist reports (authors as in Level IV text).

FILE 13:   RLH 79: Experimental lathe turning of shale. Experimental tool production (A. M. Errington, D. Sloper, P. J. Woodward).

FILE 14:   RLH 79· The animal bone, the computerised record print-out (J. Coy, Faunal Remains Project, Southampton University).

FILE 15:   RLH 79: Correspondence (PJW/78/12) together with correspondence for the Dorset Monograph with Norden and Ower (PJW/83/63).

The 1979 Excavations

A single excavation trench was located within a roughly north-south grid aligned at 'right-angles' to the cliff-edge fence, and at the centre of the settlement (as defined by the trial excavations, fig. 68). The trench opened up was an area of about 30m by 10m, running away from the cliff edge. This excavation was designed to establish the damage caused by ploughing as well as the potential and degree of preservation of the sealed archaeological deposits, especially in relationship to its undoubted future disappearance in the next 100 years as a result of cliff-edge erosion. The fence along the coastal cliff path was likely to be moved 5m inland in the next few years, because of this erosion (Schadla-Hall, 1976).

The area was stripped by farmer Mr Vearncombe with the use of farm machinery. This comprised of a tractor and plough to loosen the heavy clay ploughsoil after a winter's fallow, and another tractor with an attached front 3m push-bucket operating at right angles to the plough-cut spits. It was possible by this means to neatly clear the area of modern plough soil and medieval lynchet soils in 20cm spits

Plate 29. Rope Lake Hole: The site location and its landscape from the east (AA26).

down to the Romano-British and Iron Age levels. By this process the spoil accumulated into two long linear tips to the east and west of the excavation. The excavation area was cleared of the clay lynchet soils by hand to a recognisable archaeological level (plate 30). The excavation trench was then laid out on a 2m grid, and cleaned down by hand with the material being collected within the 2m grid. It was clear that the structures exposed at this level related to two periods:

Period 4 (fig. 75) phase VII (Romano-British) in the northern area 540230 (plate 31).
Period 3 (fig. 73) phase V (Late Iron Age), in the southern area 540210 (plate 32).

and that the site had been eroded by medieval ploughing (much of the material was abraded and some medieval pottery occurred in this horizon, plate 30). The distribution of the material types (phase VIIC, fig. 76), although in part dispersed by later ploughing, could be used to define the functional areas of the period 3 and 4 settlement structures.

Within the time available for excavation it was only possible to totally excavate a sequence in the northern 12m of the trench, approximately 120m² (fig. 72, inset), and clean the remainder of the trench to the Iron Age levels in the area indicated in fig. 73.

A trench excavated with a tractor 1m back-bucket was used to complete a section through the site (plate 5) and clarify the relationship between the exposed horizons in the southern area of the trench and the more fully excavated area (fig. 72, inset).

The completed excavation trenches are depicted in plate 35, and inset fig. 72.

The site was backfilled by the farmer, Mr Vearncombe, in the autumn of 1979 after rain had loosened the compacted clay soil dumps. The clay soils cleared from the site by machine were almost devoid of worm activity and were fortunately removed when they were pliable in wet weather at the beginning of the excavations in early June 1979. However having cleared the site, and with the onset of another summer drought these clay plough soils set like concrete. It is likely that the military activity and the annual use of heavy farm machinery in this area has led to a soil which has been compacted and which is now intractable and not easily cultivated. Although rich in minerals and fertile it may have presented some of the same problems for cultivation in the Iron Age and Roman periods. However in earlier periods it was probably used with more moderation and fewer problems of compaction would have arisen.

The Chronology and Phasing
The primary source of dating for the site was the pottery. This established the general date range and chronology of the stratified structural horizons. The pottery (Davies, following) established four general periods of occupation, in which the structural phases could be grouped. The structural phases (Phases I-VII) are shown in the diagrammatic section through the site (fig. 70), and their association into chronological periods are as follows:
PERIOD 1: EARLY TO MIDDLE IRON AGE
Structural phase I: Dismantled and collapsed circular stone huts.
Structural phase II: Shale and flint waste tips.
PERIOD 2: MIDDLE IRON AGE

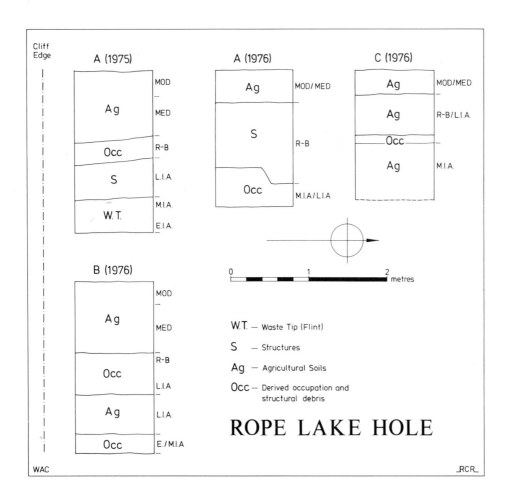

Figure 69. The Interpretative sections of the 1975-76 trial trenches, showing the location of waste-tips (WT), structures (S), agricultural soils (Ag), and occupation (Occ). The period horizons were defined from the pottery, shale waste and worked flint.

Structural phase IIIA: Accumulated soils and occupation debris, north of the stone revetment/hut walls (264/239, and 282).

Structural phase IIIB: Occupation debris, south of revetments (264/239), and including revetment walls.

Structural phase IIIC: Lower revetment wall (308) including soil and occupation accumulation to north (cuts A-C).

Structural phase IIID: Structural levels below revetment 308.

PERIOD 3: LATER IRON AGE (Durotrigian)

Structural phase IVA: Robbing (176) across phase IIIA, and phase IIIB structures and occupation. Pits cut into these robbed horizons, including burial (177) with cairn (216), and structure (238).

Structural phase IVB: Accumulated occupation soils.

Structural phase V: Circular stone huts on 'lower' terrace; huts (322) and (236).

Structural phase VIB: Pits cut through accumulated occupation soils IVB.

Structural phase VIC: Pits cut through accumulated occupation soils IVB, and sealed by yard VIA, and structure (319)

PERIOD 4: ROMANO-BRITISH (2nd-3rd century AD)

Structural phase VIA: Yard 135 and occupation debris and structure (319).

Structural phase VIIA: Yard (84) and structure (117).

Structural phase VIIB: Gulley (85) and pit (97) cut across yard (84).

Structural phase VIIC: The distribution of occupation debris across phases VIIB and V. Distribution by medieval agricultural activity.

PERIOD 5: EARLY MEDIEVAL FIELD TERRACING (12th century AD)

Structural phase VIIC: The distribution of medieval pottery at base of lynchet.

Structural phase VIII: The medieval and modern plough soils.

The samian included some late 2nd century pieces, and was all recovered from phase VIA and above. Most of the small broken pieces of Flavian date could be taken as residual.

Examination of the shale and flint assemblages (Cox and Woodward, following) showed that changes in the technology of working this material and changes in the products showed a close correlation to these chronological period divisions (1-4).

Coinage from the site was all of late 3rd century AD or 4th century AD date, and all occurred in the phase VII yard and above.

The bronze brooches (stratified in phases VIIA and V) were not particularly useful for dating. The brooch from the upper yard (84) of phase VIIA had a date range of late 1st century AD into 2nd century AD, and was presumably residual. The brooch from a level with the huts of phase V has not previously been found in well dated horizons. Phase V occupation, from its stratigraphic location and pottery, was of Late Iron Age date, but probably continued into the post-conquest period (presence of residual 1st century AD samian).

A composite photograph of the western section through

Plate 30. The exposed archaeological levels below the modern and medieval lynchet soils, from the southern end of the 1979 excavations (AB33).

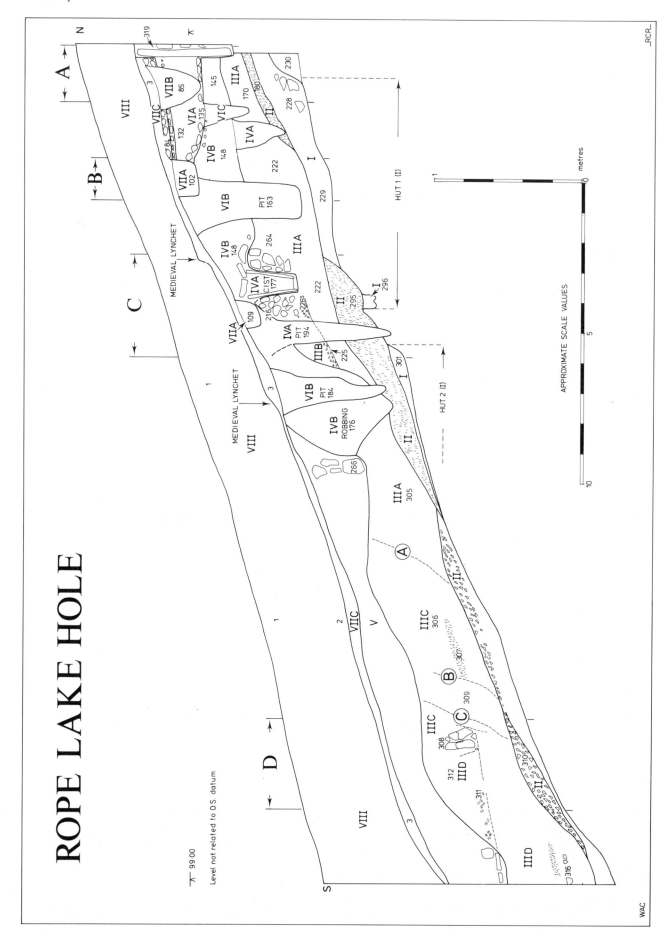

Figure 70. The North-South diagrammatic section through the 1979 excavations, showing the main structures by phase (I-VII). The vertical scale is five times that of the horizontal.

the site is shown in plate 35.

The Period 1 Occupation (Early Iron Age)

The earliest occupation horizons consist of a series of rubble-filled hollows interpreted as collapsed and robbed huts (phase I) overlain by a series of worked shale and flint dumps (phase II). These early levels are depicted in plan (fig. 72), and in detail section (fig. 71A-C). The huts themselves were only partially excavated, and it was not possible to fully define their structure. Time did not allow the examination of any internal structural arrangement that may have survived, *viz.* post-holes and internal roof support. It was felt at the time that the objectives of the excavations had been achieved in that the full chronological sequence, and the potential of the site, had been adequately identified.

Hut 1 was defined by a sharp cut through a remnant clay soil and into clay 'natural' (refer section, fig. 71A). This cut, 0.2m deep on the northern edge, and the levels suggest that the floor of the hut had been deliberately levelled and terraced into the hill slope. Limestone rubble up to 0.2m across concentrated around the cut depression (228) and could be interpreted as remnant pieces of a robbed drystone wall (plate 36). If this hollow is accepted as a hut then the structure was probably very similar to those structures identified in later phases (phase, IIIA and V) but again these later structures were also only partly understood. It is likely however that they may have been very similar to a well preserved Late Bronze Age example excavated at Rowden (Woodward, 1981) and elsewhere. It is possible that the internal arrangement of roof supports may have been a post-ring as at Rowden, but this can only be speculation, and no post-settings could be identified on the eastern side of the hut excavated. Also no post-ring (as in the houses at Eldon's Seat 1km to the east) could be identified along the edge of the cut hollow, which suggests that the construction of these huts, if they are huts at all, may have been rather different. The depression was filled (229) and (248) with shale, flint and limestone debris. The latter was probably derived from the original walling, but the flint and shale pieces were worked, and both could

be associated with shale fabrication. The flint must have been brought to the site from some distance (the chalk ridge or more likely Warbarrow Bay) for use on site. The assemblage exhibited an extremely crude knapping technique and no standardised tool product could be identified, although some secondary edge trimming and snapping of flakes was identified. It is not likely that this material was originally knapped or worked within the hut but that it derives from surrounding occupation levels after abandonment.

Virtually no burnt flint or shale could be found in these internal deposits excavated, but the two deposits (261) and (269) on the southern edge of the postulated hut 1 contained burnt clay (possibly briquetage), much burnt shale and limestone fragments, and a concentration of pottery and occupation debris. It is possible that these levels are derived from a hearth on the southern side of the hut. This would be similar to the hearth arrangement in the Rowden hut with the hearth on the south-west side adjacent and to the west of the entrance. The huts at Eldon's Seat had 'centrally' placed hearths. No large entrance post-settings could be identified on this side of the hut apart from feature (296); a double post-hole of roughly 0.3m diam. x 0.2m deep, and 0.2m diam. x 0.1m deep. This would have been rather insubstantial for a post-setting associated with a hut. However, the rubble of this 'hut' is apparently cut away just to the north of this post-hole (plan fig. 72B, and section fig. 71B), and infilled with shale waste dump (295). Limestone rubble and burnt shale (291) and (292) tip into the depression at this point. It is likely that the absence of any structural detail at the entrance to hut 1 is a result of this later cutting. In addition two linear cuts were recorded to the south-west of (295). This cut (240) partly through (269) and (261), (plate 39), and was infilled with limestone rubble flint and shale and other occupational debris including a bone pin (273). This cut was probably also in part responsible for the lack of detail in this area of hut 1. Feature (240) has been recorded with shale dump (295) in phase II (fig. 72B).

The estimated diameter of hut 1 can be suggested as 7-8m.

Plate 31. The exposed yard levels and features of Phase 7, after Phase 7C grid collection (AA14).

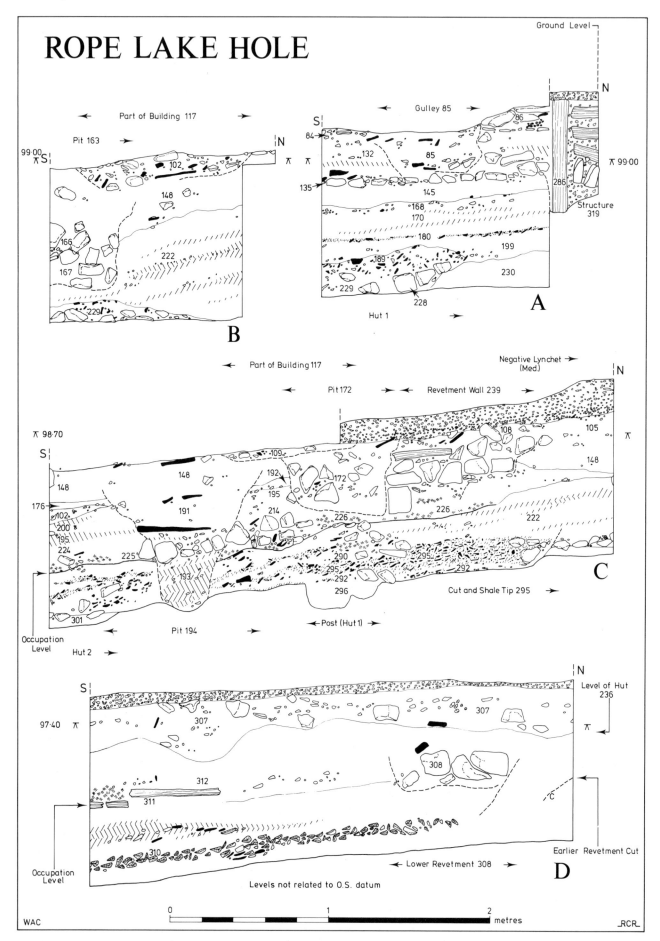

Figure 71. The Detail sections A-D, showing the main structures and occupation horizons. The location of these sections is shown on the diagrammatic section (fig. 70) and on the site plans by period (figs 72, 73 and 76).

More substantial post-pits were identified to the east (220) and to the south (288) of this hut. Pit (220) was not easily identified from the surrounding clays, but its clay fill was notably darker. It contained large limestone packing, charcoal flecks burnt clay (briquetage) and shell; 0.4m diameter 0.5m deep with a vertical edge profile and rounded base. Pit (288) was similarly filled but was more ovate in its upper dimension, but had similar vertical sides 0.8m diameter and 0.6m deep. These could be pits for quite substantial posts, but no post-pipes were identified in section.

To the south and east of these features another concentration of rubble (267) and (301) were recorded in addition to a short cut edge. These may be indicators of a second hut position; HUT 2. However if this was a hut it is now substantially eroded away, and was not recognised in the machine trench running south. Some pottery, animal bone, worked flint, shell, and shale were recovered from (301). A similar material assemblage to that in the depression, hut 1, to the north.

The cut and infilling rubble (280) to the west was somewhat similar to (229), infilling HUT 1, and it is possible that this may be the beginnings of another large diameter depression or hut.

The rubbish tips across the northern part of the site were primarily of shale, (188), (180), (245), (300) and (295) (fig. 72 B). The dump of flint (310) at the southern end of the excavation trench was identified in the section of the machine trench (fig. 71D).

Sections through dumps (180), (295) and (310) and (300) are depicted in the detail sections (fig. 71A-C, and fig. 74). Shale dump (180), partly excavated, is shown in plate 37. The shale dumps were primarily concerned with the preparation of armlet rough-outs. Contrasts between dumps (180) and (188) suggest that these came from two functionally different areas of shale preparation. The large number of perfect concoidal fractures in dump (245) also point to a separate batch of preparation. The later stages in the handworking process probably took place elsewhere on the site, possibly in closer association with the contemporary huts. Larger numbers of armlet rough-outs (presumably unsuccessful attempts) were found in dump (300) and the infill of the hut 1 depression.

The flint industry could be directly associated with that of shale armlet production, although the techniques used are not well understood.

The flint dump (310) to the south of the shale dumps was almost entirely composed of primary preparation flakes. A higher percentage of utilised flakes was noted in the shale dumps to the north, and in the hut depressions of Phase I.

No structures were identified with these phase II shale working tips.

The Period 2 Occupation (Middle Iron Age)

The period 2 occupation consisted of a series of structural groupings running the whole length of the site (phases IIIA-IIID). These are illustrated in plan (fig. 73A) and in detail section (fig. 71). A full impression of their inter-relationship can be seen in diagrammatic section (fig. 72).

Although the function of these stone structures cannot be fully understood since the area of excavation was insufficient to examine complete units, it is likely that the curved stone walls reveted occupation waste (possibly industrial) and soil accumulations. It is clear that these walls were frequently reconstructed and replaced (c.f. structural sequence of walls (260), (281) and (282)), and that they could have been an intrinsic part of hut structures. However as a result of later robbing and disturbance in the areas examined little of the occupation levels associated with these structures survived.

Interpretation of the machine trench section in the southern half of the site was difficult and a full understanding of all the deposits clearly impossible. However, the recognition of defined horizons, the identification of the main stone-wall structural alignments, and the location levels of shale and flint dumps did permit some interpretation, which clearly indicated that the structures were part of a cohesive system of terraces, which were apparently modified on several occasions; *viz.* a series of tip lines in IIIC (fig. 70) can be compared with the sequence of replaced revetments previously mentioned (fig. 73A). It can perhaps be suggested that the relative position of revetment wall (239)/(264) and the revetment (308) represent the position of two hut-terraces. This would mean a terrace width of 14m.

The similarity between deposits (305) and (222)/(142) also suggests that the upper revetment (239)/(264) had been cut into a pre-existing accumulation of soil which had previously been held

Plate 32. The exposed hut structure (236) – Phase 5 from the south, below Phase 7C collection (AE37A).

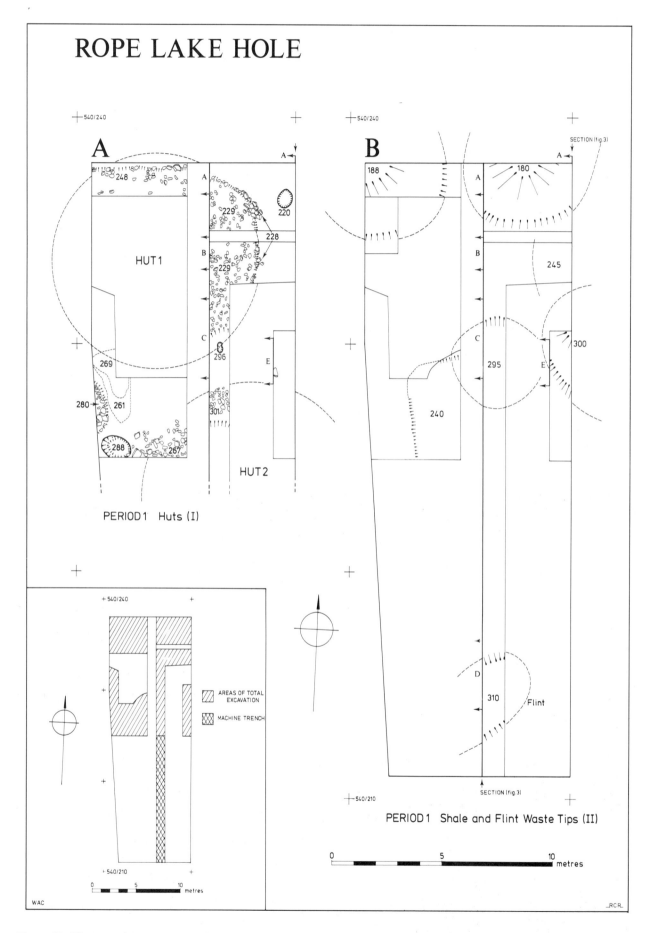

Figure 72. The Period 1 structures and waste tips. The inset shows the areas of total excavation. Plan A shows the phase I huts and Plan B the phase II tips and cuttings.

back by a series of revetments A-C (fig. 70) and finally in revetment (308). The sequence of revetted soils being: (222)/(142) and (305) held at A, (306) held at B, 309 at C and finally by (308). The revetment wall (239)/(264) is therefore last in the sequence, and indeed stratigraphically overlies the sequence of walls (282), (281) and (260). The latter three walls perhaps echo events described above (i.e. (282) with A, (281) with B, . . .), but cannot be directly related due to incomplete excavation. These problems can only be resolved by area excavation.

The earliest sediment deposit in phase IIIA has been grouped under context numbers (222) and (142), but was in no respects a cohesive or single deposit. It was composed in general terms of a mid grey-brown clay loam with numerous red and grey-black ashy lenses with red clay flecking and the usual array of coarser inclusions: limestone, shale, pottery and other occupation deposits. Occasionally more specific bands of clay were recognised, and a single post-hole was identified in section. The complexity of this deposit made excavation difficult, and the dryness of the site during excavation and the lack of water supply made recognition of post-holes in plan impossible. The nature of this deposit was identical to that of (305), and was clearly related to some industrial/occupation activity. It had no similarity to an agricultural soil, and gave the impression of having been deliberately tipped. This deposit may, in this respect, be more closely similar to the shale dumps which it seals.

The earliest revetment walls, cut into this accumulation (142)/(222), composed a sequence (282), (281) and (260) (plates 38 and 39). It would appear that the first of these was (282) which survived as two courses of limestone, 0.3m in height. The limestone blocks varied in size from 0.4m to 0.2m across. They were roughly squared and in general horizontally bedded at the back of the wall with the larger pieces at the front and small wedges between. These were probably not the original front face which had since collapsed. Wall (282) survived two courses in height. The limestone tumble (246) in front of this wall was generally of smaller size, 0.1-0.2m, than that of the base stones. The second wall (281) in front of the rubble tumble of (282) was similarly constructed but survived to a height of 0.5m in places and was of four courses. The stones of this wall were generally smaller than those large base stones of (282), and the front stones were in places well bedded and may represent the original face. The width of the wall could therefore be estimated at 0.6m. The third wall (260) was less distinct and was not easily defined in the rubble collapse behind and in front, but was composed of blocks from 0.2-0.3m across, and of two courses up to a height of 0.4m. Only part of these walls were seen in plan (fig. 73A), but it should be noted that some stretches were linear, with slight curves in evidence towards the edge of the trench, reminiscent of the earlier cut (240).

It was apparent that the alignment of (282) and (281) was cut away when the later wall (239) was built. It was certainly clear that this later wall was bedded into the top of (282), where this junction was examined (plate 10). Wall (239) (detail, plate 11) was not otherwise excavated, apart from examining its front and back surfaces. A section through it was however recorded where it was cut away by pit (172) (fig. 73B).

At this point the wall was constructed on a slight slope with three horizontally bedded courses at the front to a height of 0.3m, with a rather less defined rubbly structure at the back, and with a total width of 0.9m. Shaley limestone-slabs were sometimes used in this construction (fig. 71C).

At this point, where the later pit (172) (fig 73B) cut through the earlier levels, the exact relationship between this wall (239) and that to the east, wall (264), had been lost. However it is clear that wall (264) is very much wider than (239), and so can be said to be a separate unit of construction and that there was a break, gap or perhaps entrance at this point (plate 40). However, this, at the

Plate 33. The cutting of machine-trench through site (AK16A).

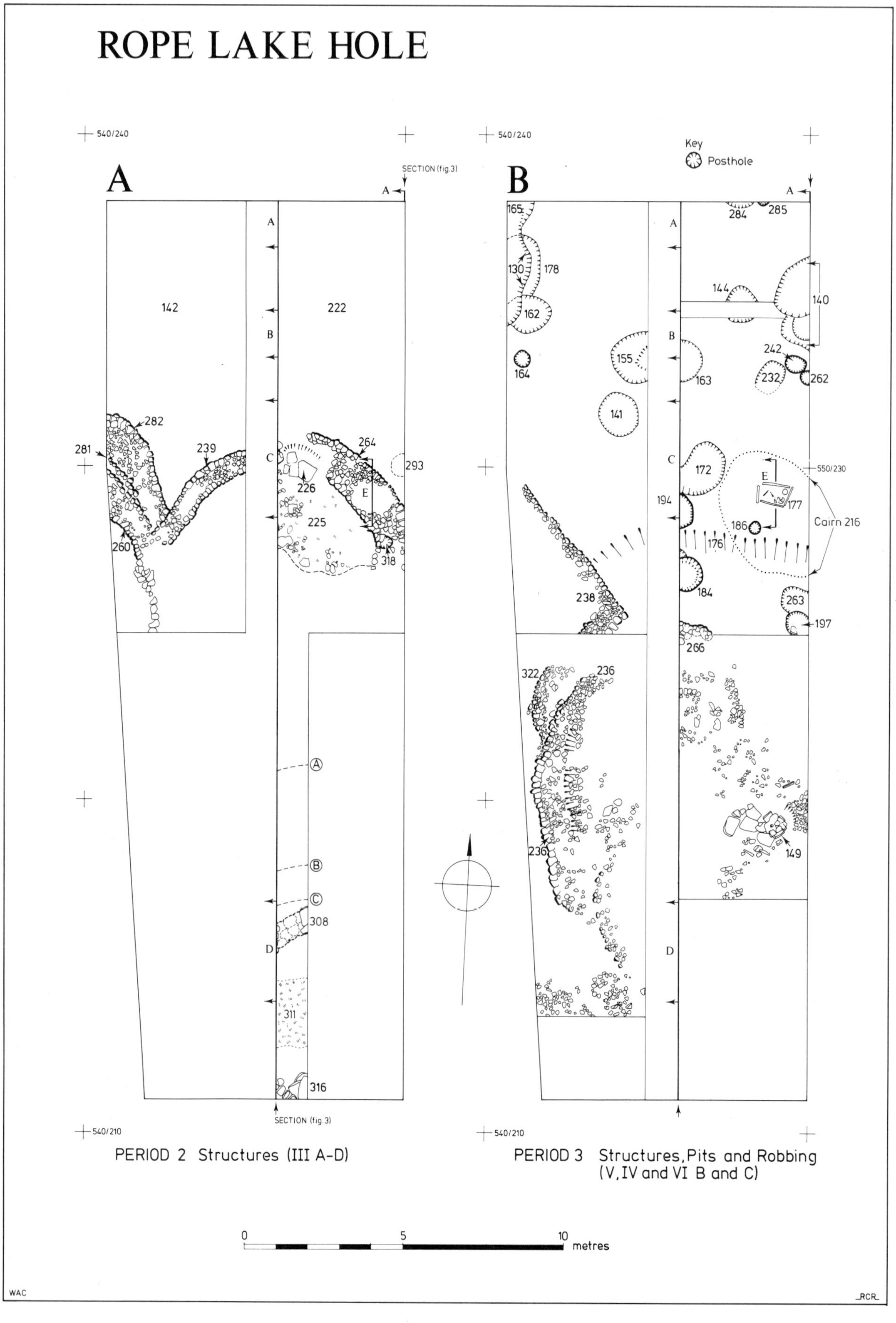

Figure 73. The Period 2 and 3 occupation horizons. Plan A shows the structures of phases IIIA-D (Period 2). Plan B shows the structures of phase V, and the pits and robbing of phase IV, and VIB-C (Period 3).

northern side, would be extremely unusual if these walls were those of a hut, but might be acceptable if the walls were thought of as lynchet terrace walls, with gaps facilitating access from one terrace to another. Pit (172) had cut down to a level which was composed of shaley limestone-slabs (226), (plate 40). These slabs were set in a slight cut into (222), and were contiguous with a trampled clay 'floor' (225), which butted to wall (264). The latter two features were certainly contemporary, but the cut for (226) may relate to an earlier feature (240), to the west. Among the occupation debris with floor (225), was a shaley limestone-slab with worn circular grooves, perhaps for some rotary mechanism (?). The construction of wall (264) can be seen in fig. 74, and a section through floor (225) in fig. 71B.

Wall structure (239)/(264) had been substantially removed to the south by a robbing trench (176), and with the construction of a later linear wall (238). A wall (266) located on the edge of the hand-excavated area probably belonged to a hut part exposed to the south, phase V. The robbing across the face of these phase IIIB structures was probably carried out when these phase V huts were constructed in the Later Iron Age (period 3).

The machine trench cutting through the site to the south exposed a series of structures and sediments, whose relationship to the hand excavated levels of phase IIIA has been previously described. The lower terrace revetment (308) can be seen in detail section, fig. 71C, and again a trampled clay and limestone occupation floor can be seen to the south of this revetment. Within this occupation level a remarkable armlet with plaited cord motif was recovered (fig. 92, 124).

The Period 3 Occupation (Later Iron Age)
The period 3 occupation consisted of a series of levels, pits, and structures which cut across and levelled the earlier terraced horizons. These are depicted in plan (fig. 73B), in detail section (fig. 71A-C), and a full impression of their stratigraphic inter-relationship in diagrammatic section (fig. 70).

This period is essentially composed of four phases; IVA, IVB, V, and VIB/C (previous). The removal (176) of the earlier hut terrace, the construction of a new linear wall (238), and the general occupation horizon (148)/(145), all of which clearly erode the earlier terraced dumps, have been grouped as phase IVB. The pits, post-pits, and burial cyst which are cut in, or below the occupation horizon (148)/(145) as IVA. The pits, cut from the top of this occupation horizon, e.g. (141), are grouped as phases VIB and C. All this occupation activity lies to the north of at least three stone-walled structures (238), (322), and (236)/(266), which are grouped as phase V. These were not fully excavated, but could be considered to be contiguous with the phases IVA/B, and VIB/C. The robbed stone from the earlier terraces would undoubtedly have been used in the construction of the hut structures of phase V, (236) and (322), and the linear wall of phase IVB, (238).

The occupation soils, (148) and (145), were an undifferentiated grey-brown clayey loam with frequent inclusions of broken shale, flint, briquetage, and other occupational debris. The robbing and rubbish tip (176) across the face of the old terrace had a similar matrix sediment, but with larger pitched debris and waste included behind and to the north of (266). The wall (238), the pits and working depressions, and burial cyst (177) could all be taken as contemporary with this general occupation horizon although as previously mentioned the level at which they were cut within this horizon varied (General section, fig. 70).

The pit features of phases IVA, V, VIB, and VIC, could be divided into four categories:

Working hollows/depressions: (130), (165) and (178).

Post-holes and pits: (164), (194), (184), (186), (242), (262) and (285).

Pits (functions various): (140), (141), (144), (155), (162), (163), (172), (197), (232), (263) and (284).

Burial cists: (177), and probably (149).

The working hollows associated with pit (162), formed a

Plate 34. The complete excavation trenches looking south, prior to back-filling (AM35).

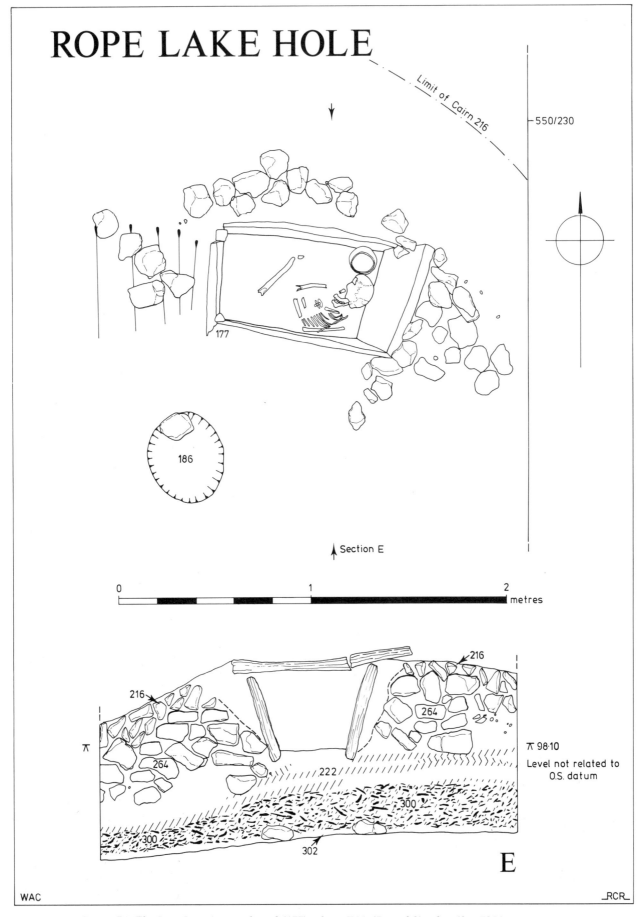

Figure 74. The Late Iron Age cist burial (177), phase IVA (Period 3), plan (fig. 73B), section E.

TABLE 21: The period 3 pits (IVA and VIB).

PHASE	PIT NUMBER	SHAPE	BASE DIAM. (metres)	DEPTH (metres)	RUBBLE FILL (Large)	COMPACTED CLAY	ASH/ BURNT CLAY	POTTERY	BONE	FLINT	FLINT (Kite-tools)	SHELL	SHALE	LATHE-SHALE (A cores)	LATHE-SHALE (6L armlet)	BRIQUETAGE	SLAG	BURNT STONE	BRONZE
VIB	140	C	0.6	0.7	×		×	×	×	×			×	1		×	×	×	
VIB	141	C	1.3	0.2	×		×	×	×	×		×	×			×	×	×	×
VIB	144	II	1.2 (recut)	0.7	×	×		×	×	×									
VIB	155	U	0.8	0.6	×			×	×	×		×	×						
IVA	162	U	1.3	0.2	×			×	×	×		×	×			×			
VIB	163	C	1.1	0.8	×			×	×	×	2	×	×⊕	5		×		×	
VIB	172	IF	0.7	0.4	×			×	×		1		×	5		×			
VIB	197	C	0.6	0.5	×	×		×				×							
IVA	232	C	0.9	0.4		×		×	×				×			2			
IVA	263	U	0.5	0.4	×														
VIC	284	U	0.8	0.3	×														

C = Cylinder, vertical sides flat bottom.
U = 'U' shaped, rounded sides and bottom, near vertical sides.

I = Irregular, with flat (F) or Irregular (I) bottom.
⊕ includes shale slab

stratigraphic sequence: in chronological order (165), (178), (162) and finally (130). These varied in depth from 0.1-0.2m and were not steep sided. That these levels were associated with shale working (as the whole of phase IV) is certain, and hollow (130) was stratigraphically separated from the other hollows by a tip of broken shale (161).

A number of features in this area could be distinguished as small post-holes: (164), (186), (262), (242) and (295). Two larger features could be interpreted as post-pits since they contained pitched limestone-slabs, which may have acted as post-wedges: (184) and (194). The dimensions were as follows:

feature	diameter	depth
(164)	0.45m	0.10m
(184)	0.64m	0.63m
(186)	0.44m	0.30m
(194)	0.30m	0.90m
(242)	0.50m	0.10m
(262)	0.40m	0.40m
(295)	0.20m	0.20m

One of the stones used as a post-wedge in post-pit (184) was a shallow circular socketted stone (refer to architectural fragments, and portable stone objects in this report). A section through post-pit (194) occurs in fig. 71C.

The array of post-holes uncovered was insufficient to group as a structure, and in this phase are unrelated to any stone walling, and may therefore not belong to buildings.

In addition to these post-features were a series of other pits. These probably provided for a variety of functions and some at least were probably storage pits. Their shape, fill and contents are summarised in Table 21. Two of the pits contained ashy burnt deposits, and it is more likely that pit (141) functioned as an 'industrial' hearth. The base of this pit was packed with burnt stones, and some slag, burnt shale, and a piece of melted bronze were recovered.

The industrial waste from the working of shale was present in most pits, and lathe technology was clearly demonstrated by the correspondence and presence of kite-shaped tools and shale lathe-cores (category 4A; Calkin, 1953).

The large shale slab found in pit 163 was probably the sheet waste from which discs were cut, and is the only large example of this category of waste on the site.

The burial cist (177) (plate 41) was cut into the underlying revetment wall (264), (plate 40). It was roughly rectangular, 1.1m x 0.8m and the sides lined with four shaley limestone-slabs; the bottom was flat but unlined, and the burial sealed with a large rectangular slab. The vast quantity of rubble (216), (plate 42) remaining in this area across the robbed lynchet was suggestive, and it is perhaps likely that a burial of this type would have been covered with a stone cairn to protect it from the deprecations of both wild and domestic animals. The burial is depicted in fig. 74, and was severely mutilated and disturbed by small animals. It is likely that the whole skeleton was never deposited. The burial was accompanied by an open pedestalled bowl of the 1st century AD. This burial can be compared with others in Purbeck; at Tynham (RCHM, 1970, 613 (41)), Cleavel Point Ower (Woodward, this volume), and at Herston (Jarvis, 1982).

The stone walls to the south of this pit complex are probably from a sequence of structures. In chronological order these are (238),

(322) and (236)/(266). Only the wall (238) was fully excavated, and this had been clearly robbed to the west for later constructions, and only survived as a single aligned course of stones (fig. 73, and plate 38); its apparent sharp corner is probably misleading, and perhaps a result of later disturbance. Its relationship to later buildings is not known.

The two buildings (322) and (236) were only examined in upper surface plan (plate 14), and a single machine section. A southern return wall was not recognised for either structure, but wall (266) of three courses may define the northern curved wall, perhaps to a circular hut. The absence of a wall at the southern end of the machine trench may indicate an entrance position.

The cist (149), (plate 15), to the east of (236) was of unknown function. It consisted of squared pitched limestone slabs (0.4m square) on two sides, the others perhaps collapsed outwards or were robbed. A pierced shaley limestone-slab was laid at the base. This was reminiscent of the entrance post-holes of the buildings at Cleavel Point, Ower (Woodward, this volume), although it is equally likely to be a robbed out burial cist. Beneath the pierced limestone slab was a carefully crafted circular limestone slab (fig. 93, 136). Perhaps this post/cist had some ritual function, or was a foundation post or pit for the building (236).

The distribution of briquetage across the walls (322) and (236) of phase V (plate 32), was recorded in the 2m grid squares of VIIC (fig. 76). This showed a relatively high concentration in this area compared with that in the upper yard levels of phase VII in the northern trench area. The percentage of briquetage was also notably lower in the area of phase IVA and B, in comparison with the phase V huts. It would appear that the briquetage, as in phase VII, was more closely associated with the internal areas of buildings as opposed to the surrounding yard areas.

The phase VIIC distribution of material survived at the base of the medieval terrace soils. It is also clear (also see following) that the southern two thirds of the site had been severely eroded by this medieval agriculture. The areas of late Iron Age activity, not sealed by the phase VI and VII yards, are clearly damaged; as a result of medieval ploughing if not by the subsequent Romano-British developments.

The Period 4 Occupation (Romano-British)

The period 4 occupation consisted of a series of levels and structures, of which the second phase could be securely identified with the manufacture of shale armlets. The earlier yard, pitched stone structure and occupation debris were grouped together as phase VIA. This was overlain by a sill-wall building and the yard with a concentration of lathe turned shale waste and flint chisel tools, phase VIIA. This latter yard was cut by a pit and a gulley, which were grouped as phase VIIB. Above these structural levels the material was collected on a 2m grid basis for the whole trench. This material was at the base of the medieval lynchet soils and the modern plough soil, but nevertheless was able to depict the functional areas of the underlying archaeological levels, phase V (previously mentioned) and phase VIIA. This material distribution was denoted as phase VIIC. The occurrence of abraded medieval pottery in this phase VIIC collection attested to its being a later 'plough-touched', and 'manured' horizon. The two yard levels and their associated structures (phases VIIA and B) are depicted in fig. 75, and the material distributions (phase VIIC) in fig. 76. Their stratigraphic relationship to earlier levels is shown in the general-

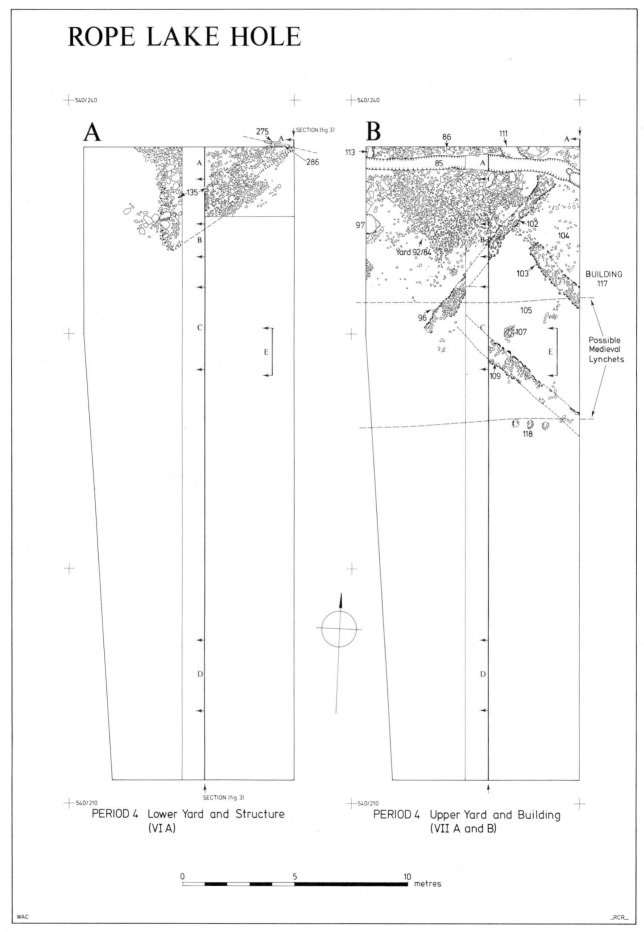

Figure 75. The Period 4 yards and structures. Plan A shows the yard and pitched stone structure of phase VIA. Plan B shows the yard, building and gulley of phases VIIA-B.

ised section fig. 70, and details of the yard levels and structures in sections A and B, fig. 71.

The lower yard (135), fig. 75A and plate 44, was composed of laid limestone flags and broken limestone pieces. The flags were up to 0.3m across, some of which spread outside the kite-shaped shaped yard area. This yard was to some extent cut into the lower levels, and was particularly marked on a straight edge on the south-east, and the west. Within the yard depression the sediment tips, to a depth of 0.25m, were extremely ashy and contained quantities of burnt shale, burnt lenses of red-brown clay and briquetage. In contrast to the upper yard there was little hand-worked or lathe turned shale waste at this level. Of the 296 lathe turned waste pieces of phase VII only eight came from yard (135).

The flint waste and tools were similarly few in number.

On the northern edge of the yard (135) in the north-east corner of the trench were a series of vertically-set stones to which yard (135) butted (plate 36). One was a perfectly circular limestone slab (286), 0.7m in diameter and 0.1m thick, which was water worn, but exhibited no evidence of working or use. Behind this slab was another pitched shaley limestone slab, and a large category 4B core (275) (0.21m in diameter, see specialist report below), and another circular limestone slab to the east. Behind these vertical slabs were horizontally bedded shale and limestone pieces. This enigmatic 'platform' was not otherwise excavated.

Above the ashy occupation deposits of phase VIA were the levels of phase VII; a series of compacted broken limestone horizons. The

Plate 35. The structural sequence as shown on the western section through the site (composite photo). Top right is north.

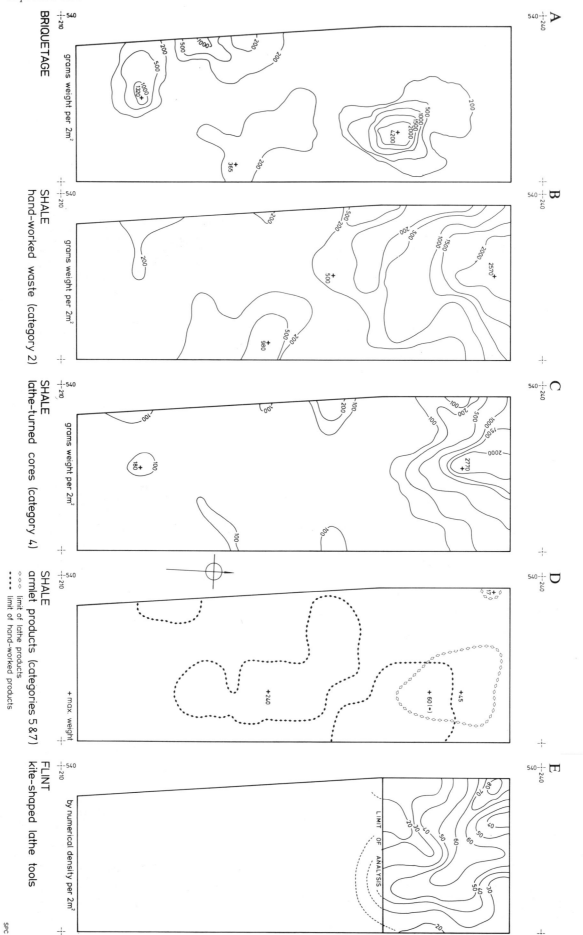

Figure 76. The Period 4 material distributions, phase VIIC. Plan A: Briquetage, Plan B: Category 2 shale waste, Plan C: Category 4 shale lathe cores, Plan D: Categories 5 and 7 shale products, Plan E: Flint lathe tools.

lowest (92) was of small to medium limestone and broken shale fragments; few lathe cores were noted at this level, and the surface was rather discontinuous. Above was a thin lense (30mm deep) of mid-grey brown clayey loam (91) with trampled concentrations of pottery, and above a rubble surface of large limestone slabs (up to 0.6m across) and smaller broken limestone (84) (fig. 75B). Yard (84) contained rough shale lumps, cores and flint lathe-working debris, and across this level the phase VIIC collection on a 2m grid was made.

Abutting yard (84) to the south-east were the linear wall footings of rectilinear building (117), (plate 45). These footings were little more than concentrations of broken limestone rubble and grey-brown clay loam, and sometimes were only apparent as slight depressions, 50-100mm in depth, cut into the underlying strata (detail sections fig. 71, B and C, for sections through (102) and (109)). These footings were probably originally edged (at least on outer walls) with larger stones (fig. 75, (109)), and were perhaps the base for horizontal floor plates of a box-frame timber building. This building is cut away on the south side by the later agricultural lynchet, and its relationship to the pitched stone structure (319) is not known, since the wall footing (102) is cut away at this point by a later gulley (85) of phase VIIB, although footings to the north of the gulley were not apparent (fig. 75B). Internal floor levels within building (117) did not survive although the phase VIIC distribution of material across this area did indicate that briquetage was concentrated across the building, whilst the shale was scattered across the yard (fig. 76). The two rectangular areas within the walls (104) and (105) contained areas of briquetage concentrations. However, the areas contrasted in that the briquetage in area (105) was concentrated around feature (107), a circular briquetage dump, whilst in (104) the briquetage was evenly distributed. The briquetage patch (107) was roughly circular, 0.4m in diameter, and 0.2m deep. However it is possible that the material within the area of the building may be derived from earlier levels, i.e. phase IVB. (Also phase VIIC distributions of hand-worked shale products and briquetage).

Across the yard and building two features were cut: a gulley (85), and a shallow pit (97). These were grouped together as phase VIIB. Gulley (85) was 0.6-0.8m wide with steep sides and a flattish bottom (section, fig. 71A), but was rather more irregularly dug at the eastern end (fig. 75B). It was 0.3m deep, and filled with a grey-brown clay loam with broken limestone and a large quantity of lathe-shale cores, and other lathe-shale working debris (shale report). The pit (97) on the western edge of the site was shallow (0.1m depth) and had an apparent diameter of 0.9m. It was steep sided and edged with pitched limestone and shale slabs, mainly on the northern edge; perhaps the remnants of a large post pit. In addition two features to the north of the gulley (85) were also partly examined; these were not fully understood because of the limited area available at the end of the trench. The pitched limestone slabs running north-south in feature (113) were suggestive of a drain (width 0.5m, depth 0.15m) which would have run into (85). This resembles a similar feature discovered in the upper level of trial pit A (76); orientated north-west to south-east. Both together are suggestive of part of a series of covered drains. Feature (111) was a series of steep sided cuts through the yard area (86) to the north of gulley (85). These cuts were up to a depth of 0.3m. Conjoining samian sherds from (111) and (85) demonstrate contemporaneity.

Above this level was the remnant occupation debris, which was collected across the trench as a whole on a 2m grid basis and grouped as phase VIIC. The resulting distributions of the flint lathe tools, the category 2 shale preparation waste, the category 4 lathe-turned shale cores, the lathe products, and the briquetage are shown in fig. 76A-E. It is clear that this material, which was at the base of the later ploughed lynchet horizons, relates to the exposed late Iron Age and Romano-British occupation horizons of phases V and VII.

The conclusions from these distributions are in general self-evident, and have been noted in the foregoing text where relevant. The location of the shale lathe-turning yard can be surmised from distributions C, D, and E. The location of areas where the hand-working of shale is taking place is indicated by distributions B and D. It is interesting to note that these distributions closely follow those of the briquetage which is associated with the buildings of phase V and phase VII. It is possible that the briquetage and shale material from the area of building (117) in phase VIIA, may be derived from earlier horizons (only the footings of (117) were recorded, and the building was severely eroded with no floor levels surviving, (previous description). The hand-worked armlet products in distribution D are almost certainly of late Iron Age date.

The Period 5 Field Lynchets (Early Medieval)

The presence of abraded early medieval, 12th-14th c. AD pottery types within the phase VIIC material collection has already been noted and is probably derived from the manuring of fields belonging to the settlement to the east (refer introduction). This worm-sorted horizon can be seen in plate 30.

A detailed examination of the section and a careful record of levels indicated the presence of two lynchet cuts. These are shown in plan (fig. 75B), in the general interpretative section (fig. 70) and detail section (fig. 71C).

The form of these medieval field terraces is now lost owing to

Plate 36. The earliest structure (229)/(228) and post-pit (220) – Phase 1 from the south-west, with the overlying stratigraphy in section (AF13).

Plate 37. A 'half'-section through the upper levels of the shale dump (180) – Phase 2, from the south-east (AD5).

Plate 38. Wall sequence on first exposure: (267) – Phase 1, (260)(281) (282) – Phase 3A, (239) – Phase 3A, and (238) – Phase 4A from the south-east (AF34).

Plate 39. Junction detail of wall (239) and (260) – Phase 3A, underlying cut (240) – Phase 2, and hut structure (267) – Phase 1, from the south (AJ11).

later site activity (refer introduction), and the nature of the modern plough-soil has already been described (see the 1979 excavations).

The medieval pottery recovered from these excavations and the trial trenches has not been described here.

THE SITE INDUSTRIES AND TRADING CHARACTERISTICS

The basic chronological development of this settlement has been described and established in the previous sections. This site was concerned primarily with the salt (briquetage) and shale industries. The status of these industries (local consumption and/or export), the associated domestic and trading characteristics of the site will be discussed here.

A crude comparison of fluctuations in the importance of shale and salt is shown in fig. 77A and B (analysis by J. Hawkes and P. W. Cox). Table B can be considered as a very simplistic representation of the relative importance of two materials (shale and briquetage) against the intensity of domestic activity (pottery) on the site, but should be carefully viewed against the structural evidence. If the briquetage is also taken to reflect 'domestic salt consumption', then the comparative importance of the shale industries through time (fig. 77B) can be seen in sharper perspective. The shale industry fluctuations then closely follow changes in the periods defined by the ceramic assemblage, and correlates closely to the structural evidence.

The early hand-working shale industries concentrate in phase II when the sites of earlier houses were used for waste-dumps, but a return to more 'domestic' activities for the site in phase III (fig. 77A and B) is indicated. Domestic activity and occupations throughout periods 1 and 2 could be identified in the worked bone assemblage (points, pins, gouges ....., Table 28), and in the cutting and working of antler. However the lack of spindle whorls and querns, at least in the excavated area of the site, for all periods contrasts strongly with the neighbouring site at *Eldon's Seat* (Cunliffe, 1968). The introduction of the lathe in the Late Iron Age is associated with an increasing use of shale on

site, together with an increasing occurrence of briquetage (fig. 77A); subsequent decline probably indicates a drop in site activity in the Late Iron Age/Romano-British period. This may correspond with an arable or abandonment phase. Subsequently shale turning becomes the primary site activity in the late 2nd century AD (phase VII).

The analysis of the shale and flint from this final shale-working phase (VII) indicates that it was not simply domestic production, since the waste-cores occur in quantity and are primarily of a single type (Calkin type 4C), and the flint lathe-tools were made to a standard specification and prepared in quantity for continuous and extended periods of lathe-turning. This lathe-turning is primarily concerned with armlet production (see specialist report). Analysis of the flint lathe-tools also indicates that the area examined was on the edge of a more extensive working floor. If large quantities of armlets were being produced, it is not apparent what commodities were being traded into the site during the Romano-British period.

The lack of coinage, and the near absence of amphora and luxury goods, suggests that the profits from shale armlet production were being distributed and taken elsewhere. Coinage comparisons with other sites in Purbeck (Woodward, 1981) and the relationship of this armlet production to other Purbeck industries (marble, salt and pottery production) can be used to suggest the status of the site within Purbeck and a carefully organised trading network.

The centralisation of the regional (Durotrigian) pottery industry on Poole Harbour in the Late Iron Age and the subsequent development of BB1 pottery for export throughout Britain in the Romano-British period is well known (Williams, 1977). The use of the tourmaline-rich clays to manufacture some of the middle Iron Age haematite wares found at Rope Lake Hole indicates that a local distribution of coarse wares based on Wareham-Poole Harbour had already begun at an early date (see specialist report). The growth of the pottery industry after the conquest was accompanied by a rapid growth in other manufacturing industries, based on the local mineral resources (principally

Percentage comparision of material types

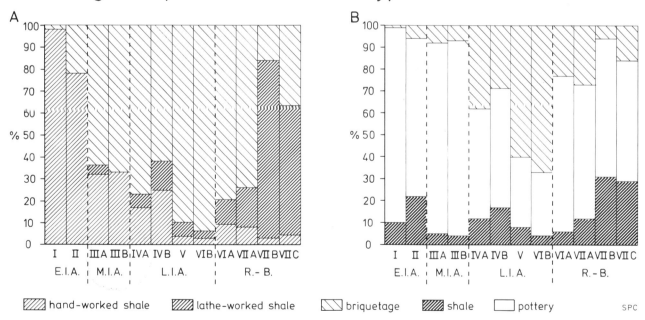

Figure 77. A comparison of industrial activity and occupation intensity. A. A rough numerical comparison of briquetage (salt production), handworked shale waste (Categories 3, 5C, 6C and 7C) and lathe shale waste (Categories 4, 5L, 6L and 7L) (primarily armlet production). B. A rough comparison (by number) of industrial waste (shale and briquetage) with occupation (pottery).

Kimmeridge shale and Purbeck marble). The sites engaged in the manufacture of pottery around Poole Harbour, such as *Ower* (Woodward, this volume), *Redcliffe* (Farrar, 1979-82) and *Norden* (Sunter, this volume), and these may have also been the centres from which the pottery was distributed; in the case of Ower and Norden of other goods as well (*Ower:* mudstone tesserrae, salt, and possibly shale; *Norden:* Purbeck Marble (mortars), chalk and mudstone tesserrae, shale (armlets, furniture, vessels)). It is possible that the production of BB1 in response to Roman military and civilian demand, acted as a stimulus for local Durotrigian entrepreneurs to exploit other minerals and manufacture a wide range of new products for sale to new urban and civilian populations, under the *Pax Romana.*

A comparison between the coinage of these two sites, Ower and Norden, and that at Rope Lake Hole (Woodward, 1981), shows that on the available evidence these two sites were wealthier and engaged in trade for a longer period. It is perhaps probable that the armlet-products of Rope Lake Hole were taken to more complex industrial-distribution centres in North Purbeck. Rope Lake Hole was probably at the bottom of an industrial hierarchy of sites, and is, interestingly, located on a site close to sources of mineral extraction.

That the Purbeck villa sites may have also taken the profits from industrial production has been discussed by Farrar, in relation to the salt industry (Farrar, 1975, 15). However, the coinage suggests that the trading wealth may have also remained within the more complex industrial sites, such as Norden.

The armlet working floor at Rope Lake Hole is probably quite late in date (3rd century AD), and may have been in operation for a long period. This armlet production occurs when both the salt industry (Farrar, 1975), and Purbeck marble industry (Beavis, 1970, 204) are in decline. Purbeck marble shows a steady decline after AD 150. The BB1 pottery industry probably continued in peak production until AD 367, when it ceased to be traded with northern markets (Williams, 1977, 206), but production levels may have begun to fall from the 2nd century onwards with competition from other ceramic centres (Williams, 1977; Farrar, 1973).

Of the Purbeck sites engaged in the working of shale which were listed by Calkin (1953, 69), the following show the characteristics of the Rope Lake Hole phase VII production site, i.e. the occurrence exclusively of 'C' type cores, and of standardised flint lathe-tools: the *Kimmeridge* sites (1-3), *Rope Lake* site (9b), *Gallows Gore* (16), *Blashenwell* (17), *Acton* (19), *Kingston* (20), and *Compact Farm* (26). These are also depicted in the introduction, Kimmeridge Sites (4, 5 and 7), Rope Lake Site (9), Gallows Gore (24 and 25), Blashenwell (33), Acton (28), Kingston (16), and Compact Farm (26) (fig. 1).

Almost all settlement sites in Purbeck probably worked shale to some extent during the Late Iron Age and Romano-British period, but only some of these were concerned with the systematic and 'factory' production of consumer products. However more detailed work and further excavation of shale working sites would be required to establish their status and manufacturing characteristics. Further work is also required on Purbeck sites to establish the inter-relationship, and the status of sites, against a background of industrial organisation, trading patterns, and rural settlement.

The Settlement, general considerations

Rope Lake Hole shows continuity of settlement from the Early Iron Age onwards. The occupation characteristics of each phase (I-VII) within the period chronology (1-4) varied quite considerably.

The Iron Age occupation accumulations were confined within a structural system related to the hill-slope topography. This was probably a series of deliberately constructed stone terraces; the buildings and habitation focus periodically shifting within the terraced system, with abandoned hut-sites being used as dumps (phase II), or being cut by later pits (phase IVA), and perhaps periodically reverting to arable (phase IVB). This system of shifting structures and terracing can be directly compared to the habitation site at *Eldon's Seat,* about a mile to the north-east. At this site the sequence began in the Late Bronze Age. The structural sequence (hut-sites) continued into the Late Iron Age, when the site reverted to an arable terrace belonging to a Late Iron Age/Romano-British settlement, probably located uphill or 20m to the east.

At Rope Lake Hole, the 'terraced' system was apparently abandoned in the Romano-British period, when a rectilinear building was constructed at 45° to the terrace and the hill slope (phase VII). This 2nd-3rd century AD building was constructed across a disturbed horizon (phase IVB), and a damaged and disturbed burial cairn located on an earlier 'terrace' wall. It is probable that the Late Iron Age settlement buildings (phase V), and associated pits (phase IVA), were ploughed and abandoned prior to the insertion of the Romano-British buildings and associated shale-working floors. This reorganisation of the arable fields and the 'taking-in' of the habitation site and terrace during the 1st century AD, can be linked directly with the reversion to arable at Eldon's Seat, during a Durotrigian/Romano-British phase.

It is probable that those two sites and the immediate settlement lands were organised and managed in tandem. The faunal remains from the two sites are comparable and indicate that both concentrated on cattle and sheep husbandry. The intervening fields and terraces were probably continuous and managed on systems of arable and pasture rotation, but no visible trace now remains. However, the function of the two sites within this matrix of fields probably contrasted and varied at any one time, and a comparison of

Plate 40. Detail of wall (264) and laid slabs (226) – Phase 3A, and cut of burial cist (177) – Phase 4A (AJ15).

Plate 41. Burial cist (177) and post-pit (186) – Phase 4A from the east (AD17A).

Plate 42. Accumulated stone cairn (216) around burial cist (177) – phase 4A from the south (AE18).

Plate 44. Lower yard (135) and pitched stone (286) of structure (319) – Phase 6A. From south-west (AB21).

Plate 45. The upper yard (92) and building (117) – Phase 7A from the south-east (AA30).

the structures and artefacts found on the two sites suggests this.

The complete hut-structures and hearths at Eldon's Seat, with the rich artefactual assemblage demonstrates a *'domestic'* focus. The soils and terracing suggest that this focus lay within a system of arable fields. In contrast at Rope Lake Hole; with the periodic dumping of extensive waste tips (shale and flint), the absence of spindle whorls, grain-rubbers and querns, and the burnt and tipped character of the sediments and soils, a function other than purely 'domestic' should perhaps be suggested.

The function of the Rope Lake Hole site may be perhaps described as 'industrial', and directly linked to the shale industry and perhaps the extraction of salt. However it must be borne in mind that both these excavations, at Eldon's Seat (300m²) and at Rope Lake Hole (150m²), were small scale sample excavations. The composition and function of each focus is only partly understood. It would only be possible to fully understand the interrelated patterns and rhythms of change by much more extensive excavation and associated fieldwork.

THE FINDS

The finds from the site are described below the relevant material headings. An exhaustive list of exact stratigraphic locations has not been published, these can be referred to in the level III archive. The finds have however always been given a phase and sometimes a feature location, where this is particularly apposite, e.g. in the dating of occupation/phase horizons.

No overall correlation table has been published for the finds by phase or feature. These have been summarised by period/phase in a series of tables and histograms (tables 21-30, and figs. 87 and 94). The detailed analysis of the horizontal distribution of material was only attempted in the upper levels of the site, phase VIIC. The distribution of the material types at this level which are relevant to the discussion of functional areas are discussed in the site description, and depicted in fig. 76A-E. The bulk comparison of pottery, briquetage and shale, which have been taken as indicators of industrial and settlement intensity through time is described in fig. 77A and B, and discussed above (Site industries and occupation characteristics). Unless others stated the reports are by P.J.W.

In some cases the full material analyses by specialists have been stored in level III archive and only summaries published here. This has been noted in the text where applicable.

All the finds, together with the original site record and level III archive have been deposited in the Dorset County Museum, Dorchester. A microfiche copy of this record has been copied for the Wessex Archaeological Committee and the Department of the Environment. The thin sections of the pottery have been retained in the reference collections of the Department of Archaeology, Southampton University.

THE SAMIAN
Hedley Pengelly

All the samian, about a quarter of which was in small featureless fragments and minute scraps, was recovered from phase VII levels apart from a single sherd from phase VIA and eight from the post-Roman phase VIII. The distribution of the samian by sherd number and date within these phases is summarised in Table 22. Approximately 33.5 per cent of this material is South Gaulish (probably Neronian-early-Flavian- to late 1st or early 2nd century); 66 per cent Central Gaulish (early 2nd century to mid- to late-Antonine) and 0.5 per cent Central or East Gaulish (Antonine or later). No specifically 3rd-century pieces were noted. The assemblage as a whole includes the following recognisable forms (all Dragendorff, except where stated) with the quantity of each shown in brackets:

South Gaulish (La Graufesenque):
Form 29(1), 37(1), Knorr 78(1), 15/17 or 18(1), 36(1), 18/31R (probably 1).
Central Gaulish (Lezoux):
Form 37(3), 33 or 33a(3), 18/31 or 31(2), 18/31-31(1), 37 or 30 rim (1), 42(1), beakers with 'cut-glass' facets (probably 1).
Central or East Gaulish:
Form 38(1) (burnt).

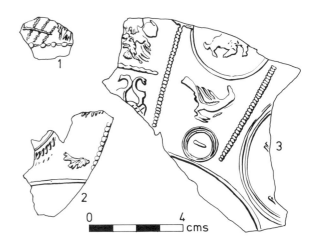

Figure 78. The Samian pottery, 1-3 at 1:2.

TABLE 22: The Samian Pottery by date and phase.

PHASE	1st c. AD	2nd c. AD Early	Middle	Late	Unassigned	Unassigned	
VIII	1	–	3	4*	–	–	
VIIC	3*	2	2	1	3	2	
VIIB	–	–	1*	–	–	–	
VIIA	3	–	2	–	2	–	
VIA	–	–	1	–	–	–	
TOTAL	7	2	9	5	5	2	30
TOTALS	7	21				2	30

*Illustrated Sherd.

Plate 43. Dismantled/robbed cist (149) – Phase 5 with shale slab (fig. 26, 136) exposed at the base. From the north-east (AD4).

TABLE 23: The coarse pottery vessel forms by fabric and period.

		BOWLS AND DISHES																			JARS															MISC.					
Period	Fabric	1	2	3	4	5	6	7	8	9	10	11	12	13	14	15	16	17	18	19	20	21	22	23	24	25	26	27	28	29	30	31	32	33	34	35	36	37	38	Total	Period Total
1	1		1																			1			2															4	
	2		3	2	2																4						1													12	
	3																																							—	
	4		4	2	20	1	1														1				1		1													31	
	5		1		6	1	1															1																		10	
	6				8																				1															9	
	7				2																																			2	
	8	1																																						1	
	9			1	1																1																			3	
	10																																							—	
Period Totals		1	9	5	39	2	2														6	2			4		2														**72**
2	1		1	2	2																																			5	
	2				2																	2																		4	
	3																																							—	
	4		1	1	47	1		1															1		3			1												56	
	5		1		22		4	1	1												1	4			2		1		3											40	
	6				7	2		1																																10	
	7		1	2	4		1																																	8	
	8																																							—	
	9		1		1	1																			1		1													5	
	10				3			1													1						1													6	
Totals			5	5	88	2	7	1	2	2											2	8	3		2		3		4												**134**
3	1					1																1							1											2	
	2		1		5																1																			7	
	3																														1									1	
	4		1	2	16					1											1			1		6										1				29	
	5				7																1				3		1		1											15	
	6			1	14								1	1		1	2								1		1		10	8	5	3	4		6					58	
	7			1	3				1			4	1			6	5	6	1	3					2				15	21	22	7	7		5					110	
	8																																							—	
	9																																							—	
	10		1	2	13		2						2	1	1						3				3				4	3	9	5	5							54	
Totals			3	6	58	3	4	2	1	1		1	9	7	10	1				3	6	1			7	3	1		35	34	36	16	16		11	1				—	**276**
4	1																																							—	
	2			1	2																																			3	
	3																																							—	
	4		4																																					4	
	5	1																																						1	
	6																				3														3					6	
	7			1	1		39				1		6	1	12	12	7	34				1			1				9	16	18	3	7	1	74	4	2	2	1	254	
	8																																							—	
	9																																							—	
	10			2																						1														3	
Totals		1	6	5	39						1		6	1	12	12	7	37				1	1		9	17	18	3	7	1	77	4	2	2	1	1					**271**

No potters' stamps were present, and only three vessels merit description and illustration (fig. 78):

1 Knorr 78, South Gaulish, with lattice and leaf-tip decoration. c. AD 65-80 (above gulley (85), phase VIIC). (Archive ref. 1).

2 Drag 37, Central Gaulish, in the style of Casurius of Lezoux. The panel shows toothed medallion (Rogers, 1974, E25) and curved leaf (ibid, H167). c. AD 160-190 (Med/Modern lynchet, phase VIII). (Archive ref. 5).

3 Drag 37, Central Gaulish. Two adjoining fragments of a small, thick-walled bowl with panels giving: (i) Pan Mask (Déchelette, 1904, 675; Oswald, 1936-7, 1214) over astragaloid divider over twin dolphins on a basket (Rogers, 1974, Q58); (ii) festoon with kneeling horse over bird (Oswald 1936-7, 2250A) over medallion with poor astragalus; (iii) a large double-medallion. The horse was unknown to Déchelette and Oswald, but more recently its origins have been assigned to the potters working at Les Martres-de-Veyre and Lezoux in Trajanic and early Hadrianic times, especially the 'Donnaucus group' and in particular Potter X-13 (e.g. Stanfield and Simpson, 1958, pl. 42, 487). Assuming the existence of at least one main lineage, it was also used by a number of potters or groups of potters whose close links and chronological overlaps are not wanting: X-13 – Sacer i, Sacer i – Attianus ii, Cerialis ii – Cinnamus ii and Cinnamus ii at Lezoux and Vichy (Terre Franche). This bowl is generally reminiscent of Cinnamus ii (at the former) and probably falls c. AD 150-165 (phase VIIB, 111 and 85). (Archive ref. 29).

THE COARSE POTTERY
Susan M. Davies

A total of 5,063 sherds weighing some 90.5kg from the stratified deposits on the site was examined. The pottery from the ploughsoil was not examined in detail and does not form part of this report.

The collection was initially sorted into fabrics on the basis of type and/or size and density of macroscopic inclusions, identified visually with the aid of a hand lens. As will be noted below some ten fabrics were defined, falling into three broad groups: those with shell and/or limestone inclusions (group A; fabrics 1, 2 and 9); those with flint inclusions (group B; fabrics 3 and 8); and those with predominantly quartz sand inclusions (group C; fabrics 4, 5, 6, 7 and 10). Limited petrological analysis was carried out (see Williams below) on a small number of haematite coated shards. These were selected from a preliminary examination of haematite coated sherds by phase. The results of the petrological work are appended to the relevant fabric descriptions (fabrics 2, 4 and 5) and discussed in more detail by Williams. A correlation of the analysis, fabrics subsequently defined, contexts and phasing may be found in Table 23.

During the fabric sorting and recording all diagnostic sherds, including decorated types, were isolated and a formal vessel form series established (see below). Table 20 shows the correlation of vessel form and fabric through time, as well as absolute numbers of vessels in each period. Table 24 shows the co-occurrence matrix of the various forms, of all periods, and is discussed below. Figs. 79-81, illustrate by period a selection of the forms present in each period, as well as the decorative range. The following sections discuss in detail the fabrics and vessel form and refer as appropriate to surface treatment and decorative motifs. These are followed by a summary and discussion of chronology, parallels and so forth. All details of number, weight, surface treatments, form and decoration were recorded initially by context, and summarised by phase and period; these may be found in the site archive.

The Fabrics
A. Predominantly shell and/or limestone-tempered types:
1. Orange-grey, slightly soapy, but well-fired fabric. Plate-like sub-rectangular fossil shell inclusions up to 5mm fairly common; rounded limestone up to 4mm fairly common; and sparse fine quartz. May be haematite-coated, or sometimes grassmarked or wiped. Considerable variation within fabric.
2. Mid-dark grey, again fairly hard and slightly soapy. Shell inclusions up to 3mm common to abundant; sub-rounded limestone 2mm or less rare; sparse fine quartz. Basically a much finer version of fabric 7, with thinner sherds (up to 4mm) and a better-sorted fabric. May be haematite-coated.
A thin-section report by Dr D. F. Williams on two sherds showed:
(i) frequent inclusions of well-sorted quartz 0.05-0.4mm; fossiliferous shell and small limestone fragments;
(ii) frequent inclusions of fossiliferous shell and limestone scattered throughout the fabric; a few quartz grains and some argillaceous material and a clean clay matrix.
9. Orange-grey, soapy or slightly sandy, hard fabric. Fine-medium quartz sand rare to fairly common; shell inclusions up to 1.5mm fairly common; surface voids sparse to fairly common. May be haematite-coated. Variation on 2, but with finer and more dense clay matrix.

B. Predominantly flint-tempered types.
3. Hard, mid-grey fabric, slightly soapy. Well-sorted angular calcined flint up to 0.5mm common; up to 3mm sparse to fairly common. Sparse fine quartz and occasional organic inclusions up to 2mm. Rarely haematite-coated.
8. Highly fired buff-grey fabric with sandy feel. Well-sorted angular calcined flint up to 0.75mm fairly common, up 2.5mm sparse. Fine quartz sand common. Sherds tend to be quite thick, *c.* 10mm, but fabric is comparatively light in weight. Rarely haematite-coated.

C. Predominantly quartz sand inclusions.
The distinction between fabrics 4, 5, 6, 7, and 10 is based on size and density of quartz. Although fabric 5 is very distinctive, the others may be less easy to identify in small sherds, especially since quartz size is variable within one vessel or even sherd.
4. Usually orange or buff with a grey core and inner surface, fairly hard. Fine quartz and coarse quartz fairly common, the latter being well-sorted throughout the fabric. Rare limestone, or flint inclusions up to 2mm. Commonly haematite-coated.
Thin section analysis by Dr D. F. Williams on two sherds showed:
(i) fairly clean clay matrix, with a scatter of large grains of quartz and quartzite up to 1.6mm, plus a little limestone and a few grains of tourmaline.
(ii) numerous grains of ill-sorted quartz up to 0.8mm with some tourmaline grains.
A heavy mineral analysis produced an assemblage rich in tourmaline.
5. Buff, orange or grey, hard-fired and slightly sandy. Coarse quartz common and fairly well-sorted; very coarse quartz up to 2mm+ common; sparse fine quartz. May be haematite-coated.
Thin section analysis by Dr D. F. Williams showed a fairly clean clay matrix, a scatter of large grains of quartz and quartzite 1.5mm and a little flint and limestone. Heavy mineral analysis again produced an assemblage rich in tournmaline.
6. Dark grey grey-brown, hard-fired, fairly smooth finish. Fine-medium quartz fairly common; rare limestone inclusions up to 1.5mm. Fine, well-sorted fabric, variations within the tradition of BB1 and its precursors. May be haematite-coated.
7. Dark grey, hard-fired, smooth-slightly sandy. Well-sorted medium quartz common–abundant; rare coarse quartz; limestone and shell. Typical Poole Harbour BB1 fabric, but also occurs in earlier periods when it is rarely haematite-coated.
10. Dark orange to dark grey, smooth to slightly sandy hard fabric. Coarse quartz, 0.75-1mm, common to abundant and

well-sorted; coarse quartz 2mm+ sparse and ill-sorted. Rare limestone inclusions. Basically a very coarse variant of 7. Quartz grains frequently tinged pink or brown. May be haematite-coated.

The relative proportion of the fabrics through time is shown on the histogram, fig. 83, which presents the percentages by number and weight for each period. The results from number and weight are generally very similar, except on rare occasions (usually where a single particularly large sherd might be involved), indicating that either could be used as a basic quantifying method with equal validity.

Several points are immediately apparent from the histogram. The flint-tempered fabrics, which form less than 4 per cent of the Period 1 assemblage, are thereafter virtually non-existent, except perhaps as residual material in later groups. The shell/limestone group are again most prevalent in Period 1, where they form *c.* 30 per cent of the assemblage, but thereafter become progressively less common and probably only occur in Periods 3 and 4 as residual. This group bears general similarities to Class I and II fabrics described by Cunliffe from Eldon's Seat (Cunliffe, 1968, 206f) and probably reflects small scale localised production using clay sources close to hand.

The quartz-tempered group invariably forms the largest in any phase but really dominates from Period 2 onwards, to the virtual exclusion of all other types in Period 4. There are, however, significant changes in 'importance' of fabrics through time, with a fairly even split in Period 1, where fabrics 4 and 5 are the largest group; to Period 3 where fabric 7 becomes more common, and ending in Period 4 where fabric 7 dominates the collection. This may well be a reflection of the increasingly standardised 'factory' production centres of the Poole Harbour region, such as Ower (site report this volume), emerging from the late Iron Age to dominate production in the Romano-British period, and taking over from the more localised 'craft' production centres using the clay and temper available nearer the site. This should not, however, be taken to imply that BB1 production in the Romano-British period is totally dependent on one fabric. As evidence from elsewhere such as Poundbury (Davies and Hawkes in prep.) shows, there are many BB1 'fabrics' which probably reflect dispersed, if large-scale, production, utilising various sources within the Wareham-Poole Harbour area. As demonstrated by the petrological work (Williams, 1977 and below) the quartz fabrics probably all derive from this area, implying a degree of 'importation' even in the earlier periods of the Iron Age.

Rope Lake Hole is situated on the Kimmeridge Clay deposits and the flint source may be found within five miles of the site, hence there is no reason to suspect anything other than a local origin for all the fabrics, as the limited petrological work suggests. It might well be profitable, however, to examine petrologically well-stratified material from all other Purbeck Iron Age sites, with a view to defining more general patterns through time, in combination with more detailed typological analysis as discussed below (p.48).

Vessel Form
The following type series encompasses the whole chronological span at Rope Lake Hole and includes forms of most periods already fairly well-known from the area, as well as one or two more unusual ones, such as forms 1 and 10. The series divides broadly into 'bowl-forms', 'jar-forms' and miscellaneous types (e.g., flagons and skillets). A selection of forms common in each period is illustrated on figs. 79-82, by period and context group. Correlation between form number and illustration are bracketed at the end of the relevant vessel form description. The chronological occurrence of the form is tabulated in Table 20 and discussed below. The Table also shows the form: fabric correlation. Since the numbers in the table are absolute numbers of sherds, the importance of some forms (e.g. form 4) may appear exaggerated. However, it is often very difficult, if not impossible, to identify sherds from one vessel. Another point which should be borne in mind is that in some cases certain sherds could fall into several categories, especially when small fragments are concerned, and hence some types may be over- or under-represented.

The vessel form type series (Bowls, 1-19; Jars, 20-34; Others, 35-38):
1. Steeply-angled, probably carinated, bowl with cordon below inclining rim. Incised-line and stabbed-dot decoration infilled with white paste. Haematite-coated (fig. 79, 15).
2. Steeply-angled carinated bipartite bowl often with beaded rim. Unusually haematite-coated, rarely decorated above carination. Usually small diameter, *c.* 12cm, but occasionally up to *c.* 30cm. (fig. 79, 8, 9, 10, 12, 13, 14, 17; fig. 80, 28, 29; fig. 81, 53).

TABLE 24: Co-occurrence matrix of vessel forms (all periods) (Diagonal represents number of contexts).

	1	2	3	4	5	6	7	8	9	10	11	12	13	14	15	16	17	18	19	20	21	22	23	24	25	26	27	28	29	30	31	32	33	34	35	36	37	38
1	1	1	1	1																1																		
2	1	8	6	11	2	5		1												1		2	1	5			1	1	1	1	1		1			1		
3	1	6	17	10		3							1		2				1	2	5			2			3	3	3	2	3		3			1		
4	1	11	10	50	3	11	1	4	2	1			2	1	5	1	1	1		5	10	1	3	5	8	4	10	8	7	4	9	1	6			1		1
5		2		3	3	1														1	1		1		1													
6		5	3	11		12		1		1			1	1		1		1		3	3		2	1	2	1	3	4	3	3	2	1	2			1		1
7				1			1																1	1	1													
8		1		4		1		18	1				5	1	6	6	2	2	10		3		2				6	5	8	1	5	1	13	2		1	1	
9			2	2				1	4						1					1							2	2	2	1	1		1					
10			1	1		1				1			1		1					1							1	1	1	1								
11											2	1							1	1							1	1	1	1			1					
12											1	1															1	1	1	1								
13			1	2		1		5		1			11	1	3	1	1	1	5		3			1			3	3	3	2	2		5		1			
14				1		1		1		1			1	3	1	1			1		1			1			3	3	3	2	2		1					
15			2	5				6	1				3	1	14		4	1	3	1	1			1			4	4	5	2	1		7	1	1	1		
16				1		1				1			1	1		1											1	1	1	1								
17				1				6					1		4		7	1	5								4	3	4	1	2		7	2	1	1		
18				1		1		2					1		1		1	4	1					1			2	2	1	2	1	3	1	1	1			1
19			1					10			1		5	1	4		5	1	14		2						3	1	4	2	4		13	2	1	2	1	
20	1	4	2	5	1	3														5			2		1													
21		1	5	10	1	3		3					3	1	1	1			2		14			3			2	1	2	1	1							
22		1		1															2	3		3	1	1			1				1							
23		2	3	1		2														2	1		3	1	2													
24		1	2	5			1	1					1	1	3					3	1		1	9	1		1	1	2	2	3		2					
25		5		8		1	2	1												1	2	1	2	1	9	1	1						1					
26		1	2	4			1	1											1				1	1	1	4	2	1	1	1	2	1	1					1
27		1	3	10		3		6	2	1	1	1	3	3	9	1	4	1	3		2		1	1	1	2	22	14	17	9	14	1	12			1		
28		1	3	8		4		5	2	1	1	1	3	3	6	1	3	2	1		1		1				14	19	14	7	10	1	9			1		
29		1	3	7		3		8	2	1	1	1	3	4	8	1	6	2	4		2		2			1	17	14	20	9	10	1	11			1		
30		1	2	4		3		1	1	1	1	1	2	2	2	1	1	1	1		4			1		2	9	7	9	13	7	1	7			1		1
31		1	3																												18							
32				1		1		1											1								1	1	1	1	1	1	1	1				1
33		1	3	6		2		13	1		1	1	5	1	10		7	3	13		1			1	1		12	9	11	7	10		25	1		1		1
34								2							1		2	1	2														1	3	1			
35															1		1	1	1														1	1	2	1		
36		1	1	1		1									1		1		2								1	1	1	1			1		1	3		
37																			1																		1	
38			1	1															1								1	1	1	1	1	1	1	1				1

3. Steeply-angled carinated bowl with short upright neck, often with beaded rim. May have fingernail impressions on rim and/or carination. Frequently haematite-coated. Diameters vary from 10-30cm, the latter being less common. Often difficult to distinguish from shouldered-jar forms. (fig. 79, 11, 18, 20; fig. 80, 31, 41, 42).

4. Carinated bowls, with 'low-slung' carination and flaring rim, usually slightly, but sometimes greatly flared. Diameters usually in the region of 15-16cm. Usually haematite-coated (fig. 79, 5, 6, 7; fig. 80, 23, 24, 25, 26, 27, 30).

5. Furrowed carinated bowls, with slightly flared rim as form 4. Usually haematite-coated (fig. 80, 25).

6. Open bowls with 'hooked' or internally-flanged rim, frequently flat on top. Rim usually has an almost triangular section, but may be sub-rectangular. Frequently haematite-coated inside and out. Could be argued that these may be lids rather than bowls. Diameters *c.* 24-36cm (fig. 79, 4; fig. 80, 33, 34, 35, 36; fig. 81, 51).

7. Open bowl with plain rim, straight-walled. Diameters 15-30cm. Frequently burnished in later Durotrigian and Romano-British periods. (fig. 80, 32).

8. Open bowl with dropped internal flange. One burnished example only (fig. 80, 37).

9. Plain open bowl, with flat-top rim (fig. 81, 52).

10. Small 'basket-like' bowl, with pierced lug-handle pulled up above rim. Haematite-coated (fig. 81, 50).

11. Round-bodied cordoned bowl, with everted rim (fig. 81, 60).

12. Round-bodied bowl with everted rim (fig. 81, 61).

13. Round-bodied open bowl, with beaded or square-sectioned rim with groove on top (fig. 81, 58, 59; fig. 82, 78).

14. Round-bodied open bowl with internal dropped-flange or lid-seating (fig. 81, 57).

15. Bead-rimmed high-shouldered bowl (?jar) (fig. 81, 55, 56).

16. Bead-rimmed high-shouldered bowl (jar?) with countersunk rod handles (fig. 81, 54).

17. Open round-bodied bowl with rolled flange rim (fig. 82, 79).

18. Flange-rim dish or 'platter', precursor of 19 frequently burnished and with typical BB1 types of decoration (see below).

19. Dropped-flange rim dish or 'platter', frequently decorated with typical BB1 decoration (fig. 82, 80).

20. High angular-shouldered jar with flaring rim (fig. 79, 21, 22).

21. Slack-profile jar, slightly inclining rim, wall thickening towards rim (fig. 79, 16, 19; fig. 80, 45, 46; fig. 81, 65).

22. Slack-profile, bag-shaped jar, with slightly everted rim (fig. 80, 44, 47).

23. Carinated jar, high, angled shoulder, plain inclining rim, probably knife-trimmed (fig. 80, 39).

24. Large necked storage jar, knife-trimmed rim. May be haematite-coated (fig. 80, 48, 49; fig. 81, 64).

25. Large shoulder jar with short upright neck and beaded rim. May be haematite-coated (fig. 80, 38, 40; fig. 81, 67).

26. Large, slack-profile jar with very short upright neck (fig. 81, 66).

27. Slack-profile jar, with stubby everted rim (fig. 81, 62, 63; fig. 82, 76, 77).

28. High round-shouldered jar with incipient bead rim. Rarely haematite-coated (fig. 81, 68).

29. Bead rim jar, with groove below rim. May sometimes have flat top rim (fig. 81, 71).

30. Globular jar with developed or pulled bead rim (fig. 81, 72).

31. Globular-jar, rim expanded internally forming triangular section. Exterior groove to define rim edge (fig. 81, 69, 70, 73).

32. Jar with stubby upright neck and plain rim, and paired countersunk-rod handles (fig. 82, 81)

33. Everted rim jar or 'cookpot'; rim becoming more splayed and body comparatively narrower with time (fig. 82, 83).

34. Large storage jar with added, everted rim. One example with at least six holes drilled through base (fig. 82, 82).

35. Flagon or jug, all types (not illustrated).

36. Fragmentary 'sieves' (not illustrated).

37. Skillet or 'frying pan'. Fragment of flat handle only, with single incised line around edge. Skillet handle of this type also at Ower (site report in this volume) (not illustrated).

38. Beaker, small round bodied (not illustrated).

Discussion

The Period 1 assemblage comprises a collection of carinated bowl and jar forms, fairly limited in number (forms 1, 2, 3, 4, 5, 6, 20, 21, 25 and 26). The vessels, particularly the bowls, are frequently haematite-coated, but rarely decorated apart from occasional examples of incised-line, stabbed-dot, fingernail and fingertip impressions (which occur 5, 1, 6 and 3 times respectively). The sole example of combined line-and-dot occurs on form 1. Otherwise decoration, mainly incised line or fingernail, is limited to forms 2, 3 and 4, and body sherds. Surface treatment, other than haematite-coating which may be burnished, is limited to wiping or smoothing, though in general the finish and firing is good.

Period 1 pottery can be paralleled well, both locally at Eldon's Seat and Kimmeridge (Cunliffe 1968), and over a wider area in southern England. This fits into the 'early Iron Age' tradition of well-finished, technically well-produced types, though perhaps also encompassing conservative local traditions, such as limited decoration or unusual forms, like the internal flanged-rim, form 6. The 'dating' of the period must rely at present, on subjective comparison with other sites, though at some point in the not too distant future it should be possible to produce a relative chronology, perhaps by seriation analysis, based on co-occurrence matrices as in Table 21. However, for the time being manual seriation analysis is not feasible and a computer not available. However, the bowl forms 2 and 4 may be used to suggest a provisional date. The squat bipartite type (form 2) occurs slightly more commonly in Period 1

than Period 2, in relation to form 4 bowls with flaring rim. Form 2 types are also rare at Eldon's Seat II but more common at Kimmeridge II (Cunliffe, 1968, 22). At Eldon's Seat the predominant forms are flaring-rim bowls (form 4), and Cunliffe suggests that the difference between Eldon's Seat II and Kimmeridge II is chronological – the latter being earlier and the phase more or less absent at Eldon's Seat. This might suggest therefore that Period 1 at Rope Lake Hole is either comtemporary with or more probably in author's view slightly earlier than Eldon's Seat II, slightly post-

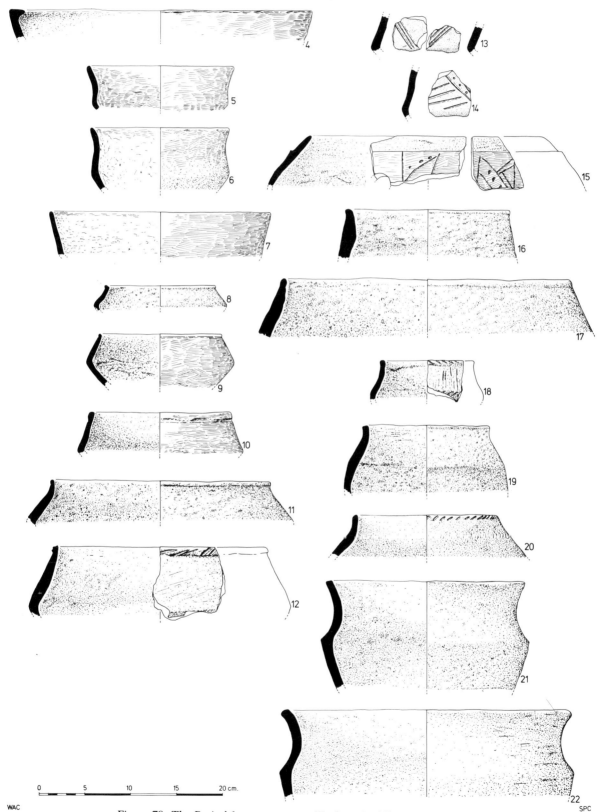

Figure 79. The Period 1 coarse pottery (Early to Middle Iron Age), 4-22.

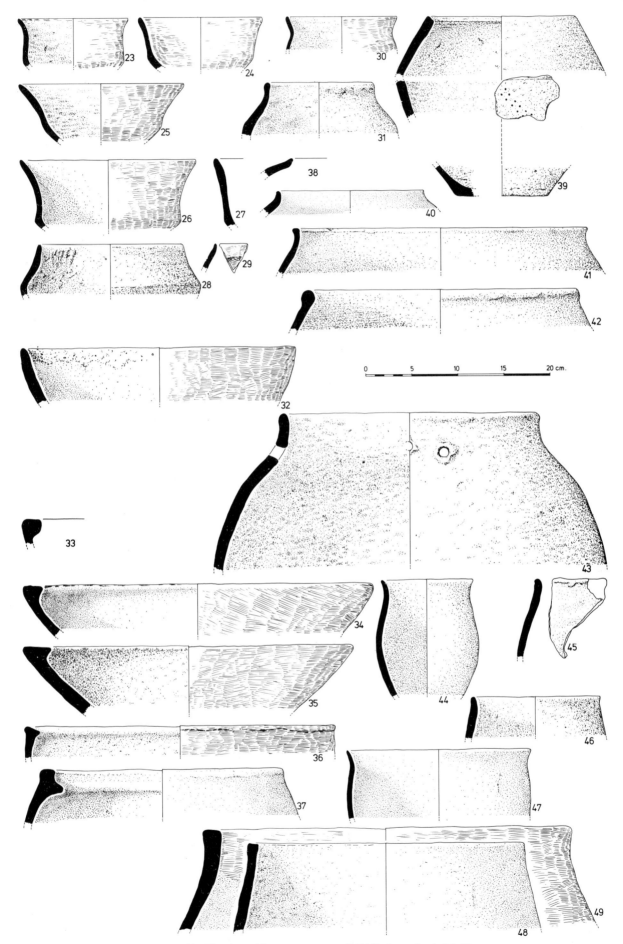

Figure 80. The Period 2 coarse pottery (Middle Iron Age), 23-49.

dating the Kimmeridge II assemblage. Cunliffe suggests a date in the 6th century for Eldon's Seat II, and this, together with evidence from elsewhere might suggest a date of 8th-6th century for Rope Lake Hole, Period 1.

Period 2 brings in a slightly wider variety of forms, with a moderate increase in both bowl and jar forms. Again form 4 bowls with flaring-rims are most common (well over 50 per cent), similar to Eldon's Seat II. The squat bipartite bowls (form 2), theoretically diagnostic of period 1, are proportionally less common, perhaps even residual in this period. Generally, as in period 1, bowls form by far the largest proportion of the collection, a trend noticed elsewhere in the earlier Iron Age.

The 'tradition' of plain undecorated wares continues with even fewer decorated examples than for Period 1. Six decorated sherds occur altogether. Of these three, incised line, fingernail and fingertip occur on body sherds. Otherwise two form 4 bowls have incised-lines and one form 23 jar has stabbed-dot decoration. Haematite-coating, however, continues to flourish with roughly the same proportion slipped in Period 2 as in Period 1. Otherwise surface treatment, except for one finely-burnished, non-haematite coated example, is again limited to wiping and smoothing. Probably because of the increase in the number of sherds in Period 2, the number of less-well finished examples has also increased, though in general the forms, especially the bowls, continue to be well-finished.

The range of Period 2 forms, comparable with the Eldon's Seat II assemblage, and sites in central southern England, and the slight differences with Period 1 would suggest a date range of *c.* 5th-3rd century BC, though there may well be overlap between the two periods.

Period 3, culminating in the full tradition of the late Iron Age (Durotrigian), brings a distinct increase in the number of vessel forms, as well as continuing standardisation of fabrics used. The number of vessel forms increases to twenty-six, of which fifteen are completely new types, and the rest, mainly residual. One haematite-coated vessel may be anomalous in Period 3. Form 10 (fig. 81, 50) has only one parallel, from an early Iron Age context at Wallingford, Oxon., (*pers. comm.* John Barrett) and does not fit well with either the preceding periods' types or those of period 3. However the general trend is for jar-forms to become dominant over bowls, and for the tradition of carinated vessels of the earlier Iron Age to give way to round-bodied forms (e.g., 13 and 14) of 'Durotrigian' type with classic beaded and everted rims. The increasing range obviously indicates a functional change in the pottery assemblage and probably also the more widespread availability of 'low-class' storage and cooking ceramics centrally produced, in contrast to the limited range of 'high-class tablewares' and few storage vessels of earlier periods.

A number of traditions are maintained including haematite-coating, which continues to be used on 'classic' Durotrigian forms. There are, however, changes in surface finish and decoration, notably towards the end of the period, which probably spans the later 2nd-1st centuries BC and the early 1st century AD. A far higher number of vessels are well-burnished or very well-wiped, rather than merely smoothed. Towards the end of the period decoration also becomes more common and more varied, incorporating Durotrigian types, such as impressed handles and BB1 types of lattice and arc decoration. However, it should be stressed that even in this period decoration is not at all common – there are only twenty-one examples (including body sherds) in all.

The Period 4 pottery shows a fully developed industry in the 'classic' tradition of Black Burnished Ware with its typical range of jar, bowl and dish types, as well as occasional oddities. It sees the introduction, at Rope Lake Hole, of seven new types. These include flagons, skillets and dishes, which were previously unrepresented but which are well-known in the area, e.g., Poundbury, Ower and so forth. As well as the most common BB1 types, the collection contains the most common BB1 decorative range – lattice decoration (especially on form 33 jars and form 18 and 19 dishes) and single or intersecting arcs (especially on form 19 dishes). Many of the vessels are well-burnished, or very well-smoothed/wiped, and may be slipped – notably forms 33 and 19. The everted rim jars, form 33, are commonly slipped on the upper body and rim, above an unslipped, plain panel of lattice decoration (e.g., fig. 82, 83). The dish forms are more commonly slipped on the inside. The date range for Period 4 is probably 2nd-late 4th century AD.

The Rope Lake Hole pottery therefore represents activity on the site from approximately the 8th century BC to the late 4th century AD. Through time there is a change from more 'local' pottery production, possibly even on-site work, with a limited importation

of 'tableware', leading up to the emergence of the BB1 industry of Poole Harbour as totally dominant in the later periods. It is interesting to note that the earlier Iron Age periods, 1 and 2, appear to show greater 'wealth or status', in terms of pottery, than the later ones. The fine haematite-coated bowls are obviously 'specialist' products, though even these are perhaps not of the highest quality, lacking the highly decorated types commonly found elsewhere, e.g., Old Down Farm, Hants (Davies, 1981), in central southern England. This may indicate a local conservative tradition. Nevertheless there is also a contrast with the later Iron Age and Roman types which represent only the most common, and functional types, with few unusual or highly decorated forms. This 'paucity' in periods 3 and 4 is also reflected in the lack of other types of imported ceramics – only two amphorae types commonly found (unidentified) were found, relativley little samian and an extremely small amount of later Roman imports, such as New Forest or Oxfordshire ware – and presumably indicates a 'low-status' site, possibly not permanently inhabited throughout the year.

The Illustrated Coarse Pottery

Period 1: fig. 79.

4. Type 6 flanged bowl; haematite-coated, fabric (from 288, phase I).
5. Type 4 bowl, haematite-coated, fabric 4 (from 189, phase 1).
6. Type 4 bowl, haematite-coated, fabric 4 (from 188, phase II).
7. Type 4 bowl, haematite-coated, fabric 4 (from 189, phase I).
8. Type 2 bowl, haematite-coated, fabric 2 (from 269, phase I).
9. Type 2 bowl, haematite-coated, fabric 2 (from 269, phase I).
10. Type 2 bowl, haematite-coated, fabric 5 (from 189, phase I).
11. Type 3 bowl, fabric 2 (unstratified).
12. Type 2 bowl, fabric 1 (from 199, phase I).
13. Type 2 bowl, fabric 4 (from 261/287, phase I).
14. Type 2 bowl, fabric 4 (unstratified).
15. Type 1 jar, haematite-coated, fabric 7 (from 269, phase I).
16. Type 21 jar, fabric 5 (from 248, phase I).
17. Type 2 bowl, fabric 2 (from 245, phase II).
18. Type 3 bowl, fabric 4 (from 248, phase I).
19. Type 21 jar, fabric 1 (from 199, phase I).
20. Type 3 bowl, fabric 4 (from 261, phase I).
21. Type 20 jar, fabric 2 (from 269, phase I).
22. Type 20 jar, fabric 2 (from 240/269, phase I).

Period 2: fig. 80.

23. Type 4 bowl, haematite-coated, fabric 7 (from 142, phase IIIA).
24. Type 4 bowl, haematite-coated, fabric 4 (from 142, phase IIIA).
25. Type 4 bowl, haematite-coated, fabric 6 (from 260, phase IIIA).
26. Type 4 bowl, haematite-coated, fabric 7 (from 142, phase IIIA).
27. Type 4 bowl, haematite-coated, fabric 5 (from 181, phase IIIA).
28. Type 2 bowl, fabric 1 (from 247, phase IIIA).
29. Type 2 bowl, haematite-coated, fabric 9 (from 181, phase IIIA).
30. Type 4 bowl, haematite-coated, fabric 4 (from 181, phase IIIA).
31. Type 3 bowl, fabric 7 (from 142, phase IIIA).
32. Type 7 bowl, haematite-coated, fabric 5 (from 187, phase IIIA).
33. Type 6 bowl, haematite-coated, fabric 9 (from 181, phase IIIA).
34. Type 6 bowl, haematite-coated, fabric 4 (from 298, phase IIIA).
35. Type 6 bowl, haematite-coated, fabric 5 (from 227, phase IIIA).
36. Type 6 bowl, haematite-coated, fabric 5 (from 170, phase IIIA).
37. Type 8 bowl, burnished int. and ext., fabric 5 (from 196, phase IIIA).
38. Type 25 jar, haematite-coated, fabric 5 (from 196, phase IIIA).
39. Type 23 jar, fabric 5 (from 196, phase IIIA).
40. Type 25 jar, fabric 5 (from 196, phase IIIA).
41. Type 3 bowl, probably haematite-coated, fabric 1 (from 170, phase IIIA).
42. Type 3 bowl, probably haematite-coated, fabric 7 (from 298, phase IIIA).
43. Type 25 jar, fabric 4 (from 227, phase IIIA).

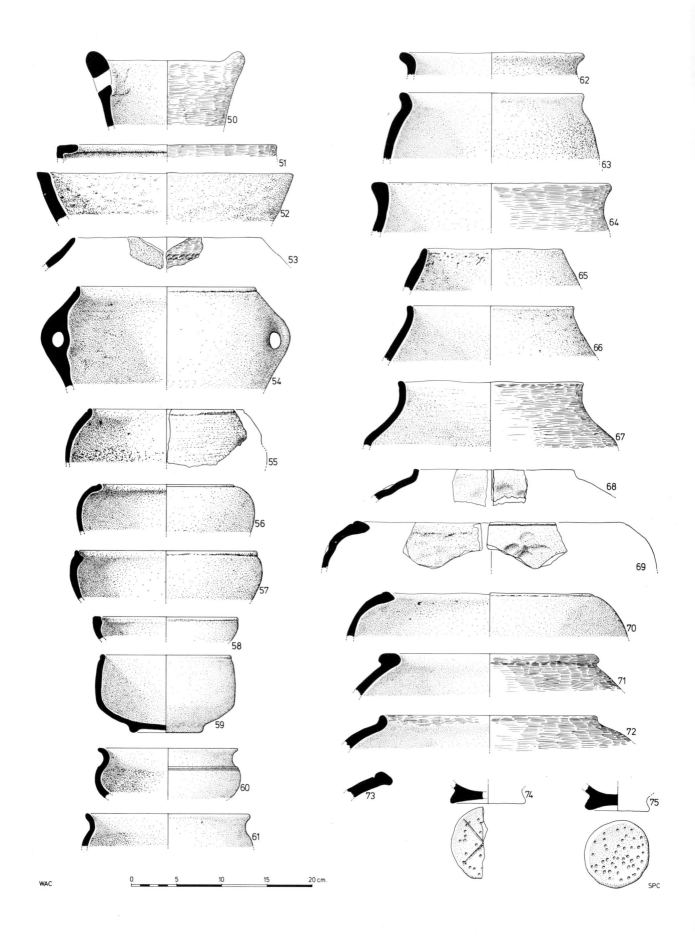

Figure 81. The Period 3 coarse pottery (Late Iron Age, Durotrigian), 50-75.

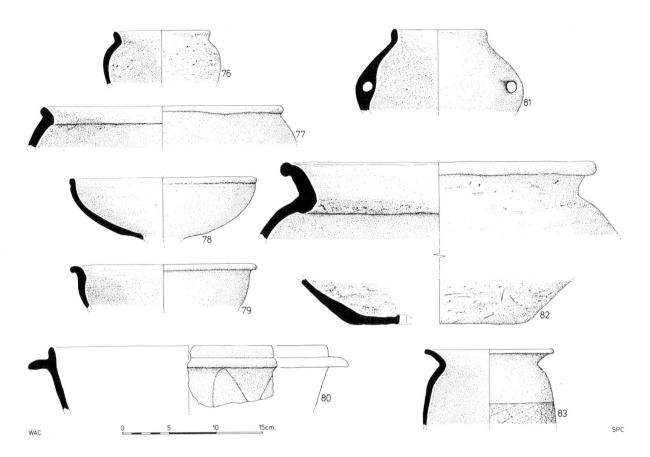

Figure 82. The Period 4 coarse pottery (Romano-British), 76-83.

44. Type 22 jar, fabric 4 (from 196, phase IIIA).
45. Type 21 jar, fabric 9 (from 187, phase IIIA).
46. Type 21 jar, fabric 5 (from 187, phase IIIA).
47. Type 22 jar, fabric 4 (from 219, phase IIIB).
48. Type 24 jar, fabric 10 (from 221, phase IIIB).
49. Type 24 jar, fabric 5 (from 196, phase IIIA).

Period 3: fig. 81.

50. Type 10 bowl, haematite-coated, fabric 4 (from 176, phase IVB).
51. Type 6 bowl, haematite-coated, fabric 10 (from 176, phase IVB).
52. Type 9 bowl, fabric 1 (from 143, phase IVB).
53. Type 2 bowl, haematite-coated, fabric 4 (from 223, phase V).
54. Type 16 jar, fabric 7 (from 176, phase IVB).
55. Type 15 jar, burnished, fabric 7 (from 172, phase VIB).
56. Type 15 jar, fabric 6 (from 172, phase VIB).
57. Type 14 bowl, ext. burnished, fabric 7 (from 129, phase IVB).
58. Type 13 bowl, burnished fabric 7 (from 217, phase V).
59. Type 13 bowl, burnished, fabric 7 (from 183, phase IVA).
60. Type 11 bowl, burnished, fabric 6 (from 235, phase V).
61. Type 12 bowl, burnished, fabric 6 (from 235, phase V).
62. Type 27 jar, fabric 4 (from 148, phase IVB).
63. Type 27 jar, fabric 6 (from 148, phase IVB).
64. Type 24 jar, haematite-coated, fabric 10 (from 168, phase IVB).
65. Type 23 jar, fabric 4 (from 216, phase IVB).
66. Type 26 jar, fabric 4 (from 216, phase IVB).
67. Type 25 jar, haematite-coated, fabric 5 (from 151, phase IVB).
68. Type 28 jar, haematite-coated, fabric 10 (from 178, phase IVA).
69. Type 31 jar, burnished, fabric 7 (from 172, phase VIB).
70. Type 31 jar, burnished, fabric 7 (from 172, phase VIB).
71. Type 29 jar, haematite-coated, fabric 10 (from 151, phase IVB).
72. Type 30 jar, haematite-coated, fabric 3 (from 223, phase V).
73. Type 31 jar, fabric 10 (from 129, phase IVB).
74. Solid footring base, with impressed decoration, fabric 7 (from 223, phase V).
75. Solid footring base with impressed decoration, fabric 6 (from 143, phase IVB).

Period 4: fig. 82

76. Type 27 bowl/jar, burnished, fabric 7 (from 92, phase VIIA).
77. Type 27 jar/bowl, fabric 7 (from 85, phase VIIB).
78. Type 13 bowl, burnished, fabric 7 (from 101, phase VIIA).
79. Type 17 bowl, slipped (?), fabric 7 (from 132, phase VIA).
80. Type 19 bowl, interior burnished, fabric 7 (from 127, phase VIA).
81. Type 32 jar, fabric 7 (from 105, phase VIIA).
82. Type 34 storage jar, fabric 7 (from 91, phase VIIA).
83. Type 33 jar, slipped and part-burnished, fabric 7 (from 132, phase VIA).

THE PETROLOGICAL ANALYSIS OF THE 'HAEMATITE WARE'

D. F. WILLIAMS, PhD and S. M. TOLFIELD
(DoE Ceramic Petrology Project, Department of Archaeology, University of Southampton).

Five samples of 'haematite ware' were submitted for examination under the petrological microscope. The object of the analysis was to try and determine whether the pottery was locally made, and also to compare sherds from two periods (1 and 3), to see how the fabrics compared. Two of the sandy sherds, fabrics 4 and 5, were selected for heavy mineral separation. The contexts from which sherds were selected and the results are summarised in Table 25, and for ease of reference the detailed microscopic descriptions have been placed with the macroscope descriptions in the coarse pottery report.

The five sherds of 'haematite ware' could be divided into two basic fabric groups, A and B. Fabric A contained frequent inclusions of fossil shell and limestone, and was represented by two sherds from Period 1 (Table 25). Rope Lake Hole is situated on Kimmeridge Clay deposits, close by to Portland limestone beds, and there seems no reason on the present evidence to suspect anything other than a fairly local origin for these two sherds. Fabric B was predominantly sandy, with conspicuous tourmaline present, and is represented by one sherd from period 1 and two sherds from

TABLE 26: The briquetage types by phase and period.

PERIOD	PHASE	RIM	CORNERS/ BASES	BODY	LEGS/ KILN BARS	TOTAL
1	I			1		1
	II		2	20		22
2	III		4	110		14
	IV	6	51	570	1	628
3	V		42	379		421
	VIB	6	92	355		453
	VIA	1	8	108	1	118
4	VIIA	3	39	455		497
	VIIB		1	26	3	30
	VIIC	3	22	827	2	851
5	VIII	—	2	47	1	50
TOTALS		19	263	2898	8	3188

period 3. The high tourmaline content of the heavy mineral residues recalled the tourmaline rich fabric of certain Durotrigian late Iron Age vessels and Romano-British BBI, shown to have been made in the Wareham-Poole Harbour Tertiary Sands area of Dorset (Williams, 1977, Group 1). A similar origin is possible for the latter three sherds from Rope Lake Hole.

Previous petrological work on haematite pottery from Wessex has suggested that much of it was probably made close by to the find-site (Gale, 1977; Hodges, 1968; Partridge, 1974). However, there is a little evidence that some haematite wares enjoyed a wider distribution than this. At Gussage All Saints there were a small number of haematite wares which were characterised by oolitic inclusions, and which were in all probability made at some distance from the find-site. A tourmaline rich haematite fabric similar to that recognised at Rope Lake Hole has already been noted at Eldon's Seat, about a mile to the south-east of the former site (Partridge, 1974). This might suggest some form of fairly localised distribution of haematite ware centred on the Wareham-Poole Harbour area, since this distinctive fabric has not been recognised outside of the Purbeck area.

THE BRIQUETAGE
JOHN HAWKES

All briquetage was unwashed (reserved for a project of detailed chemical investigation), and consequently only a very limited analysis could be carried out. Analysis of the fabric was not carried out and weighing was considered impractical. It was however possible to undertaken a preliminary typological study of the assemblage. Table 26 summarises by phase the sherd categories.

The Vessels
The method of manufacture makes it difficult to distinguish rims from body sherds. Rims were not individually formed but are simply cut with knife or wire or scored and snapped whilst the vessels are in a leather-hard state presenting a flattened if often jagged surface not immediately recognisable on unwashed sherds. Rims may therefore be under-represented.

Angle sherds (fig. 84, 84-86) could be interpreted as the corners of rectangular vessels of 'Hobarrow pan' type (terminology after Farrar 1975) but are perhaps better considered as base sherds, possessing the characteristic groove along one surface adjacent to the angle found to be diagnostic of bases in the assemblage at Cleavel Point (Hawkes in Woodward, this volume). The apparent absence of corners, taken with the occurrence of a number of base sherds of varying curvature (fig. 84, 87-90), suggests straight-sided vessels with an oval or sub-rectangular plan, paralleled at Hobarrow (Farrar, 1975) but rather less angular than the Cleavel Point and other Poole Harbour examples. Sherd thicknesses in excess of 15mm suggest that all material belongs to vessels of this type, thin-walled round profiled vessels of 'Fitzworth trough' type being absent. On the limited evidence available it is not possible to identify any typological change through time, although the briquetage from Iron Age levels is perhaps somewhat thinner than the later material. The standard fabric of medium to coarse quartz sands could not be more closely specified but appears basically unchanged through all phases.

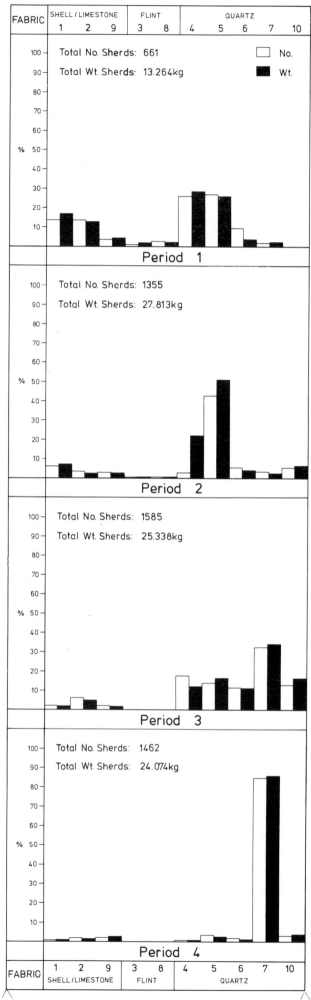

Figure 83. The coarse pottery fabrics through time (percentage histograms by period).

TABLE 25: The petrological analysis of the 'haematite ware'.

PERIOD	PHASE	CONTEXT	LOCATION	FABRIC NUMBER (macroscopic, Davies S.)	FABRIC GROUP (Thin section/mineral separation, Williams D.)	HEAVY MINERAL SEPARATION
1	I	248	Hut 1, fig. 72A	2	A, limestone/fossil shell	
1	II	300	Shale Dump, fig. 72B	2	A, limestone/fossil shell	
1	II	295	Shale Dump, fig. 72B	5	B, Sandy/tourmaline	×
3	IVB	176	Robbing trench, fig. 73B	4	B, Sandy/some tourmaline	
3	IVB	216	'Cairn', fig. 73B	4	B, Sandy/tourmaline	×

Kiln Bars/Briquetage Legs:

Eight examples of irregularly shaped bars of untempered fired clay were recovered. Two examples (one illustrated, fig. 84, 91) had a groove along one end suggesting they may have been uprights supporting a horizontal member, but otherwise there are no indications of function or usage. Other examples (fig. 84, 92-94) are not complete. Comparable items have elsewhere been suggested as kiln props and bars (e.g. Farrar, 1975), but there are no features which support a hypothesis that either pottery or briquetage vessels were being made on site – it may be that these objects were concerned with the production of the salt itself rather than the pottery containers, and acted as supports for vessels in heating or boiling brine.

THE COINS

Identifications by Richard Reece (1979 excavation),
and Rosemary Maw (1976 trials)

The four coins recovered from the 1979 excavation are described and listed in the order of site small find number. The abbreviated references used in these identifications are:

RIC, *Roman Imperial Coinage,* H. Mattingley and E. A. Sydenham (Eds.), 1923.

HK, *Late Roman Bronze Coinage,* R. A. Carson, P. Hill, J. Kent, Vol. I, 1960.

CK, as above, Vol. II.

The condition of the coins varied from extremely corroded to quite good. The only well stratified coin (from above yard 135, phase VIIA) was badly corroded (coin small find 100). The coin 122 was found in the grid collection of phase VIIC downslope from the working floor and yard levels, at 443141. This was probably in this position and condition as a result of later ploughing.

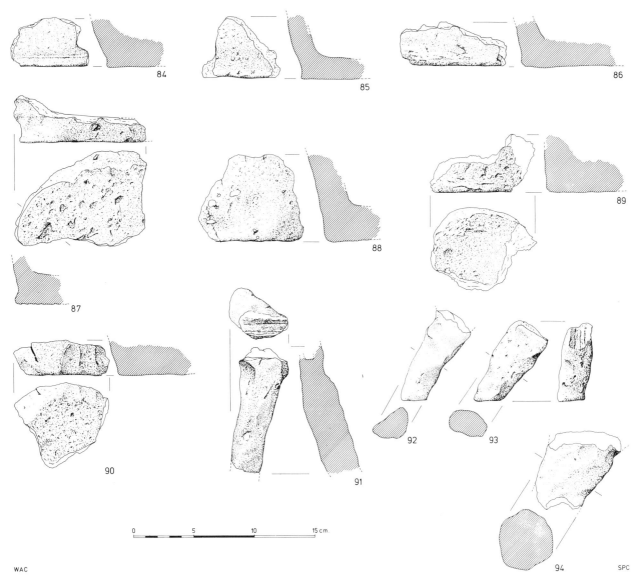

WAC

SPC

Figure 84. The briquetage and legs/kiln bars, 84-94, 1:3.

SSF 82: RIC 100, Claudius II, 268-70 AD, from (2), phase VIII (Medieval/Modern lynchet).

SSF 100: Completely corroded, 3rd-4th *c.* AD, from (91) above yard (92), phase VIIA.

SSF 120: CK8, Magnentius, 350-360 AD, unstratified.

SSF 122: Barbarous Radiate (*Rev Pax*), 270-290 AD, from (61), grid collection phase VIIC.

A single coin was recovered from the earlier trial trenches: Maw (1976) C (R-B agricultural levels, see previous fig. 2). This was an AE3 of Constans 335-7 AD (HK 95).

THE BROOCHES
D. F. Mackreth

Three copper-alloy brooches were recovered from the site. Their location by phase is shown in Table 27. All are illustrated. Figure 85.

Colchester Derivatives:

95. From layer (87), phase VIIA yard.

The pin was hinged, its axis bar being housed in the wings which are cylindrical in section. One of them bears traces of having two grooves at its end. The top of the bow has a step in it on whose face are two short grooves inclined towards each other. The lower bow, with the catch-plate, is missing.

The step at the head of the bow recalls a trait to be found on brooches which belong to south-west England. The manner of handling the decoration varies, but the chief feature is the way in which it tends to form a panel across the head (cf., Pitt Rivers, 1888, 120, pl. XCVIII, 1) rather than to run down the bow. Close parallels are perhaps not to be expected and the date is not well-established: a date in the second half of the 1st century may be suggested, although it may have extended into the second.

96. From layer (273), phase V.

The pin hinged as in 89. The back of the wings is rounded and each had a flat front with two grooves at the end. The bow has a triangle at its centre defined by grooves and with a triangular cell filled with discoloured enamel in the middle. The upper bow tapers out from the triangle, has a marked median arris with a series of cross-cuts, and rises in a peak above the wings. The peak is crowned by a disc with a round depression in front and the trace of another on the back. The lower bow has a median arris and tapers to a small projecting foot.

The brooch is clearly related to a group which belongs virtually exclusively to the south-west of England and which has few ornamental variations. Examples from Nor'Nour (Dudley, 1967, 34, fig. 13, 37-46) have a central lozenge instead of the triangle with either two enamelled triangles by themselves, or with a third cell between. They also show that the disc on the head was sometimes pierced and it may be that that was always the intention and examples such as the present should be regarded as being faulty castings. The dating is again difficult and one from Gadebridge Park, Hemel Hempstead, Herts. (Neal, 1974, 125, fig. 54, 18) seems to have no more secure dating than being probably before

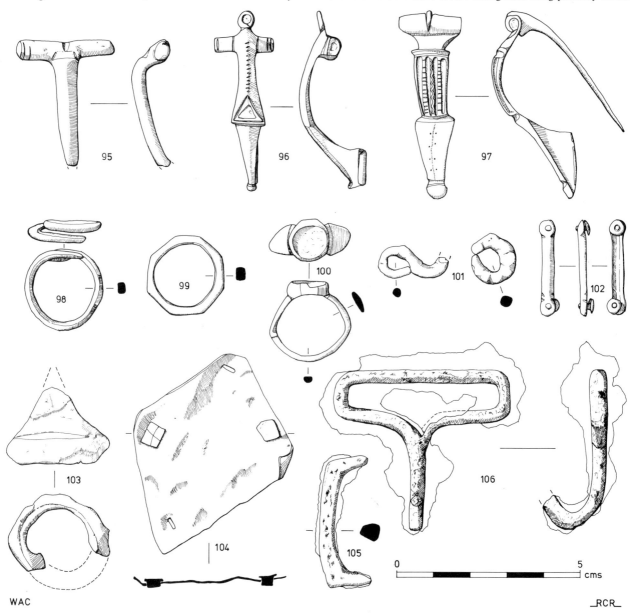

WAC   RCR

Figure 85. The metalwork, bronze brooches (95-97), bronze rings (98-100), other bronze objects (101-104), ironwork (105-106), 1:1.

the middle of the 2nd century.

Hod Hill:

97. From layer (2), medieval field lynchet (VIII).

The axis bar of the hinged pin is housed in the usual rolled-over head. The bow design is in two parts. The upper consists of five ridges divided by flutes. The central ridge has been distorted by a punch to form a regular wavy line, and the ridge to each side has a beaded top. Above and below the ridges is a cross-moulding. The lower bow is broad at the top where there is another cross-moulding, and tapers to a foot-knob with a weak moulding above. On the flat face is an incised line down each side and a line of punched dots down the middle with four pairs of extra dots along the line. The brooch was once tinned or silvered.

Relatively elaborate Hod Hills seldom have more than a few close parallels and it is clear that there is no chronological significance in the differing developed designs occurring in Britain. No Hod Hill has yet been published from a pre-Conquest deposit and it seems that those found in Britain arrived at or after the Conquest and that they were most probably at the end of their manufacturing life. There had been a marked fall-off in the numbers in use by *c.* 60 AD and very few were still in use by *c.* 70 AD as the small number found in the lands taken into the Province by Cerialis shows.

THE COPPER-ALLOY OBJECTS
The identifications were provided by Dr Martin Henig.

Apart from the three fibulae, fifteen other copper-alloy objects were recovered from various levels of the site (Table 27). All these are of Iron Age or Romano-British date, and the diagnostic pieces are illustrated (fig. 85).

98. Ring with overlapping ends, and hoop of ovoid section. This is the normal late Iron Age type of ring. Compare to examples at *Maiden Castle* (Wheeler, 1943, 226 and fig. 86). From (223), phase V.

99. Finger ring with octagonal hoop and rectangular section. Examples of the type can be found at *Gatcombe* (Branigan, 1977, 120 and fig. 26, 517), at *Lowbury* (Atkinson, 1916, 40, No. 5, pl. XI). European examples can be cited from the Rhineland (Henkel, 1913, 71, 651-662). From medieval lynchet soils, phase VIII.

100. A finger-ring with triangular shoulders and raised octagonal-bezel for a gem or paste setting. A typical 3rd century AD type (Henig, 1975, 58).

101. S-shaped link and small segmental ring. Iron Age from (187), phase IIIA.

102. A copper-alloy sheet strip with swollen ends, each pierced by a rivet attached to a circular disc. This is probably a belt mounting, and similar (but larger) examples can be cited from *Verulamium* (Wheeler, 1936, 218 and pl. LXIIIA).

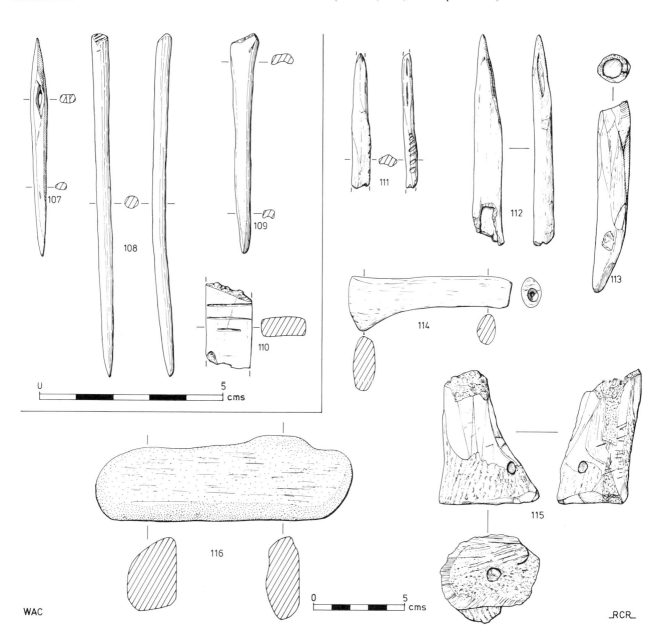

Figure 86. The bone, horn, and antler, objects (107-115). The honestone, 116.

TABLE 27: The Stratigraphic location by phase and period of the metalwork.

PERIOD	PHASE	BRONZE OBJECTS BROOCHES	RINGS	BELT/ MOUNT	RIVETTED PLATES	BAR/ ROD FRAGS.	FRAGS./ LUMPS	OTHER OBJECTS	LEAD OBJECTS	NAILS A	NAILS B	UNIDENT. BARS & RODS	STAPLES/ HOOKS	LINKS	BROOCH (?)
1	I														
	II														
2	III						2	2**							
3	IV						2					1			
	V	1*	1*											1	
	VIB						1								1
4	VIA									1		1			
	VIIA	1*				1				1	1	2	2*		
	VIIB														
	VIIC					1		1*		4	2	7	3*	3	
5	VIII	1*	2**	1*	1*				2						
TOTAL		3	3	1	1	2	5	3	2	5	4	11	5	4	1
				18					2			30			

*Illustrated object.

103. Copper-alloy band with triangular projection. Bronze bands were employed for bindings at *Fishbourne* (Cunliffe, 1971, 120, fig. 53, Nos. 180, 181). This however might have been used as a goad, though these were no doubt usually of iron. From (34), phase VIIC.

104. Rhomboidal sheet with two rivets in position and two rivet holes: as used to repair bronze vessels and other objects. From medieval lynchet soils, phase VIII.

THE LEAD OBJECTS

Two lead objects were recovered from the site, both from the machine clearance above the archaeological levels. Neither was particularly diagnostic, but both could be derived from the Romano-British settlement horizon. The objects are described as follows (not illustrated):

One short piece of rod worn in the centre, and of circular cross-section 0.7cm diameter and 5cm long. Possibly a small slug of lead for fishing weight.

A small roll of lead sheet 4cm long, ovate in section, and from 0.6-1.2cm across; a single roll. Possibly used as a net or line weight for fishing. Similar objects have been found in Romano-British levels; *Portchester* (Cunliffe (1971); fig. 123, 167), and *Ower* (Woodward, this volume).

THE IRONWORK

Of the 30 iron objects recovered from the site 65 per cent came from phase VIIC, and 70 per cent were nails or unidentified bars (refer Table 27). The paucity of iron objects below VIIC does suggest that some of these items may be derived from the medieval occupation. Some broken fragments may be parts of medieval spectacle buckles, but those are too fragmentary for certain attribution. The links, which were ovate (all roughly the same size 50mm x 40mm), are also not necessarily of Romano-British origin. The nails have been divided into two groups (none illustrated):

A: Nails with sub-rectangular/rounded head in plan, flat in cross-section.

B: Nails with narrow rectangular head in plan, flat in cross-section.

These were not very diagnostic and some are likely to be of medieval origin.

Only four pieces of ironwork were reasonably well sealed; those were the items in phases VIA, VIB and IV, which are layers not susceptible to contamination from medieval levels. The only diagnostic piece was a small bent triangle of very corroded ironwork which may be the clasp from a small brooch (not illustrated).

Two objects of probable Late Iron Age and Romano-British origin are illustrated (fig. 85). These were identified by Dr Martin Henig.

105. Small iron dog. Comparable objects were found at *Croft Ambrey* (Stanford, 1974, 172-5, fig. 81), where it is suggested that they were used for the repair of cooking pots, but no doubt they had other uses (e.g. fastening wood and leather, staple). From yard (84), phase VIIA.

106. Ring of ovoid shape with hook projection. An object of this type has been found in a Late Iron Age context at *Danebury*, Hampshire (Lynn Selwood pers. comm.). Similar objects in bronze can be found at *Hengistbury Head* (Bushe-Fox, 1915, 61 and plate XXIX, 7 and 8). From (21) phase VIIC.

THE GLASS

JUNE B. JOHNSTONE

Five fragments of glass were recovered, and their stratigraphic locations by phase are shown in Table 28. All five fragments were of a type of natural blue-green glass used throughout the the the Roman period for bottles and other containers. Only one fragment was sufficiently complete (from layer (16), phase VIIC) to suggest a vessel type.

This fragment was from a flat-sided, mould-blown bottle; at the junction where the shoulder slopes inwards from side of vessel towards the neck. This type of bottle was probably used for the transportation and storage of liquids; made in a rectangular shape for the convenience of crating. This type of bottle, although more common in the first two centuries AD, did continue in use to a lesser degree in the later Roman period, c.f. *Verulamium* (Charlesworth, 1972, fig. 75, No. 13), *Fishbourne* (Harden, 1971, fig. 143, Nos. 94 and 97), and in Isings (1957).

THE WORKED ANTLER, HORN AND BONE

Twenty-three pieces of worked antler, horn and bone were recovered from the site, and of these only nine were recognisable types, and of the remainder were from broken points or pins. The stratigraphic location of these objects by phase and period is summarised in Table 28.

Seventy-five per cent of the worked bone came from pre-Roman contexts, and only one broken bone point and a bone pin (fig. 86, 107-116) came from the latest levels of Romano-British occupation.

The extensive use of bone for tools and decorative objects is well attested on Iron Age sites in Wessex, and parallels for this small array of objects can be found at *Eldon's Seat* (Cunliffe, 1968), *Gussage All Saints* (Wainwright, 1979), *Maiden Castle* (Wheeler, 1943) and *All Cannings Cross* (Cunnington, 1923).

A double ended bone needle (fig. 86, 107) recovered from phase III is of a type which may perhaps be considered as part of a shuttle, used in weaving (Leeds, 1927). Another broken pin fragment, probably of this type, was associated with the areas outside the huts of phase V.

The two polished bone pins are of a similar type, and the well polished example (fig. 86, 108) may be for dressing hair et al.

Of the number of broken points and pins, that with notches was notable (fig. 86, 111). Notching was otherwise only noted on a piece of antler and the broken object (fig. 86, 110).

TABLE 28: The Stratigraphic location by phase and period of the bone antler and horn, glass objects, and the slag/cinder.

PERIOD	PHASE	NEEDLES	PINS	BROKEN POINTS/PINS	GOUGES	HANDLES	OTHER OBJECTS	WORKED ANTLER	WORKED OTHER BONES	GLASS	SLAG/CINDER GROUPS 1-3	GROUP 4	GROUP 5
1	I		1	1									
	II			3					1				
2	III	1*	1*			1*	N1	1	1		3		
3	IV	1			2*			1	2		9		
	V		1				N1*				2	1	
	VIB							1			3	1	
4	VIA			N1*		1*		*1N		1	1		
	VIIA									2	5		1
	VIIB		1*										
	VIIC			1						2	11		1
5	VIII												
TOTAL		2	4	6	2	2	2	4	4	5	34	2	2

*Illustrated objects.   N Notched.

Two gouges were noted on the site, one made from a sheep radius (fig. 86, 112). Gouges of this type were common at *Eldon's Seat*. One other point from a broken gouge was also noted from phase IV (post pit 184).

Two knife handles were recovered from the site, made from antler (?) (fig. 86, 113) and an antler tine (fig. 86, 114). Both were cut and polished.

The antler tine was sawn and bored for the haft-end. The hole to receive the tang was 0.6m in diameter narrowing to a point. The haft-end was polished with rounded edges.

The squared polished rib-bone with sawn notches was clearly part of a larger object, of indeterminate type (fig. 86, 110).

Four pieces of worked antler tine were recovered from the site. The object from period VIA was sawn at the base of the tine and had a straight bored hole at an angle through to the centre of the base (fig. 86, 115). The side was cut, notched and smoothed in places, but otherwise broken higher up the bowl. It is likely that this was attached to another piece of a composite object, but little otherwise can be said.

The other antler was scored along its length and was probably the raw material for the manufacture of small pins and other items.

A sheep/goat metatarsus, half-split and smoothed, was recovered from phase IVB. This was probably utilised for making pins, points and needles; a long fine straight bone. Another worn fragment of a large mammal was found in general occupation layers of phase II. A smoothed portion of sheep/goat tibia was recovered from feature (176) of phase IVB, and a smoothed cattle metatarsus (proximal end) was recovered from phase IIIB.

THE ARCHITECTURAL FRAGMENTS AND PORTABLE STONE OBJECTS

Three stone objects found in Late Iron Age contexts, have been classified as architectural fragments. Although none were in primary contexts two at least had direct affinities with stones used in the construction of buildings on other Late Iron Age and Romano-British settlements in Purbeck. These stones are described as follows (not illustrated):

1. A pierced semi-circular limestone slab at the base of cyst (149) – phase V, refer site plan (fig. 73B): 3cm thick, 62cm diameter, with pierced hole of 6cm diameter. The use of pierced slabs at the base

of slab-lined post-pits can be seen in one of the buildings excavated in 1978 at *Ower* (Woodward, this volume); there interpreted as door-posts. Below this slab was a horizontally bedded shale disc (fig. 92, 136). This was a remarkable object and suggests that this feature (149) was of some importance, since the shale disc was deliberately laid (refer Kimmeridge shale, and site report).

2. A slab with central socket from post-pit (184) – phase VIB, refer site plan (fig. 73B): Limestone, slightly domed with flat base, 40cm in diameter and a greatest thickness of 8cm. Centrally on the upper surface was a small pecked circular hole 11cm across, with a slight curved profile and 1cm in depth. In Purbeck socketted stones were commonly used as post-pads for post buildings. Examples can be found at *Ower* (Woodward, this volume) and at *Studland* (Field, 1966).

3. A broken slab with curved wear-marks from the base of robbing (176) – phase IVB, and above floor (226) – phase IIIA, refer site plan (fig. 73B): Limestone slab, broken and 4cm thick, has on one side an arc of curved and recessed wear marks 0.8cm in depth and roughly 48cm in diameter, but not truly circular. Slab stones showing arc wear patterns have been found in door-thresholds at Bucknowle Villa (3rd-4th century AD), Field (1977), but no other examples have been noted in earlier houses/huts. The partial survival of this item makes any other interpretation difficult; e.g. rotary wear marks from lathe-turning . . .

In the later Romano-British phase two large circular slabs, pitched vertically from structure (319) – phase VA, refer section and plan (figs. 70/71A and 75A): these slabs have been cut/sawn into circular shape and roughly pecked/split into requisite thickness. Both are about 65cm in diameter, and 8cm thick. No other working or indication of use could be traced on the surfaces. It is possible that their location to revet the platform structure (319) was secondary, and that they may have been designed as large ground slabs for columns, probably of wood.

Portions of circular chalk slabs again apparently unused were found in the industrial Romano-British phase at Ower (Woodward, this volume).

Only one portable stone object (unstratified) was recovered from the excavations, a hone-stone. This was little more than a regularly used (and as a result 'squared' in places), elongated, and waterworn beach pebble (fig. 86, 116). The stone was a red quartzite/sandstone. Stone of this type occurred from phase IVB onwards (petrological identifications by Paul Ensom, Foreign stone).

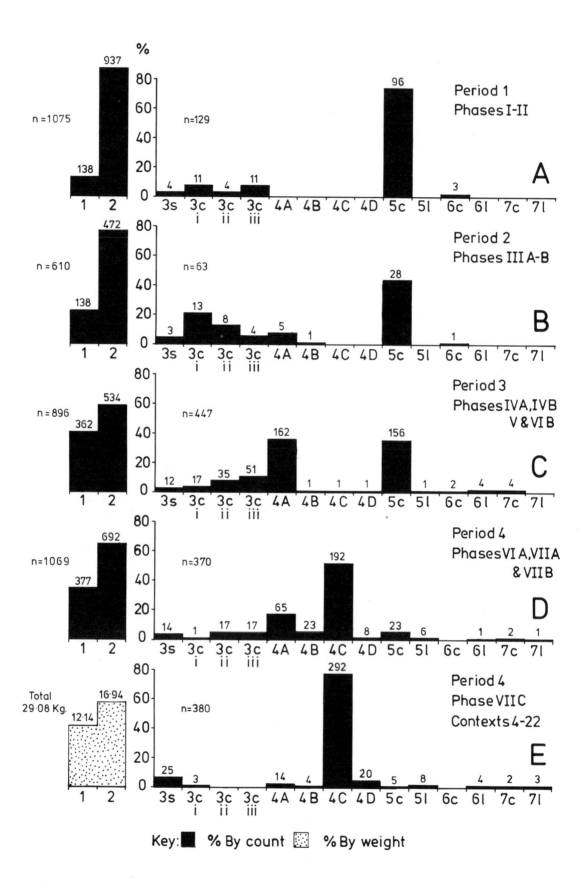

Figure 87. The worked Kimmeridge shale by period (percentage histograms). A. Period 1 (Early-Middle Iron Age), phases I and II. B. Period 2 (Middle Iron Age), phases IIIA-B. C. Period 3 (Late Iron Age, Durotrigian), phases IVA and B, V and VIB. D. Period 4 (Romano-British), phases VIA, VIIA and B. E. Period 4 (Romano-British), phase VIIC (working floor distributions, contexts 4-22).

THE KIMMERIDGE SHALE

PETER COX AND PETER WOODWARD

Considerable quantities of Kimmeridge shale working debris and waste products were recovered from all phases of the site's use. In total there were 1,511 pieces of identifiable production waste material and in excess of 4,000 fragments of primary preparation debris. The nature of deposits containing shale included discrete dumps of shale waste in Period 1, occupation levels, disturbed material in pits and soil accumulation levels of Periods 2 to 3, and large groups of lathe-waste material in successive yard levels associated with Period 4. The distribution of material in phase VIIc (fig. 76) defines the working areas in the excavation for the phase V and phase VII structures.

As at *Ower* (Woodward, this volume), the assemblage was analysed on the basis of the following categories:

1. 'Unworked' raw material, exhibiting no identifiable working (saw/chisel marks or conchoidal fracture). Often laminated and with rough edge fracture.

2. Worked shale waste showing conchoidal fracture, chisel and saw marks.

3. Circular prepared pieces (measurable) for armlet production. Sawn (3s) for machine-turning and chiselled waste from hand-made armlets (3ci-3ciii).

3s: 'Sawn' disc blanks for lathe mounting.
3ci: shale sheets with punched or cut holes.
3cii: shale sheets with part cut chisel incised circles.
3ciii: chiselled waste discs.

4. Calkin (1953) type lathe mountings on prepared shale discs and lathe waste cores, showing.
A. Central 'square' hole.
B. Central 'square' recess.
C. Paired circular bored hollows.
D. Three or more circular bored hollows.

5. Rough armlet products with little smoothing or polishing, unfinished.
c: hand-chiselled.
l: lathe-turned.

6. Finished armlet products.
c: hand-chiselled.
l: lathe-turned.

7. Other shale products and vessel core waste.
c: hand-chiselled.
l: lathe-turned.

Categories of material derived from hand-working/chiselling only are: 3ci, 3cii, 3ciii, 5c, 6c and 7c. Categories of material from lathe-preparation and lathe-turning are: 3s, 4A, 4B, 4C, 4D, 5l, 6l and 7l. Classes 1 and 2 are primary preparation debris and are not generally diagnostic of either method of production. The proportion of each category by period is shown by percentage histogram, fig. 87. It may be safely assumed that raw shale slabs were extensively mined from specific and suitable strata in the cliff face around Rope Lake Hole. No evidence for such activity has survived owing to the erosion of the cliffs through time. Occasional collection of shale from beach deposits is indicated by the occurrence of several water-worn shale beach pebbles in stratified deposits within the site.

The Shale Dumps (Period 1, Phase II)
Five excavated shale dumps (180), (188), (300), (295) and (245) are shown on fig. 72B. Random samples were taken from three of these deposits on site, sieved and sorted. Each sample represented less than 1 per cent of the total volume of any dump, although the full extent of each deposit was not known. Only categories 1 and 2 shale preparation debris were recovered from these sieved samples, although partially worked 'armlet' fragments (categories 3 and 5) were represented in the material collected from the excavation of the unsampled portions. All identifiable pieces were products of hand-working.

Results from sieved samples of dump (180) indicate an average content of 21.6 per cent category 1 and 5.1 per cent category 2 shale by weight. Samples from dump (188) produced averages of 2.4 per cent category 1 and 17.8 per cent category 2 by weight. One sample from dump (300) produced 7.7 per cent category 1 and 4.7 per cent category 2 by weight. In all cases soil, stones and other finds accounted for the bulk weight of each sample. The relative importance of category 1 in (180) and category 2 in (188) may be indicative of separate functional areas dealing with the initial preparation of shale slabs in the manufacturing process. Occupation levels were identified containing shale from later stages in the

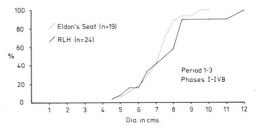

Figure 88. The diameter (internal) of Iron-Age (Period 1-3) hand-made armlets as a cumulative frequency graph, category 5c and 6c material: only 24 of 315 were measurable (comparative data from Eldon's Seat).

hand-working process. The numbers of category 5c shale waste that occurred in the excavation of these deposits were; from shale dump (300), 22; from the infill deposits of hut 1, 13; from shale dump (180), 10; from shale dump (188), 6. The average from any other context in Period 1-3 was approximately 4 pieces.

The Hand-working Industry
The nature of the hand-working industry is characterised by the perforation of sub-rectangular shale blocks, most probably with crudely formed flint flake tools (see discussion of flint assemblage below). This perforation can be achieved by one of two methods:

1. by the bifacial chiselling out of a circular central core;
2. more simply, by gouging out a small circular hole from one face which is then extended outwards.

Specific waste products from these processes are classified as 3cii and 3ciii for method 1 and 3ci for method 2. Waste core material from method 2 is indistinguishable owing to its fragmentary nature. Examples of method 1 are illustrated from excavations at *Eldon's Seat* (Cunliffe and Phillipson, 1968, plate VI, 197). No stratigraphic differences suggesting chronological developments between the two piercing methods were apparent.

Once perforated, further trimming of the internal and external edges of the shale would reduce it to an armlet ring. From waste dump (245), some 180 shale flakes with conchoidal fracture were recovered, and of these flakes, 96 per cent exhibited pressure rings and slight bulbs of percussion at right angles to the laminae and with the laminae running the length of the flake; 4 per cent had the laminae running across the breadth of the flake. This indicates that where possible the shale was trimmed by preferentially removing flakes in the plane along and parallel with the laminae of the shale. This would produce the minimum of stress within the body of the shale ring.

This characteristic of conchoidal fracture was not recorded in the trimming waste in the other dumps. This could be for either of two reasons: that the waste in dump (245) resulted from a distinct stage in armlet production, or that the shale in dump (245) had particular physical properties and was obtained from a separate source. Since the content of all the dumps was similar – waste derived from the production of armlet roughouts – the latter is more likely to be the case. It has not been possible to obtain suitable shale from the beach or cliff face replicating this distinctive conchoidal fracture (D. Sloper, pers. comm.).

Roughly-formed 'armlet' wasters are numerous from the site and attest to the fragile nature of the material in the trimming stage. Two examples of partially complete 'armlets' show fine tooling, particularly on the inner face which has almost achieved an acceptable final surface prior to polishing (fig. 92, 117 and 118). Completed hand-made 'armlets' (fig. 92, 119-124) vary in cross section and design, often only distinguishable from later lathe-turned products by their asymmetry.

The relative occurrence of internal diameters of measurable part-formed and finished hand-made armlets shows no great disparity with production from lathe-turned examples (compare figs. 88 and 89, A-D). Similarly, 'armlets' from Eldon's seat (Cunliffe 1968) display a regularity in sizes produced (fig. 88). Approximately 80 per cent of measurable examples from Rope Lake Hole were of diameters in excess of 6 cm; presumably the minimum size required to travel over an adult hand. 20 per cent were too small to be considered adult-sized and were possibly for children or alternative forms of adornment, such as pendants. A mature male skeleton from Tollard Royal was found with a shale bracelet around his left wrist (Wainwright, 1968), the internal diameter was 5.6 cm. A shale bracelet on the arm of a male skeleton less than 15 years old in a Middle Iron Age context at Winnal Down possessed an internal diameter of approximately 5.5 cm (Fasham 1985, 84). The *Tollard* 'armlet' seems particularly small to travel over an adult hand and it must be considered a possibility that such items may have been worn from a relatively young age. The similarity in dimension between the *Tollard* and *Winnall* examples and the corresponding ages at death of the skeletons lend credence to this possibility. However, the requirement of an adult market is demonstrated by the occurrence of an armlet with a diameter around 6.8 cm on the right arm of a skeleton in the Belgic War Cemetery at *Maiden Castle* (Wheeler, 1943; fig. 92, 10).

The hand-worked shale assemblage at Rope Lake Hole indicates a production process almost entirely concerned with 'armlet' manufacture. Alternative products are represented by three examples of other shale items from Late Iron Age (Period 3) contexts (fig. 92, 133, 135, and 136), and may represent occasional use of the mineral on a smaller scale.

The Lathe-turning Industry

Whereas in the early phases of the site's use the flint-like qualities of conchoidal fracture in shale were exploited, the introduction of the lathe in the later Iron Age phases (Period 3) enables a different aspect of shale's physical properties to be utilised. In particular, the fine grain and softness of the better quality shale most resembles the properties of wood and when lathe-turned and polished could produce very fine armlets, ornaments and objets d'art.

Fine products in shale have the appearance of ebony or jet, and have often been mis-identified as the latter in archaeological interpretation (Bussell, Pollard and Baird, 1982). Such products would have been sought after for personal adornment despite attendant problems of brittle fracturing.

This change of technology can be clearly demonstrated on this site (fig. 87); the beginning of lathe-turning is shown by the occurrence of waste and finished lathe-turned shale items (categories 4A-D, 5l and 6l) in Period 3. The presence of hand-working waste and semi-finished products in Periods 3-5 may be residual, but may also indicate that this mode of production continued to make some contribution to the site's output.

The nature of the flint tool industry associated with lathe-turning is discussed below.

The initial preparation of shale prior to lathe-mounting involved the cutting of blank discs from shale sheets. A large slab from pit (163) had a disc of 16 cm diameter cut from one side. Occasionally, category 2 waste debris may exhibit cutting lines from this process. Discs of this type are classified as 3s, and a total of 58 from all phases were recovered. Diameters of discs, lathe-cores (all types) and armlets are shown in fig. 89 from selected phases from periods 3 and 4. The occurrence of several discs with diameters of 11-12 cm might indicate that more than one 'armlet' could be produced from the same core. However, the average disc size was around 8 cm while the average core size was 4.8 cm. This appears to be too narrow a working margin and would seem to indicate that it is improbable that taking two or more 'armlets' from one disc was a regular method of production.

Armlet diameters in phases VIIb and VIIc show similar trends in production size. Both groups reveal proportions of 60 per cent: 40 per cent for 'armlets' with diameters greater than, and less than 6 cm respectively. No 'armlet' or 'armlet'-core greater than 8.5 cm diameter was recorded, a fact probably owing more to market demands that technological limitations. Nevertheless, one example of a category 4B core (275) was recovered with a diameter of 21 cm (not illustrated). This core had fine-chiselled surfaces on both sides and may indicate that the core was being prepared as a small tray or platter. Indications of lathe-cutting on the outer edge are consistent with the removal of a large ring (?armlet), enigmatic unless the product was a neck-ring.

A variety of cross section and decoration is exhibited on 'armlets' from the site. Finished and semi-finished 'armlets' are illustrated in

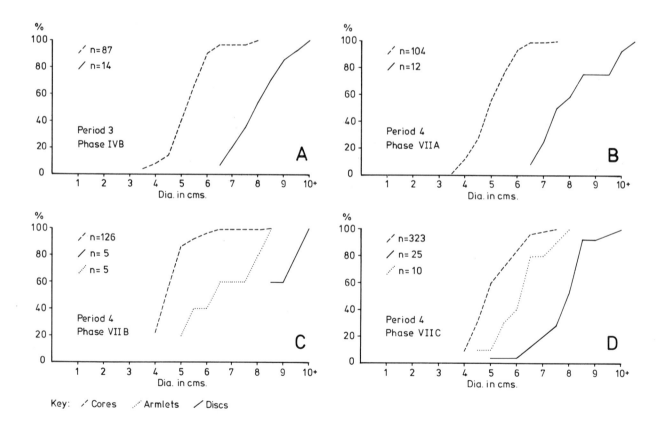

Key: ⟋ Cores   ⟋ Armlets   ⟋ Discs

Figure 89. The diameter (cm) of measurable lathe-discs, lathe-cores, and armlets from Period 3 and 4 phases, as cumulative frequency graphs. A. Phase group IVB (Period 3, occupation levels). Cores: $\bar{x} = 5.13$, n = 87. Armlets: two examples at 7.0. Dics: $\bar{x} = 7.9$, n = 14. Standard deviation (cores) = 0.77. B. Phase group VIIA (Period 4, upper yard levels). Cores: $\bar{x} = 4.9$, n = 104. Armlets: −, n = 2. Discs: $\bar{x} = 8.0$, n = 12. Standard deviation (cores) = 0.74. C. Phase group VIIB (Period 4, gulley 85). Cores: $\bar{x} = 4.5$, n = 126. Armlets: $\bar{x} = 6.45$, n = 5. Discs: $\bar{x} = 8.9$, n = 5. Standard deviation (cores) = 0.69. D. Phase group VIIC (4-22) (Period 4, working floor debris). Cores: $\bar{x} = 5.0$, n = 323. Armlets: $\bar{x} = 6.05$, n = 10. Discs: $\bar{x} = 7.75$, n = 25. Standard deviation (cores) = 0.82.

fig. 93, 125 to 132.

Other lathe-turned products include vessel fragments (fig. 93, 137 and 138) and a spindle-whorl (fig. 92, 134), possibly as a re-used core. Vessel production was certainly undertaken at Rope Lake Hole although only two specific cores attributed to this process were recognised, in phases VIIA and VIIC. Two small shale roof tile fragments were recovered from phase VIIC.

Lathe-fixing Techniques – A Summary
It would appear from the evidence at Rope Lake Hole that lathe technology was introduced into the site in the Late Iron Age. Initially, the fixing technique employed for lathe-mounting was wholly by means of near-square, chisel-cut holes or recesses in the shale disc (categories A and B respectively). Later, in the 1st

century AD a change in fixing technique occurs, eventually almost to the exclusion of other methods. This new method involved fixing the core or disc to the revolving spindle by means of two pegs inserted into the back of the core. The core types are well described in Calkin, 1953 and his classification is used here (category 4, A-D). It would appear that this form of fixing (category 4C) may possess certain advantages over the square-cut hole, although at this stage the precise nature of such benefits remains uncertain.

Detailed measurements of 292 category 4C cores from phase VIIC distribution above yards (4)-(21) inclusive and 86 category 4A cores from phase IVB were taken in order to answer specific questions relating to lathe techniques. The two groups of material were taken to be derived directly from closely defined lathe-working areas. This is substantiated by an examination of industrial

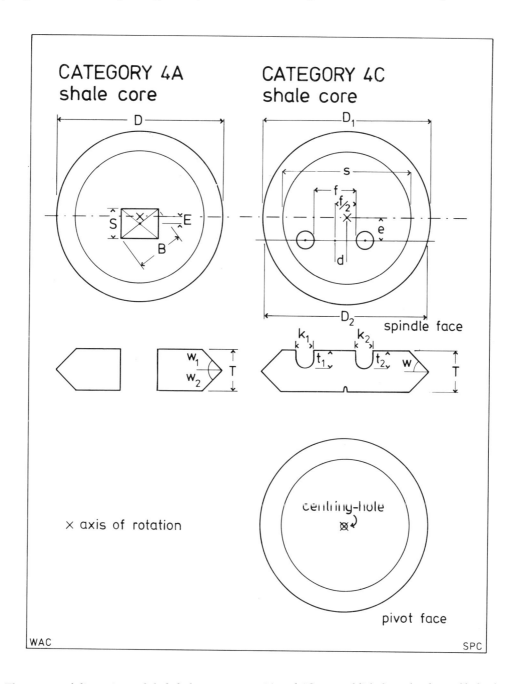

Figure 90. The measured dimensions of shale lathe-cores types 4A and 4C, to establish the technology of lathe-fixing techniques and lathe characteristics. A. Core type 4A: D: Diameter of core. S: Minimum side dimension of fixing-hole. B: Minimum diagonal of fixing-hole. T: Maximum thickness of core. W: Working angle on edge of core (two measurements). E: Measured eccentricity of axis of rotation from centre point of fixing-hole. B. Core type 4C: D_1: Diameter of core through lathe-centring hole. D_2: Length of chord through peg-holes. f: Distance between peg-holes. k_1: Diameter of 1st peg-hole. k_2: Diameter of 2nd peg-hole. t_1: Depth of 1st peg-hole. t_2: Depth of 2nd peg-hole. e: Eccentricity of chord D_2 from axis of rotation (centring-hole). d: Eccentricity of peg-holes from axis of rotation (centring-hole). S: Minimum working diameter on chuck side of core (related to size of lathe-chuck). w: Final working angle on chuck side of core (may relate to size of lathe-chuck).

debris across the excavated area (fig. 76), and an examination of wear patterns (Errington, 1981) on associated flint lathe tools suggested that the material across the yards of phase VIIB was on the edge of a lathe-turning area and that flint and shale debris had accumulated in a dump peripheral to and derived from the working area.

The attributes measured for each core, and the nomenclature adopted for recording are shown in fig 90. It was hoped that these measurements would show variations which might describe the lathe-spindle/chuck configuration more definntely, and in turn perhaps reveal the number of lathes involved. Although these may ultimately be modified by experimentation, several specific attributes of the waste-cores were identified which may have considerable bearing on future experimental research into lathe-fixing techniques.

The 4C Cores

f- value; spacing between the peg holes. The range of values (fig. 91A) shows a normal distribution between examples of 0.5 cm and 2.75 cm peg spacing. The arithmetic mean is 1.5 cm and standard deviation 0.38 cm. Interpretation of this result is difficult. With a fixed peg configuration as suggested by Calkin (1953) it might be expected that a more limited range of values would have existed if all the cores had derived from one lathe. However, there is no indication of how many lathes the sample is derived from or how much the spacing of peg holes might vary and still allow a core to be fixed and turned. The two extremes would therefore be *one* lathe possessing an adjustable fixing method from 0.5-2.75 cm, or *several* lathes each with a different fixed peg position. Since we are probably dealing with the commercial mass-production of armlets (below), then it is probably more likely that a lathe-fixing technique which would allow for flexibility in peg positioning would be preferred.

d- and e- values; the two eccentricites. The e- value was very small, 80 per cent less than 3 mm, but with measured variations up to 6 mm. Variations in d- values were similarly small. This perhaps suggests that tolerances in the lathe-spindle/chuck were small but

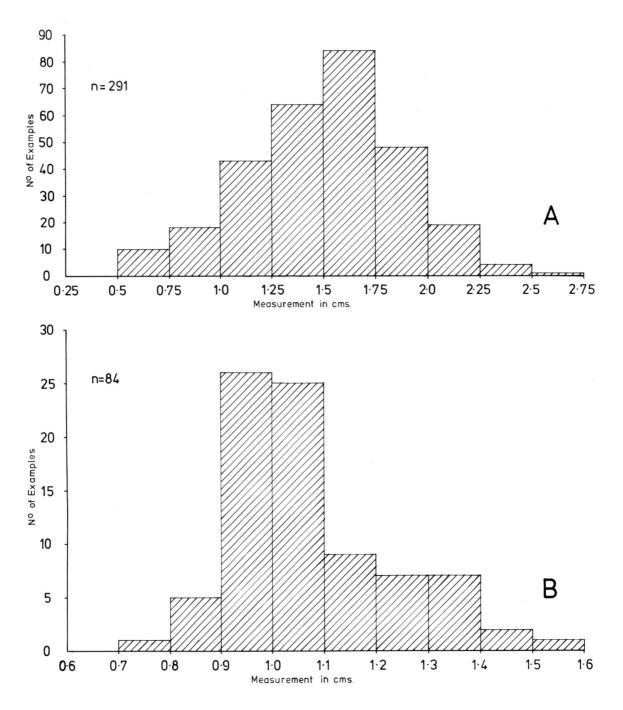

Figure 91. A. The range of 'f' values on type 4C cores, from phase VIIC (4-22) (Period 4). n = 291, x̄ = 1.5, s.d. = 0.38. B. The range of 's' values on type 4A cores, from phase IVB (Period 3), n = 84, x̄ = 1.02, s.d. = 0.16.

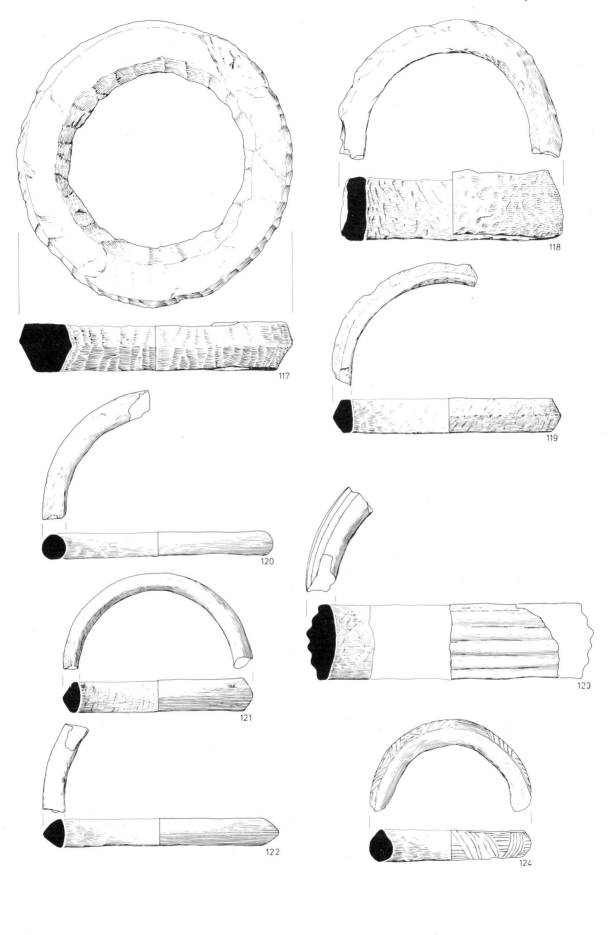

Figure 92. The Kimmeridge shale objects, 117-124, 2:3.

that they were of sufficient size to require no high degree of precision in the fitting of the shale disc to the spindle/chuck. Variations in other measurements were of a similar order. A record of these is in the Level III archive.

If the lathe-chuck was capable of accommodating a wide variation in the positioning of fixing holes it follows that:

1. The simple measurement of lathe-cores will not in itself be able to distinguish individual lathe characteristics since the tolerance to variations in the fixing method is high for all machines.

2. A chuck/spindle with fixed peg positions would not have been used.

3. The pegs attaching the core to the chuck/spindle were first attached to the shale disc and then positioned on the chuck/spindle. A chuck fixing technique using simple binding of both the spindle-shaft and wooden pegs to the spindle-shaft proved sufficient in experiments to turn an armlet and would produce the characteristic variations in d, e, and f values identified at Rope Lake Hole (D. Sloper pers. comm.).

The 4A Cores

E- value; eccentricity of the square centre hole from the axis of rotation. This was always very small indeed, 2 mm or less, suggesting that the core was through-fixed directly onto the lathe-chuck/spindle as an intrinsic part of the spindle.

The S- value; the shape of the hole was near square with side measurements (S) within the range of 7 mm to 16 mm in an approximately normal distribution, (fig. 91B).

These two measurements suggest that:

1. The eccentricity (E- value) is too small to identify individual lathes.

2. Lathes had spindles which could accommodate a range of dimensions in the fixing hole; perhaps by employing a tapered spindle or, by wedging the disc prior to turning. This measurement (S- value) in itself would not identify an individual lathe.

Lathe Technology – Conclusions

The complex nature of these cores and their size variations require more analysis and experimental research. Further study should perhaps direct itself in two main areas:

1. The lathe and the fixing technique. Why was a two-hole core technique developed? Preliminary research on the time consumed in armlet production using the square-hole and two-pin fixing technique shows little advantage to either method (D. Sloper pers. comm.). The use of a square-hole technique continued throughout the Romano-British period, particularly for turning vessels and larger discs. The preference for the two-pin technique, perhaps specifically related to armlet production should therefore be more fully examined. Such an investigation might also be able to suggest approximate production levels for sites such as Rope Lake Hole.

2. The lathe techniques themselves and wear patterns both on the residual core and the flint tools should be examined in more detail to assess the nature and requirements of the turners' skills, and the properties of the materials involved.

Currently, research is being undertaken by D. Sloper on the lathe and practical techniques (D. Sloper, forthcoming), and summarised in Sloper (1981). A preliminary study of flint tool wear patterns has been carried out as a dissertation at the Dorset Institute of Higher Education (Errington 1981 A and B).

Sample groups of worked shale from phases I, II, IVB and VIIC and finished products from all phases have been conserved to enable further research into the nature of the two modes of shale working, and in particular into the specific problems and limitations of lathe technology outlined above. It has not been possible to conserve all the worked shale from this important assemblage. However, all shale has been retained for further petrological analysis (J. Evans for Ancient Monuments Laboratory).

Discussion

That shale was worked on almost all recorded Romano-British sites in Purbeck is well known (RCHM, 1970). Although more analysis is required to produce inter-site comparisons between the range of products, waste characteristics and technical considerations, a few preliminary observations can be made.

Primarily, the waste at Rope Lake Hole is standard and specialised with few 3-pin or 4-pin cores (class 4D non-standard fitting), and few vessel cores.

In contrast at the industrial site at Norden, Corfe Castle (Sunter, this volume), contemporary with the Romano-British phase at Rope Lake Hole, the waste and products were more variable. No class 4C cores were discovered. At this site, luxury items such as table legs, tablets, trays and vessels were being produced. Perhaps for these items the traditional square-hole fixing (4A and 4B) was retained. Only three classifiable waste-cores were recovered; two of class 4A and one of class 4B. However, twelve shale armlets (4 from 1st century AD levels, 7 from 2nd century levels) were identified, some of which were unfinished and exhibited a wide range of internal diameters. This fact suggests that they were made on the site.

At Cleavel Point, Ower (Woodward, this volume) a small shale working industry was also identified on a site that was producing BB1 pottery (possibly also the case at Norden) mudstone tesserae, and salt as indicated by briquetage. Here the shale waste was again more variable than at Rope Lake Hole, with a larger variation in core type. Only four pin-fixed cores (Category C and D) were present from a total of 18 cores recovered in Romano-British contexts. At Ower, vessels and trays were being turned in addition to smaller objects and armlets. This lack of specialisation in core type is also exhibited in the Romano-British levels on the Villa site at Bucknowle, Corfe Castle (D. Sloper pers. comm.).

The specialisation of shale core type at Rope Lake Hole is accompanied by a specialised flint industry (specialist report, follows), where the kite-shaped tool type was produced to a high degree of standardisation, but with low levels of utilisation (Errington, 1981). In contrast at Norden and Ower, the flint industry was extremely 'unsophisticated' with tool types exhibiting more frequent retouch and utilisation, but which was of a more irregular type.

From the foregoing it can be suggested that the shale and flint wastes on the phase VII working floor were extremely specialised. It is most likely that the industry at Rope Lake Hole in phase VII represents the final phase of a specialist industry specifically devoted to the large scale manufacture of shale armlets.

The following shale objects have been illustrated in figs. 92 & 93 to show the range of products:

The Illustrated Shale Objects:

117. Partially completed hand-made 'armlet', category 5C, from (300), phase II.

118. Partially completed hand-made 'armlet', category 5C, from (300), phase II.

119. Fragment of plain, part polished, unfinished (?), hand-made 'armlet', from (192), phase IVB.

120. Fragment of polished, part finished, hand-made (?) 'armlet', from (147), phase IVB.

121. Fragment of polished, finished, hand-made (?) 'armlet', from (189), phase I.

122. Fragment of polished, finished, hand-made 'armlet', from (237), phase IIIB.

123. Fragment of polished, finished, hand-made 'armlet', from (248), phase I.

124. Fragment of finished hand-made 'armlet', from (311), phase IIID.

125. Fragment of polished, unfinished, lathe-turned 'armlet', from (16), phase VIIC.

126. Fragment of polished, unfinished lathe-turned 'armlet', from (86), phase VIIA.

127. Fragment of polished, ?finished, lathe-turned 'armlet', from (16), phase VIIC.

128. Two conjoining fragments of polished, finished lathe-turned 'armlet', from (232), phase IVA.

129. Fragment of polished and finished 'armlet', from (11), phase VIIC.

130. Fragment of polished and finished 'armlet', from (11), phase VIIC.

131. Fragment of polished, finished, lathe-turned 'armlet', from (28), phase VIIC.

132. Fragment of polished, finished, lathe-turned 'armlet', from (147), phase IVB.

133. Fragment of tapering 'bar' with smoothed rounded edges and skewered profile, hone stone? from (143), phase IVB.

134. Spindle whorl. ?Re-used vessel core with re-bored hole, from (85), phase VIIB.

135. Small perforated disc, and worked, from (176), phase IVB.

136. Circular cutting board with opposed rectangular slots in outer edge. Inscribed marking-out lines on both faces, central pivot hole, but no indication of lathe-turning. Score lines from use on both faces (refer architectural fragments, and site report), from (149), phase V.

137. Straight-walled dish fragment with cut, chiselled and partially smoothed surfaces. Lathe turning, striations on outer surface

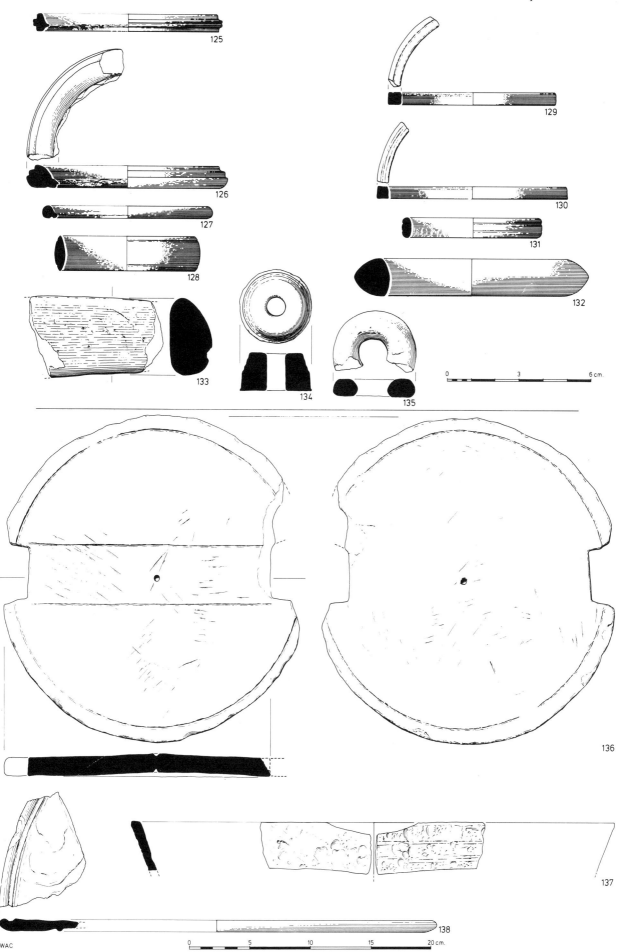

Figure 93. The Kimmeridge shale objects, 125-138, 1:3.

WAC

TABLE 29: The analysis of the Iron Age flint industry by structure and phase (phases I-IV).

PERIOD/PHASE DESCRIPTION	'Hammer' Stones	Cores Worked lumps	Irregular	Regular	Tools	Non-retouched flakes Primary cortical	Other	Retouched flakes Primary/cortical	Other	Snapped	Broken/snapped flakes	Kite-shaped tools	Burnt/calcined	TOTAL	Edge utilisation analysis of flakes with retouch Point	Edge trim	Snapped with retouch on snapped edge
PERIOD 1																	
PHASE I Hut occupation levels	13	56	28	6	–	118	434	17	66	10	54	–	43	845	24	79	2
PHASE I Hut associated levels outside	–	1	1	–	–	18	52	1	4	–	4	–	2	83	2	4	–
PHASE II Other general occupation	2	2	–	1	–	14	31	4	2	–	3	–	–	59	1	6	–
PHASE II Shale dumps	1	9	2	4	2	19	41	3	17	5	20	–	7	130	8	19	2
PHASE II Flint dump (310)	15	3	2	–	–	56	126	8	19	1	38	–	1	269	9	23	–
PERIOD 1 TOTAL	31	71	33	11	2	225	684	33	108	16	119	–	53	1386	44	131	4
PERIOD 2																	
PHASE IIIA Associated occupation levels	1	–	2	–	–	–	4	–	4	1	3	–	4	19	1	5	–
PHASE IIIA Material behind revet	2	15	8	2	–	40	131	1	11	1	21	–	33	265	2	11	–
PHASE IIIB Tumble in front of revet	3	5	2	–	–	20	72	1	8	3	7	–	14	135	–	12	–
PERIOD 2 TOTAL	6	20	12	2	–	60	207	2	23	5	31	–	51	419	3	28	–
PERIOD 3																	
PHASE IVB General occupation levels	1	12	5	–	–	26	67	2	6	1	17	–	12	149	2	8	–
PHASE IVA and VIB Pits	1	3	2	–	–	12	27	1	5	1	6	4	8	70	3	5	–
PERIOD 3 TOTAL	2	15	7	–	–	38	94	3	11	2	23	4	20	219	5	13	–
TOTALS	39	106	52	13	2	323	985	38	142	23	173	4	124	2024	52	172	4

and on flat top rim, from (109), phase VIIA.

138. Rim fragment of partially finished lathe-turned platter with footring, from (12), phase VIIC.

THE FLINT
P. W. COX and P. J. WOODWARD

A considerable quantity of worked flint was recovered from all phases of the site. Flint does not occur immediately on the site of Rope Lake Hole but could have been collected from the chalk ridge to the north, a minimum distance of approximately four kilometres. The nearest exposed outcrop at Worbarrow Bay is some six kilometres distant. Rolled pebble-flint occurred on the site, and the beach may have provided a more readily accessible supply of raw material. The worked flint normally exhibits a grey patina.

Knapped flint occurs in the majority of contexts, and particularly in association with shale waste. Discrete flint groups were excavated from within phase I hut and occupation levels, phase II shale dumps and the phase II flint dump (310). More dispersed deposits of knapped flint occurred in period 2, phase IIIA-B build up. Smaller quantities were recovered from pits and general occupation levels attributed to period 3. Large quantities also occurred in period 4 in particular some 2,200 pieces wholly from above the latest yard levels, phases VIIB and C.

Knapped flint almost invariably occurs on Late Bronze Age to Romano-British sites in Purbeck where shale working is evident (Calkin; 1948, 1953, Davies: 1936, Cunliffe and Phillipson, 1968). Only one site in Dorset is recorded where flint-knapping techniques of a later Iron Age – Romano-British character occur without any apparent associated shale working activity (Palmer, 1967). The correlation between flint and shale-working and the absence of any other surviving suitable implements in alternative materials strongly indicates that flint was indeed the shale-workers' prime source for cutting and trimming tools.

It is apparent from earlier studies (Calkin; 1948, 1953 and Davies; 1936) that there exists a distinct differentiation of flint-knapping techniques and their resultant tool products from Iron Age as compared with Late Iron Age and Romano-British phases of shale working. This would appear to be directly related to changes in shale-working technology, discussed above. The development from hand-working to the lathe-turning of shale would certainly have required specific modified tool types.

Accordingly, analysis of the early to late Iron Age excavated flint assemblage has been undertaken separately from the later Romano-British levels associated with lathe-turned shale, in an attempt to characterise the nature of an unsystematic industry (see particularly Calkin 1948, 38, Cunliffe and Phillipson 1968, 226).

The Iron-Age Industry (Periods 1-3)
Table 29 shows the analysis of 2,024 pieces of worked flint from all contexts of periods 1-3.

1. Hammerstones. The large number attributed to this category may be false owing to the occurrence of rolled, battered beach pebbles giving the appearance of hammering. This battering is not normally localised and in many examples occurs across the entire surface of the flint lump. Of a total of 39 'hammerstones', 31 had subsequently been broken and may have been utilised as crude cores. One hammerstone from phase I hut level (229) exhibits brown patination indicating the re-use of an earlier hammerstone or core.

2. Cores. Of 171 pieces in this category, 106 may be classified as worked lumps. A further 52 cores exhibit two or more striking platforms and may be irregular or unsystematic. Thirteen exhibit single platforms and had been utilised in a systematic manner. Flake beds are commonly deep and display hinge-fracturing c.f. *Norden* (Bradley, this volume).

3. Core tools. Two core tools were recovered from period 1 contexts and may be described as chopping tools (one illustrated, fig. 95, 152).

4. Non retouched flakes. The largest proportion (65 per cent) of the total knapped flint assemblage may be attributed to this category. Flakes are generally squat and many terminate with hinge-fractures. Battering on some cortical flakes results from the use of beach pebbles as cores, or broken hammerstones. Mis-hits were also frequent.

5. Retouched flakes. Only 203 flakes of a total of 1,812 exhibited secondary working or retouch (examples illustrated fig. 95, 139-147). One white patinated flake (fig. 28, 151) has retouch through an earlier patination indicating re-use of earlier knapped material. Analysis of the edge utilisation of secondary-worked flakes (Table 25 and fig. 96) is attempted in order to demonstrate the character and function of tools within the assemblage and is discussed below.

Three attributes of edge utilisation were examined:
1. retouch on a snapped flake surface
2. point retouch
3. edge retouch

The number of separate occurrences of each is shown on Table 29 and expressed as a percentage of all utilised edges in fig. 95.

1. Retouch on a snapped edge: Calkin observes that the

snapping of flakes and utilisation of the junction between the old and new flake edge is a recurring feature at Kimmeridge (Calkin, 1948). However, of 23 flakes exhibiting 'voluntary' snapping, only four snapped edges appear to have been utilised in this manner at Rope Lake Hole, one is illustrated (fig. 95, 147). It does not therefore appear to be a diagnostic characteristic of this assemblage. Other flakes exhibiting snapped or 'voluntary' fractures have no retouch or utilisation. The importance of this technique in the development of the flint industry is discussed below.

2. Point retouch. Fifty-two examples exhibit point retouch and may be considered as tools for the purposes of gouging or piercing shale in the initial stages of armlet rough-out manufacture (see shale above). Three examples of these tools are illustrated (fig. 95, 149-150). As much as 84 per cent of all flakes with retouched points were excavated from period 1 contexts. Several exhibit wear on the working point (in particular fig. 95, 150).

3. Edge retouch. Within the context of this assemblage many flakes might have satisfied the requirements for use as a tool in shale working without necessarily requiring retouch or exhibiting obvious wear. However, a significant number fall within this category of apparent edge utilisation. Both long and squat flakes have been retouched in a manner that might normally warrant their consideration as scrapers. While there is no indication that these are residual in these contexts, their common occurrence must relate to methods of trimming shale for which a scraping tool is well suited. Ten examples are illustrated (fig. 95, 139-147, 151) to demonstrate the variability in the proportions, edge utilisation and bulk of the tools. It is difficult to suggest specific functions for these tools, although a general description as trimming, chiselling or scraping tools within the shale production process may be applicable.

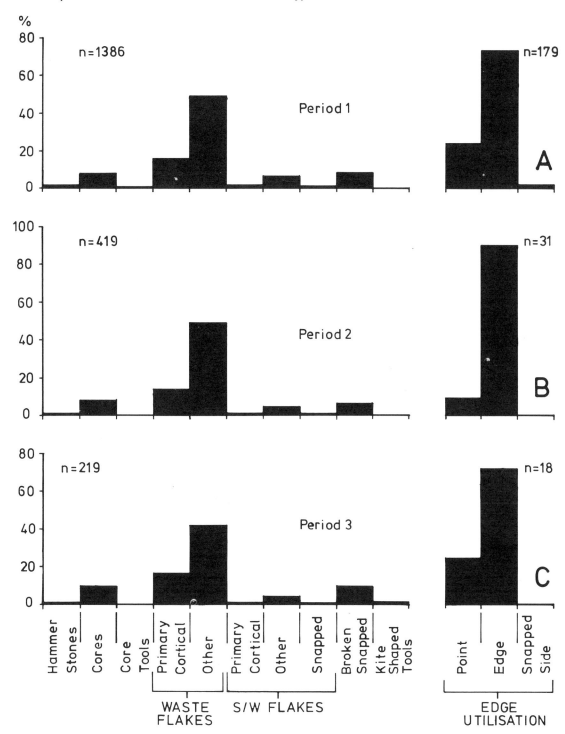

Figure 94. The Iron Age flint industry by period (percentage histograms). A. Period 1 (phases I and II). B. Period 2 (phases IIIA-B). C. Period 3 (phases IVA and B, VIB).

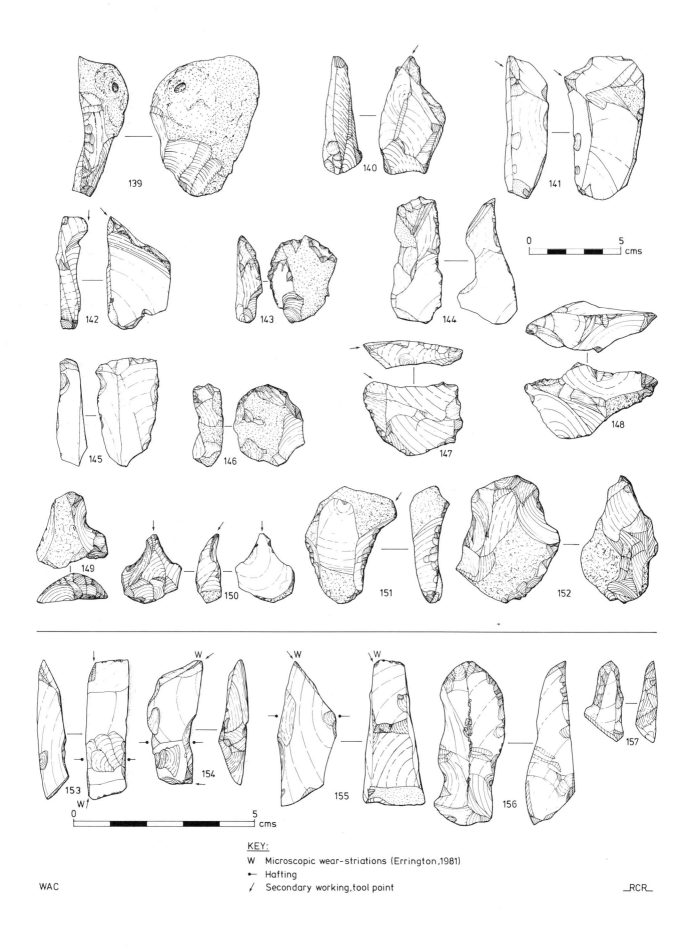

KEY:

W   Microscopic wear-striations (Errington,1981)

←   Hafting

╱   Secondary working, tool point

WAC

RCR

Figure 95. The Iron Age flint tool types (139-152), and the Romano-British tool types (153-157), at 1:2.

An analysis of the assemblage by period, as a percentage of period totals is shown in fig. 94. It is apparent that this otherwise unsystematic industry is essentially consistent in represented types through periods 1-3. The occurrence of two chopping tools in period 1 may be significant in that they are both derived from phase II shale waste dumps and may therefore be tools associated with the primary preparation of shale slabs. Snapped flakes occur in similar proportions throughout all periods although the four 'kite-shaped' tools from period 3 are from phases of the site where the first occurrence of significant amounts of lathe-turned waste (category 4A cores) is evident (see fig. 87).

In terms of the development of the flint industry at Rope Lake Hole the occurrence of snapped flakes is important. These exhibit the specific trait dominant in the manufacture of lathe chisel tools from the later Iron Age. Although few examples from the earlier assemblage exhibit wear, microscopical examination might yet reveal utilisation of pieces on the junction of the snapped and original surfaces. Indeed, such analysis of lathe tool points indicates that working shale with flint implements gives rise to very slight and discontinuous signs of wear on the contact surface (Errington, 1981 – see below).

The Romano-British Industry (Period 4)

The production of flint lathe tools and associated preparation waste has long been recognised from industrial sites of this period in Purbeck. The industry is characterised by a modified blade technique involving the snapping of narrow blade segments for hafting as chisels for the lathe-turning of shale discs. This process is discussed fully elsewhere and need not be repeated in full (ref. Calkin, 1953; Palmer, 1967).

The analysis of knapped flint from period 4 has concentrated on a stratified group from the surface of the upper yard level, phase VIIC, contexts (4) to (22). Here, the material is closely associated with shale working debris (fig. 76) and may represent accumulation across a shale working surface.

Fig. 96 shows the analysis of knapped flint from phase VIIC, (4)-(22). Of 109 cores recovered only 31 may be considered specific to the systematic preparation of long flakes. The presence of cores on the working floor may indicate that the preparation of flint tools was being carried on alongside lathe-turning. The high proportion of squat/intermediate to long flakes suggests both the discarding of unsuitable flakes for tool preparation and the utilisation of long flakes for later stages of the process. This ratio is consistent throughout phase VIIC grid squares. In grid square (12) the ratio of intermediate/squat: 56:1. Furthermore, only five long flakes exhibit retouch and have been utilised in any manner other than for lathe-tool production. However, expressed as a percentage of the total number of flakes recovered, secondary worked long flakes amount to a proportion almost identical to secondary worked intermediate/squat flakes.

A total of 557 butt and distal end flake remnants have been identified, of which 25 (4.4 per cent) have visible secondary working or wear. These are not necessarily waste products and may have made quite adequate lathe tools, as was observed at Ower (Woodward, this volume).

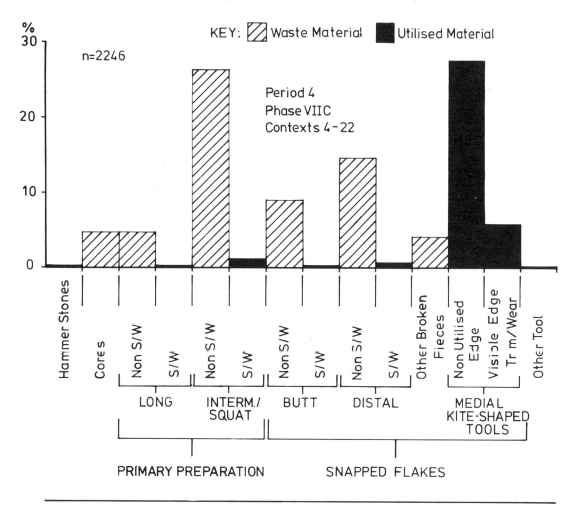

Figure 96. The Romano-British flint assemblage from across the working floor (phase VIIC, 4-22), (percentage histogram).

Some 752 snapped flake segments may have been utilised as lathe tools. Many conform to the classic kite-shaped tool most suited to hafting. Three are illustrated (fig. 95, 153-155). All illustrated examples exhibit retouch for hafting, microscopic wear to working edges and the removal of retouch or pressure flakes on working points. The dimensions, utilisation and wear of these tools are discussed below.

Three other tools were recovered from phase VIIC. They consist of one hammerstone and two gouge/point working tools (one broken). Both point tools are illustrated (fig. 95, 156-7).

The high ratio of waste to utilised material from the working floor (fig. 96) indicates that flint was brought to the site before tools were manufactured on the working floor. Similar proportions of waste to utilised material were recovered from two sample squares ((6) and (12)) which were selected for micro-wear analysis (Errington, 1981).

The Lathe Tools

The flint lathe tool assemblage is of great significance. It is the largest group of such material yet excavated, demonstrating a large range of waste products in tool manufacture. It is particularly important since the group is in direct association with a shale working floor and may allow detailed analysis of the development of both the shale and flint working industries in their final stages (phase VIIc).

Measurement of 121 tools was undertaken from sample squares (6) and (12). Length was measured as corresponding to the width of the original flake, width as the portion of the original flake measured longitudinally along it, and thickness as the maximum perpendicular distance between the ventral and dorsal surfaces of the original flake. The following results were obtained from the two sample squares, expressed as an arithmetic mean and standard deviation of the dimensions;

Length (6) 3.42 cm ± 0.53 cm, (12) 3.00 cm ± 0.63 cm.

Width (6) 0.98 cm ± 0.26 cm, (12) 0.91 cm ± 0.30 cm.

Thickness (6) 1.09 cm ± 0.30 cm, (12) 1.00 cm ± 0.28 cm.

While these measurements alone cannot define a regularity in the tool proportions, they indicate a tolerance within which each attribute might vary. The tools might therefore have been made within standard specifications.

Flint lathe tools occur across the entire working floor in varying densities (fig. 76). In total, the ratio of lathe tools to shale lathe cores was 2.3:1. This is rather low compared to other excavated groups from shale working sites on or around the shale deposits such as *Gaulter* (Calkin, 1953), 5:1 and *Gallows Gore* (Calkin, 1953), 8:1. However, at *Ower* (Woodward, this volume) and *Norden* (Sunter, this volume) the ratio of flint tools to shale lathe cores was 1:2.5 and 1:2 respectively. The observed ratio at Rope Lake Hole may be due to one of several reasons. First, shale lathe cores may be under-represented in the sample. There is evidence for the use of shale as a fuel in most phases of activity on the site. Shale cores on the working floor might therefore only represent debris from the final activity in this phase, previous accumulations having been burnt elsewhere. This phenomenon would also account for under-representation of lathe cores on other sites noted above. Secondly, lathe tools may be over-represented on this area of the partially excavated work floor. Of two sample squares examined, Errington (1981) noted that grid square (12) contained more 'malformed' and broken tools than sample (6). She suggests that as (12) is towards the edge of the work floor as excavated, the deposition of flint may be in the form of dumping of waste material. Towards the centre of the work floor (6), well formed and utilised tools are more abundant. The relative excess of lathe tools may therefore be due to the discarding of broken, useless or worn tools. Indeed, a higher proportion of lathe tools exhibit visible edge wear in grid squares 14-22. Finally, Errington suggests that experiments with freshly made tools indicate the rapid occurrence of a high degree of wear to the working point. Tools would therefore only have a short life before discard, even if the tool was re-hafted to use a second facet.

Problems in replicating shale turning with flint tools were exacerbated by difficulties in obtaining suitable shale. Exploitation of shale in antiquity would have been directed towards quarrying of the best, oil-bearing deposits least likely to fracture in turning. Even after burial, much of the shale waste discovered at Rope Lake Hole was soft and unlaminated. Few deposits of this nature are currently available in cliff exposures. Accordingly, much of the wear analysis carried out by Errington was derived from harder, more slatey material which must have affected resultant wear patterns. Nevertheless her results may be summarised thus:

1. Many excavated tools exhibit no microscopic wear. These examples may not have been utilised.

2. Wear on excavated tools was generally slight and discontinuous. Some tool tips had apparently broken in use in varying degrees. Calkin (1953) suggested that this feature was through intentional re-sharpening.

3. Wear on replicated tools was directly related to the pressure exerted. Efficient cutting-tool edges which required least pressure exhibited the finest striations on the surface of the flint. Tools requiring most pressure revealed the deepest and most continuous striations.

4. Even less efficient cutting edges could be used for turning shale with greater lathe speed and pressure exerted by the turner during experiments. However, once a tool tip had fractured, the tool became useless and was discarded.

The nature of the flint assemblage at Rope Lake Hole details the development of a sophisticated knapping technique specifically related to the working of shale and modified in response to major technological changes in the mode of shale working. Furthermore, the tools were produced in large quantities to a regular, standard specification (c.f. irregularity of tools at *Norden* and *Ower*). That such large quantities were being prepared in advance for an industry predominantly using a single lathe fixing (4C) method to mass produce armlets indicates a well-organised industrial process rather than the small scale or 'cottage' industry that appears elsewhere. The flint assemblage is also important since it dates to a period in time when the regular exploitation of flint for tools would otherwise appear to have ceased.

The Illustrated Flint

The following flint objects have been illustrated in fig. 96.

139. Deep, cortical retouched flake (from (229) phase I hut levels).

140. Retouched flake (from (229) phase I hut levels).

141. Deep, retouched flake (from (229) phase I hut levels).

142. Retouched flake, with retouch on hinge fracture (from (189), phase I hut levels).

143. Cortical, retouched flake (from (295) phase II shale dump).

144. Long end 'scraper' (from (301) phase I hut levels).

145. Long end 'scraper' (from (199) phase I hut levels).

146. Cortical end 'scraper' (from (299) phase I hut levels).

147. Retouched flake with retouch on snapped edge and point (from (295) phase II shale dump).

148. Point tool with retouch on snapped face (from (189) phase I hut levels).

149. Cortical point tool (from (220) phase I hut levels).

150. Small point tool (from (130) phase VIB pits).

151. Re-utilised flake tool with retouch through surface of earlier patination (from (225) phase IIIA accumulation).

152. Cortical chopping tool (from (188) phase II shale dump).

153. 'Kite-shaped' lathe tool (from (12) phase VIIC (Errington tool A)).

154. 'Kite-shaped' lathe tool (from (6) phase VIIC (Errington tool B)).

155. 'Kite-shaped' lathe tool (from (6) phase VIIC (Errington tool H)).

156. Gouge/trimming tool (from (19) phase VIIC).

157. Broken point tool (from (15) phase VIIC).

THE SLAG AND CINDER

LEO BIEK

(Ancient Monuments Laboratory, Department of the Environment)

Thirty-eight pieces of slag/cinder were examined visually and microscopically (x40): for their location see Table 28. Several categories of material were present:

1. Fuel-ash Slag: A number of up to egg-sized pieces, very light and vesicular with off-white to pale-grey glassy surfaces, were found scattered over the site. Such material would be produced at elevated temperatures from sintering shale ash under aerobic conditions, as on an open hearth. Although the general term 'fuel-ash slag' applies, it need not restrict the context (which could include a fierce accidental blaze) or imply an industrial purpose.

2. Charred Shale Cinder: A similar quantity was found equally randomly distributed. This material corrresponds to wood charcoal and is formed on heating shale in a restricted supply of air, but could have come from the same fire(s) as the 'fuel-ash' slag – transitional states are present and the two forms are clearly complementary.

3. Mineral Slag: A number of lumps consisted of material which was similar to group 1 but less vesicular, not glassy and much denser.

4. Glassy Slag: Several pieces were examined, one of which (151) looked superficially like a fragment of blast furnace slag and from its phase V context was certainly intrusive (Table 25). The specimen from pit (140) – phase VIB – looks similar, but not identical: it need not necessarily be intrusive; in common with the rest of the pieces in this group it consists of a continuous phase of glass containing vesicles and inclusions. It eludes precise interpretation at this stage, beyond suggesting hot spots in a fire where a fairly fluid glass had run over miscellaneous mineral debris.

5. Hearth Buns: Two small examples of 'hearth bottom buns' were present, such as are formed during smithing.

The examination indicates that shale was burnt – most probably as a fuel, and/or incidentally – and that some smithing took place possibly quite nearby. However the collection is unusual. All the pieces – except for group 5 – could be fitted into a general picture of 'burning shale'.

In particular, the green colour in the glassy phase is evidently due to iron and could come from the pyritic component of the shale (see below; and Bussell *et al.* 1982); also, the bituminous oil present would aid the establishment of reducing conditions during initial firing. But a more detailed understanding must await fuller examination with other comparative material (see also Ower, this volume).

THE HUMAN SKELETAL REMAINS
JULIET ROGERS

The inhumation (177), figs. 73 and 74.

The bones received for examination were fragmentary with abraded surfaces, and in most instances the articular ends of the long bones were missing. Because of this, accurate measurement was not possible but approximate lengths were obtained for a right clavicle and a right humerus. The bones present were:

1. Skull – frontal, parietal, occiput; right mastoid, temporal, zygoma and maxilla. Also right mandible. Reconstruction not possible owing to post-morterm distortion.
2. Clavicle. Right Diaphysis. Lateral end abraded. Approximate Diaphyseal length, 102 mm.
3. Fragment of right scapula.
4. Three vertebral fragments; one from cervical vertebra two from thoracic vertebra.
5. Ten rib fragments.
6. Humerus. Right diaphysis. Approximate diaphyseal length, 217 mm.
7. Femur. Shafts only. Pair of femoral diaphyses – much abraded.
8. Four very abraded fragments of long bone shafts. Probably 2 ulna, 1 radius and one possible fibula.

The bones belong to one individual child. The stage of eruption of the second maxillary and mandibular molar teeth suggests an age of between 11 and 12 years old. This is confirmed by the disphyseal lengths of the clavicle and humerus, which fall into the range for 10 to 11 year olds. Tooth eruption is however more accurate for ageing.

No sex can be assigned to this skeleton because no pelvic bones survived.

The only observable abnormality in this skeleton was the presence of a minor degree of orbital osteoporosis in the roof of both eye sockets. The presence of this condition is possibly due to iron deficiency anaemia (Ortner and Putschar, 1981). X-ray examination confirmed the absence of other skeletal abnormalities in the bones present.

These bones were the fragmentary remains of an 11- or 12-year-old child, who may have suffered from iron deficiency anaemia.

In addition to this inhumation six fragments of human bone were also recovered from the following contexts; 148 (phase IVB), 199 (phase I), 217 (phase V), 176 (phase IVB), 114 (phase VIIA) and 85 (phase VIIB). Detail descriptions of these can be found in the Level III Archive. Osteologically these bones are from a minimum number of 4 persons; 2 young adults and 2 newborn infants. However as these bones are from six archaeological contexts from six different phases it is likely that they derive from six different individuals; 2 young adults and 4 newborn infants.

ANIMAL BONES AND MARINE MOLLUSCS
JENNIE COY

A total of 5,333 bones and 3,685 shells from the 1979 excavations were examined. The 1976 material was scanned and appeared to be of a similar nature but, as detailed stratigraphic information was not available, were not included in this account.

Recording was by the Ancient Monuments Laboratory's system (Jones *et al.* n.d.). The OP numbers contributing to this sample, and their phasing within the different periods, are given in archive.

Table 30 lists the bones of domestic mammals which form the bulk of the finds. Tables in archive give the distribution of anatomical elements for the major ones in the different phases.

TABLE 30: Bones of domestic mammals.

	horse	cattle	sheep*	pig	dog	c-size	s-size	TOTAL
horn core	–	6	12	–	–			18
cranium	1	67	47	7	6	40	17	185
maxilla	2	22	21	14	2	2		63
mandible	5	103	227	30		24	2	391
hyoid		7	3					10
vertebra	2	43	44	1	4	62	22	178
ribs	2	80	68	2		121	230	503
sternum							1	1
scapula	4	46	44	16	2	37	5	154
humerus	5	40	75	10	2	16	3	151
radius	1	29	163	9		21	1	224
ulna	3	22	27	7		2		61
pelvis	3	40	44	4		9	4	104
femur	1	21	49	2	1	15	18	107
tibia	4	25	259	10		30	7	335
fibula				4				4
carpal/tarsal	4	58	38	7				107
metapodial	8	98	286	12	1	6	3	414
phalanges	3	62	39	6				110
loose teeth	47	233	532	64	4	2		882
l. b. fragment						476	556	1032
other frags		1	3	2		123	112	241
TOTALS	95	1003	1981	207	22	986	981	5275

*sheep includes all identifications to sheep or goat.

Species Represented

The major part of the material consists of the bones of domestic cattle, sheep (there is no evidence for goat) and pig (Table 30). The first would have provided the major meat source although the second provides most fragments in all phases. Pig remains provide a low but constant proportion throughout the period of settlement and this compares closely with results from Eldon's Seat (Cunliffe and Phillipson, 1968, 227: Coy, in press). The relative role of cattle and sheep is discussed in the next section.

There are a few bones of domestic horse, dog and domestic fowl. The first are included in the archive. Both dog and fowl appear in phases IVA, IVB, VIIA and VIIC, dog also appears in phases IIIA and VIB and fowl in IIIB and V. No butchery was recorded for dog although there was skinning evidence in VIIA. The few bones of wild species (mammals, birds, and amphibians) are detailed in Tables 31 and 32. It is unlikely that the rabbit bone is contemporary with the occupation.

Marine molluscs retrieved by conventional excavation in the different phases (Table 33) were unevenly deposited in the settlement and consisted mainly of the limpets and periwinkles found on this part of the coast today. In addition there were finds of oyster in period 4 and single shells of common whelk, *Buccinum undatum* (VIB); top shell, *Gibbula lineata* (phase VIIA) and edible cockle, *cardium edule* (phase VIIC).

TABLE 31: Bird bones.

	1	2	3	4	5	6	7	8	9	TOTALS
sternum	1									1
coracoid			1							1
scapula	2									2
humerus		1			1					2
radius	1						1	1		3
ulna					1			1	1	3
carpometacarpus	1		3							4
femur	1									1
tibiotarsus	1							1		2
tarsometatarsus								2		2
TOTAL	7	1	3	1	1	1	1	5	1	21

Key to species: 1. domestic fowl, *Gallus* (domestic) sp.; 2. curlew, *Numenius arquata*; 3. woodcock, *Scopolax rusticola*; 4. herring or lesser black-backed gull, *Larus argentatus/fuscus*; 5. guillemot, *Uria aalge*; 6. duck, *Anas* sp.; 7. buzzard, *Buteo* sp.; 8. wagtail cf. *Motacilla* sp.; 9. unidentifable bird.

TABLE 32: Other wild vertebrates.

	1	2	3	4	5	6	7	8	9	TOTAL
antler	7									7
scapula		1	1							2
humerus				1						1
tibia					1					1
other						1		1	1	1	4
TOTAL	7	1	1	1	1	1	1	1	1	15

Key to species: 1. red deer, *Cervus elaphus*; 2. roe deer, *Capreolus capreolus*; 3. rabbit, *Oryctolagus cuniculus*; 4. badger, *Meles meles*; 5. ?ulna proximal end of large baleen whale (not the lesser rorqual); 6. frog, *Rana* sp.; 7. frog or toad, *Rana/Bufo*; 8. Ballan wrasse, *Labrus bergylta*; 9. unidentified fish.

TABLE 33: Marine molluscs – numbers of individuals.

Phase	oyster *Ostrea edulis*	winkle *Littorina littorea*	limpet *Patella vulgata*
I			13
II			9
IIIA			43
IIIB			59
IVA		4	76
IVB		46	566
V		398	270
VIB		5	805
VIA		5	7
VIIA	1	256	41
VIIB		4	7
VIIC	7	728	321
TOTALS	8	1,446	2,217

TABLE 34: Specific proportions period by period. Figures given are fragment numbers (percentages in brackets).

A. ROPE LAKE HOLE

period	date	cattle	sheep	pig	total
1	early-mid IA	137(44)	152(49)	22(7)	311
2	middle IA	134(35)	222(58)	29(7)	385
3	LIA Durotrigian	402(37)	616(56)	74(7)	1092
4	RB 2nd-3rd c. AD	330(23)	994(71)	84(6)	1408
Overall		1003(31)	1984(62)	209(7)	3196

(See Table 35 for a detailed breakdown of these figures.)

B. ELDON'S SEAT

Period	Date	Cattle	Sheep	Pig	Total
I	LBA	508(53)	408(43)	35(4)	951
II	Durotrigian	140(29)	305(64)	31(7)	476
Overall		648(45)	713(50)	66(5)	1427

Specific Ratios

The overall ratios for the major domestic species compare well with those which can be calculated from the figures for Eldon's Seat. These comparisons should be treated with some reservations as the methodology used at the two sites was not comparable but they are both presented in Table 34 so that the similar specific ratios and the apparent trend towards a greater importance in sheep in the later period can be seen.

At Eldon's Seat bones not identifiable to species and loose teeth were discarded. The fact that all bones from Rope Lake Hole were saved and are included in these analyses makes it possible to rule out some possible other causes (other than a change in husbandry emphases) for specific ratio changes. These include the type of deposit and the degree of fragmentation.

Some deposits, in different periods, have identical specific ratios (Table 35). This might be because similar factors went into their accumulation. Chi-squared testing shows no significant difference even at the 75 per cent level ($\chi^2 = 2.35$, 6 d.f.) between these results for different periods.

TABLE 35: Specific proportions in different context types. Figures given are fragment numbers (percentages in brackets).

Period	Phase	Cattle	Sheep	Pig	Totals	Context type
1	I	62(42)	75(51)	11(7)	148	stone huts
	II	75(46)	77(47)	11(7)	163	waste tips
2	IIIA	94(37)	142(55)	21(8)	257	accum/occup
	IIIB	40(31)	80(62)	8(7)	128	occup below A
3	IVA	15(42)	17(47)	4(11)	36	robbing III
	IVB	218(37)	318(54)	51(9)	587	accum occup
	V	119(36)	199(60)	13(4)	331	stone huts
	VIB	50(36)	82(59)	6(4)	138	pits
4	VIA	23(38)	35(57)	3(5)	61	yard/structure/occ
	VIIA	152(26)	411(69)	29(5)	592	yard/structure
	VIIB	7(19)	27(75)	2(6)	36	gulley and pit
	VIIC	148(21)	521(72)	50(7)	719	occ + ploughing
Overall		1003(31)	1984(62)	209(7)	3196	

There is a significant link between the proportions of species and both Phase and Period (at the 0.1 per cent level in both cases) when all the results are tested by chi-squared. Most of the contribution to the chi-square value is from the results for cattle and sheep in deposit VIIC where the values for cattle are unexpectedly low and those for sheep high. This deposit has been subjected to ploughing and may also contain medieval contamination and is for these reasons likely to give different results from all other deposits at the site.

Once again, therefore, deposit type is seen to be a major factor in producing apparent changes in specific ratio in the Iron Age, perhaps not so dramatically as for Maltby's results for Winnall Down, Hampshire, where overall results for phase 3 and 4 material showed an increase in sheep in the latter phase but pit results showed little difference in species representation (Maltby, 1981, 166). The result of this analysis of deposit type is therefore to cast doubt on the postulated trend for an increase in the importance of sheep in the later periods at Rope Lake Hole.

A number of indices were calculated to see whether the figures for numbers of fragments in the different phases had been influenced by differences in preservation or fragmentation.

Altogether these results demonstrate that the period 4 deposits (especially phase VIIC) showed higher overall fragmentation than the rest of the material. Bias in fragmentation between large and small species was also visible. Adjustments made to the figures for specific ratios taking this into account would reinforce rather than oppose the theory of an increase in the importance of sheep in the later phases.

State of Preservation

The actual state of preservation of much of the bone was good. Carnivore-gnawing was seen on 21 per cent overall, the values ranging from 9 to 30 per cent in the different deposits.

A very high proportion of bones were 'ivoried' (16 per cent overall) compared with most other sites studied in Wessex.

In contrast, erosion was recorded on only about 3 per cent of all bones. This figure is quite low compared with that on some other Iron Age sites in Wessex and is an essential monitor of bone condition if detailed site comparisons are to be made.

The tibial index calculated by Maltby (pers. comm.) for other Wessex sites shows a high value for shaft fragments of sheep tibia compared with articular ends of the same bone (85 per cent) although the relative preservation of proximal ends to distal is not as low as for some sites (proximal ends tend to disappear before distal ends in this bone).

Altogether these results suggest that fragmentation at Rope Lake Hole was high (much of it probably as a result of action by dogs) but that if bone survived these ravages they may have stood a good chance of preservation in some deposits.

Utilisation of the Major Species

Horse

Of the 7 cases of cuts on horse bones, two are probably related to jointing and meat removal (scapula, ilium, and proximal ulna, respectively) and the rest might be from skinning practices.

A horse metapodial in OP 192 (period 3) was probably worked rather than butchered as a sharp blade had been used to trim the central projection of the distal condyle flush with the rest of the condyle surface.

TABLE 36: Sheep jaw ageing data compared with that from Eldon's Seat.

Stage (Grant)	Eldon's Seat No.	%	Rope Lake Hole Periods 1-3 No.	%	Period 4 No.	%
1-17	5	9	23	33	9	19
18-31	26	48	24	35	11	23.5
32+	23	43	22	32	27	57.5

Apart from the incisor of a 1-2 year old horse from the disturbed plough layers in period 4 only horses aged 8 to 16 years are represented according to the tooth evidence available.

Measurable bones mostly compare well with those of a modern New Forest Pony of *c.* 132 cm withers height (13 hands). There was a much smaller, but unmeasurable, humerus fragment in OP 105, period 4.

Cattle, Sheep and Pig
The figures for the relative balance of meat-bearing and non-meat-bearing bones for the three major species appear to be roughly equal in all periods for all three species. But the pattern behind these results is complex with the disposal of mandibles being irregular (large numbers in some deposits, none at all in others), possibly a lower efficiency of retrieval on-site for sheep carpals, tarsals and phalanges; and a relative dearth of cattle metapodials – perhaps reflecting their usefulness for working.

Knife cuts were recorded on about 5 per cent of bones, overall, and chopping with a heavier instrument on 2 per cent.

Cattle, Sheep and Pig Ageing Evidence
Using the methods of Grant (1975) and stages which coincide with the easier methods used for Eldon's Seat (Cunliffe and Phillipson, 1968) the same three divisions were used to compare RLH periods 1-3 with Eldon's Seat for sheep jaws (Table 36). The much higher figure at Rope Lake Hole for immature jaws may be a chance one as some deposits at Rope Lake Hole had virtually no immature jaws. The high value for the oldest group in period 4 is much influenced by the phases disturbed by ploughing. This suggests that a high figure for this older group may merely be indicative of their higher likelihood of preservation.

Results of the detailed tooth wear stage analysis, which allows greater detail to be recorded once all three molar are in wear (stage 32+) and uses Grant's methods, was compared with results for all three species with other Wessex results. For sheep, the mode for the older animals at Rope Lake Hole was a mandibular wear stage of 38/9 which compared well with the results for Roman Portchester (Grant, 1975) and Middle Iron Age Wessex (Maltby, 1981, 173).

The large number of loose teeth throws great doubt on the validity of such tables as Table 36, for the investigation of mortality data but a preliminary comparison of the details of individual tooth wear stages with those given by Grant in her recent more detailed work (Grant, 1982) suggest that detailed tooth wear data is the major way we have of ultimately defining differences in husbandry and genetic relationships in animal stocks in Wessex. Larger samples of jaws from Dorset would be useful. This is also a possible way of eventually detecting seasonal use of settlements.

Although similar details were recorded for cattle and pigs so few jaws produced a mandibular wear stage that it is not wise to comment on these results.

Pigs, sheep and cattle were all undoubtedly domestic and within the size ranges already seen elsewhere in Iron Age Wessex. A detailed review of measurements is not given although these are available in computer archive. Some large bones in phase VIIC could be later medieval contamination.

Pathological Changes
There were a small number of pathologically altered bones recorded, including a dog humerus with a healed fracture and several sheep jaws with periodontal disease.

Conclusions
The remains described here suggests a husbandry based mainly on cattle and sheep (all 'sheep or goat' bones have been consistently referred to as 'sheep' throughout this account) with a constant minor pig component. There is some evidence that wild species of mammal, bird, fish and marine molluscs were exploited.

There is a suggestion of an increase in the importance of sheep over cattle in the later periods. This seems to be so even if the more dubious plough collections in VIIC, which may contain medieval contamination, are excluded. This result gives support to the results for Eldon's Seat while providing a carefully collected sample which can, in addition, satisfy some of the essential checks on fragmentation, level of identification, and preservation, necessary when investigating specific ratios. It is still not clear, however, to what extent this apparent increase in sheep is due to the different disposal practices of the later periods (Maltby, 1981; Coy and Maltby, n.d.).

Whatever the vicissitudes of cattle and sheep husbandry, pig was a constant factor throughout although fragments were few, as at Eldon's Seat and Tollard Royal (Bird, 1968). This contrasts with the much greater importance of pig at some other Wessex Iron Age sites such as Groundwell Farm, Wiltshire (Coy n.d. 1) and Cleavel Point, Ower, Dorset (Coy n.d. 2) where rich valleys and saltmarsh may have played their part (Coy, in press). Low results for pig are more in line with the results for the Hampshire chalkland sites studied by Maltby (personal communication).

THE CHARCOAL IDENTIFICATIONS
RICHARD THOMAS

A total of only 35 fragments were recovered from 15 separate layers; all were small and fragmented. The low number makes intrepretation uncertain, and the original timber usage unknown. The species present and their stratigraphic location are summarised in Table 37.

TABLE 37: The wood identification (charcoal) by phase and period.

Period	Phase	BLACKTHORN (*Prunus spinosa*)	HAWTHORN (*Crataegus sp.*)	GORSE (*Ulex sp.*)	BIRCH (*Betula sp.*)	HAZEL (*Corylus avellana*)	WILLOW (*Salix sp.*)	OAK (*Quercus sp.*)	ASH (*Fraxinus excelsior*)
1	I								
	II								
2	III	O			T	T	T	M	
3	IV						T	O	T
	V								
	VIB					O		O	
4	VIA								
	VIIA				O				
	VIIB								
	VIIC	T	O	M		O			
	TOTAL: 35 fragments								

T: Twig, O: Large roundwood, M: Mature timber

Despite the low numbers it is worth noting the trend towards scrub and recolonisation species in the period 4 levels:

Blackthorn (*Prunus spinosa*), Hawthorn (*Crataegus* sp.), Gorse (*Ulex* sp.): can be taken as indications of scrub.

Birch (*Betula* sp.), Hazel (*Corylus avellana*), Willow (*Salix* sp.): can be taken to indicate secondary growth in woodland and recolonisation.

Oak (*Quercus* sp.), Ash (*Fraxinus excelsior*): can be taken as primary woodland species. The Ash species is a weak first coloniser or late coloniser, and seldom occurs in secondary woodland (*c.f.* Rackham, 1978, 32-36).

THE 'FOREIGN STONE' AND PEBBLES
based on macroscopic identification
PAUL ENSOM
and a contribution from Leo Biek on the iron pyrites

A large number of beach pebbles and stone erratics occurred on the site and were probably brought here as a result of settlement. The majority of the beach pebbles were from the Purbeck series, but some were derived from older sedimentary and volcanic deposits. The origin of this foreign material is probably the south-west of England, although continental sources could be considered. The reasons for the arrival of material on the site, 200 ft above sea level and a little inland from the coast, is less easily suggested. Some of the smoothed pebbles may have been used as rubbers/polishers. One long beach rolled pebble of a red quartzite/sandstone (possibly from Budleigh Salterton Pebble Beds, Devon, or from Chesil Beach (derived)) could be firmly identified as a honestone (see stone objects), and one piece of diatomaceous Kimmeridge limestone was scoured, with parallel grooves, and may have been used for sharpening and polishing bone (not illustrated). The bulk of the material may have moved to the site by chance as an incidental result of trade. Exotics on the Kimmeridge shore today are considered to be recent ballast.

Pebbles were found in all phases of the site. The following foreign stones were recorded (Purbeck and Portland series stones are not included):

PHASE I: (229), (?) volcanic origin.

PHASE IVB: (143), basic igneous, (?) gabbro, south-west England, (129), Iron-rich Old Red Sandstone, purplish colour, well cemented, probably North Devon/Somerset.

PHASE VIB: (233), fine-grained sandstone, (?) south-west England, (233), coarse reddish (? due to burning) gritstone, (?) south-west England.

PHASE VIIA: (105), Igneous rock.

PHASE VIIC: (16), (?) Budleigh Salterton Pebble, (7), quartzite, south-west England, (36), sandstone/siltstone pebble.

In addition to these 'foreign stones', several pieces of iron pyrites were identified. These specimens undoubtedly originated in the Kimmeridge Clay. In the absence of any evidence of smelting, it is unlikely that this mineral was collected as a source of iron, although it has recently been demonstrated (Tylecote and Clough 1983) that it can be used as such, even when it is rich in sulphur. Where unweathered, it can be made to produce sparks when struck with iron, although there is no evidence to suggest that the pieces collected were so used. Four pieces were recovered from period 1; one from period 2; ten from period 3; and seven from period 4.

ACKNOWLEDGEMENTS

These excavations were undertaken by the author whilst employed as archaeological field officer, Dorset Archaeological Committee; and were carried out to evaluate the potential and preservation of the site in the light of Tim Schadla Hall's coastal erosion report to the Wessex Archaeological Committee. The excavations were funded by the Department of the Environment.

The excavations would not have been possible without the permission and interest of the landowner Major Mansell of Smedmore House, and the co-operation, interest and help of the farmer John Vearncombe and his son Robert, whose assistance in towing caravans, providing a water supply, camp site, and help in many other small ways eased the problems of excavation on this isolated site.

The excavations were carried out with field assistant Peter Cox, with whom much of the post-excavation work was organised and researched, and with whom many hindsights into Purbeck industries were gained, and ideas developed. The excavations were carried out with a core of post-Weymouth College archaeological students, Colin Tracey, Karen Upton (finds), Peter Irvine, Dawn Eldridge, Martin Papworth, Jeannie Poulsen and Ian Brookes, together with a small team of diggers who started work in slippy mud, which subsequently baked in the hard sunshine of late July, and included Stephen Sherlock and Verna Care. Thanks are also due to the Poole Museum Service for the loan of the caravans, and to John Beavis for agreeing to tow the recently acquired caravan of the DAC, and who provided much valuable background information on Purbeck sites; also to Brenda Beavis for providing a welcome supper and tea at Kingston for tired and dirty diggers; Rosemary Maw and her family for their valuable assistance on the excavations; all those specialists who carried out detailed work on the excavated material and all those who visited this isolated site and made the excavation so enjoyable.

The excavation report was completed as part of the Wessex Archaeological Committee's publication programme; the publication drawings were executed by Stephen Crummy and Robert Read. The author would also wish to thank Leo Biek and Susan Davies for comments and discussion on the text.

REFERENCES

Addy, S. O., 1898, *Evolution of the English House.*

Andrews, W. R. and Jukes-Browne, A. J., 1894, 'The Purbeck Beds of the Vale of Wardour', *Quart. J. Geol. Soc.,* 50, 44-71.

Arkell, W. J., 1933, *The Jurassic System in Britain,* Oxford.

Arkell, W. J., 1947, *The Geology of the Country around Weymouth, Swanage, Corfe and Lulworth* (Memoir of the Geological Survey of Great Britain, nos 341, 342 and 343).

Arthur, P. and Marsh, G. (eds), 1978, *Early Fine Wares in Roman Britain,* BAR 57, Oxford.

Aspinall, A., 1977, 'Neutron Activation Analysis of Medieval Ceramics', *Medieval Ceramics* 1, 5-16.

Atkinson, D., 1916, *The Romano-British site on Lowbury Hill, Berkshire,* Reading.

Austen, J. H., 1859-60, 'On Kimmeridge "Coal Money" ', *Purbeck Papers,* 221-230.

Baily, C., 1851, 'Note on stone object from Mincing Lane, London', *J. Brit. Archaeol. Ass.* 6, 442-443.

Baker, R. S., 1970, 'A circular Kimmeridge shale tray from Wareham', *Dorset Proceedings* 92, 148-149.

Baldwin Brown, G., 1915, *The Arts in Early England 4: Saxon Art and Industry in the Pagan Period.*

Ball, D. F. and Williams, W. M., 1968, 'Variability of soil chemical properties in two uncultivated brown earths', *J. Soil Science* 19, No. 2, 379-391.

Bayley, J., forthcoming, 'Notes on the composition of coloured glass' in S. Campbell, P. Bennett *et al.,* *The Archaeology of Canterbury, Vol. III: Excavations in the Cathedral Precincts, I.*

Beavis, J., 1970, 'Some aspects of Purbeck Marble in Britain', *Dorset Proceedings* 92, 181-204.

Beavis, J., 1981, Determination and computation of amino-acid compositions of two buried soils and related surface soils from Holme Moor, Dartmoor, unpublished MSc thesis, University of Reading.

Bestwick, J. D. and Smith, T. A., 1974, 'The surface finish of samian ware', *Science and Archaeology,* 12, 21-31.

Bidwell, P., 1977, 'Early black-burnished ware at Exeter', in Dore, J., and Greene, K. (eds), *Roman Pottery Studies in Britain and Beyond,* BAR Sup. Ser. 30, Oxford, 177-187.

Biddle, M., 1967, 'Two Flavian burials from Winchester', *Antiq. Journ.* 47, 230-250.

Biek, L. and Bayley, J., 1979, 'Glass and other vitreous materials', *World Archaeology 11,* 1-25.

Biek, L., *et al.,* 1980, 'Enamels and glass pastes on Roman-period bronzes found at Nornour, Isles of Scilly', *Proc. 16th Symp. Archaeometry,* 1976, 50-79, espy. 63 ff.

Biek, L., 1983, 'The ethnic factor in archaeotechnology', *Proc. 22nd Symp. Archaeometry, Bradford, 1982,* 303-15.

Bird, P. F., 1968, 'Animal bones from Tollard Royal', in Wainwright, G. J., 'Excavations of a Durotrigian farmstead near Tollard Royal in Cranborne Chase, Southern England', *PPS* 34, 146-7.

Boessneck, J. A., von den Driesch, A., Meyer-Lemppenau, U. and Wechsler-von-Ohlen, E., 1971, 'Die Tierknochenfunde aus dem keltischen Oppidum von Manching', *Die Ausgrabungen in Manching, 6,* Wiesbaden.

Boessneck, J. A. and von den Driesch, A., 1979, *Die Tierknochenfunde aus der neolithischen Siedlung auf dem Fikirtepe bei Kadiköy am Marmarameer,* Inst. f. Palaeoanatomie, Munich.

Boon, G. C., 1957, *Roman Silchester.*

Boon, G. C., 1967, 'Micaceous Sigillata from Lezoux at Silchester, Caerleon and other sites', *Antiq. J.,* 47, 27-42.

Bourdillon, J. and Coy, J., 1980, 'The animal bones', in *Excavations at Melbourne Street, Southampton,* 1971-76 (P. Holdsworth) Council for British Archaeology, Research Report 33, p. 79-121.

Brailsford, J., 1958, 'Early Iron Age "C" in Wessex, Part I The Durotrigian Culture', *PPS* 24, 101-114.

Brailsford, J. W., 1962, *Hod Hill, Volume One, Antiquities from Hod Hill in the Durden Collection.*

Branigan, K., 1977, *Gatcome, The Excavation and Study of a Romano-British Villa Estate,* Brit. Arch. Rep. 44, Oxford.

Brassington, M., 1971, 'A Trajanic Kiln Complex near Little Chester, Derby, 1968', *Antiq. Journ.* 51, 36-69.

Brent, J. (Jun.), 1868, 'Account of the Society's Researches in the Anglo-Saxon Cemetery at Sarre, Part 3', *Arch. Cant. 7,* 307-21.

Briard, J., Giot, P.-R. and Pape, L., 1979, *Protohistoire de la Bretagne,* Ouest France,, 1979.

Briggs, D., 1975, *Sediments: sources and methods in geography.*

Brodribb, A. C. C., Hands, A. R. and Walker, D. R., 1971, *Excavations at Shakenoak Farm near Wilcote, Oxfordshire,* Vol. II, privately printed.

Brodribb, A. C. C., Hands, A. R. and Walker, D. R., 1973, *Ibid*, Vol. IV.

Brunskill, R. W., 1971, *Illustrated Handbook of Vernacular Architecture.*

Bugler, J., 1966, 'The Poole Harbour "Causeway" ', *Dorset Proceedings* 88, 158-160.

Bugler, J. and Drew, G., 1973, 'Roman Dorset', *Dorset Proceedings* 95 (1973), 57-70.

Bushe-Fox, J. P., 1915, *Excavations at Hengistbury Head, Hampshire 1911-12*, Oxford.

Bushe-Fox, J. P., 1949 *Fourth Report on the Excavations of the Roman Fort at Richborough, Kent*, Oxford.

Bussell, G. D., Pollard, A. M. and Baird, D. C., 1982, 'The characterisation of Early Bronze Age jet and jet-like material by x-ray fluorescence', *Wiltshire Arch. and Nat. Hist. Mag.* 76, 27.

Calkin, J. B., 1935, 'An Early Romano-British Kiln at Corfe Mullen, Dorset', *Antiq. Journ.* 15, 42-55.

Calkin, 1948, 'The Isle of Purbeck in the Iron Age', *Dorset Proceedings* 70, 29-59.

Calkin, J. B., 1953, ' "Kimmeridge Coal Money" The Romano-British Shale Armlet Industry', *Dorset Proceedings* 75, 45-71.

Calkin, J. B., 1959, 'Some archaeological discoveries in the Isle of Purbeck, Part II', *Dorset Proceedings* 81, 114-123.

Calkin, J. B., 1968, *Ancient Purbeck*, Dorchester.

Calkin, J. B., 1972, 'Kimmeridge Shale Objects from Colliton Park, Dorchester', *Dorset Proceedings* 94, 44-48.

Carson, R. A. G., Hill, P. and Kent, J. P. C., 1960, *Late Roman Bronze Coinage*, parts I and II.

Castle, S. A. and Warbis, J. H., 1973, 'Excavations on Field No. 157 Brockley Hill (Sulloniacae?), Middlesex', *LAMAS Trans.* 24, 55-110.

Charlesworth, D., 1961, 'Roman jewellery found in Northumberland and Durham', *Arch. Ael., fourth ser.* (1961), 1-36.

Charlesworth, D., 1966, 'Roman square bottles', *J. Glass Studies 8*, 26-40.

Charlesworth, D., 1970, 'The dating and distribution of Roman cylindrical bottles', 6-8, in *Studies in Glass History and Design* (Committee B), 8th International Congress on Glass, London, July, 1968.

Charlesworth, D., 1972, 'The glass', 196-215, in S. S. Frere, *Verulamium, Excavations, Volume I;* Oxford.

Clarke, R. R., 1939, 'Norfolk in the Dark Ages; Part 2', *Norf. Archaeol.*, 215-249.

Clay, R. C. C., 1925, 'A gun-flint factory site in South Wiltshire', *Antiquaries Journal V*, 423-426.

Clifton-Taylor, A., 1972, *The Pattern of English Building*, London.

Cook, M., 1980, *An analysis of the manufacturing methods of Roman roof tiles and the construction of roofs using them*, unpublished Dissertation Cert. Arch. (Dorset Institute of Higher Education and Southampton University), June 1980. Microfiche copy in National Monuments Record.

Corder, P., 1928, 'The Roman Pottery at Crambeck, Castle Howard', *Roman Malton and District Report*. I.

Corder, P., 1959, 'The structure of Romano-British pottery kilns', *Arch. Journ.* 114, 10-26.

Cox, E., 1980, *The level of lead in Romano-British burials – a demographic study*, dissertation submitted for the degree of BEd (Southampton University), at Dorset Institute of Higher Education.

Cox, P. W., 1985, 'Excavations on Furzey Island, an interim note', *Dorset Proceedings* (107), for 1985, publication in prep.

Coy, J. P., 1969, Report on the animal bones from the North-West and North-East entrances of Bury Wood Camp, *Wilts Arch. & Nat. Hist. Mag. 64*, 47-8.

Coy, J. P., 1982, The animal bones, in 'Excavation of an Iron Age enclosure at Groundwell Farm, Blunsdon St Andrew, 1976-7', *Wilts Archaeol. Mag.* 76, 68-72.

Coy, J. P., n.d.1., *Animal Bones from Groundwell Farm, Blunsdon St Andrew, Wiltshire 1976*, Ancient Monuments Laboratory reports nos 3591 and 3594, Department of the Environment, London.

Coy, J. P., in press, 'The role of pigs in Iron Age and Roman Wessex, in Fieller, N. R. J., Gilbertson, D. D. and Ralph, N. G. A, (eds), *Paleoenvironmental Investigations and Paleobiological Investigations*, BAR, Oxford.

Cram, C. L., 1973, The animal bones, in Brodribb, Hands and Walker, 1973.

Cram, C. L., 1978, The animal bones in *Excavations at Shakenoak Farm, near Wilcote, Oxfordshire. Part V: Sites K and E* (A. C. C. Brodribb, A. R. Hands and D. R. Walker), British Archaeological Reports, pp. 117-178.

Crummy, N., 1979, 'A chronology of Romano-British bone pins', *Britannia X*, 157-163.

Cummings, K., 1980, *The Techniques of Glass Forming*, London.

Croft, P., 1979, The mammalian bones from feature 1. In Partridge, 'Excavations at Puckeridge and Braughing 1975-79', *Hertfordshire Archaeology*, 7, 73-92.

Cunliffe, B. W., 1962, 'Excavations at Fishbourne, 1961', *Antiq. Journ.* 42, 15-23.

Cunliffe, B. W., 1963, 'Excavations at Fishbourne, 1962', *Antiq. Journ.* 43, 1-15.

Cunliffe, B. W. and Phillipson, D. W., 1968, 'Excavations at Eldon's Seat, Encombe, Dorset, England', *PPS 34* (1968), 191-237.

Cunliffe, B. W., 1971, *Excavations at Fishbourne 1961-69, The Finds*, Soc. Ants Res. Rep. XXVI, Vol. 2, Leeds.

Cunliffe, B. W., 1974, *Iron Age Communities in Britain.*

Cunliffe, B. W., 1975, *Excavations at Portchester Castle, Volume I: Roman*, Soc. Ants. Res. Rep. 32, London.

Cunliffe, B. W., 1976, *Excavations at Portchester Castle – Vol. 2 Saxon*, Soc. Ants. Res. Rep. 33, Oxford.

Cunliffe, B. W., 1978, *Hengistbury Head.*

Cunliffe, B. W., 1980, 'Hengistbury Head, Dorset: 1979 and 1980', *Dorset Proceedings* 102, 85-88.

Cunliffe, B. W., 1981, 'Hengistbury Head, Dorset: Iron Age Project 1981', *Dorset Proceedings* 103, 122.

Cunliffe, B. W., 1982, 'Britain, the Veneti and beyond', *Oxford Journal of Archaeology*, Vol. 1, No. 1, 39-68.

Cunnington, M. E., 1923, *All Cannings Cross,* Devizes.

Curle, J., 1911, *Newstead: A Roman Frontier Post and its People*, Glasgow.

Curle, J., 1917, 'Terra Sigillata: some typical decorated bowls', *Proc. Soc. Antiq. Scot.* 51, 130-76.

Dannell, G. B., 1977, 'The Samian from Bagendon', in Dore, J. and Greene, K. (eds), '*Roman Pottery Studies in Britain and Beyond'*, Oxford, 229-234.

Darby, H. C., 1979, 'Dorset' in Darby, H. C. and Welldon Finn, R. (eds), *A Domesday Geography of South-West England*, Cambridge, 63-131.

Davies, S. M., 1981, 'Exavations at Old Down Farm, Andover', *Proc. Hants. Field Club Archaeol. Soc.* 37, 81-163.

Davies, S. M. and Hawkes, J., forthcoming, 'The Coarse Pottery' in Green, C. G. S., *Excavations at Poundbury 1968-80*, DNHAS Monograph Series.

Déchelette, J., 1904, *Les vase céramiques ornés de la Gaule romaine*, tome ii, Paris.

Detsicas, A. P., 1963, 'Excavations at Eccles, 1962', *Arch. Cantiana* 78, 125-141.

Detsicas, A. P., 1965, 'Excavations at Eccles, 1964', *Arch. Cantiana* 80, 69-91.

DCM, Dorset County Museum Catalogue.

Dilke, O. A. W., 1971, *The Roman Land Surveyors*, Newton Abbott.

Dimbleby, G. W., 1978, *Plants in Archaeology.*

Dore, J. and Greene, K., 1977, *Roman Pottery Studies in Britain and Beyond*, BAR 30, Oxford.

Down, A. and Rule, M., 1971, *Chichester Excavations, Volume I*, Chichester.

Down, A., 1978, *Chichester Excavations, Volume III*, Chichester.

Down, A., 1981, *Chichester Excavations, Volume V*, Chichester.

Dudley, D., 1967, 'Excavations on Nor'Nour in the Isles of Scilly, 1962-6', *Arch. J. 124*, 1-64.

Dunning, G. C., 1949, 'The Purbeck Marble Industry in the Roman Period', *Arch. Newsletter*, I, 11, 15, reprinted 6, 12, (1960), 290-1.

Dunning, G. C., 1968, 'The Stone Mortars' in Cunliffe, B. W. (ed.) *Fifth Report on the Excavation of the Roman Fort at Richborough, Kent*. Soc. Ant. Res. Rep. 23, 110-114.

Dunning, G. C. and Evans, D. M., forthcoming, 'Pound Lane, Caerwent'.

Edlin, H. L., 1949, *Woodland Crafts in Britain*, republished Newton Abbott, 1973.

Ellison, A., 1981, *A Policy for Archaeological Investigation in Wessex, 1981-85*, Wessex Archaeological Committee (now Trust for Wessex Archaeology), Salisbury.

Errington, A., 1981A, 'Flint tools associated with the turning of shale braclets on lathes', *Bulletin of Experimental Archaeology*, Volume 2, 18-19.

Errington, A., 1981B, *A Study of Flint Tools Associated with Shale-turning, Based on Material from the Excavations at Rope Lake Hole*, unpublished dissertation for Cert. Prac. Arch., Dorset Institute of Higher Education, Weymouth, 1981.

Ettlinger, E., 1973, *Die römischen Fibeln in der Schweiz*, Berne.

Farrar, R. A. H., 1949, 'Corfe Castle, Fitzworth Point', *Dorset Proceedings* 71, 62-3.

Farrar, R. A. H., 1951a, 'Evidence for activity in the vicinity of Corfe Castle in the Roman period', *Dorset Proceedings* 73, 86-91.

Farrar, R. A. H., 1951b, 'A Romano-British kiln or oven and remains of occupation at Cleaval Point in the Ower peninsula, Poole Harbour', *Dorset Proceedings* 73, 91-2.

Farrar, R. A. H., 1952, 'Romano-British sites and two round barrows in Purbeck, recorded by Mr P. A. Brown', *Dorset Proceedings* 74, 93.

Farrar, R. A. H., 1954, 'A Romano-British building and shale armlet manufactory, near the Obelisk, Encombe, Corfe Castle', *Dorset Proceedings* 76, 80-1.

Farrar, R. A. H., 1955, 'The Romano-British occupation site at Matcham Clay workings, Norden, Corfe Castle', *Dorset Proceedings* 77, 126.

Farrar, R. A. H., 1959A, 'The Romano-British site on West Hill, Corfe Castle', *Dorset Proceedings* 81, 108.

Farrar, R. A. H, 1959B, 'Three cist burials near Kimmeridge', *Dorset Proceedings* 81, 94-97.

Farrar, R. A. H., 1962, 'A note on the prehistoric and Roman salt industry in relation to the Wyke Regis site, Dorset', *Dorset Proceedings* 84, 137-144.

Farrar, R. A. H., 1963a, 'Romano-British occupation of the castle mound, Corfe Castle', *Dorset Proceedings* 85, 104.

Farrar, R. A. H., 1963b, 'Roman and possibly pre-Roman remains at Rempstone, Corfe Castle', *Dorset Proceedings* 85, 103.

Farrar, R. A. H., 1964, 'The Romano-British site at Norden, Corfe Castle', *Dorset Proceedings* 86, 116-7.

Farrar, R. A. H., 1965, 'A Romano-British shale "panel" from Norden, Corfe Castle', *Dorset Proceedings* 87, 111-112.

Farrar, R. A. H., 1966A, 'A Quernstone from Norden, Corfe Castle', *Dorset Proceedings* 89, 144.

Farrar, R. A. H., 1966B, 'Cist burials at Ulwell, Swanage', *Dorset Proceedings* 88, 120-21.

Farrar, R. A. H., 1967a, 'The Brenscombe Villa, Corfe Castle', *Dorset Proceedings* 89, 144.

Farrar, R. A. H., 1967b, 'A stone cist at North Castle, Norden, Corfe Castle', *Dorset Proceedings* 89, 145.

Farrar, R. A. H., 1970, 'Industrial and other remains from the Romano-British site at Norden, Corfe Castle', *Dorset Proceedings* 92, 156-7.

Farrar, R. A. H., 1972, 'Romano-British finds near St Edward's Bridge, Corfe Castle', *Dorset Proceedings* 94, 88.

Farrar, R. A. H., 1973a, 'The Techniques and Sources of Romano-British Black-Burnished ware', in Detsicas, A. P. (ed.) 'Current research in Romano-British pottery', *Council for British Archaeol. Res. Rep.* 10, 67-103.

Farrar, R. A. H., 1973b 'Some Recent Archaeological Discoveries in Dorset', *Dorset Proceedings* 95, 101-102.

Farrar, R. A. H., 1975, 'Prehistoric and Roman saltworks in Dorset', in de Brisay, K. W. and Evans, K. A. (eds), *Salt: The Study of an Ancient Industry,* Colchester, 14-25.

Farrar, R. A. H., 1977, 'A Romano-British Black-Burnished ware industry at Ower in the Isle of Purbeck, Dorset' in Dore, J., and Greene, K. (eds), *Roman Pottery Industries in Britain and Beyond,* BAR Sup. Series 30, Oxford, 199-228.

Fasham, P. J., 1985, *Excavation of a prehistoric settlement at Winnall Down, near Winchester, Hampshire 1976-77,* Trust for Wessex Archaeology, Salisbury.

Ferdière, A. and M., 1972, 'Introduction á l'étude d'un type ceramique: les urnes à bord moulure Gallo-Romaines précoces', *Revue Archéologique de L'Est et du Centre-Est.* XXIII, fasc. 1-2, pp. 77-88.

Field, N. H., 1958, 'A Romano-British Burial and Pits near Bryanstone School, Blandford', *Dorset Proceedings* 80, 109.

Field, N. H., 1965, 'A Romano-British settlement at Studland, Dorset', *Dorset Proceedings* 87, 142-207.

Field, N. H., 1977, 'Excavations at Bucknowle Villa, Corfe Castle', 'Dorset Archaeology in 1977', *Dorset Proceedings* 99, 120.

Field, N. H., 1978, 'Roman villa at Bucknowle Farm, Corfe Castle – an interim note', *Proc. Dorset Nat. Hist. Arch. Soc. 100,* 112, *et seq.* 1979-1982.

Fingerlin, I., 1971, *Gürtel des hohen und späten Mittelalters,* Berlin.

Fowler, P. J., 1968, 'Excavation of a Romano-British settlement at Row of Ashes Farm, Butcombe, North Somerset', *Proc. Spel. Soc. 11,* 209-236.

Fulford, M., 1975, *New Forest Roman Pottery,* BAR 17, Oxford.

Gale, F. E., 1979, 'The ceramic fabrics', in Wainwright, G. J.,

Gussage All Saints, DoE Arch. Rep. 10, 49-56.

Geraint, and Davis, T. Alun Jones, R. T., n.d., 'Computer Based Osteometry. Data capture user manual I. Unpublished Ancient Monuments Laboratory Report No. 3342.

Gillam, J. P., 1970, *Types of Roman Coarse Pottery Vessels in Northern Britain,* Third ed., Newcastle-upon-Tyne.

Gillam, J. P., 1976, 'Coarse fumed ware in Northern Britain and beyond', *Glasgow Arch. J.,* 58-80.

Gilmore, G. R., *et al.,* 1986, 'Scientific examination of the glass beads', in Hurst, S. M., *An Saxon Cemetery at Sewerby, E. Yorks,* York University Monograph 4, 77-85.

Goh, K. M., 1972, 'Amino acid levels as indicators of palaeosols in New Zealand soil profiles', *Geoderma I,* 33-47.

Goudinea, C., 1968, *Le Céramique Arétine Lisse,* Fouilles de l'école Française de Rome et Bolsena (Poggio Moscini) 1962-1967, tome iv, Paris, 1968.

Gould, J. T., 1967, 'Excavations at Wall, Staffs., 1964-6, on the site of the Roman forts', *Transactions of the Lichfield and South Staffordshire Archaeological and Historical Society,* VIII, 1-40.

Gourvest, J. and Hugoniot, E., 1957, 'Un Emporium Gaulois à Chateaumeillant: l'Oppidum de Mediolanum', *Ogam,* Vol. IX, pp. 342-345.

Graham, A., 1971, *British Prosobranchs and Other Operculate Gastropod Molluscs.*

Grant, A., 1971, 'The animal bones', in Cunliffe, 1971, 337-388.

Grant, A., 1975, 'Appendix B: the use of tooth wear as a guide to the age of domestic animals', in Cunliffe, 1975.

Grant, A., 1982, 'The use of tooth wear as a guide to the age of domestic ungulates', in Wilson, B., Grigson, C. and Payne, S. (eds), *Ageing and Sexing Anima Bones from Archaeological Sites,* BAR 00, 91-108.

Green, K. T., 1974, 'The Samian Pottery', in Casey, P. J., 'Excavations at Segontium, 1971', *Archaeologia Cambrensis* 123, 62-7.

Greene, K., 1979, 'Invasion and response: Pottery and the Roman Army', in Burham, B. C. and Johnstone, H. B. (eds), *Invasion and Response, the Case of Roman Britain,* BAR Brit. Series 73, Oxford (1979), 99-108.

Greene, K., 1979, *Usk Excavation Report: The Pre-Flavian Fine Wares,* Cardiff.

Guido, Margaret, 1978, *The Glass Beads of the Prehistoric and Roman Periods in Britain and Ireland,* Soc. Ants. Res. Rep. 35.

Harcourt, R. A., 1979, 'The animal bones', in Wainwright, G. J., *Gussage All Saints: An Iron-Age Settlement in Dorset,* DoE Archaeological Report 10, 150-160.

Hall, J, 1983, 'The threat of coastal erosion to archaeology in the Isle of Purbeck', in Cox, P., and Hawkes, 'Purbeck Survey', Trust for Wessex Archaeology, Salisbury.

Harden, D. B., 1947, 'The Glass', in Hawkes and Hull, 1947, 287-307.

Harden, D. B. and Price, J., 1971, 'The Glass', in Cunliffe, 1971, 317-68.

Haskins, L. E., 1978, The vegetational history of South East Dorset, unpublished PhD Thesis, Southampton University.

Haverfield, F. and Taylor, M. V., 1908, 'Romano-British Shropshire', in *VCH Shropshire I,* Oxford, 205-78.

Hawkes, C. F. C. and Hull, M. R., 1947, *Camulodunum, First Report on the Excavations at Colchester 1930-39,* Soc. Ants. Res. Rep. XIV,m Oxford.

Henderson, J. and Warren, S. E., 1983, 'Prehistoric leaded glass analyses', *Proc. 22nd Symp. Archaeometry 1982,* Bradford 168-180.

Henig, M., 1975, 'An intaglio ring from Halstock Villa, Dorset', *Dorset Proceedings* 96, 58.

Henkel, F., 1913, *Die römischen Fingerringe der Rheinlande,* Berlin.

Hermet, F., 1934, *La Graufesenque (Condatomago),* Paris.

Hinchcliffe, J. and Williams, J. H., 1982, Excavations at Wilderspool, *Cheshire County Council Monograph.*

Hodges, H., 1964, *Artifacts.*

Hodges, H. M. W., 1968, 'Thin sections of pottery', in Cunliffe, B. W. and Phillipson, D. W., 'Excavations at Eldon's Seat, Encombe, Dorset', *PPS* 34, 191-237.

Holwerda, J. H., 1941, *De Belgische Waar in Nijmegen,* Beschrimjuing van de verzameling van het Museum G. M. Kam te Nijmegen (II), Hague.

Horsey, I. P., forthcoming, *Excavations at Poole, Dorset, 1972-83,* DNHAS Monograph Series.

Horsey, I. P. and Jarvis, K., 1980, 'Excavations at Lake Fortress', in Grew, S. O., *et al.* (eds), 'Roman Britain in 1979', *Britannia* II, 391.

Hughes, M., 1972, 'A Romano-British sacred well at Norden, Corfe Castle', *Dorset Proceedings* 94, 76-77.

Hughes, M., 1973, 'Second Interim Report on the Romano-British Well Site at Norden, Corfe Castle', *Dorset Proceedings* 95, 91.

Hyslop, M., 1963, 'Two Anglo-Saxon cemeteries at Chamberlains Barn, Leighton Buzzard, Bedfordshire', *Archaeol. J., 120*, 161-200.

Isings, C., 1957, *Roman Glass from Dated Finds*, Groningen.

Innocent, C. F., 1916, *The Development of English Building Construction*, Cambridge.

Jarvis, K. S., 1982, 'Three cit burials at Herston, Swanage', *Dorset Proceedings* 104, 192-194.

Jenkins, J., n.d., *The Wood-Turner's Craft*, National Museum of Wales.

King, A., 1978, 'A comparative survey of bone assemblages from Roman sites in Britain', *Institute of Archaeology Bulletin* 15, 207-232.

Knorr, R., 1919, *Töpfer und Frabriken verzi:·ºrter Terra-Sigillata des ersten Jahrhunderts*, Stuttgart.

Knorr, R., 1952, *Terra-Sigillata-Gefässe des ersten Jaⁿ. ᵇunderts mit Töpfernamen*, Stuttgart.

Koch, U., 1974, Mediterrane und fränkische Glasperlen des 6. und 7. Jahrhunderts aus Finnland, in G. Kossack and G. Ulbert (eds) *Studien zur vor- und frühgeschichtlichen Archäologie*, München: C. H. Beck, 495-513.

Koch, U., 1977, Das Reihengräberfed bei Schretzheim, in *Germanische Denkmäler der Vökerwanderungszeit*, A. 13.

Layard, N. F., 1907a, 'Anglo-Saxon cemetery, Hadleigh Road, Ipswich', *Proc. Suff., Inst. Archaeol.*, 13, 1-19.

Layard, N. F., 1907b, 'An Anglo-Saxon cemetery at Ipswich', *Archaeologia, 60*, 325-52.

Leeds, E. T., 1927, 'Excavations at Sutton Courtenay', *Archaeol. J.* 36.

Leeds, E. T. and Harden, D. B., 1936, *The Anglo-Saxon Cemetery at Abingdon, Berks:* Oxford.

Liversidge, J., 1955, *Furniture in Roman Britain*.

Liversidge, J., 1968, *Britain in the Roman Empire*.

Liversidge, J., 1969, 'Furniture and Interior Decoration', in Rivet, A. L. F. (ed.), *The Roman Villa in Britain*, London, 127-172.

Liversidge, J. and Peters, R., 1960, 'A Roman shale table-leg from Dorset', *Antiq. J.* 40, 72-3.

Loeschcke, S., 1909, 'Keramische Funde in Haltern' in Ausgrabungen bei Haltern, *Mitteilungen der Altertums-Kommission für Westfalen V.*

Maltby, J., 1981, 'Romano-British and Anglo Saxon animal husbandry: a review of the faunal evidence', in Jones, M. and Dimbleby, G. (eds), *The Environment of Man: The Iron Age to the Anglo-Saxon Period*, BAR (British Series) 87, 155-203.

Manning, W., 1976, *Catalogue of the Romano-British Ironwork in the Newcastle-upon-Tyne Museum*, Newcastle.

Martin, J., 1942, 'L'evolution des vases sigillées de Lezoux au 1ᵉʳ siècle de notre ère, *Bulletin His. et Scient. de L'Auvergne*, LXII, 181-209.

Martin, T., 1974, 'Deux Années de Recherches Archéologiques à Montans (Tarn)', *Revue Archéol. du Centre*, 13, 123-43.

Mattingly, H. and Sydenham, E. A. (eds), 1923, *Roman Imperial Coinage*.

Maw, R., 1975, 'Interim report on an excavation at Rope Lake Hole near Kimmeridge, Dorset', *Dorset Proceedings* 97, 51.

Maw, R., 1976, 'Kingston Russell (*erratum:* read Kingston)', in Keen, L. J. K. (ed), 'Dorset Archaeology in 1976', *Dorset Proceedings* 98, 58-59.

Maw, R., 1981, 'Swalland Farm (Kimmeridge) and the lost location of Chaldecots', *Dorset Proceedings* 103, 136-7.

May, V. J., 1968, 'Reclamation and shoreline change in Poole Harbour, Dorset', *Dorset Proceedings* 90, 141-154.

Maynard, D. G., 1981, *Surface collection of archaeological sites – A study of the potential and an example of the use of the technique*, unpublished dissertation for BA (Archaeo.), Sheffield University.

Meiggs, R., 1960, *Roman Ostia*, Oxford.

Moule, H. J., 1900, 'Dorset-found Celtic and Roman Bronze Objects in the Dorset County Museum', *Dorset Proceedings* 21, 102.

Neal, D. S., 1974, *The Excavation of the Roman Villa in Gadebridge Park, Hemel Hempstead, 1963-8*, Soc. Ants. Res. Rep. 31, Leeds.

Noddle, B. A., 1979, 'The animal bones', in Gracie, H. S. and Price, E. G., 'The Frocester Court Roman Villa: Second Report', *Trans. Bristol and Gloucs. Arch. Soc.* 97, 56-60.

Ordnance Survey, 1956, *Map of Roman Britain*, Third ed.

Ortner, D. J. and Putschar, W. G. J., 1981, *Identification of pathological conditions in human skeletal remains*, Washington, USA.

Oswald, F., 1937, 'Carinated bowls (form 29) from Lezoux', *Journ. Rom. Studies* XXVII, 210-214.

Oswald, F., 1936/7, *Index of Figure-Types on Terra Sigillata*, Liverpool.

Oswald, F. and Pryce, T. D., 1920, *An Introduction to the Study of Terra Sigillata*.

Partridge, C., 1975, 'Braughing', in Rodwell and Rowley (eds), 1975, 139-157.

Partridge, C., 1981, *Skeleton Green, A Late Iron Age and Romano-British Site*, Britannia Monograph Series 2.

Partridge, P. T., 1974, *The haematite wares of Wessex; A petrological study of some aspects of their production*. Unpublished dissertation, Southampton University.

Pascual, R., 1977, 'Les anforas de la Layetonia', *Ecole Française de Rome*, 32, 47-96.

Peacock, D. P. S., 1971, 'Roman amphorae in pre-Roman Britain', in Jesson, M. and Hill, D. (eds), *The Iron Age and Its Hill-Forts*, Southampton, 169-188.

Peacock, D. P. S., 1977, 'Pompeian red ware', in Peacock, D. P. S. (ed.), *Pottery and Early Commerce*, 147-162.

Périchon, R., 1974, *La Céramique Peinte, Celtique et Gallo-Romaine*, Centre d'études foreziennes. Thèse et Mémoires no. 6 (Roanne).

Pirling, R., 1979, Das römisch-fränkische Gräberfeld von Krefeld Gellep, III, 1964-5, in *Germanische Denkmäler der Völkerwanderungszeit*, B10, Taf. 76.

Pitt-Rivers, A. H. L. F., 1887, *Excavations in Cranborne Chase*, Vol. I (privately printed).

Pitt-Rivers, A. H. L. F., 1888, *Excavations in Cranborne Chase*, Vol. III (privately printed).

Pitt-Rivers, A. H. L. F., 1892, *Excavations in Cranborne Chase*, Vol. III (privately printed).

Pliny, *Natural History IX,* Book XXXV.

Pliny, *Natural History X,* Book XXXVI.

Poncet, J., 1974, 'Observations sur des Céramiques Gallo-Romaines Précoces de Roanne', *Rev. Archaèol. de l'Est et du Centre-Est.* XXV, fasc. 1.

Porter, G., 1980, *The characterisation of soil profiles from Ower, Dorset*, Unpublished Dissertation, for Cert. Prac. Arch. (Southampton University), Dorset Institute of Higher Education (Weymouth), Microfiche copy in NMR, London.

Price, J., 1975A, 'The Glass Vessels from the Cremation Groups'., 18-22, in A. E. Johnson, 'Excavations in Bourton Gardens, Thornborough, 1972-3', *Records of Bucks*, XX, 3-56.

Price, J., 1975B, 'The Glass', 12-14, in M. J. Green, *The Bradwell Roman Villa*; Milton Keynes.

Price, J., 1977, 'The Roman Glass', 154-61, in A. Gentry *et al.*, 'Excavations at Lincoln Road, Enfield', *Trans. London and Middlesex Archaeol. Soc.*, 28, 101-89.

Purchase, W. R., 1904, *Practical Masonry; a Guide to the Art of Stone Cutting*, 5th edition.

Rackham, O., 1978, *Trees and Woodland in the British Landscape*.

Rainey, A., 1973, *Mosaics in Roman Britain*, Newton Abbot.

Richmond, Sir I., 1968, *Hod Hill, volume two, Excavations carried out between 1951 and 1958 for the Trustees of the British Museum*.

Rigby, V., 1978, 'The Early Roman Fine Wares', in Down, 1978, 190-216.

Riha, Emilie, 1979, *Die römischen Fibeln aus Augst und Kaiseraugst*, Forschungen in Augst, Band 3, Augst.

Ritterling, E., 1912, 'Das frührömische Lager bei Hofheim in Taunus', *Annalen des Vereins für Nassauische Altertumskunde und Geschichtsforschung*, XL, Wiesbaden.

Rodwell, W. and Rowley, T. (eds), 1975, *The Small Towns of Roman Britain*, BAR 15.

Rogers, G. B., 1974, *Poteries sigillées de la Gaule centrale*, tome i, Les motifs non figurés, *Gallia*, Supplement XXVIII, Paris.

Rooksby, H. P., 1964, *Phys and Chem. Glass 5*, 20-25.

RCHM, 1960, 'Excavations in the west bailey at Corfe Castle', *Med. Arch.* 4, 29-55.

RCHM, 1970, *An Inventory of the Historical Monuments in the County of Dorset, Vol. 2, South-East.*

Santrot, M. H. and J., 1979, *Céramiques Communes Gallo-Romaines d'Aquitaine*, CNRS, Bordeaux.

Sauvaget, R., 1970, 'Le potier Servus II de Lezoux', *Revue Archéol. du Centre*, 9, 127-142.

Schadla-Hall, T. M., 1976, 'Coastal erosion, a rescue problem on the Dorset Coast', Wessex Archaeological Committee Field Officer's Reports, June 1976, September 1976, Salisbury.

Schindler, M. and Scheffenegger, S., 1977, *Die glatte rote Terra sigillata vom Magdalensberg*, Klagenfurt.

Schuler, E., 1959, 'Ancient Glassmaking techniques: the Moulding process', *Archaeology, 12,* 47-52.

Scott, L., 1938, 'The Roman villa at Angmering,' *Sussex Arch. Coll.* 79, 3-44.

Singer, C., Holmyard, E. J., *et al.*, 1957, *A History of Technology,* Vol. 3, Oxford.

Sloper, D., 1981, 'Experiments in lathe-turning shale armlets and vessels', *Bulletin of Experimental Archaeology 2,* 4.

Soil Survey of England and Wales, 1983, *Legend for the 1:250,000 Soil Map of England and Wales,* Rothamsted Experimental Station, Harpenden.

Stanfield, J. A. and Simpson, G., 1958, *Central Gaulish Potters.*

Stanford, S. C., 1974, *Croft Ambrey*, Hereford.

Stead, I. M., 1976, *Excavations at Winterton Roman Villa and other Roman Sites in North Lincolnshire 1958-67,* Department of Environment Archaeological Reports, No. 9.

Strong, D. E., 1966, *Greek and Roman Gold and Silver Plate.*

Stuart, M. G., 1887, 'The proceedings of the Dorset Natural History and Antiquarian Field Club during 1886', *Dorset Proceedings* VIII, xxxix-xl.

Suggett, P. G., 1954, 'Excavations at Brockley Hill, Middlesex, March 1952 to May 1959', *LAMAS Trans.* XI, pt III, 259-276.

Suggett, P. G., 1955, 'The Moxom Collection (A Romano-British Pottery Group from Brockley Hill, Middlesex)', *LAMAS Trans.* 18, pt 1, 60-64.

Swan, V. G., 1973, 'Aspects of the New Forest Late Roman Pottery Industry', in Detsicas, A. (ed.), *Current Research in Romano-British coarse pottery, CBA Res. Rep. 10,* London, 121.

Swan, V. G., 1975, 'Oare reconsidered and the origins of Savernake ware in Wiltshire', *Britannia* 6, 37-61.

Taylor, H., 1959, *The Green Island Causeway, Poole Harbour,* published privately for the County of Dorset Boy Scouts Association, 25th June, 1959, Copy in Dorset County Museum.

Tchernia, A., 1971, 'Les amphores vinaires de Tarraconaise et leur exportation au debut de l'empire', *Archivo Espanol de Arqueologia,* 44, 38-85.

Tebble, N., 1966, *British bivalve seashells,* British Museum (Natural History).

Timby, J. R., 1980, 'Early Roman finewares from Chester', manuscript for M. Ward, Grosvenor Museum, Chester.

Thomas, C., forthcoming, 'Trade and Industry in the Isle of Purbeck, Dorset, in the Iron Age and in the Roman Period'.

Thorpe, W. A., 1935, *English Glass.*

Tylecote, R. F. and Clough, R. E., 1983, 'Recent Bog Iron Ore: analyses and the smelting of iron pyrite nodules', *Offa,* 40, 115-118, Proc. 1980 Conf. Com. Sid. Anc. d'Union Intern. Étud., Pré-et Proto-hist., Senkelmark, Schleswig.

Vauthey, M. and P., and Martinet, Y., 1967, 'Répertoire des poinçons style et art décoratif du potier arverne Servus II', *Revue Archéol. du Centre,* 6, 230-56.

Vertet, H., 1961, 'Céramique Commune de l'Officine de St. Rémy-en-Rollat, Allier', *Gallia* 19, fasc. 1, 218-226.

Vertet, H., 1962, 'Les vases calciformes gallo-romains de Roanne et la chronologie des fabriques de terre sigillée de Lezoux au début du 1er siécle', *Gallia* 20, 351-80.

Vertet, H., 1963, 'Vases sigillés moulés de Lezoux au début du 1er siècle, *Actes 88ième Congrés national des Societés Savantes,* 105-19.

Vertet, H., 1967, 'Céramique sigillée Tibérienne de Lezoux', *Revue Archéol.,* 255-86.

Vertet, H., 1968, 'Influences de céramiques italiques sur les ateliers Arvernes au début 1er siecle', *Revue Archéol du Centre,* 7, 23-34.

Von Saldern, A., *et al.,* 1974, *'Gläser der Antike: Sammlung Erwin Oppenländer',* Mainz. Nos 284, 320 – both illustrated in colour.

Wainwright, G. J., 1968, 'The excavation of a Durotrigian Farmstead near Tollard Royal in Cranborne Chase, Southern England', *PPS* XXIV, 102-147.

Wainwright, G. J., 1979, *Gussage All Saints, an Iron Age settlement in Dorset,* DoE Archaeol. Rep. 10.

Ward-Perkins, J. B., 1941, 'The pottery of Gergovia', *Archaeol. Journ.* 98, 38-87.

Webster, G., 1973, 'Introduction and notes on the pottery of the 1st century AD in use by the Roman Army', Detsicas. AP(ed.), *Current Research in Romano-British Pottery,*CBA Res. Rep. 10, 1-5.

Wedlake, W. J., 1958, *Excavations at Camerton,* Somerset, privately printed.

Wheeler, R. E. M. and Wheeler, T. V., 1936, *Verulamium, A Belgic and Two Roman Cities,* Soc. Ants. Res. Rep. 11, Oxford.

Wheeler, R. E. M., 1943, *Maiden Castle, Dorset,* Soc. Ants. Res. Rep. XII.

Wheeler, R. E. M. and Wheeler, T. V., 1932, *Lydney Park Excavations,* Soc. Antiq., London.

Wild, J. P., 1973, 'A fourth-century potter's workshop's and kilns at Stibbington, Peterborough', in Detsicas, A. P. (ed.), *Current Research in Romano-British Coarse Pottery, CBA Res. Rep. 10,* 135-137.

Williams, A., 1950, 'The excavations at Allard's Quarry, Marnhull, Dorset', *Dorset Proceedings* 72, 20-75.

Williams, D. F., 1977, 'The Romano-British Black-Burnished industry; an essay on characterisation by heavy mineral analysis', in Peacock, D. P. S. (ed.), *Pottery and Early Commerce,* 163-220.

Williams, D. F., 1978, 'Petrological analysis of arretine and early Samian: a preliminary report', in Arthur, P. and Marsh, G. (eds), *Early Fine Wares in Roman Britian,* BAR 57, 5-12.

Williams, D. F., 1981, 'The Roman amphora trade with Late Iron Age Britain', in Howard, H. and Morris, E. L. (eds), *Production and distribution: A ceramic viewpoint,* BAR International Series 120, Oxford, 123-132.

Wilson, D. R. (ed.), 1973, 'Roman Britain in 1972', *Britannia 4,* 316.

Wilson, D. R. (ed.), 1974, 'Roman Britain in 1973', *Britannia 5,* 455.

Wishart, D., 1982, *Clustan, User Manual Version 2, Release 1.*

Woodward, P. J., 1980, 'A comparison of coin groups from Romano-British settlements in Purbeck – a reflection of their contrasting status?', *Dorset Proceedings* 102 (1980), 102-103, corrected table in *Dorset Proceedings* 103 (1981), 130.

Young, C. J., 1977, *Oxfordshire Roman Pottery,* BAR 43, Oxford.

Young, D., 1973, 'An Iron Age and Romano-British settlement at Broadmayne', *Dorset Proceedings* 95, 44-9.